TOEFL iBT

To high-achieving test-takers, the TOEFL iBT Writing Section is, essentially, a vehicle for demonstrating their sound grasp of the American language and their insight into the American life.

十天突破

新托福 ESSAYS

慎小嶷 / 编著

The Ten-Day Step-by-Step Guide to
the TOEFL iBT Writing Module

机械工业出版社
CHINA MACHINE PRESS

本书是出国考试类畅销书作者慎小嶷老师的又一力作。

本书紧扣官方资料要求而编写，所涉及资料均选自美国本土出版的最新资料。

本书将探讨中国留美考生在准备新托福作文过程中急需解决的大量实战问题：如何选择写作中真正需要的美语词汇；怎样才能写出灵活多样的地道英文句子；哪种段落结构才符合美国人的审美观；为什么必须果断放弃已经被用烂了的经典人物，而改举 Made in the U. S. 的新例子；偏题、难题的高分素材和段落；北美作文同义词替换合集等。

书中加分词汇和例句都为大家录制了光盘，可以边听边记。因此在准确把握北美议论文写作风格的同时，您将发现本书也是您正式开始积累地道美式英语的 milestone。

图书在版编目（CIP）数据

十天突破新托福 Essays / 慎小嶷编著. —北京：机械工业出版社，2010.1（2013.1 重印）

ISBN 978 - 7 - 111 - 29675 - 1

Ⅰ. 十… Ⅱ. 慎… Ⅲ. 英语-高等教育-自学参考资料 Ⅳ. H310. 41

中国版本图书馆 CIP 数据核字（2010）第 014728 号

机械工业出版社（北京市百万庄大街22 号　邮政编码100037）

策划编辑：孟玉琴　　　责任编辑：孟玉琴

版式设计：张文贵

责任印制：杨　曦

保定市中画美凯印刷有限公司印刷

2013 年 1 月第 1 版·第 9 次印刷

184mm×260mm·24. 5 印张·500 千字

37 001 - 42 000 册

标准书号：ISBN 978 - 7 - 111 - 29675 - 1

　　　　　ISBN 978 - 7 - 89451 - 419 - 6（光盘）

定价：56. 00 元（附赠 MP3 光盘 + 便携手册）

凡购本书，如有缺页、倒页、脱页，由本社发行部调换

电话服务　　　　　　　　　　　　网络服务

社 服 务 中 心：（010）88361066　　门户网：http：//www. cmpbook. com

销 售 一 部：（010）68326294

销 售 二 部：（010）88379649　　教材网：http：//www. cmpedu. com

读者购书热线：（010）88379203　　**封面无防伪标均为盗版**

If winning isn't everything, why do they keep score?

— Vince Lombardi
American Football Coach

推荐序

地道美语与短期应试相结合的典范

这 本书是 Pat 老师在国内出版的第三本书。原本以为在《十天突破雅思写作》与《十天突破雅思口语》两部作品仅在中国大陆的销量就已经突破 32 万册的情况下，对作者来说本书将是信手拈来。但让我始料未及的是：《十天突破新托福 Essays》的创作过程竟比 Pat 此前的著作耗时更久而且着力更多。从去年慎老师完成本书纲要，直到今年 1 月他从美国把全书最后的 Bibliography 传送给我，历时长达 1 年零三个月，并且作者为了搜集第一手资料还多次往返于中美之间。我自己有幸见证了本书中每段文字的破茧而出，方知"慎式写作法"的良苦用心。

同为留学语言类考试，新托福作文和雅思作文却有着深刻的不同。除了英美议论文在语言风格上存在明显差异之外（在本书中您将看到这些差异体现在题目表述、文体、句法、谋篇布局直至具体单词拼写等诸多方面），新托福作文还更多地涉及到了文化的层面，即学生对于美式价值观的理解和认同。

Pat 本人有长期的北美生活经历，并且他在北京从事英语教学期间批改过数万名中国学生的作文，这些都为他完成这本精彩纷呈的新托福写作书打下了坚实的基础。

给我印象极深的一个细节是：本书附录中所收入的 66 道难题由 Pat 原创的高分范文在 Pat 与他的美国朋友们一起进棚录音时，几个"老美"在朗读范文后都对文风给出了 two thumbs up，让我们再次庆幸自己找到了一位真正值得信赖的合作伙伴。更为难得的是：本书中的全部例句都是作者结合书中语言点遴选自美国 2009 ~ 2012 年的最新出版物，其使用价值已经超出了单纯的语言学习，而渗透到美国生活的方方面面。

在北美出现了这样中英双语均能挥洒自如的年轻人，并在近两年内其作品始终稳居国内新华书店英语应试类图书总排行单科书籍的第一名，与一些经典词汇用书并驾齐驱，不啻是海外军团对 two-fisted writer 一词的最好诠释。

李超群

作 者 自 序

For all of you out there who have set your hearts on studying in American institutions, an advantage of preparing for the TOEFL iBT Writing Test is that you become acutely aware of what was wrong in your past essays, which leads to fresh incentives to reorient yourselves. The reorientation effort, in turn, propels you to gain new knowledge about essay writing in American English.

For TOEFL instructors, exploration into the multiple layers of techniques for the TOEFL iBT essay test has long been a "sleeper" that more than meets the eye. Even prep instructors often underestimate the scope of this exploration. It not only allows a closer examination of the hidden aspects of the general problem of English writing competency, but caters to the entire spectrum of a TOEFL iBT candidate's personal needs as well. Throughout this book, I hope you will sense my wariness that any instructor can ever offer "infallible panaceas", and my deep conviction that any test-preparation technique should be viewed, at the very least, with a moderate dose of skepticism.

Also, since this book is meant for a unique audience — readers with a shaky grasp of English vocabulary and rhetoric but still pressed for study time, it does away with the conventional means of teaching English essay writing, such as dauntingly long word lists, baffling grammatical points and convoluted sentence patterns, which I believe hurt more than they help. Instead, this book will illuminate clearly, and often light-heartedly, the most intricate issues on the TOEFL iBT Writing Test, i. e., the complexities of test questions, the generation of new ideas, proper diction, correct mechanics and the construction of tightly knit paragraphs. You will even find sections dedicated to collections of earthy buzzwords and catchphrases in American English, whose meanings are far away from what you may expect if taken literally. Feel free to think of this book as a no-frills guide seeking to demystify the TOEFL iBT Writing Module for you.

As Alfred Adler aptly observed, referring to the school he had founded in Vienna, "The students teach the teachers." In the same vein, I do not see how I can be anything but deeply grateful for what I am daily taught about the issues on the test by those who are called my students.

Xiaoyi
(*a. k. a. Pat*)

From the Author to the Reader
致 读 者

新托福写作到底考什么?

ETS 在 O. G.（第三版）中所给的数据明确显示：以中文为母语的 TOEFL iBT 考生写作平均成绩*仅为 20 分，而申请美国顶级名校理想的成绩是每项均达到 25 分或以上。因此，新托福写作教师的任务就转化成了如何能有效地消除或者缩短这 5 分的差距。

（一）本书的实质是一本 test-prep book，95% 以上的内容都是讲解如何在短期内提高英语写作技能，特别是如何提高美式英语写作技能的。具体来说，在本书中我们将对以下领域进行深入探讨：

（a）彻底摆脱缺乏写作素材的困扰。对很多国内考生来说，见到简单的作文题目还好，但一旦遇到难题或者"怪题"就不知如何入手，甚至在考试时因为想不出素材而让宝贵的时间白白流走。本书 Day 2 与附录 E 专门为大家提供常规题目与难题、怪题的实用解法和素材，迅速突破 idea conception。

（b）提高语法知识的灵活度和准确度。很多国内考生的语法"内功深厚"，而且对语法现象的专业术语耳熟能详，但是实用性却偏低，导致写出句子来很"干"。Day 3 和 Day 6 将为大家集中展示真正适应实战要求的写作语法，并总结出必须避免的常见语法错误。对于写作考试来说，我们完全可以把 Benjamin Franklin 的那句"A penny saved is a penny earned."改为"An error avoided is a point earned."。

（c）总结出真正实用的核心词汇。考前准备写作单词理论上来说是"没有最多，只有更多"的。但适合短期突破的核心词汇却一定是有限的。Day 4 为大家展示新托福写作的真正必备分类单词，而且还系统归纳了北美考试作文中常用的强势动词、抽象名词与抽象形容词。而附录 F 则为大家提供了新托福作文同义词全面替换表。

（d）提高句式变换的能力。很多考生都有过这种经历：高分作文看着很好，想要模仿却很难。其中的原因除了国内的英语水平考试普遍重视阅读、听力这样的输入型测试却比较忽视写作和口语这类输出型考查外，另一个重要原因就是地道英文中的句式变化对多数考生来说缺乏可把握的规律性，甚至让一些孩子在学习写作时产生了严重的挫败感。我们在 **Day 5**，**Day 6** 和 **Day 7** 三天里将彻底掌握英语句式变换的各种手法，而且关键是做到七个字：考场能用得出来，否则理论再好听也只是忽悠人的空话。

（e）例证频繁是美式作文与"欧版"作文的一个重要差异。我在北京的 5 年半时间里，经常发现国内同学们痴迷于哥白尼、曼德拉、水门事件、Mother Teresa 或者波士顿倾茶事件这些"陈年老例"，却完全无视连印加传说中的"2012 doomsday"都已经快要到来（或者将被证伪）的事实。本书附录 A 就专门为大家介绍 21 世纪的"美人"怎么举例。

（f）对于很多考生来说，独立作文的逻辑往往是套模板的"副产品"。这其实是一种本末倒置（put the cart before the horse）的学习方法。**Day 8** 和 **Day 9** 会以前所未有的深度帮助大家彻底读懂英语议论文的逻辑结构。而对于基础过于薄弱、"胸无大志"、只打算套模板的那部分苦孩子，也必须好好研究一下这两天的内容，彻底理解新托福作文的逻辑到底应该怎样去展开，才能实现"源于模板而高于模板"。

（g）与比较偏重生活的独立写作部分不同，新托福的综合写作部分则是严格的 academic writing，"套路无罪，模板有理"。但问题是怎样才能拥有真正高质量的综合写作模板呢？**Day 10** 将为大家深入揭示美式综合写作考试的本质。

> 此外，本书中还将为大家提供开头、主体、结尾的大量高分实例，172 部经典"美句"、名人们如何看待新托福作文话题……备考时间特别紧张的同学还可以先重点研读书中页边侧有 V 字标记的重点章节。

（二）在切实提高写作基本功的同时，想写好新托福作文很难完全躲开美国的社会背景，这也是新托福写作教师必须帮助学生突破的瓶颈。

新托福老师讲作文的时候，多半会提到"美国人喜欢怎样的写法"。其实这种说法本身就非常值得推敲：

（a）在美国的 K-12/K-14 和大学低年级阶段通常会提供一门课叫 creative writing，门教学生怎么写出有个性、真正能表达自己想法的作文。其实只有这样才符合常理：萝卜白菜，各有所爱（Different strokes for different folks.）。怎么可能大家都喜欢一样的写法呢？

很多人喜欢唱许巍的《蓝莲花》，可我偏喜欢他那首并不算太火的《那一年》。有人欣赏刘莉莉，就一定有人支持张绍刚。有明星是"高帅富"，就一定也有名人是"土肥圆"。有人爱去三里屯儿，就一定也有人去后海或者南锣鼓巷。这就是 sociologists 笔下的"个人偏好多样性"（the diversity of individual preferences）。

在美国也是这样，或者说在美国更是这样，因为它是彻底的 capitalism in action（也是所有工业化国家中唯一没有全民医保的国家，前年获得通过的 Health Care Bill，其象征意义超过它的现实意义。事实上，如果实行全民医保，美国的 family physicians 家庭医生在今后多年内都将处于短缺状态）。Milton Friedman 对当代美国社会的影响超出大家的想象：有 demand，就一定会有 supply；有 the need for expression，就一定会有 the means of representation。

比如很多同学都会知道，新托福考试中有大量关于 Success 的考题（最近四年大陆与北美的完整机考题库请大家参考附录 C 和附录 E 以及 blog. sina. com. cn/toeflwizard）。但美国社会对于成功的定义远比中国社会更加多元化，像 William Hung 和 Sanjaya Malakar 这样如果生在 Elvis 时代会连话筒都无法靠近的人，在当代美国却都曾让 American Idol 的评委意见和 public votes 彻底决裂。如果完全不了解这种背景，就容易在讨论 success 话题时把范围限制得过窄。

又比如，新托福作文中有大量关于 Education 的题目。像小学生就近入学这样在北京根本不会是问题的问题，美国家长们则至少有 public school /private school/charter school/Catholic school 甚至 homeschooling 可以选择。如果考生能适当了解美国人对教育问题的真实看法，无疑可以让自己的 essay 更加贴近考官的审美观。

本书中的大量美语实例，就是大家了解与新托福作文考题密切相关的美式思维的快捷键。

11 年前，精力过剩的我曾从美国东海岸一直开车到西海岸，又沿着不同的路线返回。可以毫不夸张地说：对于任何一个美国人的某一种偏好，一定就有和它完全对立的其他偏好在美国合法地存在着。所以我们真的不能说，"美国人都喜欢什么样的写法"。

（b）更重要的是：到底什么是美国人？美国有 3. 05 亿人，人口是中国的 1/4 不到，但构成却异常复杂，很多人你根本说不清到底是从哪儿来的。比如上届总统竞选期间，愣是有小报记者提出大量证据说明 Barack Obama 和 Brad Pitt 是远亲，而 Hillary Clinton 则是 Angelina Jolie 的 cousin。这个例子不仅可以用来作"是否应该相信新闻来源的真实性"这道新托福作文题的论据，而且不可否认小报记者们敢去这样编故事也确实体现了美国社会惊人的民族多元化（racial and ethnic diversity）和文化多元化（cultural pluralism）。而今年的总统竞选热门人物 Mitt Romney 则是摩门教徒，而且他年轻时还在法国当过摩门教传教士（Mormon missionary），所以在 Nevada，Arizona 等摩门教徒人口较多的州就特别受欢迎。美国人口构成是如此难描难述，所以就更不该说"美国人民都喜欢什么样的写法"。

（c）但另一方面，200 多年来，美国人民从来都是一个追求 the will of the majority 的民族。大家如果有时间研究一下美国史和 the separation of powers（这里的 power 要加 s，指三权分立制度），就会看出美国版的 checks and balances 核心理念就是不管多聪明的人也一定会犯错，所以多数人的意见必须得到尊重，即使它看起来可能是幼稚的（naive）甚至可笑的（ludicrous）。

因此，不管是老托儿还是新托儿，TOEFL 从来都是对将要进入美国境内的外国学生进行文化同化的重要环节。也正是由于新托福对美国核心价值观的这种集中体现，才让貌似完全无法把握的 TOEFL iBT essay raters 的偏好具有了相对的确定性。

> 学生是否具备扎实的美语写作功底，以及对美国社会的适当了解，就是新托福写作考查的核心，也是新托福写作教师必须帮助学生有效突破的瓶颈。

本书其他参与协助编写工作的人员有：朱燕麟、于雷、宋朝晖、杨雅琳、朱卫红、张静、周晖、李梅、高路、董明明、张中华、魏林、王玲、尚彬、孔梦洋、孟若冰、冉鹏飞、苏惠心、宋文顺、袁进、杨毅、张红燕、王军、黄洋、李纲、李晨光、王向雨、董倩、谢冰、闫文健、刘菲、陈洁、于辉、张洪霞、汪洋、高峰、袁诗宁、刘盈、毛润卿、张哲、阎密、陈江升、孟玉琴、沈刚、朱卡亚、李玉亚、李杰、范喻欣、刘瑾辉、陈蕲春、谷明义、尹东临、毕骁、陈宏、齐函芝、郭东岚、董月、叶彤彤。

In fashioning this volume that will hopefully fill a void in prep-book publishing, I continue to profit from the advice of distinguished experts. Special thanks go to Professor M. C. Wilcox and Dr. J. T. Borg for their laborious critique of the manuscript. I am equally indebted to Ms. Meng Yu-qin, the CMP editor of this book, for prodding and cajoling me into completing this book as promptly as possible. A special note of appreciation to Whitney Liu, for the touching up of the Chinese text I wrote in the first and the second drafts and for giving me hints on how to make this book more meaningful in the Chinese context.

I am thankful for，as always，the loving support from my parents，my sister，Meg，and friends of mine，without whom I would not have embarked upon this "cottage industry".

2012 年 9 月于 NYC

＊ 请注意 mean 是美国生活中谈到统计数字时的常用概念，它与 average（平均值）是一样的意思，但和 median（中位值）不同。median 是指各有 50％的调查对象在这个数值之上和之下，相对来说更加客观；而 mean 是总数除以总人数，比较容易由于"顶级大牛"或者"小白级菜鸟"的存在导致数据不客观。比如美国的 median household income 在前年为 52,029USD，而同一年的 mean household income 却达到了 556,300USD。大家从中可以看出，Bill Gates，Warren Buffett 和 Mark Zuckerberg 这些 multibillionaires 严重干扰了美国家庭收入的平均值。☺

目　录

推荐序

作者自序

引言

致读者

Day 1　i 的初体验

国内新托福考生很难回答的 10 个问题 / 3

My Answers / 4

Day 2　思路的尽头

3 种快速解题方法 / 23

　　分类法 / 23

　　替代法 / 25

　　裸奔法 / 27

测测你的进展 / 30

学有余力 / 31

课后练习 / 31

Day 3　无糖语法

正确理解 5 种句子成分 / 35

有效区分 3 种句子 / 38

有效避免 7 类语法错误 / 40

来自"老托儿"的启示 / 43

学有余力 / 44

课后练习 / 45

参考答案 / 46

Day 4   词汇不是纸老虎

（上）Pat 对新托福作文核心词汇的总结 / 51
　　新托福写作完整加分词库：1180 词 / 51
（下）Pat 关于精确使用写作词汇的心里话 / 100
　　中国考生最容易失手的写作单词总结 / 100
　　新托福作文抽象加分词总结（非牛人请飘过）/ 103
　　那些让你的论证更强有力的 verbs（高分内容）/ 107
　　《那些花儿》/ 113
　　魅力四射拉丁族 / 120
　　Pat 总结的美国人表述自己的价值观时最喜欢用的 12 个词 / 121
　　在北美长大的孩子必须面对的 8 大挑战（高分内容）/ 123
学有余力 / 124
课后练习 / 124

Day 5   轻松玩转 linkers

新托福作文复杂句主、从关系完全透视 / 130
　　因果关系 / 131
　　举例关系 / 132
　　类比与对比关系 / 133
　　让步关系 / 136
　　假设关系 / 139
　　修饰关系 / 139
　　限定关系 / 140
　　下定义关系 / 140
　　不是关系的关系 / 141
学有余力 / 142
课后练习 / 142

Day 6 给你的句子一点颜色

（高分内容，非大牛留个脚印即可）

状语前置 / 147

句中做手脚 / 149

副词领路人 / 150

倒装是进步的阶梯 / 151

强调但不强势 / 152

虚拟不等于忽悠 / 152

抽象画法的 of / 152

被动也疯狂 / 153

变性表决心 / 153

副词排成队 / 155

用点、线勾出层次感 / 155

"the＋形容词" 的语法可没错 / 156

双重否定就是肯定 / 156

学有余力 / 157

课后练习 / 158

参考答案 / 158

Day 7 该出手时就出手：考场里真正实用的写作句型

北美写作 172 句型 / 163

前进类（论证 positive 方面常用）/ 163

倒退类（论证 negative 方面常用）/ 172

中间类（论证不好不坏/可好可坏方面常用）/ 178

6 个俗不可耐却依然没被美国人淘汰的句型 / 188

课后练习 / 189

Day 8 显微镜下的开头、主体与结尾

（上）万事开头未必难 / 193

什么是开头段 / 193

美式议论文写 Introduction 的十四种方案 / 194

课后练习 / 205

（中）Body 的诱惑 / 208

　　Body Paragraphs 的展开路径详图 / 208

课后练习 / 221

（下）蛇尾还是豹尾 / 224

　　结束全文的五种方式 / 224

学有余力 / 229

课后练习 / 229

Day 9　独立作文的结构与解构

最简单也最困难的 "一边倒" / 234

　　"一边倒" 范文分析 / 235

　　真的要是写 High 了怎么办？（仅适合考前 Dove 摄入过多的童鞋们）/ 238

中立但不中庸的 "折中式" 写法 / 239

　　"折中式" 范文分析 / 239

致 "反动派" 们的一封信（只适合基础薄弱或者备考时间极短的小白）/ 244

　　新托福作文模板工具箱 / 244

学有余力 / 252

课后练习 / 252

Day 10　那些年，我们一起追的综合写作模板

Integrated Writing 的结构与怎样编写个性化模板 / 263

综合写作模板之解构版 / 264

综合写作模板同义词替换全集 / 265

The Devil Is in the Details（高分内容）/ 269

学有余力 / 271

附　录

附录 A　美国考官喜欢看什么样的例子 / 274

　　妙手举例子 / 274

　　建立起属于自己的作文例子库 / 282

　　学有余力 / 290

　　课后练习 / 291

附录 B　新托福写作中的偏题、难题原创素材库（高分内容）／ 293

　　新托福作文偏题、难题的 66 个高分段落／ 293

　　Bonus Samples ／ 312

附录 C　新老作文话题总 PK（上）／ 314

　　2006～2011 年大陆机考话题全集／ 314

附录 D　新老作文话题总 PK（下）／ 320

　　老托福的 185 话题／ 320

附录 E　北美在行动／ 327

附录 F　新托福写作 211 同义词重点替换词全集（适合骨灰级玩家）／ 331

　　写作 211 同义词重点替换词全集／ 332

附录 G　名人眼中的新托福写作／ 353

附录 H　新托福写作常用备考网站／ 365

结束语／ 368

参考文献／ 370

Day 1

Getting Your Feet Wet
i 的初体验

Some people are afraid of what they might find if they try to analyze themselves too much, but you have to crawl into your wounds to discover where your fears are.

——Tori Amos
American singer-songwriter

有个成语叫"涉世未深"，Pat 常想：为什么一定要用两个带水的字形容年轻人进入社会的过程呢？是在暗示前面的险滩（social intrigues）？

美语中也有一句常用语，"Get your feet wet before you jump in." 是说在完全投入地做某事之前应该先体验一下之后再做决定。

读完本章的深度分析之后，您将可以明确把握 TOEFL iBT 写作的特点，并更加坚定考新托福（至少是写作部分）的信心。

国内新托福考生很难回答的 10 个问题

10 Questions That May Well Put You on the Spot

☆ TOEFL iBT 写作部分与 GRE, GMAT, IELTS 的写作部分有哪些本质不同?

☆ 我是否应该通过旧托福的 185 作文题库来准备新托福写作考试?

☆ 准备 TOEFL Writing Tasks 时是否需要提前储备专业知识?

☆ 新托福作文的评分标准很好很强大,但是我无法充分理解怎么办?

☆ 新托福作文观点的"深邃"或者新颖重要吗?

☆ 准备独立作文是否需要准备模板?

☆ 独立作文应该写一边倒式还是折中式?

☆ 新托福独立作文是不是难词越多分数越高?

☆ 作文应该采用哪种格式写?

☆ 独立作文是否需要写标题?

Bonus Questions

★ 是否在作文的开头段就必须表明自己的观点?

★ 怎样客观看待北美机经?

★ TPO 的价值有多大?

★ 传说中 ETS 的 e-rater 到底有多可怕?

My Answers

> *TOEFL iBT* 写作部分与 *GRE，GMAT，IELTS* 的写作部分有哪些本质不同？
> *Would it be wise for me to get acquainted with the TOEFL iBT writing tasks through the GRE Issue，IELTS or GMAT essay topic pool?*

这个问题涉及到新托福作文的本质，是大方向问题，因此必须得到及时解决。

有很多新托福考生是申请去美国读 graduate school 或者 business school 的，除了托福成绩之外，还需要再提交 GRE 或者 GMAT 成绩，所以国内才出现了"寄托"这个专有名词。

另外还有一部分同学正在考托福还是考雅思之间犹豫不决。关于新托福考试和雅思考试总分间的对应关系，部分美国大学会使用下面这个换算表：

TOEFL iBT	IELTS
0 – 8	0 – 1
9 – 18	1 – 1.5
19 – 29	2 – 2.5
30 – 40	3 – 3.5
41 – 52	4
53 – 64	4.5 – 5
65 – 78	5.5 – 6
79 – 95	6.5 – 7
96 – 120	7.5 – 9
Top Score	**Top Score**
120	**9**

一个客观事实是：如果不考虑其他三项，单就写作部分而言，新托福比 GRE，GMAT 和 IELTS 更容易准备充分。这么说并不是因为要给各位什么心理安慰，而是有真凭实据的（我们先探讨独立写作，在 Day 10 中我们再以极其详尽的笔墨研究综合写作考试）：

（A）与 GRE Issue，GMAT 或者 IELTS 作文相比，TOEFL iBT 作文从题目理解难度来看是偏低的。

◎ 我们可以从下面的详尽对比中非常清晰地看出区别：

TOEFL iBT 考题

Do you agree or disagree with the following statement?

Successful leaders should make others part of the decision-making process.

话题近似的 Revised GRE（新 GRE）Issue 考题

Claim: In any field — business, politics, education, government — those in power should step down after five years.

Reason: The surest path to success for any enterprise is revitalization through new leadership.

Write a response in which you discuss the extent to which you agree or disagree with the claim and the reason on which that claim is based.

◎ 再请认真对比下面两道题：

TOEFL iBT 考题

Do you agree or disagree with the following statement?

Most businesspeople are motivated only by the desire for more money.

话题近似的 Revised GRE Issue 考题

Some people believe that corporations have a responsibility to promote the well-being of the societies and environments in which they operate. Others believe that the only responsibility of corporations, provided they operate within the law, is to make as much money as possible.

Write a response in which you discuss which view more closely aligns with your own position and explain your reasoning for the position you take. In developing and supporting your position, you should address both of the views presented.

◎ 即使是当考题难度非常接近时，GRE 作文考题的文字表述依然要比新托福作文题的表述要难一些。请看下面这对儿：

TOEFL iBT 考题

Do you agree or disagree with the following statement?

The government should not support scientific research that may not have any practical use.

Governments should not fund any scientific research whose consequences are unclear.

Write a response in which you discuss the extent to which you agree or disagree with the recommendation and explain your reasoning for the position you take. In developing and supporting your position, describe specific circumstances in which adopting the recommendation would or would not be advantageous and explain how these examples shape your position.

准备去美国读本科的童鞋们现在一定很庆幸自己没有早生几年而沦落到必须考 GRE 的地步吧！

◎ 我们再对比着看一道 IELTS 作文题：

Some people believe that there should be fixed punishments for each type of crime. Others, however, argue that the circumstances of an individual crime, and the motivation for committing it, should always be taken into account when deciding on the punishment.

像这种题目的思辨性和题目表述难度，已经直逼下面这道 Revised GRE Issue 考题了：Laws should be flexible enough to take account of various circumstances, times, and places.

而新托福从 2005 年样题公开截止至 2012 年 9 月从未出现过如此艰深的作文话题（如果大家还不敢相信自己的幸福指数，那就请参考本书的附录 C、附录 D 与附录 E 以及 blog. sina. com. cn/toeflwizard 的全部机经）。

即使是完全相同的话题，可爱的新托福作文题通常仍然比 IELTS Academic 类作文题的用词更加直白。请看两种考试对同一道题目的不同表述：

TOEFL iBT 考题:

Do you agree or disagree with the following statement:

Schools should not pay much attention to general subjects. Instead, they should help students prepare for future jobs and careers.

IELTS 考题:

Some people think that schools and universities should provide graduates with the knowledge and skills needed in the workplace. Others think that the true function of a school or a university should be to give access to knowledge for its own sake, regardless of whether the course is useful to an employer. What, in your opinion, should be the main function of schools and universities?

(B) 不仅考题的理解难度存在本质差异，这四种留学考试对思维深度的要求同样存在本质区别。

美国本土的学生在申请 graduate school 的时候也必须递交 GRE 成绩。它除了语言测试功能外，更重要的是思维能力测试。GRE Issue 对素材和写作形式都有更严密的要求。

比如，请试着读读下面 GRE 官方满分范文的一个主体段：

Overspecialization means narrow *focii* in which people can lose the larger picture. No one can hope to understand the human body by only inspecting one's own toe-nails. What we learn from a narrow focus may be internally logically coherent but may be irrelevant or fallacious within the framework of a broader perspective. Further, if we inspect only our toe-nails, we may conclude that the whole body is hard and white. Useful conclusions and thus perhaps useful inventions must come by sharing among specialists. Simply throwing out various discoveries means we have a pile of useless discoveries. It is only when one can make with them a mosaic that we can see that they may form a picture.

幸运的是：与这种"吃脚趾头不吐脚趾甲"的杀手型作文相比，新托福作文则明显带有"拉家常"的性质，它考查更多的是 common sense 以及把这种 common sense 用并不是很艰深但比较准确的英文表达出来的能力。如果说 GRE 对素材的要求是 profound（深刻的），那么新托福对 ideas 的要求则是 reasonable（合理的）。请对比下面的新托福官方满分范文主体段：

If your friend had worn a newly-purchased dress on her birthday and energetically asked you if it was a worthy buy, would you freely express your opinion that you'd never seen a dress as the one she was wearing and just spoiled her birthday? Inarguably, hiding the truth in some situations can be quite handy indeed.

如此单纯、率真，让人想起去年在美国火得不行的 Hannah Montana 那口雪白的牙齿。不过需要提醒您注意的是，即使是表达这么简单的 ideas 其实作者也偷偷地使用了"虚拟 + 状语前置"这些在中国考生手中罕用的变换句式手法，让本来很短的篇幅却显得丰富多样（详情请看 Day 6）。

此外，对于新托福写作中的少数偏、怪、难题，您可以在本书的附录 B 中找到大量原创素材；

☆　　☆　　☆

与 GRE 作文接近，IELTS 作文也明显带有学术型作文的倾向，对 ideas 的要求虽然还没有 GRE 那么高，但是明显比 TOEFL iBT 写作更偏学术。请体会下面的雅思官方满分段落的明显差异：

I personally think that some people do have talents that are probably inherited via their genes. Such talents can give individuals a facility for certain skills that allow them to excel, while more hard-working students never manage to reach a comparable level. But, as with all questions of nature versus nurture, they are not mutually exclusive. Good musicians or artists and exceptional sports stars have probably both good training and natural talent. Without the

natural talent, continuous training would be neither attractive nor productive, and without the training, the child would not learn how to exploit and develop their talent.

如果您是"射手座＋O 型血"性格，这么拐弯抹角的论证也够您喝一壶的吧？

新托福与雅思作文的本质区别还可以用下表概括：

	新托福	雅思
1	作文话题偏重生活化	作文话题偏重学术化
2	考题的英文表述清晰易懂	相当一部分题目的英文表述难度已经接近 GRE 写作
3	写作风格比较接近生活，允许使用缩写形式，甚至官方满分作文中也出现了少量口语化词汇	语言风格带有明显的学术色彩，官方满分范文中从未出现任何缩写，看不到口语化表达
4	官方满分范文**多采用**"一边倒式"写法	官方满分范文**全部采用**折中式写法
5	官方满分范文中例证（exemplification）至关重要	官方提供的满分范文中例证很少
6	独立写作时间为 30 分钟	议论文部分写作时间为 40 分钟
7	通常在 300 字以上（但并不是像传闻的那样必须写满 400 字才能拿高分，超过 300 字以后更重要的就是看内容质量了）	字数要求在 250 字以上

在本书后面的各章节中，我们将深入地探寻新托福写作这种鲜明的个性。

下面这个表格说明了 TOEFL iBT 与 GRE 和 IELTS 这些偏重学术风格的考试间的语言风格差异：

有多少爱可以胡来？
——新托福作文允许我们做的囧事

新托福的 independent writing task 并不是严格意义上的 academic writing，即使在 ETS 提供的 top－level sample essays 中也经常出现不符合学术写作要求的"违规"行为。这些写法如果在正式的 research papers 中出现，很可能会被视为 poorly-educated 甚至 illiterate，但在新托福写作中，它们却显得如此理直气壮，尽显新托福作文"我是流氓我怕谁"的坦白与率真：

- 即使是满分官方范文也偶尔会出现一些打字或者标点错误，因为 raters 都明白这其实还只是 the first draft（初稿）。但前提是不要错得太邪乎，否则会导致考官误读。另外请国内考生注意英式拼写中的-our, -se 和-l 在美式拼写中经常会拼成-or, -ze 和-ll。比如 labor, organize 和 fulfill。更详细的英美拼写差异大家可以参考 http://oxforddictionaries. com/words/british-and-american-spelling；

- 满分托福作文中也允许使用 **I'm, don't, shouldn't** 这类常用缩写形式，这点上它跟 GRE 和 IELTS 完全不同。但请注意不要使用 OMG, LOL, BRB 这样的非正式首字缩写词（informal acronyms），更不要因为一时情绪紧张把 SF, RP, BT 这些汉语拼音缩写带入你的作文；

- 高分作文中允许使用疑问句、反问句甚至感叹句，但前提是确实有真情实感时才用，不要让人觉得你是在无病呻吟；

- 允许使用与题目相关的 proverbs（谚语）、idioms（成语）或者 quotations / citations（直接或间接引用），相关资源请看本书的附录 H；

- 官方满分作文也经常在意义正确的前提下使用 **I, we** 甚至 **you** 这些比较主观的人称代词；

- 可以使用一些口语化的表达，比如 What really counts is...（真正重要的是……），come in handy（派上用场）或者 make or break（决定成败）都曾经出现在 ETS 的满分范文中。但需要注意的是，要避免使用 wanna, drag, bender, wicked 这类在美国年轻人中经常能听到但相当不正式的俚语（但如果你对在口语考试中使用地道的美国俚语有兴趣，则可以登录 www. urbandictionary. com，这是一个极酷的美国俚语网站。而且每个单词后面的 for / against 打分可以让你精确地把握自己是否应该使用它）；

- 尽管被动语态在学术论文中是否适宜使用在北美的"叫兽"们那里并没有达成一致，往往是各执一词，但是对于新托福作文这样比较生活化的作文考试，被动语态只要看起来自然就尽管放心用。

事实上不仅仅是新托福，The SAT Writing Section，甚至一部分 GRE Issue 官方满分范文也都是以生活实践为主要分析对象的。与欧洲相比，完全撇开事实去抽象说理的写作方式，在美国这个一直都高度重视生活实践的社会中从没有成为 the mainstream practice。

Pat's Tips

申请读本科的同学应该集中准备新托福真题并深入研究新托福写作。如果不是确实精力过剩，就没必要非逼着自己跟风熬夜读 GRE 或者 GMAT 范文了，先把本书看两遍再说 hoho。计划先考 G 的筒子们可以从 GRE 的作文里搬一些好的词汇和句子过来，但同时务必牢记新托福作文的论证更加偏重生活实际。

我是否应该通过旧托福的 185 作文题库来准备新托福写作考试？*How did the Independent Writing topic pool of TOEFL iBT come about?*

很多同学都对 O. G. 中的这段经典论述记忆犹新：

"*You will see*，*on the TOEFL iBT*，*topics very similar to the actual Independent Writing topics that were eligible for use on former versions of the TOEFL test.*"

就是说托福大作文的很多话题和过去老托福的"185 话题"接近。但对于考生来说关键其

实并不在此，而是在于：到底有多接近？我们是否真的可以很放心地使用 185 话题来准备好新托福写作？

如果很关注这个问题，您不妨对比一下本书附录 C 与附录 D 的 "新旧托福作文题库大PK"，立刻就会发现如下的特点：

（a）新旧托福作文话题的大类是完全相同的，都可以用下表中的 15 类话题概括：

	话题	机考中出现频率
1	Education	★★★★★
2	Technology	★★★★★
3	Media	★★★★☆
4	Success	★★★★☆
5	Work	★★★★☆
6	Government	★★★★☆
7	Friends	★★★★☆
8	Old vs. Young	★★★☆☆
9	Transportation	★★★☆☆
10	Environment	★★★☆☆
11	Money	★★★☆☆
12	Leisure	★★★☆☆
13	Family	★★☆☆☆
14	Animals	★☆☆☆☆
15	Food	★☆☆☆☆

（b）尽管话题的大范围完全相同，但是新托福的机考写作考题完全照搬旧托福 185 原题的情况是很少出现的，反而是中国大陆和北美前一两年内的机考题目时常在近期机考中重复出现。特别是从 2008 年起，随着 ETS 新题库开发的进一步推进，尽管机考题目与旧托福重题的情况还偶然会有发生，但 185 老题完全重复出现的概率已经非常低了，即使偶有相似一般也会做些改动。

比如，请大家认真对比下面两道题目的差异：

新托福机考题：

In your opinion, which one is better, to spend money on something that lasts for a long time, such as valuable jewelry, or spend your money on short-term pleasure such as vacation?

老托福 185 题：

Is it better to enjoy your money when you earn it or is it better to save your money for the future?

Pat's Tips

很明确：练习作文最好还是利用新托福机考话题（参考本书附录 C 和附录 E 以及 blog. sina. com. cn/toeflwizard）。从 2008 年开始至今，大陆和北美的机考题重复出现的可能性远比过去的 185 老题在机考中重现的可能性大得多。当然如果您考前确实有时间，看看 185 题也并不会有害处，但是全都写一遍的必要性真的已经并不存在了。

准备 *TOEFL iBT Writing Tasks* 是否需要提前储备专业知识？*Do I need to acquire specialized knowledge prior to the Independent Writing Task?*

童鞋们应该已经很熟悉下面的 ETS 官方说法：

None of the (essay) topics require specialized knowledge. Most topics are general and are based on the common experience of people in general and students in particular.

不过，这明显属于站着说话不腰疼。如果完全不具备任何专业词汇，那么遇到某些话题你还是会感到无从下笔。比如下面这道题：

Do you agree or disagree with the following statement?

The renewable sources of energy, such as sun, wind and water will soon replace the fossil fuels such as gas, oil and coal.

再比如这道题：

Do you agree or disagree with the following statement?

Human needs for farmland, housing and industry are more important than saving land for endangered animals.

其实官方说的 "None of the essay topics require specialized knowledge." 挺不现实的，纯属是标题党，有些题目确实需要一些相关专业词汇才可能得到让自己满意的分数。

Pat's Tips

考新托福作文，你可以不是一个 specialist，但却绝对不可以是一个 ignorant person。请至少先把本书 Day 4 里的写作分类词汇好好背上 2~3 遍才有足够的筹码来谈要不要 specialized knowledge 的问题。

还有，下面这个官方表格也可以让大家对新托福写作考试的定位有更精准的把握：

新托福写作成绩与实际写作能力对照表（Source: www. ets. org）

TOEFL iBT — Writing Competency Descriptors

Competency Descriptors	TOEFL iBT Writing Score Levels (0 – 30)						
	1 – 5	6 – 10	11 – 15	16 – 19	20 – 23	24 – 27	28 – 30
I can write a summary of information that I have read in English.							
When I write in English , I can organize my writing so that the reader understands my main and supporting ideas.							
When I write in English, I can support ideas with examples or data.							
When I write in English , I can write more or less formally depending on the purpose and the reader.							
I can write an essay in class on an assigned topic.							
I can write a summary of information that I have listened to in English.							
Is can express ideas and arguments effectively when I write in English.							
I can use correct grammar, vocabulary, spelling, and punctuation when I write in English.							

Likelihood of Being Able to Perform Each Language Task:

<50%
Very unlikely

50–65%
Unlikely

66–80%
Borderline

81–95%
Likely

>95%
Very likely

> **新托福的评分标准很好很强大，但是我无法充分理解怎么办？** *A rookie's version of the rating criteria*

上过培训班的同学肯定都知道 ETS 的官方版写作四项基本原则（除非你上课的时候把全部注意力都放在前排的那个 MM 或者 SG 身上了）：

- effectively addresses the topic and task

- is well organized and well developed, using clearly appropriate explanation, exemplification, and/or details

- displays unity, progression, and coherence

- displays consistent facility in the use of language, demonstrating syntactic variety, appropriate word choice, and idiomaticity, though it may have minor lexical or grammatical errors

听起来很高深啊，可是这样的东西真的有实战价值吗？会有人一边默念这四段话一边去写文章吗？

其实牢记下面 8 字 "草根版评分标准" 就足够了：

● **扣题** 这个是指主旨	● **充实** 这个是指素材
● **严密** 这个是指论证	● **耐看** 这个是指词句和语法

📎 **Pat's Tips**

考试不是请客吃饭。我们只有半个小时去完成我们的大作文，所以必须坚决 BS 官方的 gobbledy-gook，采取更加灵活的战术。

> **新托福作文的观点 "深邃" 或者新颖重要吗？** *Is it really essential to display creativity and profound thoughts in my essays?*

到底什么是好的托福写作 ideas？这在培训界一直存在争议。我们还是必须从美国社会的特色出发才会看到实质。

(1) 先看要不要追求深刻（profound）。

在美国生活过的人一定都有体会：总体上说美国人是相当 "反智" 的（有兴趣的童鞋还可以研究 R. Hofstadter 的 *Anti-intellectualism in American Life*）。这并不是说美国人笨，而是

说虽然他们/她们在重视实践和应用上在世界上首屈一指，但却普遍对高深的理论研究兴趣不大。您也许不知道 the aircraft carrier（航空母舰）其实是英国人发明的，只不过却被美国人做到了极致。类似的欧洲人发明美国人推广的例子实在太多了，比如 TV set，fax machine 甚至 iPod！

再看美国历史上最重要的两个哲学家——杜威（John Dewey）与爱默生（Ralph Waldo Emerson），分别是实用主义（Pragmatism）和个人主义（Individualism）的代表人物，但他们的哲学跟欧洲的抽象哲学比起来属于绝对"形而下"的理论。而欧洲人提出的解构主义（Deconstructionism），本来是很深邃的哲学，一到美国就成了 Frank Gehry 式的表面文章。

甚至当 ETS 的 *Official Guide*（the Third Edition）谈到某篇作文的思想很有哲理（philosophical）的时候居然故意加上了双引号，变成了"philosophical"，调侃意味已经明显至极。

一口气跟大家讲了这么多事儿，答案却还是那个：新托福作文的 ideas 要求 reasonable，不要求 profound。

（2）再看新托福作文的素材要不要 creative。

Witty 和 LaBrant 对于 creative writing 有一段很精辟的定义：

> Creative writing is a composition of any type of writing at any time primarily in the service of such needs as
>
> a) the need for keeping records of significant experience
>
> b) the need for sharing experience with an interested group, and
>
> c) the need for free individual expression which contributes to mental and physical health.

这段话里的 creative writing 其实是美式教育中的一个专业概念，但是道理却很鲜明：作文中的创意，关键是有感而发才会好。

Pat's Tips

观点新颖不是坏事，但是从实战的角度看，对于备考时间本来就并不宽裕的国内考生来说，如果非把主要精力花在准备与众不同的素材上，却忽视自身语言表达能力的提高，很可能得不偿失。

> **准备独立作文是否需要背模板？** *Am I supposed to memorize templates in preparation for the Independent Writing Task?*

To be or not to be? That is the question.

什么叫用模板？就是写作文完全机械套用现成的模式，自己原创的部分很少或者完全没有。下面是个开头段使用模板的实例：

It is an amazing fact that technology is changing our world drastically in various ways. However, in recent years there's been controversy about the hot-button issue of whether technology is making our lives more complicated than ever before. People from different walks of life all have their own opinions. Some people approve of this statement but others strongly oppose it. As far as I'm concerned, I strongly believe that technology can help children develop their creativity. I take this view on account of the following reasons.

更为触目惊心的是，这样的开头通常还会对应下面的结尾：

All in all, as the old saying goes, ...

上面这些句子给人的感觉完全就是韩梅梅的 "I'm fine. Thank you. And you?" 的写作版。本来很简单很明白的事儿却非要绕一堆弯儿去说，让人非常质疑这位考生的心里是否有某种不可告人的秘密。

下面这个开头段使用的模板同样给读者冗长多余的感觉：

The issue of whether we should spend time with one or two close friends or a large number of friends is a complex one, since it involves a conflict of perspectives of different people. The judgment, nonetheless, is not easy to make. In my point of view, the benefits of only few close friends companion outweigh the drawbacks it brings.

再比如这个，虽然是在努力 "化解" 模板痕迹，却仍是 dead giveaway：

The twentieth century has brought with it many advances. With those advances, human lives have changed dramatically. In some ways life is worse, in other ways it's better. Changes in food preparation, for example, have improved our lives greatly.

要不要用模板的问题让孩子们长期纠结。我们从两个方面深入分析：

1) 战略上：美国人重视个人偏好的多样性，所以用模板不是好选择。如果说他们/她们有什么 commonality（共性），那一定就是 thoroughly straightforward（彻底的率真）。在到过的美国几十个城市里我发现：人们停车的时候至少 1/3 plus 都是违反规定，直接把车头直接开进停车位，这帮人才不管把车开走的时候再倒车会有多费劲。更有说服力的是美国国债 –11.8 trillion dollars 的天文数字，典型的今天花明天甚至后天的钱。理论上来说，如果大家一起找美国要债它马上就破产，只不过一般国家没有让美国破产的勇气。这种无与伦比的直率让美国人很难容忍空话连篇的模板。

2) 战术上：我们需要承认，英语并不是新托福考生的母语，所以如果英语基础确实不是很好，那么从实战的角度来看，准备一两个自己写着顺手的逻辑框架是**提高速度**的好方法。

如果大家看一下 the Princeton Review 最新出版的 *Cracking the GRE* (2010 *Edition*)，竟

然也悍然推荐了一个明显的模板：

Para. 1	The issue of... is a controversial one. On the one hand, ... On the other hand, ... I believe that...
Para. 2	One reason for my belief is that...
Para. 3	Another reason for my belief is that...
Para. 4	Perhaps the best reason is...
Para. 5	For all these reasons, I believe that...

Pat's Tips

　　作文模板其实很接近于医学里的"保守疗法"，建议基础好的同学认真学习 Day 8 的高分实例后扔掉模板自己写。换句话说：如果不具备对于词汇和写句子能力的扎实掌握，模板再彪悍也是没用的。如果实在要用模板，那么请牢记：对于新托福写作来说，最好的模板只是一个在考场里帮你控制逻辑的合理框架，而不是充满大词、200 多单词长、每句空话的"凑字儿"工具。而且最好的模板一定是在理解了文章结构后自己动手写出来的，或者是自己参与其中写出来的，这样使用的时候你才会得心应手。**基础不太好的同学可以在阅读了本书 Day 8 和 Day 9 后，仿写出属于自己的框架。**即使英文再不好，关掉你的手机和 PSP，踏踏实实地写上 2 个小时，无论如何一个框架也出来了，而且不要写得很难，适合你自己的才是最安全的。就把写模板当成自己的新托福作文处女帖吧。写完之后还可以随着考前复习的深入继续修改或者找人修改。

　　用自己编的模板，用葛优的话来说就是——"踏实"。

独立作文应该写一边倒式还是折中式？ *Am I supposed to pick one side or just straddle the fence?*

　　ETS 教导我们：It does not matter whether you agree or disagree with the topic. The raters are trained to accept all varieties of opinions.

　　从考官阅卷的角度来说，对于任何一个话题，考生无论采取 affirmative（正方）、negative（反方）还是 eclectic（折中），都是完全可以接受的。

　　不过，在美国还有一句很逗的话，"We all know what happens to people who stay in the middle of the road: They get run over, right?" 从新托福满分作文的比例分配上统计，70% 左右是使用一边倒写法的，这种倾向仍然是源于美国人与生俱来的直率与自信。

Pat's Tips

　　新托福作文的立场问题只有好写与不好写的区别，只有能不能在 30 分钟内顺利完成的区别，只有能不能让你把自己考前准备的素材、词汇、句型、例子、谚语、名言 etc. 最充分地使用出来去说服考官的区别。立场的取舍必须是从考试的实战角度出发，完全实用主义的。

> **新托福独立作文是不是难词越多分数越高？** *Will big, awe-inspiring words give me a leg-up?*

　　上文说到，新托福写作总体上是比较"拉家常"的，更加看重 common sense 的表达，所以与 GRE 或者 IELTS 相比，新托福作文的"大词"主要是用来点缀全文的，而且要用对、用准才是最关键的。比如下面的这个满分作文开头段：

　　It's surely not easy to be a good supervisor because you have to manage so many things and to deal with a lot of people, including your employees and your clients. In my opinion, the most important qualities that a good supervisor should have are discretion, finesse and impartiality.

　　本段虽然多数词都是小词，但是用三个偏大的单词一"点缀"，马上这个开头段就让人眼前一亮。

Pat's Tips

　　通过对本书 Day 4、附录 B 和附录 F 的学习，您将掌握用来有效"点缀"新托福作文的全部常用词汇。

> **作文应该采用哪种格式写？** *Are there any rules about indentation?*

　　细心的同学们应该已经发现了：ETS 给出的官方范文经常采用一种特殊格式——就是开头段的每一行都顶格写，但主体段和结尾段的第一行开头退后 6~7 个字母左右，下文则是每行都顶格写。

　　其实在美国这并不是什么"特殊"格式。写 academic papers 时，每个教授都会指定 stylebook，比如 APA 或者 MLA 等，ETS 用的这种格式就是在美国发表论文时挺常见的一种格式。

Pat's Tips

　　作文格式问题大家其实不必太过担心，用 O. G. 给出的范文格式，或者用 flush left（左对

齐，段间空行）格式，再或者用 indented（段首退 4~5 个格但段间不空行）格式，都是可以的。但需要注意的是：一些新托福考点电脑键盘上的 tab 键不太好用，所以空格时用 space 可能反而更快一点。

> **独立作文是否需要写标题？** *Do I need to come up with a title for my independent essay?*

除非您确实灵机一动想出了极度惊艳的标题，否则就不要在标题上再浪费时间了，半个小时本来就不长，更不要说您自以为"惊艳"的标题也许其实是"惊恐"的效果。

Bonus Questions（以下为高分内容）

> **是否在独立作文的开头段就必须表明自己的观点？** *Am I supposed to include my personal view in the opening paragraph?*

看似简单，其实这是一个相当专业的问题，甚至是涉及美国公立教育本质的问题。

在北美的 composition 课上，特别是在公立学校的 composition 课上，因为 school boards 一直深受 John Dewey 的 student-centered teaching 理论影响，导致教师对学生的个性往往比较宽容。老师们虽然也有自己的个人偏好，但一般不会彻底排除异己写法。而私校总体来说老师相对"大牌"一些，权威也大一些，所以少数写作教师确实有硬性规定开头、主体和结尾布局的习惯。

Pat's Tips

具体就新托福独立作文来说，ETS 给出的官方高分作文绝大多数还都是在开头段就表明了作者观点的。所以对于纯粹应试而言，还是在 opening paragraph 就表明自己倾向性的写法更加稳妥（新托福作文开头的"第 N 种写法"请仔细阅读本书 Day 8）。

> **怎样客观看待北美机经？** *How should I put the North American test-question pool in perspective?*

"北美机经"在国内是相当的 *in* 啊！北美考生们为此付出了辛勤劳动，值得喝彩。而且确实有过北美跟大陆在同一个周末考题重合的情况。就写作部分而言，Pat 统计了 2008~2011 年的大陆作文考题与同一个周末的北美写作考题，发现如下 11 次遇到 100% 重题：

2008 年 3 月 8 日	2010 年 3 月 27 日
2008 年 5 月 4 日	2010 年 5 月 8 日
2009 年 2 月 14 日 (Valentine's Day gift)	2010 年 9 月 11 日
2009 年 3 月 28 日	2010 年 11 月 13 日
2009 年 5 月 9 日	2010 年 12 月 11 日
2009 年 12 月 12 日	

因此，客观地说，同一个周末的北美作文题和大陆作文题重题的可能性不算高（6%±）。反倒是考前一年左右的北美话题（还有考前一两年的大陆题）更值得大家多花些时间去研究。

Pat's Tips

有兴趣的同学请看本书的附录 E 以及 blog. sina. com. cn/toeflwizard。

TPO 的价值有多大？ *What's your assessment of the TPO?*

TPO 大家应该都很熟悉了，就是 TOEFL Practice Online 的缩写（官方网址 http://toefl-practice. ets. org/）。在所有的现有练习题里，TPO 和真题是最接近的，特别是听力和阅读。不过单就独立作文来看，由于是属于输出型考试，所以依赖 TPO 的必要性没有听力和阅读大。

Pat's Tips

独立作文不一定非要通过 TPO 来练习。但是对于综合写作来说，因为涉及听力和阅读这些 input 环节，如果有条件就应该练习一下 TPO 的综合写作来感受一下其进程。

传说中 ETS 的 e-rater 到底有多可怕？ *How formidable is the fabled e-rater?*

对于中国考生来说，e-rater 过去只是在 GRE 作文中对大家构成威胁。但是从 2009 年开始，电子阅卷系统也开始参与新托福的独立写作，作为对人工阅卷的补充，不过主要原因其实还是为了减少人工阅卷的费用（Monaghan & Bridgeman）。

e-rater 到底有多恐怖？ETS 给出了明确解释。它从三方面考查文章：①单词使用，也包括词性和介词等的搭配；②语法准确度；③文章结构是否符合议论文常理。

所以结论就很清楚了：e-rater 的要求丝毫没有超出我们写好独立作文的常规要求，只要在考前多实践，形成好的写作习惯，e-rater 根本构不成任何障碍。

Pat's Tips

　　认真阅读本书的 Day 3，Day 4 和 Day 7 之后，您将对经受 ETS 电子阅卷软件的考验充满信心。

"全球皆应试"
——Pat摄

Day 2

When Brainstorming Is
Worse Than a Storm
思路的尽头

A mind, once stretched by a new idea, never regains its original dimension.

——Oliver Wendell Holmes Jr.
American jurist

昨天我们已经提到了 TOEFL iBT 作文和 GRE 作文是有本质不同的：前者重在语言能力测试，而后者才是实打实的思维能力测试（当然思维测试也绕不开语言这一关）。

新托福写作的大多数话题还是比较常规的，素材并不难想，而且考试时还可以在 scratch paper 上写 notes（考场里允许用的物品请参考官方报名网站上的详细信息 http://toefl. etest. net. cn/en/Information）。但在新托福考场里遇到那种从来没见过、很"雷人"的题目的可能性毕竟还是存在的，比如下面这道考题：

Do you agree or disagree with the following statement: It's easier to succeed today than in the past.

这道相当抽象的考题当时真是难倒了无数英雄。

又比如这道题：

Should a city try to preserve its old, historic buildings or destroy them and replace them with modern buildings?

据 Pat 所知，"拆还是不拆"的问题在北京和上海等高速发展的城市已经争论了很多年，直到现在专家们都还没有定论。但这道题却要求考生用 1~2 分钟把素材定下来（因为只有这样，才能有更多的时间去用准确的英文把自己想到的素材表达出来而且写到 300 多字），真有点强人所难。

关于独立写作有句很经典的话，"Independent writing is not really independent. You'll constantly need a variety of resources to help you proceed."

我们现在就来学习如何快速突破新托福作文难题的素材（您还可以在本书的附录 B 中看到大量难题的高分原创段落）。

3 种快速解题方法

分类法 A = (B, C, ...)

原理：当题目的讨论对象（A）过于广泛或者过于抽象的时候，我们就可以把讨论对象具体化，对其进行分类（B，C...）。比如分成两大类，那么素材就比原来增加了一倍，如

果分成三大类，那素材就是原来的三倍了。这样可写的内容就成倍增加了。但需要强调的是：分类法对思维清晰程度要求较高，所以分类时应该尽可能全面、科学，否则有可能出现逻辑上的问题。

具体说明如下：

○ 185 题第 65 题：

Should a city try to preserve its old, historic buildings or destroy them and replace them with modern buildings? Use specific reasons and examples to support your opinion.

提示： 老房子包含的范围非常广，直接入手有困难。从拆或者不拆的角度看，老房子可以分成几大类呢？明显是两类：应该拆的和不该拆的。相应的这道题至少可以写成四段（高分作文的结构安排我们会在 Day 8 进行彻底的分析，今天先重点讲快速突破素材的方法）。

Para. 1 Introduction 背景介绍并引出辩论的话题：城市里老房子很多。人们对是否要拆掉有争议（Old structures abound in urban areas today. But their relevance to modern life has been a highly contentious issue.）。

Para. 2 提出一些老房子应该拆，理由（即分论点）可以写 2~3 点：比如老房子已经老化了不安全（decrepit and often unsafe），还可能破坏市容（spoil the appearance of cities）；又比如城市人口激增导致需要新的高楼（The urban population boom calls for construction of high-rise structures.）。

Para. 3 提出还有一些老房子不应该拆。这一段里又可以用分类法，比如分成：有历史意义的老房子（buildings of historic value），有审美价值的老房子（historic buildings of specific esthetic value），已经成为城市标志的老房子（historic landmarks），特殊的民居（unique ethnic architecture）和名人故居（在美国一般就叫 historic houses 或者更绕弯一点，叫做 historical figures/celebrities' homes。在北京常见的翻译 famous people's residences 则很少在美国看到）等。知识面宽的考生还可以加入像 *Palais du Louvre*，the Guggenheim museum，Taliesin，*La Chapelle de Ronchgmp* 或者 the Empire State Building 这些在北美和欧洲被认为"一定不能拆的老房子"作实例。

Para. 4 Conclusion 结论：有些老房子由于城市发展必须拆掉，但是有特殊价值的不能拆而应该有效地保护（should be effectively preserved）。

分析完毕。

※ 如果你发现分析中有不认识的词汇，不用紧张，到 Day 4 我们会彻底突破新托福写作核心词汇。

再来看一道机考题：

Do you agree or disagree with the following statement: High-school graduates should go to travel or work for a year before they go to university.

提示： 直接讨论高中毕业生这个群体也许不一定能写到 300 字以上，所以我们可以把讨论对象（high-school graduates）分成准备去学文科的学生（high-school graduates who intend to study humanities or social science in university）和计划去学理工科的学生（high-school graduates who plan to study science and engineering in university）两大类。去工作或旅游对文科和理工科这两类学习目标不同的中学毕业生的影响明显是不同的甚至可能是相反的。主体段可以分别讨论两类学生进大学之前先去旅游或者工作各自的利与弊，内容就立刻增加了一倍。当然，如果学科分得更细，比如再加上艺术类（high-school graduates who will study fine or performing arts），那么可写的内容就是原来的 3 倍了。

替代法 A⇒B，C，D...

原理： 当我们发现题目当中出现 -est（形容词最高级），only（唯一的），ban/stop（禁止），never 或者 always 这五类词汇的时候，就立刻可以使用替代法了。这五类词的共同点是语气都非常绝对："最……" ／ "唯一的" ／ "完全禁止" ……听起来挺恐怖的，所以也可以把它们统称为 "黑五类"。这五类命题在逻辑上多半站不住脚，因为它们太绝对了，想证明它们正确会非常困难。但如果想证明它们错呢？很简单，举出几个反例就行。

185 题第 53 题：

Do you agree or disagree with the following statement? The most important aspect of a job is the money a person earns.

分析： 挣多少银子是决定一个工作好与不好的最重要因素吗？这也太绝对了吧！罗姆尼（Mitt Romney）先生也许会这样认为，但是占领华尔街运动（the Occupy Wall Street protests）喊出的著名 slogan 却是 We are the 99%. 最高薪的人未必在为社会做着有益的事情。虽然在美国大家不讲社会主义精神文明，但这道考题里这么明显的拜金（money-worshipping）倾向也是会被多数美国人鄙视（despise）的。

Para. 1 Introduction 引出话题（写好开头段的全部技巧我们都会在 Day 8 彻底揭秘）。

Para. 2　让步段，承认 compensation（salary 在美国的常用替代说法）确实很重要，比如从经济上回报员工（reward the employees financially）或者员工的工资也来之不易（It's hard-earned money）等。

Para. 3　举反例，提出还有其他很多方面同样重要（equally important），比如员工是否有归属感（the sense of belonging）、职业的上升空间（room for professional growth and career advancement）、工作时的成就感（the sense of fulfillment）、人际关系（interpersonal relationship）、团队精神（team spirit）等。如果只有高薪，但每天深陷于 office politics，或者被 office gossip（流言）所困扰，躺着也中枪（is an easy target for office bullying or abuse），那么肯定不是每个人都会认为这样的工作值得拥有。

Para. 4　结论："银子"只是一个方面，还有其他很多因素会影响工作满意度（job satisfaction）。

分析完毕。

我们再练习一道替代法的题目：

◎185 题第 123 题

Do you agree or disagree with the following statement? People should read only those books that are about real events, real people and established facts.

分析：only 这个词的存在说明这个命题很可能有逻辑问题！远的像 J. K. Rowling 的 Harry Potter 系列就不用说了，而这两年 Stephenie Meyer 的 *the Twilight series* 和 *Suzanne Collins* 的 *The Hunger Games trilogy* 等多本 fantasy novels 也彻底征服了北美的读者们。

如果只有 non-fiction，世界将会怎样？

Para. 1　Introduction。

Para. 2　承认 non-fiction 的一些优点，比如信息量大（informative），符合事实（factual）等。

Para. 3　举反例证明虚构情节的书同样重要，比如童话故事书可以激发孩子们的想象力和创造力（Fairy tale books stimulate children's imagination and creativity.），侦探小说充满悬念、富于娱乐性（Detective novels are entertaining because they keep readers in suspense.），科幻小说则往往成为未来科技的准确预言（Science fiction often turns out to be accurate predictions about future technology.）等反例都很好很强大。

Para. 4　结论，应该"多读书、读好书"，但不要限制自己看书的选择：Don't confine your interests about books to one particular genre（这是在北美生活中谈论艺术时极度常见的一个单词，指图书、电影、音乐等作品的种类）。

裸奔法 TM STREEC ＄

这个名字听起来很火爆吧？用起来更火爆！这种方法是新托福写作考试时最实用的方法之一，而且特别适合把抽象的难题快速具体化。这种方法需要我们快速记忆 18 个单词。

请先看下面的三组符号：

TM STREEC ＄

其中的 streec 和英文的裸奔 streak 这个单词正好发音相同，所以才叫这种方法为"裸奔法"。这三个符号可以帮助我们快速记忆下面的 9 组共 18 个英文单词。请各位同学先把下面每一行的第一个单词看一遍，每行的第二个单词先不看，请注意每行第一个单词的首字母拼在一起就是 TM STREEC ＄：

Team & Trust

Mind & Skill

Socialization（社交）& Competition

Tenacity（毅力）& Pressure

Rights & Responsibilities

Environment & Health

Employment（就业）& Efficiency（效率）

Culture & Tradition

Money & Enjoyment

这样我们通过 TM STREEC ＄ 就可以记牢每行的第一个词了。

接下来，我们又可以通过逻辑对应关系记牢每行的第二个词。每行第一个单词和第二个单词的逻辑对应关系是这样的：

团队（需要）信任

头脑（学习）技能

社交（反面）竞争

毅力（承受）压力

权利（对应）责任

环境（改变）健康

就业（要求）效率

文化（对应）传统

金钱（买到）享受

更棒的是：在实战时如果真的碰到超难的题目，需要在 scratch paper 上"裸奔"，那么为了节省时间，我们不需要把每个单词都写完整，而只要用下面的缩写提示自己就行：

TM STREEC $	
Te & Tr	Envi & Heal
Mi & Sk	Em & Ef
So & Co	Cul & Tra
Ten & Pre	Mon & Enjoy
Rig & Res	

连续记忆三到五遍之后，这 18 个单词大家肯定就非常熟悉了。不过光背不练可不行，各位抄筷子开吃吧：

◯ 185 题第 3 题

Nowadays, food has become easier to prepare. Has this change improved the way people live?

分析：这题不算难，大家自己想应该也能想出素材来，我们只把它当成中场加餐。

skill：会做饭的孩子越来越少，这肯定是坏处

efficiency：快餐在效率方面当然是好处

socialization：家人们不再一起做饭了，错过了在厨房一起合作的好机会（pass up opportunities to strengthen the family bonds in the kitchen）

health：不管 frozen or canned food 还是 TV dinner，都"灰肠"不健康

culture："厨艺"渐渐远离年轻人的生活——The culinary art（=the art of cooking）is growing irrelevant（无关的）to young people's lives.

enjoyment：美味饮食带来的享受也越来越少了——Nice cooking not only pleases the taste buds（味蕾），it pleases the eyes as well. Sadly, it seems fine cooking belongs more to to the past than to the present.

分析到这儿，Pat 真想冲向 fridge 把里面那些速冻食品全都扔出窗外，可惜俺是巨蟹座，从小就不浪费粮食……

素材确定，分析完毕。

下面增加难度，来道著名的北美考题：

> *Do you agree or disagree with the following statement: The main purpose of universities should be to teach theory rather than to teach skills that help graduates find a job.*
>
> **分析：** 大学的目的到底是教就业技能还是教知识？进入 21 世纪后，美国有一部分大学的目标确实已经变成了以赚钱为主（profit-making or even profit-oriented institutions，对这方面有更深入兴趣的童鞋还可以登录 www. becker-posner-blog. com/archives/2006/01/forprofit_ colle. html）。很多学生是花钱去上学的，所以教就业技能（employable skills）对于这部分营利性大学是很重要的。但同时，因为科技不停地变化，所以理论知识对毕业生还是有用的，因为它可以让毕业生有更新自己技能的基础。
>
> 大学教就业技能的必要性可以从 skill，efficiency，employment 和 money 几方面搞定。
>
> 大学教 theory 的必要性可以从 mind 或者 competition 方面迅速解决。

分析完毕。

今天的最后，咱们来看一道难度系数 3.8 的机考题吧。

> *Do you agree or disagree with the following statement:*
>
> *It's easier to succeed today than in the past.*
>
> **分析：** 这道题非常抽象，已经涉及到一些社会学甚至哲学的问题。但只要咱们坚信新托福写作的本质是语言能力测试而非高端思维能力测试，那就可以很快地通过绕场裸奔一周来得出如下的素材。

如果想证明过去比现在更容易成功：

1）competition：过去的竞争没有现在这么激烈（stiff/fierce）；

2）enjoyment：过去比现在的享受少，诱惑（temptation）也比较少，没有 iPod, iPhone 或者 PSP 这些"玩意儿（gadgets）"，所以人们可以更集中精力在自己的追求上（more focused on their commitments）；

3) team：过去的生产率（productivity）低，所以人们更注重合作，因而团队成功的例子多：The relatively low productivity in the past often compelled individuals to collaborate with others, which in turn made teamwork better appreciated. Thus, team success was more likely to come about（新托福写作中很常用的动词短语，在 Day 4 将会学到）.

而如果打算写现在比过去更容易成功，用裸奔法也很容易想：

1) mind：现在人们获得的教育程度更高了：Overall, we are better educated than the previous generations.

2) skills：现代社会需要的技能更加多样化了（diversified），所以很多不同领域的人们都有机会获得成功；

3) socialization：社会交往激增（multiply/increase exponentially/boom/surge），信息来源也更多，所以成功的渠道也更多（There're more avenues to success today.）；

4) pressure：社会给人的压力更大，想偷懒也难了：More pressure means fewer excuses to slack off.

汇报完毕。另外大家还可以从本书附录 A 中找到写这道难题可以举的大量例子。

测测你的进展

请用本章学到的三种方法快速确定下面作文题的主体段理由：

◎ 185 题第 173 题

It's sometimes said that borrowing money from a friend can harm or damage the friendship. Do you agree or disagree?

◎ 185 题第 131 题

Do you agree or disagree with the following statement? Only people who earn a lot of money are successful.

◎ 185 题第 23 题

In some countries, teenagers have jobs while they're still students. Do you think this is a good idea?

If you realized how powerful your thoughts are, you would never think a negative thought.

——*Peace Pilgrim*

学有余力

（适合备考时间超过三个月的"闲人"）

www. idebate. org

独立写作的本质就是辩论。点击这个页面上方的 datebase，然后选择话题的类别，马上能在每个 "This house believes…" 的后面找到与新托福作文话题极其相似的海量 topics。不过必须要提醒您：可以学习 arguments 里面的 ideas，但是绝对不要整段地把人家的帖子搬到你的新托福考试作文里，E-rater 可在那儿把着关呢。如果全盘照搬只能是"华丽丽"的"杯具"了……

课后练习

Take-Home Quiz

① 替代法的"黑五类"是指哪几个标志词？

② 请迅速填写裸奔法当中的空格对应的单词：

Team & _Trust_

Mind & Skill

Socialization & ~~respo~~ _Competition_

Tenacity & _Pressure_

Rights & _Responsibilities_

Environment & Health

Employment & _Efficiency_

Culture & _tradition_

Money & Enjoyment

③ 请用 TM STREEC $ 法快速思考出下面题目主体段可以利用的分论点，并用英文简要表述出来：

185 题第 75 题：

Some universities require students to take classes in many subjects. Other universities require students to specialize in one subject. Which is better?

参考答案

分析：既可以选择写一边倒，也可以选择写折中式（这两种写法我们都会在 Day 9 深入分析）

用裸奔法得出分论点如下：

Concentrating on one single subject helps students gain specialized knowledge more efficiently.

— efficiency

Focusing on one specific subject enables them to develop a more solid grasp of the subject.

— mind

The exploration of a wide range of subjects can expand students' outlook.

— mind

Understanding a wide variety of subjects helps students find a job more easily after graduation.

— employment

Studying subjects like music and painting deepens students' understanding of arts and culture in general.

— culture

在 2011 年的北美愈演愈烈的 Youth Culture

——Pat 摄

TOEFL
iBT Writing Test

Day 3

Diet Grammar
无糖语法

The young man knows the rules but the old man knows the exceptions.
——Oliver Wendell Holmes
American writer

Super Size Me

　　喜欢吃"巨无霸"的朋友们都该看看这部纪实电影——Morgan Spurlock 每天去吃三顿麦当劳，而且每顿都是往狠里点餐，连吃了一个月，体重上升了 24 磅（大家到美国后记得 1 磅比 1 斤稍少一点就很好算了），情绪严重失衡，而且还悲壮地出现了性功能障碍。

　　如今，各种 diet 饮料已经在美国大行其道（It's all the rage.）。其实 Pat 的看法倒是：偶尔用 burgers 和 French fries 麻醉一下自己也不是罪过。不可否认，有些 junk food 吃着确实挺香的……只是同时要注意多运动 to burn calories，才是问题的关键。

Life is like music, it must be composed by ear, feeling and instinct, not by rule. Nevertheless, one had better know the rules, for they sometimes guide in doubtful cases, though not often. ——*Samuel Butler*

TOEFL iBT
Writing Test

老 托福里单独的语法测试部分被取消后，写作考试就变成了测试新托福考生运用书面英语语法能力最重要的一个环节。

什么叫语法？语法就是说话和写作的章法。它应该是一种简明实用的东西，因为如果章法太多，那就不再是章法，而是束缚了。而且，考虑到实战的需要，我们就更不能把写作语法搞得过于学究。只有考场里能用得出来的语法才是有用的语法。

OG, *Barron's*, Kaplan, the Princeton Review, the Michigan Guide... 里面的海量高分范文无一例外地告诉我们：新托福作文需要用到的核心语法永远只有 5 种成分、3 种句子和 7 种必须避免的错误。

请一节一节地把本章看完，今天我们就彻底搞定新托福写作语法！

正确理解 5 种句子成分

英文里句子的组成成分细分起来主要有 7 种：主语、谓语、宾语（还有一种特例叫表语）、定语、状语、补语和同位语。其中，补语和同位语难度比较大，英文基础不太好的同学重点了解前 5 种就够了。

学习句子成分，真正的关键是要知道什么样的词才能作这种成分，否则就会出现错误。而这恰恰是被很多同学忽略的环节。

主 语

主语是句子要说明的人或事物。英语句子的主语比较花哨，可以由名词、代词、动名词（*v.* +ing）、动词不定式（to + *v.*）、what 从句、that 从句、how 从句等组成。

需要提醒注意：动词原形不能作主语。

请阅读下面的句子，并特别注意主语由何种成分组成。

All doctors and nurses should get vaccinated against the H1N1 flu.

Smoking is a personal choice rather than a moral issue（道德的问题）.

Being physically active can reduce stress levels and lower blood pressure.

Supporting children with mentors and after-school programs will give these children opportunities and guidance that they might not receive otherwise.

It is hard to reach a consensus（意见一致）on this affair（事件）.

In the holiday season，it's advisable to book seats at least one week in advance.（It's advisable to… 意思是"应该去……"）

It is well documented（有详细记录的）that college students tend to gain weight and suffer from many stress-related illnesses because of the strong pressure on them.

　　最后这三句话都是主语后置，把动词不定式或者 that 从句放到了句子后半部分，这样可以避免句子头重脚轻。

▌谓　语

　　谓语说明主语的动作、状态或特征。与主语的五花八门不同，英语中的谓语永远只能由动词构成。

　　请阅读下面的句子，并特别注意谓语由何种成分组成。

In this day and age，an increasing number of people agree that gambling（赌博）is an unwholesome（不健康的）hobby.

There are certainly dangers in taking time off at that important age.

▌宾　语

　　宾语表示动作行为的对象，跟在及物动词之后。能作宾语的有名词、代词、动名词、动词不定式、that 从句、what 从句、how 从句等。说白了就是什么成分可以作主语，换个句式它就一定也可以作宾语。

　　另外还有一种特殊的宾语，就是当动词是 be（am, is, are）时，be 动词后面的名词或者形容词也可以叫做表语。

　　请阅读下面的句子，并特别注意宾语（或表语）由何种成分组成。

Junk food undermines（破坏）people's health.

Studies reveal（显示）that there is a definite link（密切的联系）between obesity（肥胖症）and serious diseases such as heart attacks.

What we should do is to tell children how to think instead of how to memorize（记忆）things.（动词不定式作表语）

Life is like music, it must be composed by ear, feeling and instinct, not by rule. Nevertheless, one had better know the rules, for they sometimes guide in doubtful cases, though not often. ——*Samuel Butler*

TOEFL iBT
Writing Test

What we are concerned about（关注的是）is that to what extent tests are harmful to students' creativity（创造力）.（that 从句作表语）

Animal experiments are inhumane（残忍的，形容词作表语）.

定 语

修饰名词的成分叫定语。最常用的定语就是形容词，还有一种用句子来修饰名词的定语，就是传说中的定语从句了。

请阅读下面的句子，并特别注意定语由何种成分组成。

In recent years, the Internet has been gaining in popularity at an amazing rate.（gain in popularity 是固定短语，比 gain popularity 更常见）

Those who have spent some time earning a living or traveling to other places, have a broader view of life.

状 语

状语可修饰动词、形容词或者全句。状语可以由副词、介词短语、分词短语或者动词不定式构成。还有一种难度比较高但是特别拿分的语法现象叫做状语提前，在 Day 6 我们将会学到。

请阅读下面的句子，并特别注意状语由何种成分组成。

Outdoor activities can greatly improve our health.

Like self-awareness, this is also hard to achieve（实现）.

基础一般的读者朋友只要充分了解这 5 种句子成分就够了。如果还感到意犹未尽，可以在考完试后等签证的那段时间再恶补一下语法。

补语（只适合有野心的大牛）

所谓补语，新托福作文里主要是宾补，即下面这个结构

v. +*n.* +*n.* / *adj.* 中的 *n.* / *adj.* 部分。

新托福口语中的补语特别常用，不过在新托福作文中，宾补结构一般只用来补充说明以下动词后面的宾语：find / make / render

请阅读下面的例句：

The graduates find the job market frustrating because of the economic recession.

Some individuals are concerned the Internet will render international tourism obsolete（过时的）.

Many retailers（零售商）are worried that the upcoming new models will make these tablets（平板电脑）outdated.

People with allergies（美国人对"过敏"这个词比其他很多国家的人们更加"过敏"）are super-sensitive to things that most people find harmless, including pollen from plants, dust and food.

同位语（也只适合 pros 与 go-getters）

同位语这个名字听起来很玄，所以我们直接看例句吧：

Shopping, a necessary part of daily life, is increasingly time-consuming due to the multiplied options available to consumers.

其中的 a necessary part of daily life 就是 shopping 的同位语。

所以，同位语说白了就是一个名词的后面跟一个小短语，解释说明这个名词，在新托福作文中体现的是一种下定义或者列举的功能。

再比如 *Barron's* 中的这个句子：

In fact, the Fed is not confined by the usual check and balances that apply to the three official branches of government — the executive, the legislative and the judicial.（行政、立法和司法，美国三权分立的机制）

有效区分 3 种句子

新托福作文的句子写来写去永远就是 3 种：简单句、并列句和复杂句。

简单句

简单句就是只含主谓宾成分。而当谓语是不及物动词（只能单独用，不可以后接宾语的动词）的时候，简单句就是"主语＋谓语"了。

例句： The value of experiments is not confined to sciences.

Life is like music, it must be composed by ear, feeling and instinct, not by rule. Nevertheless, one had better know the rules, for they sometimes guide in doubtful cases, though not often. ——*Samuel Butler*

TOEFL iBT
Writing Test

简单句表达的信息简单，但是很明确，这是它的优点。所以希望大家不要不敢用简单句，其实很多时候简单句也有它的优势，特别是当你已经写了一串儿长句子的时候，一个明快的简单句反而显得生机勃勃，而且给了考官喘口气的机会。

下面我们看一个非常长的"另类"简单句：

The failure of the aspirations of the 1960s has led，in the decade since then，to perhaps the most self-centered Dream in American Society.

因为全句只有一个谓语，所以它仍然是一个简单句，但已经是"超级无敌简单句"了。

并列句

并列句就是"主谓宾 + 主谓宾"，中间用 and/or/but 3 个词当中的一个把它们串起来。

下面两个例句都是高分范文中的并列句：

Their perspective（视角） would be narrow and they would not be able to exchange views with others.

The smokers may be segregated（隔离） in a different area, but the smoke itself will drift（飘移） into the nonsmoking side of the restaurant.

复杂句

复杂句的核心结构还是"主谓宾 + 主谓宾"，但它和并列句的区别在于，句子开头或者中间的连词并不是用 and/or/but，而是用更复杂的连词。

如何写好复杂句的问题长期困扰中国考生。我们会在 Day 5，Day 6，Day 7 中彻底揭开这团迷雾。今天只要求各位先记住：写好最基础的复杂句（即一个主谓宾再加一个主谓宾，其中没有连词的主谓宾叫主句，用一个连词引出的主谓宾叫从句） 才是新托福作文最核心的造句能力。当我们把这种最基础的复杂句练习熟练之后，就会发现更难的复杂句自然地就写出来了。而如果非要一步登天，刚上来就追求两三个从句的复杂句，那只会错误连篇，在写作时产生严重的挫败感甚至心理障碍。

下面的例句都是地道的美语复杂句：

In America，people who believe in hegemony（霸权） increasingly turn to military force when their economic power begin to wane（减退）.

These survey findings may understate the crisis in Iraq as the social structure in that country begins to break down.

It would be a mistake though，to imagine that a Democratic（注意当首字母 D 大写时通常是指美国民主党的） administration would be any different.

有效避免7类语法错误

Brad Pitt 和 Morgan Freeman 主演的悬念电影 *Seven*（《七宗罪》）曾在美国连续 10 周占据票房排行榜首位。下面我们来学习语法中的"七宗罪"。

一篇文章里面即使使用了精彩的词汇和句型，但如果存在大量的基础语法错误，仍然会让考官阅读你的文章时感到很困惑，甚至可能会让他/她感到自己在阅读连小学都没毕业的半文盲写出来的、用词却十分高深的畸形文章。这种薄弱的语法基本功和用词的高难度之间不协调的情况存在于很多国内同学的文章里。

根据 Pat 的长期总结，其实国内考生常犯的语法错误只有 7 大类。如果能避免这 7 类错误，就完全可以把文章里面的语法错误减少到 3 个左右甚至 3 个以下，而这样少的错误是不会对你的分数产生任何实质影响的。

请快速找出下面句子里的语法错误：

第 1 宗罪

▶ **例题：**

Employee can get more benefits from telecommuting（远程上班）than employer.

说明： employee 和 employer 两个单词存在错误。

※ 可数名词永远不能单独使用。

什么叫单独使用呢？英语里面任何一个可数名词，必须在前面加上限定词，比如 the/an/a/this/that/my/your 这些词，否则后面就必须加复数。

正确形式： employee 和 employer 后面加上 s。

第 2 宗罪

▶ 例题 1：

Work at home using modern technology can greatly enhance（增进，提高）our efficiency.

说明：work 存在错误。

※ 英文里动词不能作主语。

正确形式：work 改为动名词 working。

▶ 例题 2：

Children who are raise in impoverished（贫穷的）families can generally deal with problems more effectively in their adult years.

说明：raise（抚养）应该用被动形式。

※ 被动的动词一定别忘了加 -ed 或者 -d。

正确形式：raise 改为 raised。

▶ 例题 3：

The problems that are created by environmental contamination（污染）is very hard to resolve.

说明：主谓不一致，主语的主干是 problems 复数，而谓语是单数。

※ 主语很长，就一定要检查谓语的单复数。

正确形式：is 改成 are。

▶ 例题 4：

Many students are like studying home economics（家政课，很多美国中学都开设的一门课）.

说明：like 是动词，前面没有必要再加动词 are。

※ 只有情态动词可以加动词原形。

正确形式：把 are 去掉。

▶ 例题 5：

Today, cultures around the world were becoming increasingly similar.

说明：时态前后矛盾。

※ 除非是在列举过去发生的例子时，否则议论文里极少会使用过去时。

正确形式：were 改成 are。

第 3 宗罪

▶ **例题**：

Intelligent students should not be treated different by their teachers.

说明：different 修饰动词，应该用副词形式。

※ 修饰名词用形容词，修饰形容词或者动词用副词。

正确形式：different 改成副词 differently。

第 4 宗罪

▶ **例题** 1：

Countries should pay attention on the disadvantages globalization may create.

说明：pay attention 介词搭配 to。

※ 另外，请牢记下面的两个介词搭配：reason for..., solution to...

正确形式：pay attention to。

▶ **例题** 2：

The Internet has instead of teachers in many classrooms.

说明：instead of 不可以当动词用，只能作副词/介词短语。

※ 动词"替代"是 replace 或者 supplant。

正确形式：用 replaced 或者 supplanted 代替 instead of。

第 5 宗罪

▶ **例题**：

Some parents do not obey traffic rules himself.

Life is like music, it must be composed by ear, feeling and instinct, not by rule. Nevertheless, one had better know the rules, for they sometimes guide in doubtful cases, though not often. ——Samuel Butler

TOEFL iBT
Writing Test

说明：代词指代复数名词有误，应该是 themselves。

※ 代词距离它所指代的名词比较远时就要看它所用的单复数是否正确，实践中有很多"大牛"也会义无反顾地犯下这类低级错误，明显是由于从小到大写英语作文的机会太少。

正确形式：himself 改成 themselves。

第 6 宗罪

▶ **例题**：

Some people think the Internet only has positive impact, other people think it also has negative influence on our lives.

说明：很明显，这句话不符合咱们对简单句、并列句或者复杂句中任何一种句子的定义。

※ 同一句话里的两套主谓宾在句首和句中都没有连接词，肯定是病句。

正确形式：在句首或句中加上 while 表示对比关系，形成复杂句。

第 7 宗罪

▶ **例题**：

There are many people think that robot workers will never replace human workers.

说明：there be 句型后面的名词再加动词时不要使用原形。

正确形式：把 think 后面加上 -ing，或者在 think 之前加上 who，形成修饰 children 的定语从句。

来自"老托儿"的启示

老托福考试里的语法这一项在 iBT 里虽然已经被取消了，但是有两个重要的语法考点仍然非常值得我们在新托福写作中注意。

A 坚决压缩冗词

什么叫冗词？就是废话。冗词不一定是大词，而大词如果有实际意义也不见得是冗词

（Geez，is this a tongue-twister or something？）。其实话说英文里有的冗词还是被广泛接受的，比如 in this day and age 在美国就是即使受过很好教育的人也时常使用的一个冗词短语。

但有些冗词在作文中用多了就确实显得累赘了，请认真思考下列说法为何需要压缩成箭头右侧的形式：

consensus of opinion ➡ consensus

The reason is because... ➡ The reason is...

new innovations ➡ innovations

more and more + *adj.* ➡ increasingly + *adj.*

例如： As children become increasingly dependent with their food choices, parents may wonder if home cooking is still necessary.

搞笑的是，有些美国的"文化人儿"也犯过类似语病：

"I never make predictions, especially about the future."

— Samuel Goldwyn
American film producer

B 平行结构

这个语法现象很多同学都听说过，说白了就是名词对名词，动词不定式对动词不定式，分词对分词……但实际写作文时很容易被忘记，请仔细体会下面例句中的平行结构：

They visited the U. S. Military Academy at West Point as well as Georgetown University.

Patrick Henry said he would rather die than lose liberty.

Many American kids prefer eating out to cooking for themselves.

学有余力

a4esl. org/q/h/grammar. html

这个网站里的语法测试特别适合在高中和大学没好好学习语法的苦孩子们补课使用。大家直接在每类 quiz 中挑 medium 到 difficult 部分的测试就好了，把 entry-level 的留给"小盆友"们吧。

课后练习

Take-Home Quiz

分析句子

正确划分下面的句子成分：

① The first step that should be taken is to improve the living conditions of all elderly people.

② Increased investments in public transport would result in a more efficient transport system.

③ Consequently, teenagers' violent activities are effectively curbed.

④ Every year millions of animals die due to the inhumane experiments performed upon them.

判断练习

判断下列句子是简单句、并列句还是复杂句。如果是复杂句，请用下划线划出从句部分：

① Today the way we consider human development is heavily influenced by genetic technology.

② Some people suggest the government take steps to combat juvenile delinquency（青少年犯罪）.

③ Schools afford education of the mind while communities provide education of the heart.

④ In theory parents should spend more time with their offspring but in reality few can spend more than three hours with their kids daily.

改错练习

利用"语法的七宗罪"规则快速找出下面句子里的语法错误：

① Conflicts may arise（出现）between tourist and local resident.

② Grow up in a poor family makes some children feel they are not as capable as other children.

③ Some events are not report by the media in a dependable way.

④ The governments of all countries on this planet is beginning to realize the severity（严重性）of water shortage.

⑤ In general, computers help students learn things more effectively, computer games may lower their efficiency.

⑥ There are numerous countries in the world suffer from poverty.

⑦ Fast food is insteading of traditional Chinese food in many Chinese cities.

填空练习

在下面的括号里填上正确的介词：

① Students should pay attention （   ） how much progress they make instead of how much time they spend on study.

② The reason （   ） the proliferation of pollution varies from country to country.

③ Scientists have presented many possible solutions （   ） the severe population problem on earth.

④ Citizens think museums and art galleries are very important （   ） them.

参考答案

Answer Key

句子分析

① 〔The first step〕〔that should be taken〕〔is〕〔to improve the living conditions of all
　　　主语　　　　　　　　定语从句　　　　　谓语　表语（be 动词后宾语的特殊形式）
elderly people〕.

② 〔Increased〕 〔investment in public transport〕 〔would result in〕 〔a more efficient〕
　　定语　　　　　　　　主语　　　　　　　　谓语　　　　　　　定语

〔transport system〕.
　　宾语

③ 〔Consequently,〕〔teenagers' violent〕〔activities〕 〔are〕 〔effectively〕〔curbed〕.
　　　状语　　　　　　　定语　　　　　主语　表被动谓语　状语　表被动谓语

④ 〔Every year〕〔millions of animals〕〔die〕〔due to the inhumane experiments performed
　　状语　　　　　主语　　　　　谓语　　　　　　　状语

upon them〕.

判断练习

① Today the way <u>we consider human development</u> is heavily influenced by genetic technology. 复杂句，下划线部分为定语从句。

② Some people suggest <u>the government take steps to combat juvenile delinquency.</u> 复杂句，下划线部分为宾语从句，that 被省略。

③ Schools afford education of the mind <u>while communities provide education of the heart</u>. 复杂句，下划线从句表示对比。

④ In theory parents should spend more time with their offspring but in reality few can spend more than three hours with their kids daily. 并列句，连接词为 but。

改错练习

① tourist 和 resident 均为可数名词单独使用，前面应该加 the 或者后面加-s。

② grow up 动词作主语，应该在 grow 之后加-ing。

③ report 被动形式应该加-ed。

④ 主语的主干名词是 governments 复数，谓语动词应改用 are。

⑤ 两套主谓宾却没有加连接词，应该在后面的从句前加表示让步的 although。

⑥ There be 句型加名词再加动词就不能用动词原形了，应该在 suffer 后面加上-ing。

⑦ instead of 不能作动词使用，应该改为 replacing。

填空练习

注意下面的介词搭配:

pay attention to

reason for

solutions to（在美国确实偶尔也能看到写 solutions for 的，但严格来说并不准确）

important to

U of T的点、线、面
——Pat 摄

Day 4

How Many Words Must
a Man Walk Down
词汇不是纸老虎

He who does not understand your silence will probably not understand your words.

——Elbert Hubbard
American writer

Accuracy Counts

　　说起用词准确度，前总统 George W. Bush 无疑是目前还在世的美国名人里用词失误率最高的人之一。这位爷曾在公开演讲里生生地造出了 misunderestimated 这个英语里根本不存在而且从逻辑上完全无法解释的怪词（under-就已经暗示是不够准确的，前面再加个表示有差错的前缀 mis-岂不负负为正又变回了正确的？）。更加恶搞的是，Bush 先生喜欢习惯性地给 Internet 加上复数，在演讲的时候经常抛出 Internets 这一崭新的概念，让 IT 界的大牛都"给跪了"。为此，英语还专门出现了一个新词叫做 Bushism，泛指他所犯下的各种用词错误。连前总统先生用错单词都难逃责任，咱普通人使用英语单词当然得更加小心才是。

（上）Pat 对新托福作文核心词汇的总结

美国人一般不叫毛主席 Chairman Mao，而是称他为 Mao。其实他老人家也曾为英语贡献过一个词组：paper tiger。比如有个句子是《纽约时报》用来形容曾经的拳王 Mike Tyson 的就很形象：Only paper tigers roar. Real tigers bite.

精准的作文用词绝不是纸老虎，而是让我们把自己的观点表达得更鲜明生动的重要手段。事实上，写作词汇一直也是新托福考生高度关注的焦点之一：背韦氏、背 GRE 词汇书、还有无数民间流传的发黄的词汇手抄本……

可惜，Pat 在北京时极度失望地发现，这些必备词中的很多在写托福作文时并不是那么能"hold 住"，甚至有相当一部分跟新托福的作文话题一点边儿都不沾。我们为什么总是在做一厢情愿的事情（wishful thinking）呢？

考前背写作单词一定要紧密结合过去 6 年里的机考真题（如果有时间还可以再加上 185 老题库）去背单词，这样才能确保考前所储备的写作词汇的针对性。

在开始阅读本章之前，请您先把自己的英汉词典锁到柜子里。斗胆说一句：Pat 在国内看到的多本英汉词典里都存在着不少翻译不够准确的词条。Pat 自己才疏学浅，也不敢妄称对下面的新托福写作核心词汇的解释全都准确，但我可以保证的是：在给出下面每一个单词的解释的时候，我都尽了最大努力去体现这些词在北美生活中的真实用法。如果您看完本章后还有没把握的条目，那么请查阅一本 2000 年后出版的带有例句的英英词典，并仔细研究其中的例句，或者就给 Pat 发邮件吧：toeflwizard@ sina. com。

▎新托福写作完整加分词库：1180 词

※ 对于基础比较薄弱的同学，同义词或者近义词只需要掌握一个就够。永远牢记：只有记得少才能记得准。

※ 即使是这个核心词汇表，也不一定要全都背诵，毕竟每个人的基础、需要的分数还有备考时间都是不同的。只要能选出你认为自己能真正记住的那些单词，并尽可能把它们背得熟一些，就是最好的选择。写作是输出型考试，记较少的词并且能准确地用出来，比记一大堆单词却都用不对（考生写作的通病）要强得多。

※ 大家如果觉得备考时间紧，就可以先把每类中好记的单词尽可能多记一些，毕竟备考永远是时间与质量的博弈。当然如果备考时间充足就最好全记下来，Pat 向毛主席保证，您背过这些词到美国之后会发现它们都是常用词，绝不会白记。

Education

assignment	*n.* 作业（请注意 homework 不可数，而 assignment 则是可数名词）
elective	*n.* 选修课（必修课则是 required courses，或者更正式地说 compulsory courses）
credit	*n.* 在教育类话题中当然是指学分
children and youth	这两个词在美国书面语里有时会连在一起写，而且后面这个一般是作为总称，所以不要加复数，所指的年龄也并不是非常具体，基本就是"青少年"
adolescent	*n.* 青少年　　*adj.* 青春期的
teaching/pedagogical methodology	教学法
adapt to sth. / adjust oneself to sth. / become accustomed to sth.	适应
adaptability	*n.* 适应能力
apply	*v.* 应用（名词形式为 application）
segregate students	把学生分开教育
team spirit	团队精神
think independently	独立思考
learn things through understanding	在理解的基础上学习
students' feedback / students' input	学生的反馈
appraise（or evaluate）their teachers' performance	学生评价老师的教学
generalist	*n.* 通才
specialist	*n.* 专才
well-rounded / versatile	*adj.* 全面发展的

contribute to social progress	为社会健康发展作贡献
humanities	*n.* 人文科学
social sciences	社会科学
arts	*n.* 艺术
liberal studies/arts	*n.* 文科总称
sciences	*n.* 理科
engineering	*n.* 工科
basic sciences	基础科学
applied sciences	应用科学
discipline	*n.* 学科（通称）；纪律　*vt.* 管教（比如：discipline their children 管教孩子）
self-discipline	*n.* 自制力
primary-level（or secondary-level/tertiary-level）education	小（中、大）学教育
vocational education（or training）	职业教育
interact	*vi.* 互动（形容词 interactive）
schooling	*n.* 学校给学生的教育（在北美经常可以听到一些家长抱怨自己的孩子受到了 schooling 却没有得到真正的 education）
parenting	*n.* 家长给小孩的教育（但如果是从孩子的角度来说，那么孩子得到的家长教育则是这个孩子的 upbringing）
curriculum（*pl.* curricula）	*n.* 学校提供的课程总称，单独的一门课只能叫 a course

⇧ **例句：**Science is an essential part of their high-school curriculum.

psychological	*adj.* 心理的
participation ≈ involvement	*n.* 参与，比如：parental involvement
distraction	*n.* 干扰（动词 distract students from…）
memorize	*vt.* 记忆（ = commit… to memory）
acquire	*vt.* 获取（后面经常跟 knowledge / skills）
teacher-centered	*adj.* 以教师为中心的
student-centered	*adj.* 以学生为中心的
be proficient in…	熟练掌握……
role model	榜样

peer	n. 同龄人
peer pressure	来自其他同学的压力
overprotective	adj. 美语中一个很重要的概念：（家长等）对孩子或者其他弱者过度保护的，一般作贬义词
motivation	n. 动力（形容词 motivated，有动力的）
frustration	n. 沮丧（形容词 frustrated）
critical thinking abilities	美国教育体系中极度重要甚至可以说是最核心的概念：用批判的眼光去看问题的能力
awareness（of）	n.（某方面的）意识
creative/original	adj. 有创造力的
be well-acquainted（with）	adj. 对……非常熟悉的
perform well	表现出色
lay a solid foundation for	为……打好基础
self-esteem	n. 自尊
dignity	n. 尊严（美国有句很拽的话：Honor is what others think of you but dignity is what you think of yourself.）
evaluation	n. 评估
mastery	n. 动词 master 的名词形式，指"对……非常好的掌握"

⇧ 例句：The kid dazzled his relatives with his mastery of dates, events and policies in the American history.

curiosity	n. 好奇心
elite	n. 精英
test-oriented education	应试教育（请注意……-oriented 是个挺常用的合成单词方法，意思是"以……为导向的"，比如：market-oriented economy）
imaginative	富于想象力的
indulge in…	沉迷于……
thought-provoking	adj. 发人深思的
ignorant	adj. 无知的
illiterate	n. 文盲；adj. 文盲的

preschooler	*n.* 学龄前儿童或者上学前班的儿童
literacy	*n.* 对读写技能的掌握
numeracy	*n.* 对基础数学知识的掌握
go astray	误入歧途
refreshing	*adj.* 给人新鲜感的
uplifting	*adj.* 令人振奋的
motivating	*adj.* 给人动力的
single-parent family	*n.* 单亲家庭
minors	*n.*（正式用法，比如法律中的）未成年人
spoil	*vt.* 溺爱
juvenile delinquency/ youth crime	青少年犯罪
bully	*vt. & n.* 欺负（当名词是"喜欢欺负人的孩子"的意思）
truancy	*n.*（正式说法）逃学，口语里"逃学"叫 cut class 或者 skip school
enlightening	*adj.* 很有启发的
formative years	成型的阶段

⇧ **例句：** Children are still in their formative years.

botany	*n.* 植物学（写出来会比较拿分的课程名）
astronomy	*n.* 天文学（写出来会比较拿分的课程名）
cultivate / foster / nurture	*v.* 培养
promote students' physical, mental (or intellectual) and emotional development	促进学生身心发展
give students motivation to do sth.	给学生以动力（近义词：motivate the students to do sth.）
impart / inculcate knowledge	传授知识
instill high moral values	灌输高尚的道德观（注意这里 value 是复数，表示价值观）
give the students inspiration	给学生以灵感

students' grasp / command of what has been taught	学生对老师所教知识的掌握
employable / marketable skills	就业技能
force-feed the students	填鸭式教法教学生
Students should not be treated as passive receptacles of predigested ideas.	学生不应该只是被动接受知识的容器。
learn things by rote	死记硬背
memorize for memorization's own sake	为了记忆而记忆
a sense of obligation/duty/responsibility	责任感
memorize equations, formulas, theorems and laws	记忆方程式、公式、定理、定律
follow sth. blindly / follow sth. indiscriminately	盲从
extinguish / stifle/constrain creativity	限制创造力的发展
dampen / sap the students' enthusiasm	打击学生的积极性（近义词：frustrate the students）
create undue pressure	产生不必要的压力
mold one's character	塑造某人的性格
adverse circumstances/adversity	*n.* 逆境
encourage the students to think critically	鼓励学生用辩证的眼光看问题
extra-curricular activities	课外活动
A school is society in miniature.	学校是社会的缩影。
indiscipline / misbehavior / mischief	*n.* 不遵守纪律
disruptive students / unruly students	违反纪律的学生

V

theoretical knowledge	理论知识
bilingual	*adj.* 双语的
nagging	*adj.* 形容人嘴特碎的，美语里经常用来形容家长或者老人
stimulating	*adj.* 有趣的（在教育类作文中经常可以用来代替 interesting）
cognitive	*adj.* 认知的
guardian	*n.* 监护人（通常指父母之外的监护者）
valedictorian	*n.* 也是很 "美" 的一个概念，指中学毕业当年成绩最优秀的学生，一般毕业典礼上要由他/她来做演讲
graduate summa cum laude	一串拉丁文肯定让您晕了吧，这是指 "大学毕业成绩最拔尖"。美国大学里拉丁文实在太常见了，属于典型的美式暧昧，最神的一个是 Phi Beta Kappa
illuminate	*vt.* 本意是照亮，新托福作文里是 "阐明，解释清楚" 的意思
autonomy	*n.* （学生）自我管理
edification	*n.* 这个词有点大，意思很接近中文的 "启迪"
syllabus	*n.* 一门课的全部授课内容在北美叫做 syllabus

○ Technology

state-of-the-art	*adj.* 这个合成词在谈 equipment 时很常用，但其实跟艺术没什么关系，而是指 "非常先进的"
cutting-edge	*adj.* 尖端的
revolutionize	*vt.* 彻底变革
automated	*adj.* 自动化的（名词：automation）
mechanized	*adj.* 机械化的（名词：mechanization）
computer-generated	*adj.* 电脑生成的，比如: computer-generated graphics
assembly line	组装线
mass-production	大规模生产
cost-effective / economical	*adj.* 省钱的
transform	*vt.* 深刻改变（名词：transformation）

breakthrough	n. 突破，注意当名词时中间没有空格。类似的形容词 ground-breaking 也是 "有突破性的" 意思
break boundaries	打破（传统的）界限
endless possibilities	无限的可能
advance	v. & n. 发展（另外，它的名词形式也可以使用 advance-ment）
information overload	信息过剩
information explosion	信息爆炸
self-sufficiency	n. 这个词跟中文的 "自给自足" 并不完全一样，Pat 通过英文例句来给大家解释吧

⇧ **例句**：Modern technology like electric wheelchairs, automatic doors and elevators has substantially increased the self-sufficiency of many disabled people.

the virtual world	虚拟世界
be detached from reality	脱离现实
webcam	n.（电脑的）摄像头
inconceivable	adj. 不可想象的
telecommunications	n. 远程通讯
productive	adj. 高生产率的（它的名词 productivity "生产率" 在科技类话题中也十分常用）
available	adj. 可利用的（名词：availability）
novel	adj. 当形容词时可不是小说，而是 "新颖的"，在美国媒体里几乎每天都能见到这个形容词

⇧ **例句**：The company adopted（= accepted and started to use）a novel approach to making their product.

durable	adj. 耐用的
user-friendly	adj. 对用户友好的，方便使用的
conventional	adj. 常规的
enhance = boost	vt. 增进，提高.
speed up/accelerate	加速（比如 the pace/tempo of life 生活节奏等）
manufacture	vt. 生产，制造

standardized	adj. 标准化的，在美国人们现在如果提到这个词一般都是持否定的态度，因为虽然它确实提高了效率，却未必能提高质量。最明显的当然就是 standardized tests
printing press	印刷机
telegraph	n. 电报
surgery	n. 外科手术
adopt	vt. 采用
telecommuting	n. 在家远程上班
online banking	网络银行（业务）
augment / enhance/ boost efficiency	提高效率
augment / enhance/ boost productivity	提高生产效率
labor-saving machinery	减少人力的机器
labor-replacing machinery	取代人力的机器
automation	n. 自动化（形容词为 automated）
biotechnology	n. 生物技术
clone	v. 克隆（名词为 cloning）
telecommunications	n. 远程通讯
space exploration / space probe	太空探索
one's genetic makeup / one's DNA programming	……的基因构成
innovations	n. 创新（形容词：innovative 有创新性的）
ingenious	adj. 有独创性的，精巧的
at a staggering rate	以惊人的速度
ultra-lightweight	adj. 超轻的
ultra-thin	adj. 超薄的
portable / compact	adj. 便携的
antenna	n. 天线

organ transplant	器官移植
pacemaker	*n.* 心脏起搏器
transactions	*n.* 交易
manned landing on the Moon	载人登月
manned spacecraft	载人航天器
telecommunications satellite	通讯卫星
weather satellite / meteorological satellite	气象卫星
launch pad	发射台
the Hubble Space Telescope	哈勃太空望远镜
bulletproof vest	防弹背心
cutting-edge technology	尖端的技术
information explosion（or overload）	信息爆炸
the information age（or era）	信息时代
the proliferation of the Internet / the extensive use of the Internet / the widespread use of the Internet	互联网的广泛使用
technological innovations / inventions / advances / progressions）	科技创新及发展

Media

curiosity	*n.* 好奇心
dependable/trustworthy	*adj.* 可靠的
coverage	*n.* 报道（动词是 cover）
make headlines	成为头条新闻
newsworthy	*adj.* 有新闻价值的
informative	*adj.* 信息量大的

entertaining	*adj.* 娱乐性强的
commodity	*n.* 商品
commercialized	*adj.* 商业化的
privacy	*n.* 隐私
ratings	*n.* 收视率
go viral	这个词组是最近两年在美国才火起来的短语：指某种事物在互联网、媒体或者公众中快速传开

⇧ **例句：** Randy Pausch, the Carnegie Mellon professor whose last lecture had gone viral on the Internet, passed away at the age of 47.

overrated	*adj.* 评价过高的
journalists	*n.* 记者
the press	新闻界
groupies	*n.* （多半指女孩子）追星族
teenybopper	*n.* 跟上一个意思差不多，但是在美国近几年用这个词的人少了
icon	*n.* 跟 idol 不同，idol 还只是偶像，而 icon 则已经成为一种文化的象征，比如不可否认 Kobe Bryant 已经是美国篮球文化的 icon 了，当然还有他著名的老婆 Vanessa Laine
make a splash	演员在影视作品或者广告中突然成功。比如下面这句话就是描述一度在美国报纸、杂志、电视等无处不在的 Robert Pattison，虽然这哥们儿实在太不像 1986 年出生的人了

⇧ **例句：** Robert Pattison made a splash in Hollywood when he played Edward Cullen in the movie *Twilight*, based on Stephenie Meyer's bestselling novel of the same name.

clarify	*vt.* 澄清
censorship	*n.* 审查
blow things out of proportion	夸大事实（这个短语在美国描述媒体时相当常用）
entirely cut off from the outside world	完全与世隔绝
sway	*vt.* 媒体影响公众意见经常会用 sway 然后后面再加宾语

commercial	*n.* 电视、收音机或者互联网上的广告
flyer	*n.* 就是那种小传单广告
billboard	*n.* 大幅广告牌（当然也是音乐排行榜的名字）
poster	*n.* 海报
tabloid	*n.* 这个跟中文的"小报儿"意思一模一样，还有个更形象的说法叫 supermarket tabloids
quiz show	有奖竞猜节目
reality show	真人秀
sitcom	*n.* 情景喜剧
soap opera	肥皂剧
variety show	综艺节目
current affairs	时事
the print media	印刷媒体
the electronic media	电子媒体
news outlets	报道新闻的机构
be awash with / be inundated with / be saturated with sth.	充斥着……
censor	*v.* 审查
delete / eliminate / excise	*v.* 删除
excessive / gratuitous violent and pornographic contents	过多的暴力与色情内容
misleading / misrepresented / distorted	*adj.* 有误导性的
fraudulent	*adj.* 诈骗性的
false / bogus	*adj.* 虚假的
report sth. in graphic detail	报道非常详尽的细节
exaggerate things / sensationalize things / blow things out of all proportions	夸大事件
objective and balanced	公正客观的

expose / reveal	*v.* 揭露
violate（or intrude on/ infringe on）someone's privacy	侵犯隐私
tarnish（or sully/ smear/ besmirch）one's reputation	毁坏某人的名誉
paparazzi（paparazzi 是复数名词）	*n.* 狗仔队
celebrities（*pl.*），a celebrity	名人
scandals	*n.* 丑闻
cover up / gloss over / whitewash	*v.* 掩盖
objective	*adj.* 客观的
biased	*adj.* 不客观的（形容词为 skewed/unobjective）
factual accounts	如实的描述
reliable	*adj.* 可信的（形容词为 trustworthy/dependable）
up-to-date / up-to-the-minute	及时的
code of ethics	职业道德准则
scrutinize	*vt.* 监督
ubiquitous / prevalent	*adj.* 形容词"无处不在的"
absurd / ludicrous	*adj.* 荒唐的，可笑的（不是 funny，而是 ridiculous）
high-profile / low-profile	*adj.* 高调的/低调的
exclusive news	独家新闻
the glitz and glamor	（明星的）光环
glamorous	*adj.* 魅力四射的
in the spotlight / in the limelight	处在公众注意力的焦点
media hype	这个完全就等于中文的"媒体炒作"
gossip	*n.* 传闻（Gossip Girl 的粉丝请举手！）
fabricated	*adj.* 捏造的

● **Success**

determination	*n.* 决心（determined *adj.* 有决心的）
motto	*n.* 座右铭
a household name	家喻户晓的名字，比如芙蓉姐姐或者 Amber Lee Ettinger（Obama Girl）
established	*adj.* 形容人时不是"建立的"，而是"有一定成就的"：an established painter。反义表达是：sb. is a flash in the pan 意思是说某个名人只是"昙花一现"
glorious	*adj.* 辉煌的，名词为 glory
despair	*n. & vi.* 绝望
adaptable	*adj.* 适应能力强的
fame	*n.* 名望（经常连用：fame and wealth）
prestige	*n.*（很高的）声望
reputation	*n.* 名声（其实不见得只是好名声，完全也可以说 a bad re-putation）
misfortune	*n.* 不幸
probability	*n.* 概率
disabled	*adj.* 残疾的（名词：disability。注意在美国因为 politically correct 的问题一般不鼓励用 handicapped 形容残疾人）
succeed in sth.	在某方面成功
attitude	*n.* 态度
tenacity / perseverance	*n.* 毅力（前者的形容词是 tenacious，后者的动词是 per-severe）
a proven and straightforward way to do sth.	一种直接而且被证明有效的去除……的方法
commitment / undertaking / endeavor	*n.* 努力去做的事情
go-getter	很有本事极容易成功的那种人，多数时候是褒义词
highly-sought-after	*adj.* 很多人都希望得到的，≈coveted
adversity / hardship	*n.* 逆境（第一个词的形容词是 adverse）

Be careful of your thoughts, they may become words at any moment.

——*Ira Gassen*

TOEFL iBT
Writing Test

have a yearning / longing / craving for sth.	很渴望得到……
upward mobility	这个词组是美国社会一直引以为傲的概念，如果真的深入谈能写本书。但用最简练的话解释就是：个人通过自身努力获得更高社会地位的可能性。比如 Bill Clinton 出身单亲家庭，又是在美国各州中经济地位倒数第三的 Arkansas 长大（Mississippi 一直稳居倒数第一），他肯定算是美国 upward mobility 的最有力证人之一了
remarkable→excellent→outstanding→distinguished	*adj.* 优秀的，这几个词都可以用来形容成功人士，而且一个比一个语气强
willpower	*n.* 意志力
setback	*n.* 挫折（当名词时中间没有空格）
rugged	*adj.* 形容人的时候指"坚忍不拔的"。美国人一般都认为 John Wayne 是 being rugged 的代表，所以连 Clint Eastwood 都用电影向他致敬
stubborn	*adj.* 这个一般是贬义：顽固的
decisive	*adj.* 决定性的，有决断力的
insurmountable	*adj.* 不可逾越的（困难等）
be adept in	某方面技能很高 经常可以代替 be skilled in… 或者 be good at…
obscure	*adj.* 不知名的，默默无闻的
status symbol	身份和地位的象征（social status: 社会地位）
strategy	*n.* 战略，行动安排
adhere to（principles, rules, a diet…）	坚持（原则、规定、某种饮食习惯等）
rival	*n.* 对手
illusion	*n.* 不切实际的幻想
indispensable	*adj.* 不可缺少的，绝对必要的
well-thought-out	*adj.* 深思熟虑的
a rags-to-riches story	这就是指那种从"一无所有到富甲天下"的成功故事，而且在美国用这个词组的时候通常都要先来一段关于 a humble（卑微的）beginning 的介绍

65

be a flash in the pan	很像中文"昙花一现"
strengths	*n.* 长处，一般用复数
weaknesses	*n.* 弱点，一般也用复数
blunder	*n.* 重大的过错
peccadillo	*n.* 可以原谅的错儿（一般与道德过失有关）
charismatic	*adj.* 这个如果只翻译成"有魅力的"太平淡，应该是像 U2 乐队的 Bono 那种万人迷级的才对

V ○ Work

clear-cut / specific goals	明确的目标
anxiety	*n.* 焦虑，形容词是 anxious
assign	*vt.* 分配
conflict	*v. & n.* 冲突
embrace	*v.* 本意是拥抱，但是美式写作中经常表示"热情地接受"

⇧ **例子**：embrace conflict as a call to change

attempt	*n. & v.* 尝试
competitive	*adj.* 竞争激烈的
accomplished	*adj.* 其实这个词并不完全是"有成就的"，而是指"技巧很高的"，比如 an accomplished pianist / painter

⇧ **例句**：He was accomplished in all the arts.

excel in...	*vi.* 在……方面很出众
blue-collar	*n.*（不用解释了）
white-collar	*n.*（也不用解释了）
negotiation	*n.* 谈判
technique	*n.* 注意这个词的准确意思不是科技，而是指做某事的方法或者技能，更接近 method / skill，比如：test-taking techniques（应试技巧，汗……）

⇧ **例句**：Techniques can be learned but talent simply can't.

triumph	*n.* 胜利（注意它和 victory 并不完全一样，victory 一般是击败对手获得的胜利，而 triumph 则也可以是指做某件重要事情自身的成功）

⇧ **例句：** Vaccinations（注射疫苗）are one of public health's greatest triumphs.

feedback	*n.* 反馈

⇧ **例句：** Their new approach has received positive feedback from the school consultants.

industrious	*adj.* 工作非常勤奋的，就是正式版的 hard-working，请注意它的拼写跟 industrial（工业的）结尾不同。而考生爱用的 diligent 那个词相当正式，不到万不得已最好不要用。还有个词叫 conscientious，是指"尽职尽责的"
constructive	*adj.* 建设性的
stressful	*adj.* 有压力的
exhausting	*adj.* 令人筋疲力尽的
high-paying jobs / low-paying jobs	（注意在美国这两个词的主动形式比被动形式 high-paid/low-paid jobs 用得更多）
upgrade	*vt. & n.* 这个词作动词大家肯定都认识，其实在地道英文里它也可以作名词

⇧ **例句：** I really hope I can give my TOEFL iBT essay-writing skills an upgrade, just as I can give one to my laptop, iPhone or wardrobe. 😊

colleague	*n.* 同事，略正式的说法
co-worker	*n.* 这个词比较生活化,在公司里用得比 colleague 还要多一些
career path	职业发展道路
staff morale	员工的工作热情
feasible	*adj.* 可行的
time-consuming	*adj.* 耗时间的
compromise	*n. & v.* 妥协
sacrifice	*n. & vt.* 牺牲
delegation of responsibilities	责任分配
workload	*n.* 工作量
psychological strain	心理压力

layoff / downsizing	n. 裁员
conscientious	adj. 尽职尽责的（这个词有点大，但是在美国还是经常看到）
approach（to）	n. & vt. 当名词时是"做某事的途径"，当动词时是"靠近"
recruit	vt. 原意指征兵，但在北美经常也指雇员工，或者更口语化地解释成"招人"吧
stiff / fierce competition	激烈的竞争
high-caliber	adj. 高水准的，招聘广告里特别常见
blunder	n. 重大错误
enthusiastic	adj. 有热情的
nuisance	n. 讨厌的人或东西
self-expression	n. 自我表达
self-image	n. 自我印象，对自己的评价
self-esteem	n. 自尊
teleconference / teleconferencing	n. 远程会议
contentment	n. 一种很知足的状态
assessment / evaluation	n. 评价，评估。两个词并不完全一样，但是新托福写作里基本可以换用
time constraints	n. 时间限制，时间上的制约
be reluctant to do sth. / be unwilling to do sth.	不愿意去做某事
profession / occupation	n. 对工作的正式说法。比如问别人做什么工作，稍正式一点就可以说 What's your profession? / What's your occupation?
career	n. 这不是一般的工作，而一定是踏踏实实长期做的工作，就像中文里的"事业"
calling	n. 这个更厉害，相当于中文里的"天职"（用宗教的讲法就是"来自上帝的呼唤"）
work ethic	一些字典把它翻译成"职业道德"，其实并不是很准确。这个词组的含义更接近中文的"敬业精神"。而且自从被 Max Webber 把这个概念炒火之后，在美国它经常还会被与 the Protestant work ethic（新教徒的敬业精神）联系到一起

professionalism	n. 并不是某种主义，而是很接近中文的"职业水准"
expertise	n. 这个也不只描述顶级专家时才能用，其实也就是"很高的专业素养"了
experienced	adj. 经验丰富的（还有个常用词叫 seasoned，可就是"老油条"了。例如：seasoned travelers, seasoned musicians, seasoned writers）
workplace	n. 美语里最接近"工作单位"的实际就是这个简单的词，而 work unit 那个词只在很少而且特定的工作部门才用
entrepreneur	n. 这个词在美国绝不只是"企业家"，而必须是白手起家、自己创业成功的那种人才能叫 entrepreneurs。美语里这类词特别多，再比如 a self-made man/woman
enterprising	adj. 这个词就是"事业心强的"意思，不一定要白手起家
daunting / formidable	adj. 两个词的语气都挺沉重的，用来修饰 task, undertaking 或者 job 时非常接近于中文"艰巨的"

⇧ **例如：** The hustle and bustle（成语：喧闹拥挤）of the holiday season can make decorating the home a daunting task.

sleep-deprived	adj. 睡眠严重不足的
idle	adj.（人）闲着的，（物品）闲置的
significant→essential→vital	adj. 这三个词的重要性逐层递增，按频率来比较写作和口语中 essential 用得更多

⇧ **例句：** Sunlight is essential to good health, but it can also be extremely dangerous.

zeal	n. 这个仅仅翻译成热情已经不够，而是对某种目标的狂热，比如 the boy's zeal to become a rock star
devoted / fervent / ardent	adj. 十分投入的
lofty / noble	adj. 高尚的，比如 lofty/noble goals
job satisfaction	工作满意度
stability	n. 稳定性
back-breaking work	非常难做的工作
nerve-racking	adj. 给人的精神压力很大的
stress-induced diseases	和压力有关的疾病

exert oneself	努力，作文里用来代替 do one's best 很不错，还有 strive to do sth. ／ strive for sth. 这两个在北美很常见的表达国内考生一般也不太爱用。此外，take pains to do sth. 也是类似的意思。例如：If they take pains to do something, it will be a success, no matter how hard it can be.
gratification	*n.* 满足感（语气比 satisfaction 强很多）
collaborate（with）	*vi.* 合作（在新托福作文的话题里基本都可以代替 cooperate）
overpaid	*adj.* 而这个则一般多用被动形式：工资过高的（多虚伪，多拿了工资就装成被逼的……）
employable skills	就业技能
interpersonal skills	人际交往能力
career prospects	职业前景
repetitive	*adj.* 重复性的
freelancer	*n.* 自由职业者
self-employed people	自雇的
personnel	*n.* 人员，员工（集合概念）
competent	*adj.* 这个词是"有竞争力的"，就是说人有本事，能力强的意思，反义词当然是 incompetent
flawless	*adj.* 完美的，这个词在作文里用来代替 perfect 挺完美的
insomnia	*n.* 失眠（形容词：insomniac）
work overtime	加班
workaholic	*n.* 工作狂
incentive	*n.* 激励物，奖励条件
reward	*n.* 奖励，回报
lead by example	这是个固定表达，很像中文的"以身作则"
solidarity	*n.* 团结
unity	*n.* 整体性，有时候也类似"团结"的意思

⇧ **例句：** Seeking unity is the basic tenet of most religions.

demanding	*adj.* 苛刻的

compensation	*n.* 其实在美国"薪酬"除了 salary 还可以用这个词表示，这时它一般要用单数（有兴趣的同学不妨到 www. payscale. com 查一查在美国 profs 们的平均薪酬，并不算高。但是 profs 们一年只需要工作九个月，而且每七年还可以有 sabbatical，所以仍然是很多留学生向往的职业）

⇧ **例句：** Some systems of compensation have been impoverishing（导致……贫穷）companies in the United States.

whine	*vt.* 一个比 complain 更痞的"抱怨"
fringe benefits/perks/employee benefits	虽然不完全相同，但这几个词都是"员工福利"的地道表达
compulsive	*adj.* 偏执的
etiquette	*n.* 礼仪（不要加复数）
collaboration	*n.* 这个词在多数新托福话题里可以用来代替 cooperation（动词表达是 collaborate with）
hectic	*adj.* 超级忙碌的

○ Government

abolish	*vt.* 废除（法律、制度等）
implement	*vt.* 实施
legalize	*vt.* 使……合法化
priority	*n.* 首要任务
establish	*vt.* 建立
alleviate = ease = relieve	*vt.* 减轻，缓解
the authorities	主管当局（作文里有时可以替换使用次数过多的 government）
forbid/prohibit	*vt.* 禁止
legislation	*n.* 立法，正式场合经常代替 law，但需要特别注意的是这个词是不可数名词，不能写 a legislation，而只能写 a piece of legislation 或者 under the new legislation
tax revenue	税收
democratic	*adj.* 民主的

efficient	*adj.* 高效率的
optimize the distribution of resources	优化资源分配
stability	*n.* 稳定
combat＝tackle＝resolve＝address＝grapple with	*vt.* 解决
stringent	*adj.* 严厉的，严格的，政府类和环境类话题里可以代替 strict（反义词 lenient 也经常用在政府和环境类话题中）
short-sighted	*adj.* 短视的
expenditure	*n.* 支出，花费
social security	在美国极端重要的概念，社会保障或称 "社会保险"，千万不要误解为 "治安"
citizens / the citizenry	*n.* 老百姓
regulate / monitor / oversee	*v.* 规范，管理
strictly prohibit / ban altogether	严禁
stringent laws / legislation	严格的法律
mandatory / compulsory	*adj.* 强制性的，按照法律或者规定必须做的
scrutiny	*n.* 监督（近义词：*v.* scrutinize，*v.* monitor）
allocate money to sth.	为……拨款（近义词：be a patron of, invest in, *v.* fund, dedicate money to sth.）
budget	*n.* 预算
the government spending/expenditure on sth.	政府开支
curtail	*v.* 削减
augment	*v.* 增加
priority	*n.* 当务之急
give priority to sth.	把……当作当务之急
duty / responsibility / obligation	*n.* 责任
arms race	*n.* 军备竞赛
self-defense	*n.* 自卫

national security / homeland security	国土安全
short-sighted policy	缺乏远见的政策
expansion / aggression	*n.* 扩张
seek / pursue hegemony	谋求霸权
a vicious circle	恶性循环
destabilising factors	地区不稳定因素
rules and regulations	规章制度
space race	太空竞赛
arms / weapons / armaments	*n.* 武器
laid-off workers / downsized workers	下岗工人
unemployment / joblessness	*n.* 失业
infrastructure	*n.* 基础设施
public transportation / transit system	公共交通系统
power grid	电网
pipelines	石油天然气管线
water supply and drainage system	给排水系统
a democratic and progressive government	民主与开明的政府
a stopgap measure	临时的应急措施（反义词组：a long-term step / plan）

Friends

detect	*vt.* 察觉到

⇧ **例如：** Spending more time with their children can help parents detect the changes in their children's mood.

appearance	*n.* 外貌
attraction	*n.* 吸引，吸引力

sociable	adj. 喜欢社交的（名词：socialization 社交）
loyal	adj. 忠实的，名词 loyalty
ambition	志向（请特别注意在北美它很多时候都是褒义词。不仅是它，甚至连 aggressive 这样传统意义上的绝对贬义词在美国有些时候都可以用来形容你认为很有能力的人。另外还有个词叫做 aspiration，这个则完全是一个褒义词了）
company	n. Friends & Family 类话题中极为重要的概念，这里不是"公司"，而是"陪伴"，为不可数名词

⇧ **例句：** During family meals, we not just enjoy nice, but the company of our loved ones as well.

handy	adj.（人）动手能力强的，（物品）轻便的
cooperative	adj. 乐于并善于合作的
organized	adj. 有条理的
intelligent	adj. 聪明的
gifted / talented	adj. 有天赋的，有才华的
athletic	adj. 体育好的
happy-go-lucky / carefree	无忧无虑的，乐天派的（optimistic 其实挺大的）
mutual	n. 相互的，比如：mutual respect, mutual trust, mutual understanding，还有在美国 2007 年亏得一塌糊涂的"基金"也是 mutual fund。另外，英文里还有个词叫 reciprocal，比 mutual 更大，但在美国也时常能见到
artistic	adj. 有艺术气息的
sincere	adj. 真诚的
candid / frank	adj. 直率的
betray	vt. 背叛
animosity / antagonism	n. 敌意
fair-weather friend	靠不住的朋友
affection	n. 很像中文的"好感，关爱"
hug	n. & vt. 拥抱

reassure sb.	*vt.* 安慰某人，近义词：comfort sb. （comfort 也可以作动词）
superficial/shallow	*adj.* 肤浅的，表面化的

⇧ **例子：** Some of the girls at the Halloween party seemed incredibly shallow. （这是去年 Pat 参加 Halloween Party 的真实感受哈，比起往年实在太没创意了，姑娘们穿的除了婚纱还是婚纱。不过当然也有挺有头脑的女孩，比如 Charlene，竟然也是 Green Day 的粉丝，而且也特喜欢 *Almost Famous* 里 Russell 从屋顶上跳进游泳池那段儿……）

eloquent	*adj.* 表述清晰的，口才好的
eternal	*adj.* 永恒的
lively	*adj.* 活泼的，活跃的
modest	*adj.* 谦虚的
awkward	*adj.* 尴尬的
self-conscious	*adj.* 这个词绝不仅仅是"自我意识强的"，它其实是美国年轻人文化中的一个重要概念，是指年轻人对自己所处的状态感到紧张或者缺乏自信的心态，比如请仔细体会下面的例句

⇧ **例句：** Teenagers may feel self-conscious about many things, like their new clothing, their weight or even their teeth.

dilemma	*n.* 两难的困境，经常搭配 in a dilemma
certainty	*n.* 确定性（反义：uncertainty）
genuine	*adj.* 真实的，真正的，很多时候可以代替 true，而副词 genuinely 也是代替 truly 的好选择

⇧ **例句：** The CEO practices leadership that is informed by a genuine sense of responsibility.

underestimate	*v.* 低估
virtue	*n.* 美德
reconcile	*v.* 调解（在美国最常听说的 divorce 理由就是 irreconcilable differences）
absurd /ridiculous	*adj.* 荒唐可笑的
irritating	*adj.* 很烦人的（=very annoying）
resilient	*adj.* 承受力或者恢复能力强的

⇧ **例子：** Children tend to be more resilient than adults after an injury.

low-profile/low-key	*adj.* 低调的
supportive	*adj.* 很支持（朋友，亲人，同事等）的
contagious	*adj.* 本来指"传染性的"，但托福作文里经常指"有感染力的"

⇧ **例句：** Attitudes are contagious so don't be a carrier of bad ones.

open-minded	*adj.* 严格来说并不是"思路开阔的"，而是"豁达的，接受能力强的"，反义词则是 narrow-minded 甚至 closed-minded
a parochial outlook toward life	狭隘的生活态度，outlook 是名词
solitary	*adj.* 喜欢独处的
reserved	*adj.* 内向的（introverted 那个词挺大的，如果打算用要悠着点）
compassionate	*adj.* 富有同情心的（比 sympathetic 的语气强）
reticent	*adj.* 不爱多说话的
bring a person out of his/her shell	让某人逐渐放得开

⇧ **比如：** Good teachers know how to bring their students out of their shells.

well-intentioned/well-meaning	*adj.* 指某人的本意是好的，一般暗含的意思其实是 have screwed it up 把事情做砸了
self-deception	*n.* 自我欺骗
deceitful	*adj.*（指人）爱骗人的（deceptive 也是欺骗性的，但指事物比较多）
assertive / self-assured	*adj.* 在美语里这两个词经常见到，可以算褒义词，接近于 confident "自信的"。当您已经实在用烦了 confident 或者 self-confident 的时候，就不妨用它们来替换
tolerant	*adj.* 容忍的（名词：tolerance）
witty	*adj.* 机灵的（名词：wit）
wise	*adj.* 有智慧的（名词：wisdom）
considerate /thoughtful	*adj.* 体贴人的
understanding	*adj.* 当形容词的时候是"理解他人的，善解人意的"
articulate	*adj.* 作形容词时指"口齿清楚的，表达能力强的"

amusing	*adj.* 很逗的（在美国这个词比 humorous 常用）
hilarious	*adj.* 极度搞笑的
egotistical	*adj.* 过于自我的（≈self-centered）
indifferent（to）	*adj.* 漠然的
isolated	*adj.* 孤立的（名词：isolation）
vain	*adj.* 喜欢虚荣的（vanity 虚荣：Vanity makes people unrealistic.）
laid-back	*adj.* 您早就对不停地到处扔 easygoing 感到厌倦了吧……
congenial	*adj.* 这个词有点大，但用在写作里很棒，"很友善的"
elegant	*adj.* 优雅的≈graceful
chum	*n.* 各位都知道 buddy，但知道 chum 的人却不多。它也是好朋友的意思，这个词稍有点正式，但可以作为 friends 的替换备选
bouquet	*n.* 花束，这个词的发音很"欧版"，请大家仔细听光盘
prominent	*adj.* 杰出的
sophisticated	*adj.* （人）老练的，（工具）复杂高端的
tough	*adj.* 顽强的
trivial	*adj.* 琐碎的

⊙ Old vs. Young

custom	*n.* 风俗习惯
energetic ≈ dynamic	*adj.* 很有活力的
promising	*adj.* 并不是"承诺的"，而是"有前途的"，另外美语里有个合成词：up-and-coming，也是类似的意思，例如 promising / up-and-coming young artists，反义表达则是：has a bleak future
conservative	*adj.* 保守的
entrenched / ingrained	*adj.* 根深蒂固的
rueful	*adj.* 悔恨的

norm	*n.* normal 的名词形式：常规，通常的做法。这个单词在日常生活里用得不太多，但在大学里的 group discussion 中极度常用
proactive	*adj.* 做事很主动的（招聘广告里特常见，老板都喜欢麻利的）
old-fashioned	*adj.* 老式的（这个是中性词，不见得一定是贬义）
antiquated/outdated	*adj.* 过时的（这两个一般都是贬义了）

⇧ **例句**：The army has decided to discard its antiquated tanks and buy new ones.

deteriorate	*vi.* 恶化
obsolete	*adj.* 过时了的，没人用了的，比如 286 电脑……
fossilized	*adj.* 僵化不变的
life expectancy	人均寿命
unprecedented	*adj.* 史无前例的（≈ groundbreaking）

⇧ **例句**：By 1949, the American economy had adjusted to the ending of the war and the country entered an unprecedented economic boom.

is/are not carved in stone	非常实用的成语：某事物并不是一成不变的
impractical / unrealistic	*adj.* 不实际的
reflection	*n.* 沉思，而且很多时候指对过去发生的事情的思考

⇧ **例句**：① Upon reflection, I recognize, sadly, my past experience of being a high-school student and those of the high-school students today are not as different as I hoped.

② In our search for knowledge, we also need to allow ourselves time for simple, quiet reflection.

nostalgic	*adj.* 怀旧的（名词形式 nostalgia，每次看到这个词都觉得它的拼写实在很唯美）
empty-nest syndrome	这个大家应该很熟悉了：小孩子长大离家后家长们的寂寞与失落状态，"空巢综合症"，而 empty-nester 则是这种状态下的家长
midlife crisis	中年危机
confused / bewildered / puzzled	*adj.* 困惑的
disoriented	*adj.* 迷失了方向的

Be careful of your thoughts, they may become words at any moment.

——*Ira Gassen*

TOEFL iBT
Writing Test

mindset	*n.* 这个词的意思很接近中文的"心态",虽然它不含 heart
maturity	*n.* 这个名词的形容词形式 mature"成熟的"大家应该很熟悉了,而 mature 的反义词则是 immature→immaturity
dynamic	*adj.* 有活力的
linger in one's mind	非常像中文的"挥之不去"
retirement	*n.* 退休状态或者退休后的时间
retiree	*n.* 退了休的老人(pensioner 使用得少一点)
retirement home	老年公寓(在国内经常说的"老年公寓" nursing home 在美国其实并不是普通的老年公寓,而是只有长期身体不好的老人才会去住的地方,甚至有些生病的年轻人也可以住 nursing home)
retirement plan / pension plan	基本相当于养老保险,比如美国的 401(k)
seniors = elderly people	*n.* 老年人(比 old people 客气,它的全称当然是 senior citizens)
seniority	*n.* 年长者
respectful	*adj.* 尊敬的
baby / infants	*n.* 大致是 1~2 岁的小朋友,不过在美国有时候七八岁的孩子了还能听到有 adults 指这些孩子说 babies
toddlers	*n.* 走路摇摇晃晃的那种孩子,也就是差不多 2 岁的样子吧
teens / teenagers	准确地说是 13~19 岁的孩子,不过也没有人算得那么清楚
kids / children	*n.* 对这两个其实每个人的定义都可能不一样,在美国常听到人说 college kids,基本上这两个词也就是指未成年人了(法律上叫 minors)。另外还有个词叫 youngster,一般也是指稍大些的 children,就是差不多十几岁的,跟中文的"年轻人"并不一样
adolescent	*n.* 这个词有点正式,严格来说是处在青春期的青少年,其实就是十几岁的孩子了
people in their 20s / 30s / 40s …	这个大家一看就能明白,还可以更具体地说 people in their early 20s / mid 30s / late 40s 等等
middle-aged people	差不多就是中文的"中年人",大概 40 多到 50 多岁
retired people / pensioners / seniors / the elderly	这 4 个词其实概念不一样,不过从考试角度看,也没必要区分太细了,基本都是老年人,pensioner 在美国用得少一些

ancestors	*n.* 祖先（一般都用复数）
reactionary	*n. & adj.* 这个不知道字典是不是翻译成"反动派"，在美国这个词也是贬义词，就指那种坚信一切变革都不好的非常保守的人，也可以用作形容词
aging society = graying society	老龄化社会
sagging skin	松弛的皮肤（白人的皮肤似乎松弛得更早，昨天在 Costco 看到一张 Brad Pitt 的最新海报，不由得感慨岁月不饶人呐）
time-honored	*adj.* 历史悠久的（传统或者风俗习惯等）
timeless	*adj.* 永恒的（后面一般跟抽象名词），比如 timeless wisdom, timeless beauty
the good old days	过去的好时光
wrinkle	*n.* 皱纹
salt-and-pepper hair / pepper-and-salt hair	在美国"盐加胡椒的头发"就是花白的头发了
distinguish right from wrong	分清是非
mutual understanding	相互了解
fade	*vt.* 有太多意思了，但在新对老的话题中就是"逝去"的意思
stagger	*vi.* 很像中文的"蹒跚"
veteran	*n.*（已经退伍的）老兵，在美国还有个 Veterans Day，在加拿大是叫 Remembrance Day，就是向老兵们致敬的，在每年的 11 月 11 号（光棍儿节？汗……），另外在北美这个词有时候还指某方面的"老手儿"
recall	*vt.* 虽然跟 remember 意思上稍有区别（recall 偏重主动努力地去回忆的含义），但写作这个词很多时候还是可以用来代替 remember
reminisce about...	这个则是特暖人心的过程了，有点像"温情回顾"

⇧ **例子：** Some U of T alumni reminisced about their college years.

the fond memories of...	这就是上面那个的名词版
pay tribute to	向……致敬

⇧ **例句：** I'd like to take this opportunity to pay tribute to all my readers for your hard work. ☺

denigrate	*vt.* 贬低

Transportation

traffic congestion	写作中经常用来代替 traffic jam
treacherous road conditions	危险的路况，在北美的天气预报里只要赶上下雪这个词组就绝对少不了
public transit	指公交的时候在北美远比 public transportation 常用
magnetically-levitated trains	磁悬浮列车（偶尔也简称为 maglev）
sky train	Vancouver 的"天车"，其实就是轻轨（light rail）
streetcar / tram / trolley	*n.* 有轨电车在北美和欧洲不同城市的叫法都不太一样，但都是指那种地上有轨道、天上有"辫子"的公交工具了，而且速度都不是很快
ferry	*n.* 轮渡，比如 Vancouver 的 seabus
road rage	名词短语，指在路上发飙，而且是横冲直撞的那种行为
aggressive drivers	蛮不讲理的司机（不过在美国大家最怕的还是 slow drivers）
reckless driving	不负责任地开车
drunk driving	在美国也可以简称为 DUI 或者 DWI：酒后驾车
culprit / offender	*n.* 肇事者
commuter	*n.* 美国社会中很重要的一个概念："通勤者"，指每天经过长距离去上班的人们，而这个去上班的过程就是 commute

⇧ **例如：** New York City residents spend an average of about one full week a year getting to work — the longest commute time in the nation among large cities.

traffic volume / volume of traffic	交通量
modes / means of transportation	交通方式
vehicle	*n.* 交通工具
decline	*n. & vi.* 下降
densely-populated	*adj.* 人口稠密的
soar	*vi.* 激增
packed / crowded	*adj.* 拥挤的

be squished up	被挤在……里，比如上下班时间的 TTC
population explosion / population boom	人口爆炸，人口激增（请注意后面这个词的拼写不是 bomb，时常看到同学们写错）
impose higher taxes on	提高征税
pedestrian	*n.* 行人，另外在美国还常用这个词组 pedestrian zone，不仅仅是一条步行街，而是一个区域都是步行区
fine	*vt. & n.* 罚款
sardine-packed	*adj.* 这个也是形容公交像沙丁鱼罐头那么拥挤
hazardous	*adj.* 危险的（名词形式：hazard，比如 health hazard 可能破坏健康的因素，occupational hazard 职业风险）
subway car	地铁的一节车厢就这么说，但整列地铁列车又叫 subway train
limo	*n.* limousine 的简称，就是加长轿车了，白人男孩追 MM 的时候有时会用到这手，北美大城市机场的出租车队里也经常见到它
fleet	*n.* 本意是舰队，但在美国也经常用来指车队
car-pool	*n. & vi.* 多人乘坐同一辆汽车，而且一般还要分担费用，至少是汽油费
metropolitan	*adj.* 大都市的，名词 metropolis
overcrowding	*n.* （一般指城市里的）过度拥挤，overcrowded 则是形容词"过度拥挤的"
collision / car accident	*n.* 撞车（口语里 car wreck 更常用）
density of population	人口密度
overpass	*n.* 美国管高架桥或者过街天桥就这么叫（但也有人管过街天桥叫 sky bridge）
underpass	*n.* 地下过街通道
internal combustion engine	内燃机
diesel engine	柴油机
steam-driven	*adj.* 蒸汽驱动的
petrol-driven	*adj.* 汽油驱动的，汽油在美国日常生活中叫 gas，更完整的说法则是 gasoline

hydrogen-driven	*adj.* 以氢气为动力的
chaotic	*adj.* 混乱的
horse-drawn carriage	马拉的那种观光车，蒙特利尔的 Old Port 有一辆特帅的，很适合整个城市的 Francophone 风格
chariot	*n.* 欧洲古代的战车

⊙ **Environment**

pollutant	*n.* 污染物
minimize	*vt.* 尽可能减少，最小化
dump	*vt.* 倾倒
recycle	*vt.* 循环使用
irrigation	*n.* 灌溉
inhabit	*vt.* 居住于……

⇧ **例句**：Some of the Inuit people inhabit the frigid（严寒的）part of Alaska.

conserve	*vt.* 节约，环境类题可以代替 save
preserve	*v.* 保护
reuse / recycle	*v.* 再利用
shortage / scarcity / dearth / lack	*n.* 短缺
pollute / contaminate	*v.* 污染
the ecosystem	生态系统（许多 eco-开头的单词都和生态有关）
eco-friendly	*adj.* 有益于环保的
environmental degradation / environmental deterioration	环境恶化
local resident / local inhabitants	当地的居民（注意与 indigenous people / aboriginal people "原住民" 相区别）
ultraviolet（UV）rays	紫外线
skin cancer	皮肤癌
sunscreen	*n.* 防晒霜（北美的紫外线不是一般的强）
poisonous / toxic	*adj.* 有毒的

non-toxic	*adj.* 无毒的
immune system	免疫系统
disposable	*adj.* 一次性的（比如 disposable chopsticks）
inhale	*vt.* （人）吸入
adverse effects	负面影响，比 negative effect 对考官来说稍新鲜点
sandstorm	*n.* 沙尘暴（在美国有时也叫 dust storm）
biodegradable	生物可降解的，或者说白了就是可以被环境吸收的（反义：non-biodegradable）
joint effort / concerted effort	联合的，协调一致的努力，concerted 这里是协调一致的
the international community	国际社会而不是国际社区
ozone layer	臭氧层
put a strain on...	对……形成压力，比如：Uninsured people in America have put a strain on the health system.
environmentally-conscious	*adj.* 有环保意识的
irreversible	*adj.* 不可逆的
chemical reactions	化学反应
tranquil and serene	在北美这两个形容词经常被连起来用："安静的，宁静的"
limited/finite natural resources	有限的自然资源
alternative energy	替代性能源
packaging	*n.* 商品包装的总称，一般不加复数
contaminate	*vt.* 污染（这个词比较大，即使在写作中也不要用得过多，前几年的"毒奶粉"在北美的报道中就是 contaminated milk powder）
carbon dioxide emission(s)	二氧化碳排放，emission 在这里是可数名词
exhaust fumes	汽车尾气，这里的 fume 作可数名词
acid rain	酸雨
glacier	*n.* 冰川（它在美语里的发音很有特色，请认真听 CD）
discharge	*vt.* 排放（污染物）
vegetation	*n.* 不是蔬菜，而是植被
photosynthesis	*n.* 光合作用

solar energy	太阳能
wind energy	风能
nuclear energy	核能
hydropower	*n.* 水电
smoggy	*adj.* 烟雾重的
respiratory diseases	呼吸系统疾病
agony	*n.* 极大的痛苦
artificial	*adj.* 人造的
alter	*vt.* 改变，变更
appropriate	*adj.* 适当的
indignant	*adj.* 愤慨的
Go green	在美国巨常听到的宣传语，这两年还出现了一个 Think green. 总之是鼓励环保
exploit natural resources	开采自然资源
rainforests	*n.* 热带雨林
erode	*vt.* 侵蚀
chain reaction	连锁反应
ripple effect	字面翻译叫"水波效应"，其实基本就是"连锁反应"，而且 chain reaction 多是用在科学领域，而 ripple effect 则是在社会和政治领域用得更多的"连锁反应"
butterfly effect	蝴蝶效应，这个其实意思也很接近"连锁反应"，但是说得更神：一只蝴蝶在地球某个地区扇一下翅膀，就可能最终在地球另一个地方产生一场飓风（产生地点从巴西到德州到南非，怎么提的都有）。Pat 的看法是：蝴蝶效应确实提示了我们保护生态系统的重要性，甚至也可以当成生活哲理来理解。但它的关键词是"may"——可能，也就是说"如果产生不了可别怪我"。用类似的思维，Pat 还可以提出：大家都应该到阿富汗或者伊拉克去度假，因为这段经历 may 对新托福作文里举例子产生帮助（到底该怎么举例请您看附录 A）
reshape our lives	彻底改变我们的生活

barren / infertile land	贫瘠的土地
fertile land	肥沃的土地
caution	*n. & vt.* 警惕
chemical fertilizer	化肥
pesticide	*n.* 杀虫剂
abundant	*adj.* 丰富的，充裕的
radiation	*n.* 辐射
wreak havoc on sth.	（多指对环境、建筑等）破坏
deteriorate/aggravate	*v.* 如果某种现象自身恶化，就可以说它 deteriorate（*vi.*）；但如果某种事物导致别的现象恶化，就用 aggravate sth. 或者用它的被动形式
ecological balance ecological equilibrium	生态平衡
sustainable development	可持续发展
environmentalists / conservationists	*n.* 环保主义者
environmentally-friendly	*adj.* 对环境无害的
countries on this planet must join forces	各国必须携手解决环境问题，近义词：<u>make a concerted effort</u> /unite/ to combat（or tackle/ resolve/ address）environmental problems
raise（or elevate）the public awareness of sth.	增强公众关于……的意识
put a strain on the resources	让资源承受很大压力（近义词：stretch resources to the limit（固定短语））
wreak havoc on natural resources	破坏自然资源
deforestation	*n.* 砍伐森林
boost crop yield	增加农产品产量
renewable resources	可再生资源
non-renewable resources	不可再生资源（包括：金属 metals、矿产 minerals、石油 petroleum、天然气 natural gas、煤 coal 等。后三种可以总称为 fossil fuels）

consume / deplete	*v.* 消耗（某种资源）
use up exhaust	*v.* 用尽（某种资源）
harsh actions/measures	*n.* 严厉的措施
the wildlife in a region	某一地区所有生物总称，近义词：the biota（=flora + fauna）of a region
biodiversity	*n.* 生物的多样性
effluent / sewage	*n.* 污水
greenhouse effect / global warming	温室效应
severe / grave / grievous	*adj.* 严重的
non-biodegradable garbage	白色污染产生的垃圾（近义词：wastes that cannot decompose or break down, inorganic trash）
condemn rather than condone sth.	谴责而不是纵容
fertile soil	肥沃的土壤
infertile soil	贫瘠的土壤
arable land / farmland	*n.* 耕地

○ Money

precious / valuable	*adj.* 珍贵的
worthless	*adj.* 毫无价值的
insecurity	*n.* 不安全感，在年轻人谈话时这个词也经常指"缺乏自信"

⇧ **例句**：Some jobs are very demanding and labor relations may be poor, which lead to insecurity rather than job satisfaction.

thrifty/ frugal	*adj.* 节俭的
economical	*adj.* （事物）省钱的
make ends meet	习语：保持收支平衡
a tight budget	紧张的预算，更形象的美语中还有 on a shoestring budget 的用法

| extravagant / lavish /luxurious | *adj.* 奢侈的 |
| stylish | *adj.* 时尚的，写作里用着比 fashionable 有意思点儿 |

⇧ **例如：** Selena Gomez is definitely one of the most stylish teen stars in 2012.

penniless	*adj.* 身无分文的
costly	*adj.* 昂贵的
upscale	*adj.* （商店或者餐厅等）高档的
amass	*vt.* 这个词接近中文的"聚敛"，后面常跟财富等宾语，偶尔也可跟 evidence 或者 information。

⇧ **例句：** Chief executives, Wall Street bankers and law-firm partners amassed ever-greater incomes, while the incomes of factory workers, teachers, office managers and others in the middle grew much more slowly in America.

exquisite	*adj.* 精致的，精美的
exorbitant price	天价（口语还可以说 The price is sky-high.）
top-end/high-end	*adj.* "高端的"，可以指服务场所，也可以指商品
low-end	*adj.* 对应上面的一组：低端的
fortune	*n.* 不仅是好运，也经常指财富例如：make a fortune
wealthy / affluent	*adj.* 富有的
impoverished / needy	*adj.* 贫穷的
the haves and the have-nots	大家可能觉得这个写法很诡异，但它确实是地道的美语：富人与穷人

⇧ **例句：** The stark gap between the haves and the have-nots is even more extreme now.

resist	*vt.* 抵抗
temptation	*n.* 诱惑，例如：resist the temptation 抵抗诱惑，或者 irresistible temptations 无法抵抗的诱惑
outfit	*n.* 美语里对 clothing/clothes 的常用替代说法之一，不同之处是 outfit 是一个可数名词
property / possessions	*n.* 财产
status symbol	*n.* 地位和身份的象征，比如 Mercedes 或者 Jaguar
patron	*n.* 顾客，是比 customer 更正式的说法

client	*n.* 公司的或者律师等专业人士的客户
demand	*n.* 需求
desire	*n.* 欲望
greed	*n.* 贪欲
jealousy	*n.* 妒忌（形容词 jealous）
irresistible	*adj.* 无法抵制的
tempting	*adj.* 有诱惑力的
generosity	*n.* 慷慨
charity	*n.* 慈善事业或者慈善组织
philanthropy	*n.* 基本就是"慈善事业"，但是比 charity 稍大些
lead a wretched existence	其实 wretched 在美国口语里还有很多别的用法，但在写作里，这个表达就是"生活很悲惨"
donate	*vt.* 捐赠（名词 donation，捐赠人则是 donor）
despise	*vt.* 看不起
denigrate	*vt.* 贬低
menial jobs	比较下等的"粗活儿"

Leisure

excursion	*n.* 旅行，而且一般是指短期的旅行
sightseeing	*n.* 观光
conducted tour / guided tour	有导游的旅行
package tour	跟团游
self-conducted tour/self-guided tour	自助游
exotic	*adj.* 意思很像中文"异域风情的"
ecotourism	*n.* 有益环保的旅游
backpacker	*n.* 背包族
tourist attraction / tourist spot	旅游景点
travel agency	旅行社

souvenir	n. 纪念品
explore	vt. 探索
relics	n. 不见得一定要是"文物"，也可以很黄很暴力，其实就是古代留下来的东东了，比如就可以讲 war relics
castle	n. 城堡
handicrafts	n. 手工制品
artifacts	n. 这个倒是更像中文里的"文物"：古代留下来的工艺品
cherish	vt. 珍惜（美语中经常把 love, honor and cherish 三字连用后面跟自己非常珍爱的东西）
collection	n. 收藏
gallery	n. 美术馆，画廊
expand one's outlook/vision	开阔某人的眼界（broaden one's horizons 已经被用得过多了）
abstract painting	抽象画
representational painting	具象画
landscape painting	风景画
still life painting	静物画
portrait	n. 人像画
oil painting	油画
mural / fresco	n. 两个不完全一样，但新托福写作里都解释成"壁画"就行
carving	n. 雕刻
Different strokes for different folks.	很接近中文的"萝卜白菜，各有所爱。"
diversion / pastime	n. 业余的消遣
recreation	n. 休闲
release stress	释放压力
trend-setting	adj. 引领潮流的
amusement park	游乐场
theme park	主题公园
rid off the worries	消除担心
get away from the daily grind	从日常琐事中摆脱出来

lift one's spirits	提振某人的精神
one's spirits sink	精神消沉（注意这个词组里 sink 不能用被动形式）
memorable	*adj.* 值得回忆的，描述旅行或者其他经历时非常常用的词
cultural heritage	一般不能加复数：文化遗产
folktale	*n.* 民间传说
ethnic minorities	少数民族
exterior	*n.* 外观，比如建筑的外立面
interior	*n.* 内部，比如建筑的室内
cosmetics	*n.* 化妆品
amateur	*n.* 业余爱好者，"票友儿"
prejudice	*n.* 偏见
fiction	*n.* 严格来说不一定是小说，任何虚构情节的书都可以叫 fiction
non-fiction	*n.* 以事实为基础的书，比如多数历史书和社会学书籍
detective novel	侦探小说
biography	*n.* 传记（自传是 autobiography）
motivational books	励志书（那些书真的感觉都长得差不多哦……）
mosaic	*n.* 马赛克
mythology	*n.* 神话
musical instrument	乐器（如果您感觉作文里总写 play the piano 太没成就感，可以考虑下这几个有特色的乐器：cello, viola, ukulele, mandolin, harmonica 或者 tambourine）
musical	*n.* 当名词时，它表示音乐剧，是美国文化的一个重要组成部分
performance	*n.* 表演（但 academic performance 可就是学术表现了）
mold one's temperament	意思很像中文的"塑造某人的性格"
capture	*vt.* 本来是抓住的意思，但是谈到艺术就经常是"捕捉"

⇧ **例句：** Photos capture precious moments for us.

calm the nerves and restore the soul	"让人放松"一个很深情的表达方式

ballet	n. 用脚趾头想也能知道：芭蕾舞
flick	n. 对 movie 不太正式的替换说法，美语中极为常用
acting	n. 演员的（表演）或者演技
predictable storyline/plot	adj. 看了开头就知道结尾的那种剧情
a happy ending	大团圆结局
animation	n. 动画片除了 cartoon，还经常可以这么叫，或者写 animated movies
special effects	特效
exhibition	n. 展览
exhibit	n. 这个词当名词时在美国有两个含义：展览或者展品
circus	n. 马戏团
light exercise	低强度锻炼
moderate exercise	中等强度的锻炼
vigorous / strenuous exercise	高强度锻炼
dirt biking	提醒大家一下：您要是在美国听到 bike，它可不一定是指自行车，其实很多时候 bike 在美国也可以指摩托车，而 dirt biking 就是越野摩托车运动，尘土飞扬时极帅
moderation	n. 适度，常用于短语 in moderation

⇧ **例句**：Drinking in moderation can actually be a healthy habit.

workout	n. 健身
aerobic exercises	有氧运动
blood circulation	血液循环
flexibility	n. 灵活性
endurance	n. 耐力
coordination	n. 协调，（身体的）协调性
marathon	n. 马拉松（北美的很多马拉松其实是为了 fundraising，所以经常有业余选手参加，气氛很轻松）
athletics = track and field	在英国这个词并不等于 sports，而是专指田径，但在美国则基本就等于 sports + exercise
exquisite tastes	高雅的品味

antique	*n.* 古董　*adj.* 过时的
gorgeous	*adj.* 超级好看的
unsightly	*adj.* 不好看的，写作里可以代替 ugly
hideous	*adj.* 巨丑的（如果说人丑，小年轻们还常说一个极损的词：butt-ugly）
connoisseur	*n.* 鉴定家，这个词发音特法国，请大家认真听光盘
pretentious	*adj.* 爱慕虚荣的
keep up with the Joneses	（idiom）攀比
multisensory	*adj.* 涉及多种感官的

⇧ **例句：** Overseas trips are multisensory experiences of foreign cultures.

appealing / attractive	*adj.* 有吸引力的
fascinating / captivating	*adj.* 极有吸引力的
indulge in…	放纵自己于……（反义词组：dabble in… 对……浅尝辄止）

⇧ **例句：** He loves wine but he doesn't indulge in it.

　对比： Al Gore first dabbled in politics when he was in university.

punch line	一个笑话最后的那句最逗的话
exhilarating	*adj.* 让人特兴奋的，比较"拽"的文科教授上课的时候有时喜欢用这个词代替被用得过多的 exciting
aesthetic	*adj.* 审美的
garish	*adj.* 艳俗的

⇧ **例句：** Her earrings are too garish for my taste.

| orchestra | *n.*（交响）乐团 |
| symphony | *n.* 交响乐 |

　下面是几种写起来有点意思的 sports/exercise：

horseback riding	骑马
archery	射箭
triathlon	铁人三项
racquetball / squash	严格来说这两种还不完全一样，但是都可以算作"壁球"
spinning	*n.* 这个现在在美国实在太火，虽然形式不同，但本质都是室内自行车运动

lacrosse	*n.* 这个暂时还无法跟美国的传统三大球相比，但有逐渐成为主流的趋势：美式曲棍球，Buick 的那款车名也由此而来

○ **Family**

elderly people / senior citizens	老年人
family bonds / family ties	亲情
family values	家庭观念
strengthen / reinforce	*vt.* 增强，加固
spouse	*n.* 配偶
offspring	*n.* 家里的孩子，请注意它的复数还是 offspring
sibling (s)	*n.* 兄弟姐妹
sibling rivalry	*n.* 在美国家庭里经常被提起的概念：兄弟姐妹间的相互竞争
cousin	*n.* 表兄弟/姐妹
household chores	家务事儿，接近 housework

⇧ **比如**：take out the trash/garbage 倒垃圾，do the laundry 洗衣服，do the dishes 洗碗等

give-and-take	*n.* 这也是个特"美"的词儿，而且有好几个不同的意思，在家庭类和 Friends 类话题中，是"相互的支持与谅解"的意思

⇧ **例句**：In any friendship there has to be some give-and-take.

personality clash	性格冲突
household appliances	家庭用品，特别常指家电，比如 washer, vacuum cleaner 等
be tied down by	被……所拖累
generation gap	代沟
one's immediate family	很接近中文的"家人"概念
one's relatives	一般指中文的"家人"概念之外别的亲戚
nuclear family	只有父母和孩子一起住的小家庭
extended family	这个就是"一大家子人" = three or even more generations live together under the same roof)
neighborhood	*n.* 社区，也经常叫做 community

attachment to... / affinity for...	这个名词在家庭类话题里不是"附件",而是很像中文的"依恋",比如 the child's attachment to his mother
family heirloom	这个就是中文的"传家宝"
family reunion	家庭团聚
Blood is thicker than water.	这句不必多解释了,大家来了北美就知道咱中国的家长真是世界上最伟大的家长

⇧ **例句:** Anna gave her son the job instead of advertising the position. Blood is thicker than water.

a sense of belonging	归属感
an attachment to sth. / an affinity for sth.	对……的依恋
single-parent households	单亲家庭
mistreat / abuse	*v.* 虐待
domestic violence	家庭暴力
addiction to drugs / be addicted to drugs	毒品上瘾
harmony	*n.* 和谐

○ Animals

companion	*n.* 伙伴
man / humans / the human race / humanity / humankind / Homo sapiens	这些都是"人类"的正确写法,但请特别注意这些词在单复数上的区别,最后一个是很正式的表达法。不用担心不加冠词的 man 指人类会有性别歧视问题,这个词作为人类的意思即使在大学论文里也很常见
abuse	*n. & vt.* 动物类话题中指虐待 (=mistreat)

⇧ **例句:** Brutal abuse of animals in the lab was disclosed by the investigation.

replacements = alternatives	*n.* 替代物(比如化妆品实验用动物作为人类的替代物)
epidemic	*n.* 爆发的传染病
captivity	*n.* 囚禁

creatures	n. 在新托福作文里这个词是用来替换 animals 的好选择

⇧ **例句：** Today, countless creatures are facing extinction because of human activities.

drive off our loneliness	驱散我们的寂寞
well-behaved	adj. 表现很乖的
preserve	vt. 保护，注意它一般是指保护某种资源，比如 wild animals, natural resources, old buildings 等
habitat	n. 栖息地
brutal / callous /merciless/ inhuman/ruthless	adj. 残忍的，虽然程度不完全一样，但是作文里都可以用来代替 cruel 这个大家在作文用得很 cruelly 的词
biodiversity	n. 生物多样性
endangered species	濒危动物
hide	n. 兽皮，兽毛的美语是 fur，近几年在美国环保主义者们示威时经常举个大牌子，上书：I'd rather go naked than wear fur（皮草）.
pharmaceutical company	制药公司
biomedical research	生物医学研究
clinical	adj. 临床的

⇧ **例如：** The medicine is undergoing clinical trials. 这种药正在经受临床试验。

laboratory	n. 实验室
simulation	n.（用实验、仪器等的）模拟
animal rights activists	动物权益保护主义者（请注意这个词组中的 right 美语惯用复数）
medical research	医学研究
cruel	adj. 残忍的，近义词：merciless, inhuman（注意和 inhu-mane "不人道" 的区分），callous, brutal
vivisection	n. 活体解剖
anesthetic	n. 麻醉（注意它的拼写虽然以 c 结尾，但是是名词）
relieve / alleviate / ease animals' pain	减轻动物的痛苦
pets are their owners' companions	宠物是主人的伙伴

V

afford their masters consolation and comfort	给主人心理安慰
poach	*v.* 偷猎（名词：poaching）
there are no replacements/ substitutes/ alternatives for sth.	某一种事物是没有替代物的（如果是单数则 replacements，substitutes 和 alternatives 要去掉 s）

○ **Food**

tasty	*adj.* 味道好的，偶知道你早已用烦 delicious 了 ☺
flavor	*n.* taste 是味道，而 flavor 则是"风味"
aroma	*n.* 这个词是指饭菜的"香味儿"了，形容词叫 aromatic，但注意它一般都是形容饭菜或者一些饮料，花香可是叫 fragrance
scrumptious	*adj.* 超级好吃的
delicacy	*n.* 虽然 delicious 已经被用烂，但这个"美味食品"仍是很酷的加分词
authentic	*adj.* 地道的，正宗的
variety	*n.* 多样性，老话说：Variety is the spice of life.
organic	*adj.* 有机的
intake	*n.* 摄入量（在美国一些教育机构的招聘人数也叫 intake）
excessive intake of...	……的摄入过多
obesity	肥胖症
coronary heart disease（CHD）	冠心病
greasy	*adj.* 油腻的
food hygiene	食品卫生
dairy products	奶制品，还包括 cream，butter，cheese 等
sedentary lifestyle	缺乏运动的生活方式（近义词还有 physical inactivity 缺乏运动）
TV dinner	基本上就是指那些很不健康的外卖或者速冻食品了，这个词组虽然简单但在美国确实经常听到
diabetes	*n.* 糖尿病

cardiovascular disease	心血管疾病
malnourished	*adj.* 营养不良的
incurable disease	无法治愈的病
treatment	*n.* 泛指治疗
therapy	*n.* （一般指非药物或者手术的）治疗
nutrition fact	在美国食品外包装上必须贴的"营养成分构成表"
nutritious / nourishing	*adj.* 有营养的
vegetarian	*n.* 素食主义者，还有一种更为极端的素食主义者叫 vegan，对鸡蛋、牛奶和 cheese 都毫不动心
frozen food	冷冻食品
canned food	罐装食品
fattening	*adj.* 一听到这个词很多美国女孩就会感到肝儿颤：让人发胖的
watch your diet	"控制饮食"就这么简单，而且连一些 dieticians（营养师）也这么讲
groceries	*n.* 美语里极其常用的词汇，经常用复数：从超市或者别的店儿里买的食品或其他小物品，grocery store 也很常用
low-calorie	*adj.* 低热量的
low-fat	*adj.* 低脂肪的
low-cholesterol	*adj.* 低胆固醇的
lose weight at a healthy pace	以不破坏健康的速度去减肥
calcium	*n.* 钙
high in fiber	*n.* 高纤维
gain weight	发胖
overweight	*adj.* 超重的
chronic diseases	慢性病
symptoms	*n.* （疾病的）症状
feeble	*adj.* 虚弱的

junkie	*n.* 对于某种饮食或者物品上瘾的人，比如 a Coca-Cola junkie / a high-tech junkie
cuisine	*n.* 请注意这个词并不是指具体一个菜，而是指某一类有特色的菜的总称，有点接近中文的"菜系"，比如：Italian cuisine / Indian cuisine
recipe	这个也容易用错，请注意它并不完全等同于中文的"菜谱儿"，而是指具体做某个菜的方法。中文"菜谱儿"的准确英文说法是 cookbook（你看多牛，一般还不叫 cooking book）。比喻用法：a recipe for success / trouble / disaster
starving	*adj.* 饿得不行了的
keep fit	很多人把它解释为"保持好身材"，其实并不完全对。"保持好身材"仅仅是 keep fit 的一个方面，在地道英文里，keep fit 很接近"保持健康"的意思。类似的还有一个短语：get in shape，也是改善自己的身体状况
invigorated	*adj.* 精力充沛的
ingredient	*n.* 原料

⇧ **比喻用法：**The development of new products is an essential ingredient of these companies'（公司的）success.

beverage	*n.* 饮料的正式说法
wholesome / healthy	*adj.* 有益健康的
balanced diet	均衡的饮食
dietary habits	饮食习惯
staple	*n.* 主食　*adj.* 主要的
cooking utensils	厨具
eating utensils	餐具
silverware	*n.* 西式餐具，其实美国人用筷子用得挺好的人也不在少数，而且也都知道 Kung Pao Chicken 和 Ma Po Tofu，虽然他们/她们心目中这两个菜的味道和北京餐馆里正宗的这两个菜千差万别……
allergy	*n.* 过敏（形容词：allergic to）

carbohydrate	*n.* 碳水化合物
protein	*n.* 蛋白质
vitamin	*n.* 维生素
mineral	*n.* 矿物质
trace elements	微量元素
supplement	*vt.* 对……提供补充

⇧ **例句**：Scott supplements his diet with iron tablets.

可以肯定地说，如果您真的可以记熟了上述词汇，并且经常思考附录 C-E 中的考题，那么在新托福写作的用词方面您已经可以算一个专家了。当然还是要强调：① 不需要每个词都记，只记你认为自己容易想到的词；② 只要打算记一个词就必须背熟，如果只是似是而非、既不熟练又不准确的记忆，那么在考场上只会导致扣分而不是拿分。

（下）**Pat** 关于精确使用写作词汇的心里话

中国考生最容易失手的写作单词总结

易错词	错误原因
benefit	benefit from 这个词组前面的主语一般是人或者机构，是"从……中获益"的意思。但如果要表示某事物"对……有益"，则可以把 benefit 直接作为及物动词使用，后面跟作宾语的人或者机构，可这时就不要再加 from 了，或者改用形容词形式 be beneficial to... 也可以
lack	这个貌似简单的小词却错得更多。在地道美语中，作动词的时候 lack 是及物动词，后面不能跟介词（它的分词 lacking 有一些特殊用法，但是建议大家考试的时候就不要用 lacking 的形式了，否则更容易乱）。lack 的另一个正确用法是它还可以作名词，这时候后面的介词必须跟 of，请不要跟别的介词（这里还是 lacking 特殊，但也不必掌握了）

Be careful of your thoughts, they may become words at any moment.

——Ira Gassen

（续表）

易错词	错误原因
affect	这个是表示"影响……"的动词，经常看到同学把它拼错
modern	这个词真的不该错，可惜我见过太多英语学习者把它错拼成了 morden，类似的容易拼错的还有 environment 和 government
research	"研究"这个词是不可数名词，不要加复数
knowledge	不可数名词，不能加复数
data	错误原因同上
information	错误原因同上
equipment	错误原因同上
be concerned about /be concerned with	这两个词组意思并不完全一样: be concerned about 在北美多数时候是表示"关注……"的意思，be concerned with 则是"关于……"的意思
rise / raise / arise	这三个词一定要分清楚。raise 是及物动词，指的是提高别的东西或者抚养孩子；rise 是不及物动词，指的是自身升高；arise 也是不及物动词，意思是某个现象出现，在托福作文里和 emerge 的意思非常接近
outweigh	请注意它的词性是动词，意思是"超过，大于"，经常在比较利弊时使用。要注意的是它的拼写词尾没有 t，Pat 经常发现大家把它和 overweight（超重的）弄混
while	这个词的常见错误是把它当成句首副词用，写成 While,……的形式。这样写的同学们明显是把它和 However,……弄混了。请注意: while 的后面一定紧跟英文，而永远不可能紧跟一个逗号
in a word	很多同学甚至教师喜欢把它放在结尾段开头，当成"总而言之"的意思，可惜在地道英文里它后面只能是一个单词，比如"The movie was, in a word, horrible."，而不能跟一个句子（但 in other words 是可以跟句子的）
nowadays	一定要注意这个词的拼写最后有一个字母 s，它的词性是副词而不是形容词，它也并没有 nowaday 这个错误的形容词形式

（续表）

易错词	错误原因
relative	很遗憾，这个词连很多英语专业的孩子也会用错。大家误以为它是"与……相关的"的意思，其实它的正确意思是"相对的"，比如常用的 the relative advantage of something 或者 the relative peace in this country，还可以说 the relative importance of natural talent。这个词的副词 relatively（相对地）也很常用，比如 Movie stars' relatively short working life may be some justification for their very high pay. 至于大家要表达的"与……相关的"，其实正确的形容词应该是 related。注意地道英文里还有常用短语 related to 或者合成词 unrelated，但是 related 极少使用副词形式
extinct	"已经灭绝的"。这个词的词性是形容词，却有很多孩子把它误用为动词。这两个写法都是正确的：become extinct 和 go extinct. 它的名词形式是 extinction，比如 face extinction
economy	注意由这个词派生的另外三种形式意思全都不同：economy 是"经济"，economics 是"经济学"，economic 是形容词"跟经济有关的"，而 economical 则是说做某种事物"省钱的"
staff	这么简单的词一不小心也会成为障碍，一定要注意它是员工的总称而不是指单个员工，所以也不能加复数-s。staff member 和 staffer 则都是单复数均可以用的，staffer 在美国偶尔能听到有人用，但不算很高频
superior	这个词意思上接近 better，很多同学的用法错误在于给它又加了比较级形式，其实它不能再加 more，而且它后面需要跟介词 to

⇧ **例句：** Scientists have repeated proven that breastfeeding is superior to formula feeding.
（这里的 formula 是配方奶，Formula 1 则是一级方程式汽车赛）

discriminate	注意这个词作"歧视"的意思时只能作不及物动词，经常看到国内的朋友们写 discriminate sb.，其实是错误的英文，必须用 discriminate against sb.

⇧ **例句：** Under federal law, it is illegal to discriminate against minorities and women.

新托福作文抽象加分词总结（非牛人请飘过）

名词部	
misery	这个抽象词的所指相当广泛，可以包括从 poverty 到 starvation 到 unemployment 到 unrequited love 等等任何值得同情的状态，难怪小说 *Les Misérables* 被翻译成中文的《悲惨世界》
wellbeing	它泛指一种比较良好的生活状态

⇧ **例句：** This movie has documented the sedentary lifestyle's influence on people's physical and psychological well-being.

mechanism	政府类常用词："机制"

⇧ **比如：** to reform the current decision-making mechanism in the government

alienation	疏远，它的形容词更加常用，be alienated from sb.
equilibrium	很像 balance，但是更加虚伪，比如：ecological equilibrium
circumstances	处境，状况

⇧ **例句：** The circumstances of an individual crime and the motivation for committing it should always be taken into account when the punishment is decided on.

similarity	相似之处，反义词：distinction
distinction	可以看做 difference 的升级版：差异。它的形容词 distinctive 是指 "很独特的"，接近 unique
disparity	这个词基本就是 gap 的升级版了：差距
remedy	这个词的本意指一种病的治疗方法，新托福作文里意思很像 solution，"解决方法"
ancestors	它多用复数，"祖先"
posterity	一般只用单数，而且前面不加 the，"后代"

⇧ **例如：** preserve resources for posterity

pursuit	这个估计各位写 personal statement 说明自己的目标的时候都已经用了 N 次吧，如果实在用烦了，就用 endeavor，commitment，undertaking，quest（后两个意思不完全相同）这些词换换吧。类似的意思，语气最强的是 aspiration

（续表）

名词部	
novelty	不再是小说，而是指非常新鲜有趣的东西，比如 Nintendo 的 Wii U
rarity	指罕见稀有的东西，比如 This antique chair is a definite rarity.
commonality	这个词挺大，不过新托福作文中也偶有使用，就是"共性"

⇧ **例句：** Some friendships grow over years. Others form in an instant. The commonality of all these friendships is — the recognition of the special things we share in common. Friends assure us that we are not alone in the world.

incidence	有点像 rate，但它一般是特指某种坏现象的发生率

⇧ **例如：** the rising incidence of obesity, coronary heart diseases and diabetes

ambience / atmosphere	气氛，氛围
necessity	必需品或者必要性
luxury	奢侈，作文里有时候也作"奢望"

⇧ **例句：** Having a garden would be a luxury in downtown Manhattan.

niceties	在美国是很常见的一个词，而且经常用复数，表示那种看起来很美但实际并不是很必要的事物

⇧ **例句：** The niceties of technology-aimed life mean little when our needs are simple: warmth when we're cold; food when we're hungry; sleep when we're tired.

形容词部	
materialistic	物质化的，非常现实的，在美国这个词经常用来描述大城市居民，比如热爱 Manolo Blahnik 的 Carrie
mediocre	平庸的，水平一般的，用来描述人或者说事物都挺拿分的
alarming	令人警觉的，比如 the alarming crime rate
disturbing	让人很烦的，困扰人的
recurring	一再出现的，一再困扰人的，后面通常跟不好的事物，比如 recurring problems, recurring pain

（续表）

	形容词部
desirable	值得拥有的，在新托福作文中是代替 good 的上乘之选，比如 Foreign language skills are highly desirable. / a desirable neighborhood（社区）/ It's desirable that you have some familiarity with computers.
adept in	固定搭配 be adept in 指某方面技能很高，经常可以代替 be skilled at/in...，有很多时候也可以代替 be good at...
abject	请注意拼写！它不是 object，而是 a 开头的形容词。它在写作中经常用在一些表示艰难困苦的名词之前加重程度，比如 abject misery, abject poverty
laborious	当然了，它是 labor 的形容词形式，但它的意义比 labor 窄很多，一般后面只能跟 task 或者 undertaking 之类表示任务或者工作的词，表示需要付出很大努力的
flawed	有缺陷的，比它更委婉的说法则是 imperfect

⇧ **例句：** People are by nature flawed. There'll always be times when our friends do things that are disappointing or hurtful to us. Sometimes these things are done on purpose；sometimes by accident.

impeccable/flawless	这两个词则是"无懈可击的" — perfect 的近义词
indiscriminate	一定不要误解，这个词跟歧视无关，而是"不加区分的，不加选择的"

⇧ **例句：** The indiscriminate use of chemical fertilizer has been causing serious problems.

discriminating	让你吃惊的是：这个词仍然与歧视无关。恰恰相反，它是个褒义词，指"有品味的，有鉴赏力的"

⇧ **例如：** discriminating shoppers

注： "歧视的"在英文里正确名词形式是 discriminatory，瞧瞧这些五花八门的英文词缀……

optional	可选择的，不是必须的，反义词：mandatory / compulsory
chronic	长期存在的（问题），慢性的（疾病）

（续表）

形容词部	
pressing	紧迫的，比如 pressing issues, pressing concerns，有时候也可以用 burning / urgent 代替它
intense	强烈的，但比 strong 更 strong，比如 intense pressure, intense emotions
exhilarating	比 exciting 程度还强，在美国有些 motivational speakers（专门做励志演讲的那种人）特别爱用这个词
bitter	很多同学知道它是"苦的"意思，但是在写作里它还经常作"辛酸的"或者"辛辣的"意思

⇧ **例如**：bitter experience / a bitter battle / bitter arguments / a bitter dispute 等

sensible	明智的，有理性的
mercenary	完全就是为了钱的

⇧ **例如**：sponsors'（赞助商）exclusively mercenary attitude toward the Olympic Games

sweeping	席卷一切的，比如 the sweeping impact of globalization
all-encompassing	包罗万象的，比如：the all-encompassing information highway
sole	这个与上个词正好相反：唯一的，意思很接近于 only，但是它只能用在名词之前

⇧ **例句**：Mothers are the sole instructor in many Americans families.

rampant	猖獗的，比如 rampant crime, rampant poaching（偷猎），rampant inflation
mounting	这个词同样是指负面现象大量存在，但它更多地是强调依然在增加：mounting pressure, mounting concerns, mounting criticism, mounting debts
burgeoning	发展迅猛的，比如：burgeoning population / burgeoning demand for energy

　　总之，抽象词汇是新托福写作的精彩亮点之一，多花些时间总结常用的抽象词汇，并且把它们用熟练、用准确，确实是一件很值得咱们做的事儿。在 Day 6 中，我们还会恶补特别拿分的副词。

Be careful of your thoughts, they may become words at any moment.

——*Ira Gassen*

TOEFL iBT
Writing Test

那些让你的论证更强有力的 verbs（高分内容）

在美语作文中，动词由于自身带有的行动意味，经常会让你的逻辑论证更加强而有力。Pat 去年听过一个在北美访问的欧洲商务与文化代表团团长作演讲，他就是用精彩的动词叠用让台下掌声不断。比如下面这段话就很动人，"Our mission is to promote business activity, foster professionalism, develop networking opportunities, enhance visibility, encourage academic excellence and advocate the prominence of our members within and outside the European-American business and professional community. "

下面这些新托福写作最常用的加分动词，大家一旦能使用准确也将让你的论证变得更加强有力。

	正方动词		
	动词	**含义**	**常见宾语或例句**
1	acquire	获取	knowledge / skills
2	afford	请注意在写作中这个词经常是 offer "提供"的意思	job opportunities 就业机会/ a sense of achievement 成就感 / protection / an uninterrupted view 没有阻碍的视线
3	allocate	分配	allocate money to … / allocate resources to…
4	anticipate	虽然与 expect 略有区别，但在新托福写作中这个极酷的词经常可以用来替换 expect	anticipate changes / developments / discoveries / difficulties
5	boost	提升，增加	efficiency 效率/ crop yield 农作物产量
6	censor	审查（多用于 Media 类话题）	films / books
7	combat / address / tackle / grapple with	解决	a problem / a situation
8	conserve	节约使用（注意和 preserve "保护"的区别）	resources / fresh water
9	cultivate / foster / nurture	培养	creativity / skills / interest

（续表）

		正方动词	
	动词	含义	常见宾语或例句
10	curb	遏制	crime / nuclear weapons 核武器
11	curtail	削减	expenses 开支 / budgets 预算
12	demolish	拆掉	buildings
13	display	展现（还可以用近义词 demonstrate / exhibit 代替）	talent / abilities / potential / skills
14	disseminate	传播（某种思想或者观念）	ideas / thoughts
15	elevate / heighten / raise	提高	citizens' awareness of 公民的某种意识 / the standard of living 生活水平
16	eliminate	消除	poverty 贫困 / injustice 不公正 / wea-pons of mass destruction
17	enhance	增进，美化	the cityscape 市容 / infrastructure 基础设施
18	enlarge	扩大	the market for products 产品市场
19	enrich	丰富	one's knowledge 知识/biodiversity 生物多样性
20	ensure	确保	social stability 社会稳定 /ethnic unity 民族团结
21	establish	建立	a system 体制 / an institution 机构
22	expand	扩大	one's outlook 眼界 / domestic demand 内需（国内市场需求）
23	exploit/utilize	使用，开发	natural resources 自然资源 / one's potential 潜能
24	explore	探索	outer space 外层空间 / other cultures（表示不同种类的文化时 culture 可以用复数）
25	fulfill	实现，完成	fulfill one's potential 发挥潜力 / fulfill one's dream 实现梦想 / fulfill one's task 完成任务

（续表）

正方动词			
	动词	含义	常见宾语或例句
26	generate	（大规模地）产生	employment opportunities / electricity / tax revenue 税收
27	harness	在新托福作文里主要是环境类话题使用：开发（某种资源）	wind energy / solar energy /natural resources
28	implement	实施	a policy 政策
29	integrate / incorporate	结合	integrate oneself into a society whose culture is so different from one's own / incorporate students' suggestions into curriculum design （课程设计）
30	intensify	强化	regional cooperation 区域合作 / cultural interaction 文化间的相互交流
31	justify	让……合理 / 证实……的合理性	It often seems that the amount of money that they are able to earn in a short time cannot possibly be justified by the amount of work they do.
32	lower	降低	costs 费用 / expectations 期望
33	maintain	维持	close links 紧密的联系/social order 社会秩序
34	motivate	给……动力	motivate students to think independently 鼓励学生独立思考 / motivate employees to work harder
35	mold	塑造	one's character 性格
36	optimize	优化	the management of sth. / the distribution of resources 资源配置
37	override	比……更重要	例句：At the moment, the government's concern about poverty overrides its other concerns. （形容词 overriding 也很常用，表示当前最重要的）

（续表）

正方动词			
	动词	含义	常见宾语或例句
38	perform / conduct	从事	scientific research 科学研究
39	multiply	成倍增加	people's choices / employees' earnings
40	pose	在议论文里不是"摆 pose"的意思，而是指对……构成某种挑战或者威胁	pose a threat to 构成威胁 / pose a challenge to 构成挑战
41	preserve	保护某种资源	natural resources 自然资源 / cultural heritage 文化遗产
42	promote / facilitate	促进，推动	healthy lifestyles / cultural exchanges 文化交流 / sustainable development 可持续发展
43	protect	保护	national security 国家安全 / citizens
44	pursue	追求	maximum profit 最大利润
45	recycle	循环利用	waste / rubbish
46	reform	改革，改造	a system /criminals
47	reinforce /strengthen/consolidate	增强	family bonds 亲情 / economic ties 经济联系 / ethnic solidarity 民族团结的另一种表达方法
48	release	释放	stress / prisoners
49	relieve / ease / alleviate	减轻	traffic congestion 交通堵塞 / poverty 贫困
50	remove	消除	the barrier 障碍 / discrimination 歧视
51	safeguard	保障（一般后面跟抽象概念）	political and social stability 政治社会的稳定 / national cohesion 民族凝聚力
52	shift	转移	one's attention to / the focus to
53	accelerate	加速	pace of life 生活节奏 / economic growth

（续表）

正方动词			
	动词	含义	常见宾语或例句
54	stimulate	激发	imagination / creativity / economic development
55	synthesize	有机结合（比 combine 或者 blend 结合得更紧密）	synthesize the Asian and the Western cultures / synthesize different sources of information
56	transcend	超越（某种界限）	national boundaries 国家的界限 / races
57	treasure / value / cherish	前两个词也都可以作名词，但当动词时三个词都是"珍视"	That old guitar is his most treasured / valued / cherished possession. ; the cultural heritage 文化遗产 / the local customs 当地风俗
58	upgrade	升级	the facilities / skills
59	uphold	支持某种事业或者价值观	our national values / justice
60	utilize	使用，利用，有些时候可以代替 use	solar energy / the newly-invented gadgets
中立或反方动词			
1	cause	产生，导致（新托福作文中一般跟坏现象）	misunderstanding 误解 / psychological strain 心理压力 / a vicious circle 恶性循环
2	corrupt	毒害	children's minds
3	degrade	是 upgrade 的反义词	the quality of sth.
4	deplete	消耗	natural resources / the ozone layer（大气层中的臭氧层）
5	disregard	无视	traditions / the law
6	distort	歪曲	facts / truth
7	disturb	扰乱	social order 社会秩序
8	exacerbate / aggravate	导致……进一步恶化	economic recession 经济衰退 / environmental pollution

（续表）

中立或反方动词			
	动词	含义	常见宾语或例句
9	erode	侵蚀	the cultural identity of a nation 一个国家的文化特性 / one's confidence 信心
10	exhaust	耗尽	energy / resources
11	fuel	本意是燃料，但是当动词用的时候，它很像中文的"激化"，后面一般跟一个抽象名词	antagonism 敌意 / conflicts 冲突
12	hinder / impede / obstruct	阻碍	the development of…
13	impose	把某事物强加给某人	impose their own will on their children / impose high taxes on…
14	involve	涉及	uncertainties 不确定因素 / the recognition that… 某种意识
15	isolate	孤立	a nation 国家 / prisoners 罪犯
16	jeopardize / undermine	危及，破坏（跟抽象宾语）	one's future / economic prospects 经济前景
17	multiply	本意是算术中的"乘以……"，但在新托福写作中经常形象地用作"激增"的意思	In warm weather, these germs multiply rapidly. / The amount of information has multiplied. / Smoking multiplies the risk of heart attacks and other health problems. （细菌在美语里不一定非要用 bacteria，germs 也很常见）
18	punish / penalize	惩罚	criminal acts 罪行
19	restrict / constrain	限制	the development of…/ one's freedom
20	rethink	反思（注意与 think 不同，rethink 后面经常可以直接加宾语）	their policy / their strategy 策略

（续表）

		中立或反方动词	
	动词	**含义**	**常见宾语或例句**
21	sap / dampen	削弱（自信等抽象名词）	one's confidence / one's enthusiasm 热情 / the market demand
22	seek	谋求	hegemony 霸权 / opportunities
23	spoil	破坏（原先很好的东西）	the cityscape
24	stifle	扼杀	creativity 创造力 / potential 潜力 / economic and social reform 经济与社会变革
25	stretch	本意是拉伸，议论文中一般指过度使用，stretch…to the limit 为固定短语	stretch natural resources to the limit / stretch students' energy to the limit
26	tarnish	玷污	one's reputation 声誉 / one's image 形象
27	violate	侵犯	citizens' rights / the law

《那些花儿》

这可是 Pat 很喜欢的歌儿，唱的是年轻时特花心的一个人成熟之后突然活明白了，变成了新好男人的故事。其实新托福作文中也有那些花儿：不知道大家发现没有，国内考生们喜欢用单个单词表达的意思，在地道英文里却经常被用一些很简洁的动词短语表达出来，让本来很灰暗的文章顿时充满生机。让俺也当回"麦霸"吧：啦啦啦啦，啦啦啦啦，那些心情在岁月中，已难辨真假……

※ 美语里的动词短语非常多，但是有相当一部分过于口语化，不太适合在新托福写作里用。如果大家有兴趣了解纯正地道的 informal phrasal verbs，请关注 Pat 将于近期完成的《十天突破新托福口语》。

	短语	**中文解释**	**例句或宾语**
1	abide by / comply with	遵守	the law 法律 / the rules / the guidelines
2	adapt to ≈ adjust to	适应	It's essential that kids adapt to their school life early on.

（续表）

	短语	中文解释	例句或宾语
3	appeal to	对……有吸引力	While the print appeals only to the sense of sight, television appeals to both sight and hearing simultaneously（=at the same time）.
4	attribute... to.../ ascribe... to	把……归因于……	They attributed their success to having a competent team working for them.
5	be geared toward...	指（产品、服务等）专门针对某种目的	The curriculum of this course is geared toward students who lack motivation in their studies.
6	be stressed out	被压垮	Many students were stressed out after the serious cramming for the finals.
7	bring about	带来	Together these brought out the recent financial crisis.
8	burn out	累垮	If I keep working like this, I'll burn out.
9	brush up on	复习过去曾经学过的技能	I'll brush up on my French before my trip to Paris this coming March.
10	carry out	开展，进行，也可以用动词 conduct 或者 perform 代替	More research on the greenhouse effect has been carried out.
11	clash with	与……冲突	The latest statement from the Pentagon clashed with prior statements from the White House.
12	come into being / take shape / come about	逐渐成形	What started out as an American military computer network program has developed into a global communication tool for millions of computer networks. That was how the Internet came into being. Regulations first came about in the U. S. to deal with services of transportation companies.

(续表)

	短语	中文解释	例句或宾语
13	come up with	给出，提出，用法很像 present	Some students came up with truly original ideas while many others just followed suit（习惯用语：跟着别人模仿）.
14	cope with	应付，处理 = handle	Some students have a hard time coping with the daily stress.
15	cut down on	削减	In America, kids between the ages of 10 and 16 spend an average of six hours a day in front of a screen. They really should cut down on the screen time.
16	draw on	借鉴	others' experience
17	drop out of	退出，尤其常指辍学	By the age of 18, he'd already left home and dropped out of school, deciding to flip burgers at McDonald's.
18	end up doing sth. / in sth. / with sth.	很"美"的一个短语，基本是"结果成了……/结果得到了……"的意思	She'll end up being penniless if she carries on spending like that.
19	face up to	勇于面对	a difficult situation
20	free up	把（能量、资源等）释放出来	The government offered to free up $120 million to create 1,500 jobs in elementary schools.
21	get across	传达，表达清楚	No matter how short an advertisement is, there's always a lot you can get across, which is really amazing.
22	give rise to	导致（某种广泛存在的负面现象）	+ unemployment 失业 / + inflation 通货膨胀 / + debate / + alienation from one another 人与人之间彼此疏远
23	give priority to	把……放在优先位置	Teachers should give priority to the cultivation of students' critical thinking ability.

（续表）

	短语	中文解释	例句或宾语
24	go about	从事	The pamphlet tells you how to go about the application.
25	hang out	这个短语实在太常用了，对成年人来说，很多时候"玩儿"其实只有用 hang out 才能准确表达	If we spent all last weekend hanging out with new colleagues, then maybe we can make time this week to have dinner with our oldest school chums.
26	hinge on	取决于	The future of the economy hinges on whether the recession can be curbed.
27	impose... on sb.	把……强加给某人	Parents shouldn't impose their own values on their kids.
28	impose on sb.	与上面的区别是 impose 后面直接跟 on，这是在美国挺常用的一个客气说法："给……添麻烦"	I just hate to impose on others.
29	infringe on	侵犯	+other individuals' rights
30	interfere with	干扰，干涉	Supervisors should try not to let their personal worries interfere with their work.
31	liven up	让……更丰富，更活跃，更口语化的说法是 brighten up 或者 spice up	They played black eyed peas' songs to liven up the party.
32	lose track of	对……失去了解或者掌控	No matter how busy you are, make sure you don't lose track of things.
33	make sense	合理	In today's media, many reports simply don't make any sense. Interestingly, people just keep listening to or reading them.

（续表）

	短语	中文解释	例句或宾语
34	make possible sth.	这个词组严格来说不算是 ph-rasal verbs，而且用法挺独特的，是 make possible 后面再跟名词，但不知道为什么就是在议论文中特别常用	The new agreement makes possible potential improvements in the employees' benefits regarding health and safety.
35	make up for	弥补	I sent her a gift to make up for my mistake.
36	mingle with	进行社交活动	She's been talking to Chris all evening — she really should be mingling with other guests.
37	nail down	把……弄清楚，确定	Sometimes it's hard to nail down exactly what the weaknesses of a system are.
38	narrow down	缩小（选择范围）	The brochure can help the customers narrow down their options.
39	nibble away at	逐渐消减	Even though inflation（通货膨胀）is low in America these days, it still nibbles away at our savings.
40	open up（opportunities）	开启	These discoveries will open up almost unlimited possibilities for our lives.
41	opt for sth. /opt to do sth.	选择（去做某事）	In view of the increasing uncertainty in the economy, the company has opted for downsizing.
42	page through	page 作动词时指一页一页地阅览	We wander through libraries, page through thick texts, spend hours at the computer, conduct painstaking research, and consult with experts.

（续表）

	短语	中文解释	例句或宾语
43	patch up sth.	修复受到伤害的关系	The couple tried to patch up their marriage.
44	pay off	回报	All his hard work eventually paid off.
45	participate in	参与	Our professor often encourages us to participate in group discussions.
46	pass up	错过，放弃（很珍贵的东西）	Jesse Jackson passed up a pro baseball contract and became a preacher instead.
47	pitch in	一起努力	If all of us pitch in together, it won't take too long to finish the project.
48	prevail over	有不同的意思，新托福作文中一般是"战胜，克服"	Our inner strength will enable us to prevail over life's obstacles.
49	refrain from	克制自己不去做某事	In almost all airports in America, I heard announcements like "Please refrain from smoking."
50	reflect on	不同语境下有不同的意思，新托福作文中一般是"认真思考"或者"反思"的意思	Every night, the writer spends some time reflecting on the things that have happened during the day.
51	scrape through	勉强混过	They just scraped through their tests even though they never did much work.
52	show off	这个大家应该很熟悉了，基本等于中文的"卖弄"	chic（时尚的）clothing / skills 等
53	sign up for	报名或者参与某种活动，很多时候像 register for	courses, classes, certain service
54	sit through	坐等……（很枯燥的某事）结束	It was the worst movie we had to sit through. The plot was worn-out and the acting was soporific.

(续表)

	短语	中文解释	例句或宾语
55	speed up	加速	pace of life 生活节奏 / economic growth
56	spring up / sprout up	短时间内大量出现	Since Westinghouse established the first commercial radio station in America, stations sprang up all over the country almost overnight.
57	spur sb. on to sth.	激励某人继续前进（注意这个 to 是介词）	This success will spur students on to greater achievements.
58	squeeze in...	把……勉强塞入……	Life is hectic（超级忙碌的）。We can barely squeeze in the time to exercise. And when we do, we feel guilty（内疚的）that we're not doing the hundred other things on our to-do list.
59	stand for	代表……意思，经常用于解释缩写	Does U. S. stand for the United States or Uncle Sam?
60	stick with sb.	留在某人身边	Your siblings are the best link to your past and the people who are most likely to stick with you in the future.
61	succumb to	屈从于某事	+temptation 诱惑 / +peer pressure 同龄人间的压力
62	take... into account	把……考虑在内	People often fail to take their own limits into account when setting goals for themselves.
63	take up	有很多意思，但在托福作文中一般是"开始某种爱好"之意	I've recently taken up jogging.
64	wind down	放松 = relax	I really need to wind down after such as hectic day.

（续表）

	短语	中文解释	例句或宾语
65	wipe out	①彻底消除 ②（被动形式）非常疲惫的	Nothing can wipe out his bitter memories of the past.
66	work out	①规划出…… ②得到解决 ③健身	work out a plan to do sth. Things will work out in the end. It's important to work out regularly.

魅力四射拉丁族 Glamorously Hispanic／Latino

这种拿分技巧很多国内孩子们还不知道，其实在美国大学里写议论文的时候，有 7 个拉丁文词汇相当常用。在新托福写作中虽然不必刻意去追求大量使用，但只要是适当而且准确地用出来，就将强烈暗示考官这是一个对美利坚底细十分了解的筒子：

i. e.（that is）

etc.（and so on）

e. g.（for example）

and/or vice versa（反之亦然）

vs.（versus: 相对于……，和……相比）

bona fide（真正的，真实的，Friends 和 Family 话题中特别常用）

the status quo（the current or the existing state of affairs：现状）

请大家看下面的应用实例：

1. All participates should submit an original piece of writing (e. g. , a short story, poem, song, play, illustrated story, essay, etc.) or artwork, including computer-generated artwork, that shows how specific individuals from specific backgrounds have contributed to the development of America.

2. Physics teachers teach students how to convert the material from its solid state to liquid state or vice versa.

3. bona fide supporters／bona fide friends

Pat 总结的美国人表述自己的价值观时最喜欢用的 12 个词（Pat's List of the Top-12 Most Frequently Used Words: When Americans Indicate Their Values）

Pat's Tips

虽然这些词在美国几乎每天都能见到或听到，但是有些时候它们并不一定被真正执行（Some Americans don't always practice what they preach.）。

❶ justice（*n.*）正义

"维护正义"在地道美语中可以写成 safeguard / uphold justice。美国人还常说一句话叫做 Justice has been done.（正义得到了伸张）。这个词的反义词 injustice 也经常能见到，但时常也被一些人拿来做寻求 funding 的借口。

❷ fulfill（*vt.*）实现，履行

比如：fulfill one's potential，fulfill one's tasks，fulfill one's promise 和最重要的——fulfill the American dream。

❸ faith（*n.*）信念

这个并不见得非要是宗教信仰。一个人对于任何事物有信念都可以说 he/she has faith in sth. /sb.，也可以包括对 spouse 或者 partner 的绝对信任。

❹ vision（*n.*）有很多意思，但一般指"远见，对未来的设想"

还有一个词在美国也经常可以看到或者听到：visionary——对未来总是有很明确设想的人，经常用来指 Larry Page 或者 Sergey Brin 这些人。

❺ altruistic（*adj.*）利他主义的，乐于助人的

近年来越来越多地被提起，这里还有个 music video 可以让你深刻领会这种精神：http://www. youtube. com/watch?v =9ylgchWR-lg。

❻ freedom（*n.*）自由

这个不用多说，无数的宪法修正案（amendments to the U. S. Constitution）都是为了它而被通过的，比如 the freedom of speech / thought / belief / religion 等等等等。如果要表达"维护某人的自由"，则可以把 secure 当成动词来用：secure one's freedom。

❼ egalitarian（*adj.*）平权主义的

这也是美国社会太常用的词汇，本质就是 the faith in individual equality。比如：strive for an egalitarian society，adopt an egalitarian approach to…，egalitarian beliefs 等。还有一个意思类似的单词：equitable，用得相对少一些，但也是用来形容资源分配是公正的。

⑧ enlightened and progressive (*adj.*) 开明的，进步的

这两个词既可以连用，也可以分开单独用；可以用来形容政府，也可以形容其他机构或者运动，比如 Pat 认识一个从 UC @ Berkeley 毕业的哥们儿就总说自己的母校 is a modern, enlightened and progressive university，但 Pat 并不喜欢有那么多 liberals 的校园。

⑨ potential (*n.*) 潜力

西方文明自从 16 世纪在 John Calvin 等众人的带领下经历了影响极其深刻的 Reformation（宗教改革）之后，开始相信个人必须努力工作才能被上帝选中（to be the few select individuals，这里的 select 一般不用被动），于是开始重视个人"潜力"这个概念。individual potential 与 Rousseau 的 social contract（社会契约观念）一样都对近代西方的社会形态产生了极其深远的影响。比如 Jeremy Lin 高中时就在 Stanford 校园对面儿打过球，却居然拿不到 Stanford 的奖学金。但最终个人潜力还是战胜了 racial stereotype，Lin-sanity 终于成为了 regular season 的黑马。又比如 Elizabeth Blackwell 在接连被 17 个牛校拒收之后最终成为第一个获得医学学位的美国女性，Rachel Carson 凭一本 *Silent Spring* 最终争取到 DDT 的全球被禁，甚至 Forrest Gump 的虚构故事，无疑都在诉说着美国人对于 potential 的信念。

⑩ rhetoric (*n.*) （中文翻译请看下文）

这个词在美国文化中实在太重要了，而且它是纯粹西方的概念。比如：Obama's rhetoric often holds the crowd spellbound（跟着了魔似的）。经常有人说在北美的华人很 shy，其实我认为这么说并不完全准确。更准确的说法应该是我们的文化很看重实干，总觉得自己做得好别人最终就一定会知道的，不是太看重 rhetorical skills。中文字典里对这个词的翻译可能是"修辞"吧，但 Pat 认为更精准的解释应该是"用言语去说服和打动别人的技巧"。比如美国的 salespeople 惯用的 sales pitch 就是典型的 rhetorical skill。但在北美掌握这种言语说服技能的高手绝不仅限于推销员。中国移民初到美国的时候一般都会对当地普通老百姓的"能言善辩"感到震惊，甚至连那种一事无成的美国人讨论问题的时候也能说得跟 nationally-televised presidential debates 似的，特有"范儿"。西方文化中这种对 rhetorical skills 的重视其实一直可以追溯到古希腊时代。切记：在美国社会里一味地傻干是不会有人说你好的。如果不学会当地人这种用嘴皮子去说服别人的技巧，那么你只能是 underachiever。

⑪ integrity (*n.*)

这个词接近 honesty，但是包含的意义更广泛，基本上是"正直、诚实而且原则性强"，集所有优点于一身。比如 Denzel Washington 的多数电影角色都可以看成是美式 integrity 的代言人。

⑫ individualism (*n.*)

说实话这个词在 TOEFL iBT 写作里其实并不是太常用。但它的的确确是美国精神的核心——个人主义。它和自私并不是同义词，虽然有时自私是它的副产品。美国公众普遍相信，个人是推动社会发展的首要力量（Individuals are the primary driving force behind social progression.）。特别是每次当共和党（Republicans）上台的时候，这种倾向就更加明显。相应的个人自由、信仰、选择和财产权等都应该得到社会尊重。在美国的私人住房外面经常可以见到一块大牌子，上面很不客气地写着：Private Property. No Trespassing.（私家财产，非请勿入）。而个人主义最突出的体现则仍是一直备受争议的"枪权"（gun ownership）。

在北美长大的孩子必须面对的 8 大挑战 Eight Gigantic Challenges Confronting North American Teens （高分内容）

在北京的五年半经历给 Pat 一个极深的感受是：很多国内的家长把美国的教育体制想象得过于完美了，同时又把中国的教育体制批判得一无是处（hopelessly bad）。Pat 却很想大胆地讲一句真话："美国的基础教育问题一点儿也不比国内少！"事实上，中国的基础教育在 literacy 和 numeracy 这两方面做得远远要更扎实，只是在鼓励学生的创造力方面确实做得太不够。而对比来看，现在北美的很多家长（绝不只是"虎妈""Tiger Mother"Amy Chua 一个人）也很担心自己的孩子"创造"了好几年却没学到扎实的基本功。

总体来说，在北美越是高级私立名校以及房价贵的好学区的公立学校，老师对孩子们的基础知识教育反而抓得越紧，而且知名高中里的学习竞争也同样非常激烈，反倒是质量一般的学校里时常会闹出家长抱怨老师管得太严的事情。

下面是在北美长大的孩子必须面对的 8 个挑战（比较容易理解的就不做深入讨论了）

❶ peer pressure 同辈间的压力。

❷ identity crisis 身份危机——如何给自己定位。

❸ drug addiction / substance abuse

在一些美国中学生和大学生中，smoke pot 真的已经不算什么，甚至还有人把 marijuana 说成是防止青少年接触更危险毒品的好方法，而被某些国内留美手册吹捧成"全美公立第一名校"的 UC Berkeley 的整个校园都弥漫着一股强烈的大麻气味。

❹ alcohol，特别是 liquor（烈酒）和 binge drinking（暴饮），导致了无数悔恨甚至迷失。当然也有好孩子，比如大家可以听听 Pat 博客里唱 *Hooray for Bear* 的 Bowling for Soup 有多乖。

❺ racial gap 这个绝不仅仅是 discrimination（歧视）的问题。当代美国的种族问题早已经远比歧视更加微妙，成为一种"隐形的冲突"（invisible conflicts）。而 Hispanics（西班牙裔）美国人的激增正让美国的种族问题更复杂化。

❻ campus violence 校园暴力，从比较轻的 school bullying 到 campus shooting）。

❼ juvenile delinquency 青少年犯罪。

❽ unwanted sex

high-school prom（高中毕业舞会）已经被很多年轻人当成纪念 the first time 的仪式了。当然也有特例，比如去年在美国红得发紫的组合 Jonas Brothers，就带 purity ring 来证明自己没有过 sexual experience。在美国特别引起家长们和全社会担心的是 unwanted sex——即未经过选择而发生的 xx，各种 party 之后往往是高发期，某些甚至导致 underage pregnancy。这种"无证驾驶"的行为在美国一直是受到大多数有良知的人士谴责的。

学有余力

www. randomhouse. com/wotd/index. pperl？action＝dly__alph_arc&fn＝word

输入这个繁琐的网址会给大家带来不小的麻烦，但是很值。一个绝对有个性的 Random House 小站，但是很多国内孩子们搞不定的词，都可以在里面找到十分靠谱的解释。比如，请试着找找在美国大学里参加 seminar 时经常能听到的 myriad 这个单词……

课后练习

Take-Home Quiz

阅读练习

请结合您在本章中学到的写作核心词汇阅读下面的短文：

The most effective way to collaborate with an irritating coworker is to first clarify their behavior, understand why he/she irritates you, and then recognize whatever degree of truth that exists in your coworker's comments before responding to their behavior in a constructive way.

改错练习

下面三个句子里各有一处用词错误，请找出：

① The environmental problems in this region are being deteriorated. The federal as well as the state government should take immediate steps to combat them.

② Some teenagers crime after they watch violent movies.

③ High-school students should be encouraged to contribute to develop their communities.

参考答案

① deteriorate 是不及物动词，不能用被动形式，应改为 are being aggravated，或者用 are deteriorating。

② crime 是名词，动词应改为 commit a crime。

③ contribute to 中的 to 是介词，所以后面的 develop 应该改为名词，the development of。

从 streetcars 的电网中拔地而起的多伦多 CN 塔，不知该用怎样的词汇形容黄昏中的她呢——是 magnificent, spectacular, imposing 还是 lonely？ ——Pat 摄

Day 5

Get the Hang of Linkers
轻松玩转 linkers

Words are just the vague shadows of the volumes we mean. Little audible links, they are, chaining together great inaudible feelings and purposes.

——Theodore Dreiser
American writer

学习作文理论的核心在于是否能够投入使用，否则，即使能让一堆专业术语 roll off your tongue 也还是写不出好文章。在这点上学英语倒是和看购物指南有相似之处。Pat 的桌上正放着一本最新的 Customer Reports 出的 Ratings & Pricing Guide。这本册子虽小，却是北美公认的买车圣经。除了全面、准确和公正之外，它还对每款车的 reliability, satisfaction 和 owner cost 都给出了清晰易懂的评价，对购车族具有很强的可操作性。比如，让我们一起翻到最近在美国本土接连出事的 Toyota Prius 那一页……

It is a mistake to look too far ahead. Only one link in the chain of destiny can be handled at a time.

——Winston Churchill

TOEFL iBT
Writing Test

在 美国有个很著名的词叫 "KISS"，四个字母都大写，等于 "Keep it simple, stupid." （简单就是美）。

即使在美国大学里写专业论文，只要一出现过长的句子，prof 们就总会毫不留情地标出来，要求简化。其实不仅仅是学生作业，即使是美国的思想家（thinkers）和理论家们（theorists）在论述高深见解的时候也都尽量在句式上接近大众的口味。

例如，我们可以看看美国历史上影响最大的哲学家之一 John Dewey 怎样论述 associated living 这样一个相当抽象的哲学概念的：

Associated living is to the mutual advantage of everyone concerned. It is like friendship. Friends help each other, exchange knowledge and insights, with the result that their lives are richer and more meaningful. Associated living is the highest ideal of social development.

像杜威这样在 20 世纪美国最有影响力的哲学大师写的句子，居然可以简短到让国内的寄托 "大牛" 们不屑的程度——除了标注出的两个词我们已经在昨天全部学过之外，已经酷似新托福作文有关 friends 话题的段落了。

我们可以对比着看一段对杜威影响深刻的欧洲大师 Friedrich Hegel（黑格尔）的一段代表性文字：

This bygone mode of existence has already become an acquired possession of the general mind, which constitutes the substance of the individual, and, by thus appearing externally to him, furnishes his inorganic nature. Culture or development of mind (*Buildung*), regarded from the side of the individual, consists in his acquiring what lies at his hand ready for him, in making its inorganic nature organic to him, and taking possession of it for himself. Looked at, however, from the side of universal mind (*qua*, the general spiritual substance), culture means nothing else than that this substance gives itself its own self-consciousness, brings about its own inherent process...

没啥说的，给跪了 + 泪奔……

在美国，用简洁文字表达深刻思想的例子实在太多，Pat 随手给您再挑一个——Columbia University 的哲学与教育学大牌教授 Jonas F. Soltis 在讨论 pedagogy and analysis 这样高深的话题时写道：

In a way, I suppose, students and teachers may feel that to ask such ridiculous questions as, "What is meant by 'education'?, 'subject matter'?, or 'learning'?" is like asking a housewife to reflect on the meaning of "cooking", "cleaning" or "washing dishes". After all, the ordinary terms which refer broadly to what students and teachers actually do each day of their lives hardly call for an unnecessary strain of brain power...

这位哥伦比亚的大腕儿同样是用极其简明的语言阐述了深刻的道理，文中标记出的两个表达我们也已经在 Day 4 中学过了。

当然，不能以偏概全。来美国读大学还是有可能碰到高深的文章的，少数"叫兽"也确实喜欢用艰深的 handouts 来刁难学生，GRE 阅读的那些段子就是最好的证明。但总体而言，美国人偏好用相对简洁的句式来表述问题却是一个不争的事实。

相应的，我们对新托福作文句子难度的要求，应该也是实用＋准确，而不应该是莫名其妙的高难度（being difficult just for difficulty's sake）。

在 Day 3 中我们提到过，所谓的英文复杂句，本质上不过就是两个（或者两个以上）简单句（就是主谓宾）和连接词的叠加。其中没有连接词引导的那个主谓宾叫做主句，由一个连接词引导的主谓宾叫做从句。结构如下：

（连词）＋主＋谓＋宾＋（连词）＋主＋谓＋宾

这就是英文复杂句的本质结构。当然，可以根据这个结构再嵌套出更复杂的复杂句，不过实战中掌握好这个基础结构才是最重要的。

一个复杂句最多只有一个主句，但可以有一个或者多个从句。主句和从句都是主谓宾结构，而主谓宾大家一般都会写，那么我们理清复杂句头绪的关键，其实不就是连接词的正确使用吗？好，今天我们就专攻连接 linkers/connectives。

在作文中特别是在主体段的支持句中，提高使用连词的准确度真的是提高托福作文分数最快的方法之一。因为每一个连词的正确使用，本质其实就是一种逻辑关系的正确使用。

美式写作最实用的连接词超不出以下 7 种。

新托福作文复杂句主、从关系完全透视

画※的连词为重点推荐连词（从实战角度每类记 1~2 个词就够了，不需要都记）

It is a mistake to look too far ahead. Only one link in the chain of destiny can be handled at a time.

——*Winston Churchill*

TOEFL iBT
Writing Test

因果关系

❶ 标志词

类型	单词或词组	解释	说明
原因	※ as	因为……	注意这两个词后面要跟从句而不能只跟一个名词
	since		
	※ due to	因为……	注意这两组词后面只能跟名词，不能跟从句
	owing to		
结果	hence	因此	用在句首和句中都可以，如果用在句中的话，则句中用分号，后面跟它们引导的从句
	thus		
	※ therefore		
	as a consequence	作为结果	用在句首比较多，后面用逗号
	as a result		
	※ consequently		
	so that	因此	用在句中
目的	thereby	以此达到……的目的	不能用在句首，而且在正式英语中后面加动名词（*v.* +ing）

❷ 本类连接词例句

Since we cannot experience everything all by ourselves, we also acquire knowledge by reading books, magazines and newspapers.

Being of the same age, children find it easier to communicate with their generation than with their parents. As a result, they learn more from their peers than from their parents.

In fact, it is difficult to determine the impact of humans on the environment as we only have been documenting weather changes for the last hundred years.

Sometimes new information contradicts our old ideas. This happens to people of all ages because learning is a lifelong process.

The IT industry is highly competitive; thus, even the slightest advantage gives a company a substantial edge over its rivals.

Habitual exercise reduces stress, prevents weight gain and improves academic performance; therefore, exercise should be made a part of any school's curriculum.

In the conventional classroom, most lessons are aimed at the middle level of ability. Thus, some students are dragged along much faster than is good for them.

Large numbers of animals and plants are being threatened with extinction, mainly as a consequence of human activities.

Parents who choose homeschooling for their children may be attacked by others — for thinking that their children are better than anyone else's, for refusing to participate in an important social institution, or even for trying to destroy the public schools.

❸ 私房秘制的因果关系 linkers（高分内容）

for the sake of 也表达因果关系。有些同学误以为它完全等于 because of，其实这是一种误解。*Longman* 里给出了准确解释 for the sake of: in order to help, improve or bring advantage to… 所以，它的意思其实更接近于英文的 for the purpose of helping/improving…

比如：

Many elderly people prefer to live in the countryside for the sake of their health.

For the sake of our health, we should aim for a healthy diet and a healthy weight.

另外还有一个表示方式的词组叫 by virtue of，意思是："通过……来……"，也属于因果关系中的高难项目。比如例句：

She succeeded by virtue of her tenacity（Day 4 中学过：毅力）rather than her talent.

The CEO has power by virtue of keeping the rules in the company.

再有，Given…, In view of… 和 In light of 三个表达都是"考虑到，鉴于……"的意思，后面跟名词或者名词短语，也是用来引出因果关系的精品：

Given the mounting pressure at work, he would sacrifice his high-paying job in exchange for more leisure time.

In view of the increasing uncertainty in the economy, the company has opted for downsizing.

举例关系

❶ 标志词

单词或词组	解释	说明
take... for example	以……为例	省略号里面只能填名词，不能填句子
※ for instance	比如……	=for example
such as	例如	后面跟名词，切记不能用在句首

It is a mistake to look too far ahead. Only one link in the chain of destiny can be handled at a time.

—*Winston Churchill*

TOEFL iBT
Writing Test

（续表）

单词或词组	解释	说明
This point is best illustrated with the example of...	这个观点可以用……的例子最有力地证明	后面跟名词
This point can be confirmed by the example of...	这个观点可以被……的例子支持	后面跟名词
consider... for example	以……为例	省略号里填入名词或者 that 从句都可以
... is a case in point.	……是一个恰当的例子	省略号里填名词

❷ 本类连接词例句

For instance, the factory should hire more inexperienced laborers to work on the part of the plant if less skill but more physical strength is needed.

Sometimes the value of a gift cannot be measured by money, such as a handmade key chain or a little souvenir from an overseas trip.

Some noise is caused by our neighbors listening to music or watching television at full volume, or using noisy power tools such as power drills, leaf blowers or lawn mowers.

In some cases when language courses demand that students practice speaking in groups, cooperative classmates will be a great assistance to achieving the goal of effective learning.

A classic example of this was the purchase of Alaska which so many people thought was a huge mistake but later turned out to be a really good deal when gold was discovered there in 1897.

类比与对比关系

❶ 标志词

（a）类比

单词	说明
※ Similarly, ...	"类似地"，一般用在句首
Likewise, ...	"类似地"，一般用在句首
By the same token, ...	"同理"，这个词组其实有点陈腐，但是偏偏就是有很多美国人喜欢加在作文里，大家将就着用吧
The same is true of...	"这对于……也适用"，一般用在句首，后面跟名词或者名词短语

（b）对比

单词	说明
※ while…	
whilst…	用在句首或者句中，表示主句和从句的对比（句内对比）
※ whereas…	
※ by/in contrast, …	用在句首，表示它之前一个句子和它后面引导的句子之间的对比（句间对比）

❷ 本类连接词例句

（a）类比

Similarly, students who have to cope with intense peer pressure may have a hard time concentrating on their academic subjects.

Our lives are pervaded（充满）with humor: Some of our most serious moments may be full of wit, just as funny situations often have serious overtones. Similarly, I have noticed that people who pull a serious face sometimes look funny.

To accomplish the assigned task, employees need to have ambition. Likewise, they need to put forth great effort.

"Some people have little power to do good, and likewise have little strength to resist evil."

— Samuel Johnson

Some of the funniest pieces of literature is actually very close to being tragic, and vice versa. By the same token（≈similarly）, try to imagine the face of a clown: One half of his face laughs and the other half cries.

The presenter didn't present any fresh ideas, but by the same token（≈ anyway）we didn't expect any from him.

（b）对比

This is based on the belief that identical twins share all the same genes whereas all the fraternal twins share only half the same genes.

While environmentalists are quick to blame the increased carbon dioxide emissions for the global warming, the truth is that nobody knows whether a similar warming — and the later cooling — occurred before the advent of temperature-related technology in the 1900s.

While print appeals only to the sense of sight, television appeals to both sight and hearing simultaneously（=at the same time）.

It is a mistake to look too far ahead. Only one link in the chain of destiny can be handled at a time.

——*Winston Churchill*

TOEFL iBT
Writing Test

Some people argue that *The Great Global Warming Swindle* is based on sound science and interviews with real climate scientists while Al Gore's *An Inconvenient Truth* is mostly an emotional presentation from a single politician.

Canadian society is described as a "Mosaic" or "tossed salad", composed of people of many different ethnocultural groups, races, creeds and colors. In contrast, American society defines its identity as a "Melting Pot" where people from all over the world come together as part of one united "American" culture, shedding their own heritage and individual identities.

Unlike the volatile (多变的) nature of stocks, which can fall apart as a group if the value of a large company drops suddenly, a home in good condition may keep its worth even if one nearby suffers a loss in value.

Homeschooled children are less likely to become involved with gangs or drugs. On the other hand, they spend much more time in the company (陪伴) of appropriate role models: parents, other adults and older siblings. (Kaplan)

On the one hand, moving large companies to the countryside may reduce the tax revenue (税收) of the city government. On the other hand, this measure can effectively relieve (减轻) the pressure on the urban transit system. (在美式作文里有时候其实 On the one hand, 也可以省略，先直接说第一方，然后用 On the other hand, 引出相对比的另一方)

❸ 私房秘制对比关系 linkers（高分内容）

对比关系中有几个一旦能用对就能拿分的表达：

On the contrary, ...

这个同学们很爱用，但是错误率高。特别需要注意不要把它和 In contrast 弄混了。On the contrary 其实更接近 Instead, ... 的意思，它后面的内容是否定之前的陈述的；而 In contrast 是表示前面的陈述和后面的陈述都是正确的，但是相互之间存在对比关系。

例句： The weather won't get any better. On the contrary, we're in for a hurricane.

Contrary to all the experts' expectations, the American economy took a nosedive.

It should be noted that not all school kids love to study. Instead, they love to explore the world around them, paying little attention to their academic work.

（这个 Instead 和 On the contrary 就非常类似）

rather than.../instead of... （而不是）这两个词组大家应该都比较熟悉了，在新托福高分范文里面特别常见，可以在不产生审美疲劳的前提下多用几次。

例句： Many American tourists go to Africa these days to see wildlife in its natural environment rather than in cages or cement pools.

At work, we should try to be ourselves rather than to be someone who we think others expect us to be.

Instead of making further requests, pessimistic customers tend to lodge complaints.

值得注意的是：地道美语中有些时候还喜欢把 rather 这个单词独立使用。"…；rather" 或者 Rather 的这种用法在大学，特别是文科（humanities）用书中相当常见：

Those recent graduates are not going to take a gap year. Rather, they will attend college soon.

Many experts claim that the recent global warming is not something that we should be concerned about; rather, it just reflects a natural course of planetary events.

Conversely 这个词就更高端了：跟在它后面的内容一般是把它前面一句话的意思完全"镜像"。虽然它在美式议论文中还算比较常见的一个单词，但因为其用法确实让新手犯晕，在考场时间太紧张的情况下，很容易出现"不是玩儿 conversely，而是被 conversely 玩儿"的惨烈局面，所以对它还是不宜有太多的感情投入。

请体会例句：

Studies have shown, for example, that reading aloud to children helps them become better readers. Conversely, children who do not have others reading aloud to them generally find it more difficult to learn how to read.

We often think, as we grow older, that if we had known in the past what we know now, we would have treated our elders differently when we were younger. Conversely, as we age (= get older), we often forget what it was like to feel and act when we were younger.

让步关系

① 标志词

单词	解释	说明
※ despite		
in spite of	尽管	后面跟名词或者代词
notwithstanding		
nonetheless	尽管如此	后面直接跟完整的句子
nevertheless		
※ even though	尽管	很多时候可以替换 although，后面跟从句，表示对已经存在的状况让步

It is a mistake to look too far ahead. Only one link in the chain of destiny can be handled at a time.

——*Winston Churchill*

TOEFL iBT
Writing Test

单词	解释	说明
※ even if	即使	后面跟从句，表示对还没有发生的状况让步
albeit	尽管	一般用在句子中间，后面跟形容词
as long as	只要	用在句子中间，不仅写作很常用，口语也常用，比如 *Backstreet Boys* 那句有名的歌词 I don't care who you are, where you're from or what you did as long as you love me. ☺

❷ 本类连接词例句

Despite many economists' claim that the surge（急速上升）in real estate value could not last, investing in real estate was considered by the average Americans to be one of the safer choices that a family could make.

Despite considerable public popularity, many of JFK's social and civil rights programs had made little progress in a Democrat-controlled but conservative Congress.

Some kinds of violence are not intended to kill, hurt or harm people. Nevertheless, people have been harmed, hurt or even killed by them.

Even though most technology has been designed for good purposes, it can also be used for evil. For example, computer networks were established in order to allow software to interface freely between computers. However, the accessibility to information on the Internet also opens the door for abuse.

Notwithstanding the concern about the adverse health effect cell phones may bring, the user base of cell phones kept soaring in America over the past decade.

Popular culture represented in the media deeply influences how young people see the world and discover their place within it. In spite of the diversity of people's background in America, the media continue to portray a Eurocentric discourse that largely ignores the knowledge, culture and contributions of the other half of the world.

❸ 私房秘制让步 linkers（高分内容）

除了上述的常规让步手段外，还有几种特殊美语用法也可以明确地表达出让步关系：

..., however + *adj.* + *n.*, ...

However 很常见，但它在这个句型里的诡异之处是它后面的从句可以省略掉动词，意思是：不管多么……

例如： Most couples, however fossilized（Day 4 学过的单词，"僵化的"）their relationship（后面省略了 is），have some interests in common.

此外，下面两种 linkers 也可以准确地表达出"不管……，无论……"的意思：

No matter how efficient they are, how safe, or how inexpensive, trains simply cannot offer the thrill that is inherent in automobiles.

No matter how tough things get, we'll deal with them more effectively with a positive approach.

No matter what your age（严格来说应该加上 is，但美语中也经常省略），it's worth taking time to understand the importance of a healthy diet.

Sometimes we just have to rely on ourselves, regardless of all the intelligent friends we have.

Some argue that the true function of higher education should be to give students access to knowledge for its own sake, regardless of whether the course is useful to employers.

还有，副词 admittedly 也可以表达让步逻辑，但要注意它引导的句子后面一般还会"话锋一转"，再来个 However, ... / But... 或者 Even so, ... 之类的句子。比如：

In determining promotions and advancements, admittedly, the employers make the final decision. However, their decisions are usually based on factors like seniority or job performance rather than on employer-employee relations.

还有一个高端让步词 Granted, ...，接近中文的"诚然"，在一些受过良好教育的美国人中被广为接受（当然前提也是别用得太频繁）。

Granted, these problems are minor at this point. But they do have the potential to develop into major headaches.

在美语中甚至有时候表示对比的 while 也可以表示出 even though 的意思，比如：

While it would be wrong to say that vaccines（疫苗）are completely free of side effects, they're much safer than the disease they protect against.

还有：

While the symptoms of these two diseases are very similar, there are important differences between them as well.

连 whether 这样通常表示选择的连词在美语中也经常引导让步状语从句：

Whether you're male or female, your risk of heart disease increases as you get older. Women tend to develop heart disease at an older age than men though.

It is a mistake to look too far ahead. Only one link in the chain of destiny can be handled at a time.

—Winston Churchill

TOEFL iBT
Writing Test

假设关系

❶ 标志词

单词	解释	说明
※ if	如果	前面或者后面的结果可以是我们希望或者不希望看到的
provided that… /providing that…	如果	前面或者后面的结果通常是我们希望看到的
unless…	除非……	前面或者后面的结果可以是我们希望或者不希望看到的
※ otherwise	否则	后面的结果多数时候是我们不希望看到的

❷ 本类连接词例句

If companies commit to building the skill sets and experience of workers in the U. S. , there's a good chance that they'll also award these employees with better-paying positions once their current jobs are done by workers in other countries.

He's welcome to come along, provided that he behaves himself.

The United States and China are the world's two largest emitters of greenhouse gases, of carbon that is causing the planet to warm. Unless both countries are willing to take critical steps in dealing with this issue, we will not be able to resolve it.

— Barack Obama

Be sure to write down what you hear during the lecture, otherwise you'll forget the details.

修饰关系

❶ 标志词

that, who, ※which, why（它的前面经常是 the reason / reasons）

其实这种关系就是定语从句了。

❷ 本类连接词例句

Supporting children with mentors and after-school programs will give them opportunities and guidance that they might not receive otherwise.

Since the Industrial Revolution, the burning of fossil fuels and other materials has greatly increased the levels of carbon dioxide, which naturally traps heat from the sun.

Large class sizes force teachers to focus on discipline, which prevents them from spending time making sure that students have the facts and skills that they need in order to perform well on these important tests. (*Kaplan*)

Regulations are created by politicians who represent either the interests of companies or consumers.

Some computer programmers who get paid good money for their day jobs come home at night and work for free for the sheer pleasure of working.

限定关系

这种逻辑关系旨在限定讨论对象的具体范围或者某种观点的适用范围，可以体现出作者逻辑思维的严密性。

❶ 标志词

单词或词组	解释	说明
※ in terms of	从……的意义上来讲	后面跟名词或者名词短语，用在句首或者句中都可以
As for...	谈起……	后面跟名词或者名词短语，用在句首
※ When it comes to ...	谈到……	后面跟名词或者名词短语，用在句首，有时根据上文意思的不同还可以在它前面加一个 But
regarding/concerning/ with respect to/ with regard to	关于……	后面跟名词或者名词短语，用在句首或者句中都可以

❷ 本类连接词例句

We all differ in terms of what we find funny, but we're all the same in terms of our interest to listen to amusing things.

These children are often spoiled, not in terms of love and attention because working parents do not have time for this, but in more material ways. (注意美语里 spoil 的过去分词是 spoiled 而不是 spoilt)

限定关系特别能体现思维的严密性，乡亲们可要多多关注。

下定义关系

就是对你提出的某个概念进行更进一步的描述或者细化。有能力有勇气去这样写的考生无疑是可以用更强的思维能力打动考官的。不过需要注意的是：考虑到新托福作文的具体特点，

It is a mistake to look too far ahead. Only one link in the chain of destiny can be handled at a time.

——Winston Churchill

TOEFL iBT
Writing Test

下定义的时候没有必要吹毛求疵（nitpicking），只要符合 common sense 就很好。

下面的几个新托福作文下定义最常用表达严格来讲已经不算是 linkers，而要算是句式。但为了方便大家学习作文中的常用逻辑关系，也放在本章中跟童鞋们一起研究吧：

A means…	意味着……
A refers to…	A 指的是……
A suggests that…	A 提示（我们）……（注意这里的 suggest 不是建议的意思）
A constitutes…	A 构成……（新托福作文中这个省略号里经常填入负面的内容，比如 violation of the law 等）
A is best characterized by…	A 最重要的特征是……
A is, essentially, …	A 本质上是……
A reflect…	A 反映了……
A represents…	A 代表了……

例句： High-caliber journalists are best characterized by their discipline, determination and dignity.

Happiness is, essentially, satisfaction of specific human desire.

A language represents the culture and the experience that are unique to the people who speak it.

不是关系的关系（暧昧关系）

暧昧……就像是 Carrie 和 Mr. Big，或者莉香和完治那样么？

在新托福作文中，玩儿暧昧就是 to paraphrase a sentence：转述前一句，貌似更深入地又论证了一句，其实仔细一看意思差异不大——但不管怎样，确实让论证看起来更充实了。

❶ 标志词

单词或词组	解释	说明
※ In other words, …	换句话说	用在句首
— that is,	那就是说	用在句中
※ — i. e.,	那就是说	用在句中

（续表）

单词或词组	解释	说明
— that is to say, …	那就是说	最好放在句中，但在美国放在句首也时有见到（很多美国人的语文基本功实在是 shaky，都是电脑和网络惹的祸）
※ By that I mean…	那样说我的意思是……	用在句首
What is meant by that is…	这样说的意思是……	用在句首

❷ 本类连接词例句

Asking for money usually requires an explanation of why it is needed. In other words, students' financial dependence on college results in dependence in other areas of life at a time when young people just begin to think for themselves. (*Barron's*)

The companies that can afford the high cost of advertising on TV can also afford to do intensive market research — i. e. , they can identify market trends in order to target a very specific consumer base.

The most beautiful lady in Greek mythology, i. e. , Helen of Troy, was the daughter of Zeus and Leda.

☆　　☆　　☆

学有余力

http://leo. stcloudstate. edu/style/transitioncues. html#forward

如果大家对英文写作的 linkers 还有更加深入的兴趣，还可以登录这个网页，学习更多的英文连接词。

课后练习

Take-Home Quiz

判断练习

请快速判断下面的段落含有哪些逻辑关系：

It is a mistake to look too far ahead. Only one link in the chain of destiny can be handled at a time.

　　　　　　　　　　　　　　　　——*Winston Churchill*

TOEFL iBT
Writing Test

(a)

Coal is the one fossil fuel whose reserves are so immense that they are not in danger of exhaustion within the near future. But rapid expansion of facilities for coal transportation is difficult. Moreover, the burning of coal poses the threat of serious pollution that /which may sharply limit its usefulness in a few years.

(b)

Contrary to "common sense", it is in the best interest of the "ordinary" people to live in a country with high tax rates, especially on incomes, as the goods and services that they can receive from the government are normally worth more than the taxes they pay. In contrast, only a small elite — i. e. / that is, those who hold large amounts of wealth, can benefit from low tax rates. As a consequence, this elite will try to talk the majority of people into accepting an economic and social order that can provide the super rich with more advantages.

(c)

Some people believe that all or most space research should be eliminated (because of) its incredible expense, (not only) in terms of money, (but also) in terms of scientific and human resources. These people point out that (even though) it costs billions of dollars to send astronauts to the moon, all they can bring back are worthless rocks. These people believe that the money and effort being wasted in outer space could be spent on more important projects, (such as) housing projects for homeless people, improving the educational system and finding cures for diseases as well.

(B. Rogers)

填空练习

请在下文的括号中填入正确的单词、词组或者标点符号，使它成为一个逻辑上连贯的段落：

I will soon have to choose between two universities that have accepted me. The first is a large one in a big city (　　) the other one is a small one in a little town, both offering some real benefits and drawbacks.

Going to the large one appeals to me. (　　) does it have more professors and more courses, it can (　　) give me access to all kinds of entertainment and cultural events. (　　), this university has a large department in my field of interest, good laboratory facilities and renowned professors. (　　) social life, there are several museums, a public library, night clubs, major athletic teams in that city and many interesting people to meet, (　　) will be of great help to me in the future when I look for a job.

Universities in little towns, (　　), have a clear focus and orientation in their academic programs (　　) a broad, integrated, balanced education bridging many areas. The professors are paid better than those in the city, (　　) the lower living costs in the town, and are expected to be excellent teachers. Besides, classes are small, (　　) allows a lot of contact among all the members of the community. (　　), it has its limitations (　　) the reputation and academic standards are high, the protective attitude of the administration (　　) the way they watch over students disturb me.

(　　) I do not consider myself wild or radical, I think the freer atmosphere in the city would make me feel more comfortable.

参考答案

whereas/while, Not only, also, Specifically, As for/When it comes to / Regarding / Concerning, which, in contrast, —, despite / in spite of, which, Unfortunately, even though, as well as, Although

Committed to Public Safety

When it comes to transit security, we can always use an extra pair of eyes. Look around. Be aware.

If you have a security concern, report it to police or a TTC uniformed employee.

今天大家所学到的linkers在北美日常生活中也都极为常用。
　　　　　　　　　　　　　——Pat 摄

Day 6

The Faces of a Chameleon
给你的句子一点颜色
（高分内容，非牛人留个脚印即可）

Journalists make it a point to know very little about an extremely wide variety of topics; this is how we stay objective.

——Dave Barry
American Journalist

很多朋友们都听说过或者读过 *The Elements of Style*，一本在美国高中和大学的写作课上常见的名著（http://www.bartleby.com/141/）。Strunk & White 在 1918 年出版的这本书确实抓住了美国人写作的很多特点。特别是它对于 clarity（清晰）和 brevity（简明）近乎偏执的追求，是非常值得我们在写学术类议论文，比如 GRE Issue essays 时借鉴的。

但同时由于种种原因，国内的朋友们可能还不太了解的一个事实是：它在当代美国已经备受争议。毕竟优秀的写作除了 clarity 和 brevity 之外，还有一个至关重要的因素：individuality（个性）。而那本书中的诸多硬性规定却难免有机械和狭隘的嫌疑，其中在当代美国最惹争议的问题就是两位作者对于被动语态的歧视。而事实上美国大学里专门有一派教授（人数还不少）明确要求写 research papers, thesis 或者 dissertation 的时候尽量少用 I, we 这类主观人称，而是用一些被动表达（具体请看本章正文）来展现学术论文的客观性。所以，有的语言学家把那本书里关于 style 的种种规定称为 personal eccentricity（个人怪癖），还有学者认为那本书太过 bossy。

Pat 的观点是：新托福作文毕竟属于比较生活化的作文考试，大家可以通过它学习到两位作者严谨的写作态度并向他们致敬，但却未必一定要让你的新托福作文变成两位老先生个人偏好的克隆。

A mos Bronson Alcott 说过，"The less routine, the more life." （同样的意思比较恶俗的版本则是：Variety is the spice of life. ）

媳妇儿或者老公肯定是不能经常换的，但要是能给新托福作文的句式多加些不同的色彩，却立刻可以让你的作文从一堆堆散发着榴莲或者二氧化氮气味的八股作文中脱颖而出，诱使考官打出高分。

那些暂时风光无限的机考霸主们（"机霸"们），不好意思，俺要把你们的句式变化秘笈全部交代了……

A 状语前置

在英文写作里，状语前置是一种相当常用的句式变换手法，遗憾的是：很多"小白"完全没有意识到这种极酷的多样化手段。

状语前置就是把一个由副词、介词、现在分词或者动词不定式形成的小短语放在句首。这种句式最大的好处是让你的句子产生了一种长短结合的跳跃的节奏感。

◎ 新托福作文状语前置用法全集

☆ Historically, in America workers have been mercilessly exploited by big corporations. For example, garment industry workers, farm laborers, railway workers and fruit pickers were suffered many hardships and paid very little.

☆ Typically, aircraft（飞行器，请注意它的单复数形式相同）are constructed of aluminum, used for its strength, light weight and low cost.

☆ Clearly, this is a positive alternative for motivated parents and their children.

☆ In reality, there's no conclusive evidence that human activity has any effect on the Earth's surface temperature.

☆ Undoubtedly, the most basic elements of writing are to be found in pictures.

☆ Without doubt（注意美语里这个 doubt 前面通常不加 a），computers have changed the way individuals interact with each other in American society.

☆ By sending operations offshore, American companies are securing their own financial future and that of the American public.

☆ By assigning（分配）household chores to their kids, parents recognize children's ability to contribute to the running of the home.

☆ Recently, several nations have begun seriously discussing a manned mission to Mars.

☆ In this way, fresh graduates can get a strong sense of the realities that await（≈ wait for）them.

☆ Many died on the way or shortly after getting here. Some persevered. A few prospered. Eventually, all these different elements combined into a people unique in the world.

☆ In America, many second-generation immigrant children can't speak their mother tongue. Luckily, now the International Language Program and many community schools have started to provide instruction in these children's native language.

☆ Parents' concerns about risk and safety of their children on the streets and outside has driven a generation of children indoors. Ironically（有讽刺意味的是）, it can be argued that now children are being exposed to a whole new set of risks.

☆ In general, it's motivating for students to receive feedback from their teachers.

☆ Time and time again, people who make internal changes that allow them to love their work find that they still feel frustrated no matter how hard they try to love their work.

☆ Simply put, people's productivity and enjoyment have suffered greatly.

☆ Simply stated, the American economy is living on borrowed time.

☆ We all have stress; it's part of life. In fact, we need some stress in our lives to keep our bodies prepared to respond to emergencies.

☆ Given the choice（如果可以选择的话）, he would sacrifice his high-paying job in exchange for more leisure time.

☆ In view of（鉴于）the congressman's proposal, they reconsidered their course of action.

☆ In light of（考虑到）the recent incidents, some cities cancelled Independence Day fireworks displays.

☆ Apart from the cost, it is not a bad option.（Please note "apart from" means "except for" here）

☆ Apart from being used as a school, the building is used for weddings, parties and meetings.（Please note "apart from" means "in addition to / besides" here）

☆ In addition to / Besides the financial benefits, the job brings intellectual rewards.

☆ Although this test only contains a small subset of expectations, students don't really know which ones will be assessed. Accordingly, they're forced to cover all expectations in breadth (跟面包没关系哈~，是 broad 的形容词：广度) but don't have time to study them in depth (深度).

☆ In an ideal world, eating a healthy diet should provide all the nutrients (营养物质) our bodies need. Unfortunately, in the real world, mealtime often means grabbing a quick bite and the food we eat don't provide what our bodies need to maintain good health.

☆ Oddly enough / Strangely enough, government investment in developing new weapons tends to leave citizens fearful.

☆ Interestingly, the educational philosophies of John Dewey and Confucius actually have a lot in common, such as the belief in moderation and the optimism about individuals' potential to change themselves.

☆ Ideally, all the weapons of mass destruction should be eliminated. But in reality, the elimination of such weapons would cause serious national security concerns.

※ 在新托福作文中常会写"理想化状态是……但事实上……"类似的配套表达还有：**In theory,** / **Theoretically,** / **Hypothetically,**（最后这个词比较正式）对应：**But in practice,** / **But in actuality, ...**（最后这个短语也比较正式）

☆ Not surprisingly, adolescents who are under constant stress in their studies tend to develop behavioral problems.

☆ Overall (总体来看), the function of a building is more important than its exterior (外观).

☆ To alleviate (减轻) traffic congestion, the municipal (城市的) government should encourage people to take the public transit.

☆ Living in sheer poverty, these people do not even have money to buy enough food.

◎ **其他经常用于状语前置的副词或词组还有：**

Basically, / **Realistically,** / **Evidently/ Apparently/ Traditionally,** / **Specifically** / **Essentially,** / **In essence,** / **Ultimately,** / **Frankly** / **Fortunately** / **Indeed,** / **Undeniably,** .../ **Indisputably,** （无可争辩） / **On the whole,** / **As a rule,** （并不是"作为规定"，而是"通常来说"） / **Consequently,** 等。

B 句中做手脚

同理，在新托福作文的句中也经常可以引入小短语，它会让句子显得更加灵活多变。请看

下面的大量实例：

☆ Shopping, a necessary part of daily life, is increasingly time-consuming（消耗时间的）in North America.

☆ We'll all die in the end, and because of this, we should cherish every moment of life.

☆ In America, those who move long distances are generally the kind of people who play the major role in holding the community together, in large part because / partly because they are more confident and have better career opportunities.

☆ The Internet is, simply, a collection of screens of information（known as webpages）that reside on thousands of computers around the world.

☆ A positive attitude, after all, is essential for a student's academic performance.

☆ Upon reflection, I recognize, sadly, my experience of being a high-school student and those of the high-school students today are not as different as I hoped.

☆ Ronald Reagan is, arguably, the most successful actor in history, who rose from a career as a movie actor and then television star into the governorship of California and finally two terms as President of the United States.

> ※ 需要特别注意：**arguably** 这个副词很多同学单看词形而误解为它是"引起争议地"的意思，其实在地道美语中正好相反，它是"有道理地，站得住脚地"。类似的还有句型 **It's arguable that...**，也是对后面的话表示支持而不是对后面的话提出质疑，这点很容易错，需要特别小心。

☆ Many scientists believe that human activity has very little, if any, impact on the recent warming trend on Earth.

☆ The costs may vary immensely, depending on the travel distances in a tour.（这个严格来说已经不算句中插入语了，但效果很近似而且非常常用，所以 Pat 还是要力荐）

◎ 此外，经常用于状语前置的单词还有：

　　fundamentally（从根本上讲）和 **namely**（"也就是……" / "即……"，后面再加上具体所指的几个名词）

C　副词领路人

　　有些表示幅度或者范围的副词，如果放在形容词的前面引导形容词，经常可以起到让它们后面的形容词更加明确的作用。

例如：The ability to speak English is increasingly important in a global society.

The medicine doesn't cure the illness. It merely （≈just）stops the pain.

The product's success can't be solely （≈ only，但注意 solely 只能作副词）attributed to the advertising.

类似的副词还有：**approximately**（大约），**markedly**（显著地），**substantially**（大幅度地，显著地，在比较正式的文章和演讲中异常常用），**considerably**（显著地，可观地），**slightly**（微小地），**marginally**（略微地）和 **fractionally**（本意是分数地，但一般就近似"微小程度地"意思）。

D　倒装是进步的阶梯

倒装这种语法现象同学们都学过，但经常想不到去积极使用。在新托福作文里如果找准机会用一次，会让考官感到一股暖流涌上心头。

☆ Not only should the parents spend more time with their children, they should also try to communicate with their children more often.

☆ Not only will kids improve their cardiovascular and muscular strength, endurance, flexibility and hand-eye coordination，but they will also learn perseverance, goal-setting and coping skills to deal with success and failure. （很牛的一句话，如果 Day 4 的单词您都已经熟记了，就会看不到一个生词）

☆ Only in this way can the problem of child obesity be effectively controlled.

☆ Under no circumstances should teachers punish their students physically.

☆ On no account should people say such things during an interview. Nor can a teacher pay much attention to any single student in a classroom of 30 or discover how individual students learn best.

☆ Strange as it may seem，parents' attention sometimes hinders （阻碍）students' academic progress.
近义词：hinder / impede / obstruct

☆ Neither of these factors is the case any longer.

☆ Never have there been more appropriate vehicles for direct marketing than the Internet and E-mails.

☆ Yes, practice makes perfect. But equally important to success in learning a foreign language is constant attention to details.

E 强调但不强势

用 It is... that... 或者 It is... who... 这两种常见强调句式，表达出类似中文的"正是……导致了……"的意思，也是在北美写作中为人们所喜闻乐见的特殊句式之一。

例如： Although friends definitely play a significant role in shaping teenagers' personality, it is the parents and siblings that have a far greater impact on the development of their personality traits.

F 虚拟不等于忽悠

虚拟语气听起来很神，其实说白了就是用过去的时态表示现在或者将来的事儿，来表示语气的弱化。虚拟语气在提建议或者表示某一句论证只是一种假设未必真会发生的时候，在新托福高分范文中极度常见。

The recent crisis could not have occurred without the participation of the biggest players on Wall Street.

By opening our community to different people, we could also expect to be exposed to new ideas that they could bring with them.

Had I lived in a small town, my life would have been confined to（被限制）very few possibilities.

接下来请允许俺引用 *Gone with the Wind* 里的一句描述 Scarlett 心理活动的名句来证明虚拟语气的威力：

Had she ever understood Ashley, she would never have loved him；had she ever understood Rhett, she would never have lost him.

※ 这本小说 Pat 看过 3 遍，而且坚定地认为这本书绝不仅仅是爱情故事。事实上就像 Margaret Mitchell 指出的，它的主题是关于 survival——在人们质疑的眼神中、绝望中、痛苦中、风言风语中、迷茫中……甚至顺境中，去让真实的自己能够 survive 的过程。

Be it learning styles, culture, race, sexual orientation, class, religion, ability, or gender — all identities should be recognized and reflected in the curriculum.（"不论是……"，通常后面跟一串儿名词或者形容词，是只有顶级大牛才需要掌握的高端句型）

G 抽象画法的 of

这种句式中国考生使用较少，但在北美却极为常见。"（be）+of+抽象名词"的意思就相当于其中的那个名词所对应的形容词，用来说明某种特征或属性。of 后常跟的抽象名词有 use / importance / help / value / interest / significance / necessity / quality 等。比如：

☆ Whether people in the developing world are suffering is of no interest to many wealthy citizens in industrial countries. (of no interest 表示 uninteresting)

☆ Fossil fuel is of great importance to the development of industry, transportation and tourism.

H 被动也疯狂

有些同学可能觉得奇怪：怎么被动都能算是句型多样化的手段了？

能！在本章刚开始 Pat 提到了：在 *The Elements of Style* 这本 20 世纪 20 年代出版的写作书中，被动语态被列为 "incorrect" 的高危句式。但是在比较偏重生活化的新托福高分范文中，被动语态依然十分常见：

例如： It has been confirmed by scientists that prolonged（延长）exposure to high levels of noise in modern cities can lead to hearing loss and high blood pressure.

除此之外，北美议论文写作中的常见被动表达还有：

It can be argued that…

It has been noted that…

It's observed that…

It's believed that…

It's commonly accepted that…

It's generally recognized that…

It is reported that… (注意这里可以用现在时)

It's estimated that…

I 变性表决心

请注意这里的变性是指"改变词性"的句式变换手法。写作中的变性主要有三种：

❶

请比较下面两句话的不同效果：

改变前： People are concerned because the traditional values are gradually disappearing from the tribes.

改变后： People are concerned about the gradual disappearance of the traditional tribal values.

说明：动词和名词间的相互转换往往可以让我们把句子写得更加灵活多样。类似的常用变化还有：

动词	名词
improve	improvement
intend to	intention
graduate	graduation
decide	decision
explore	exploration
discover	discovery
aspire to	aspiration
provide	provision

②

改变前：Some people don't fulfill their responsibilities as parents.

改变后：Some people don't fulfill their parental responsibilities.

说明：-al 是英文里一个很常见的后缀。虽然也有少数特例（比如 denial 就是一个名词，而 professional 有时候也可以作为"专业人士"当成名词来用），但大多数-al 结尾的单词都是形容词，而且这类形容词在略偏学术的文章中相当常见。下面几个词是-al 结尾的常用形容词：environmental, governmental, societal（比 social 正式一些，但在书面语中也挺常用），biological 和 technological。

下表中的词汇也都可以在形容词和名词间相互转换：

形容词	名词
mature	maturity
chaotic	chaos
generous	generosity
possible	possibility
happy	happiness
applicable	applicability
optimistic	optimism
stable	stability
disastrous	disaster

❸

Telecommuting（在家远程上班）can bring numerous benefits to both employees and employers.

Both employees and employers can benefit from telecommuting.

Telecommuting is beneficial to both employees and employers.

Both employees and employers can be beneficiaries（受益者）of telecommuting.

这一组是在名词、动词、形容词和名词派生词间做了相当灵活多样的转换。

希望大家在今后的写作和阅读中有意识地积累这类"千面词汇"。不仅是备考新托福，而且从今后大家在美国的学习和工作来看这事儿也非常值得做。

J 副词排成队

副词排成队就是把几个副词连用，形成排比。这种绝活儿会让你看起来相当有自信，对于还在摇摆不定的阅卷人有强大的震慑作用：

☆ Athletes tend to move gracefully, energetically and powerfully.

☆ Some people argue that the new instruction methodology can help students develop intellectually and emotionally.

☆ All this material is now quickly, inexpensively and readily available from the comfort of our desks and workstations.

☆ After the surgery, most young patients feel physically and mentally back to normal within a week.

K 用点、线勾出层次感

素描强调点、线、面的结合，而高分范文也经常会调动"："和"—"这两个标点，给全篇文章的"面"带来更生动的层次感。

☆ In a simpler time, advertising only called attention to the products. But now it manufactures a new product of its own：the consumers.

☆ Homeschooled children spend much more time in the company（陪伴）of appropriate（恰当的）role models（榜样）：parents, other adults and older siblings.（Kaplan）

☆ Inappropriate（不恰当的）humor with students is often viewed as a boundary violation：It's a failure to maintain a professional comportment and distance and a failure to appreciate the sensitivity that students may have to a teacher's comments.

☆ All advertising media share a common goal: to reach as many consumers as possible and convince them to buy a certain product.

☆ And what does writing mean to us today? We're surrounded by writing at every turn. We use it, often unconsciously, in daily activities — in the kitchen, at the job or on the road.

☆ Actually, cloning is only part of the dramatic aspect of the revolution taking place in the bioscience — a revolution that will give humans complete control of their biological makeup.

☆ Humor helps build bridges between cultures and individuals — It's an ideal form of promoting understanding and friendship between people who don't even speak the same language.

☆ Many public school educators believe that the learning process should be centered on the learners' needs, wants and initiatives — a precondition for students to feel happy and content.

☆ In fact, the World Wide Web is just one part of the Internet — a multifaceted communication medium that takes in anything from simple text communication by E-mail, to video-conferencing with high-quality sound and video.

☆ Universities in little towns have a clear focus and orientation in their academic programs — a broad, integrated, balanced education bridging many areas.

L　"the +形容词" 的语法可没错

例如: the rich, the wealthy, the poor, the needy, the elderly, the unknown, the unemployed, the weak, the neglected（被忽视的群体）

这些可都不是语法错误，而是英文里的一种习惯用法，泛指某一类人。并且因为是复数概念，当这些表达用作主语时也经常需要跟复数动词。比如下面的例句: The elderly are a valuable part of society and deserve to be treated as such.（Kaplan）

M　双重否定就是肯定

新托福写作中比较推荐大家用的是下面这几种双重否定:

☆ It is not unrealistic to promote more job satisfaction in any job. 意思是: 去做某事是……现实的

☆ These days, it is not uncommon that young people have a break from studying after graduating from high school. 意思是: ……的现象是挺常见的

☆ During Christopher Columbus' many voyages, it was not unusual for half of the crew to die of diseases.

☆ Not surprisingly, students who are under constant stress in their studies may suffer from mental problems or even commit crimes. 意思是：不出所料，……（严格来讲这个是"单重否定"，但因为意思比较接近双重否定，所以也列在这里）

☆　　☆　　☆

除此之外，新托福写作中还有五种异常简单但却经常被大家忽视的特殊句式，只要你稍加注意，马上就可以提高句式多样性：

序号	类型	特点
N	长短句结合	如果你使用前一章讲的那些 linkers 已经实在用累了的时候就歇一歇吧，那么短句子自然就写出来了
O	疑问句	在 Day 8（上）我们还会看到高分实例
P	反问句	ditto
Q	形容词的比较级 +……，形容词的比较级 +……	大家对它都很熟悉，但也不一定能想到去使用，最简单的例子就是：When it comes to sending in your application package，the sooner，the better！
R	合理地进行省略	有些句式在美语中可以合理地省略掉某部分，比如：No matter what your age（is），it's worth taking the time to understand the importance of a healthy diet. 不过从实战角度看，Pat 给大家的建议是：有些省略方式如果遇到有"洁癖"的考官，则有触雷的可能，所以对这类省略也不必太执着

本章已经覆盖了美语写作句式多样化变换从下里巴人一直到阳春白雪的全部"18 般兵刃"。接下来的工作就需要各位去积极实践了。

考场如战场。Pat 永远都坚信：考场里的实用性才是任何备考的终极目标。

学有余力

（适合背写作单词已经背疯了的大虾们）

www.englishpage.com/vocabulary/vocabulary.html

互联网上有很多很酷的词汇教学网站，不过说实话，多数网站的内容跟新托福作文真的没关系。上面这个网站还比较不错，有很多单词你都可以用到作文话题里。不过大家花时间去找这类网站的前提一定是要先把 Day 4 里的新托福作文核心词汇背得非常熟了，这样才能用最低的机会成本去换得最实用的备考词汇。

课后练习

Take-Home Quiz

判断练习

（A）识别下列句子使用了何种特殊加分句式：

① In terms of history, many Asian cities hold definite advantages over American metropolises（大都市）.

② It is the air quality that keeps some foreign investors away from Hong Kong.

③ Only in very few regions（区域）do the residents have enough water for their daily needs.

④ Without electricity, many of the modern inventions would have been impossible.

（B）请判断下文中的彩色字使用了何种特殊句式：

Not only was the South Beach Diet designed to help you lose weight, it was developed to improve your health as well. The idea is, contrary to weight-loss plans, that we have to learn to eat "good" carbs such as those found in vegetables while eliminating "bad" carbs — i. e., those found in processed food like bread, snacks and soft drinks. According to Dr. Arthur Agatson, our bodies could not process these kinds of food and, as a consequence, the body stored more fat than it should. The South Beach Diet has been of great interest to millions of people around the world.

（C）请判断下文中的彩色部分使用了何种特殊句式：

Not to strive, not to take advantage of the opportunities in such a world, not to succeed where success was so available — these things naturally became a sort of crime against the state. To develop the resources of a new country required energetic people, bent upon using their energies — not only for the rewards that would result to themselves, but even more importantly, to the community. So material success in the United States is not looked upon as selfish. Its results are seen to have communal value.　　　　　　（Bradford Smith）

参考答案

（A）

① In terms of history, many Asian cities hold definite advantages over American metropolises. 本句中 In terms of history 是典型的状语前置，是"在历史这方面"的意思。

2 It is the air quality that keeps some foreign investors away from Hong Kong. 本句使用了强调句，强调令一些投资者远离香港的原因。

3 Only in very few regions do the residents have enough water for their daily needs. 本句使用了倒装句，强调缺水的严重性。

4 Without electricity, many of the modern inventions would have been impossible. 本句使用了虚拟语气，表示和事实相反的一种假设。

（B）

倒装，句中插入短语，拉丁词，状语前置，of + 抽象名词

（C）

点、线技法 + 句中做手脚

Boston College 虽然叫college, 其实名气远比很多university 要响得多。因为是以文科为主，所以"Work hard, play hard." 的精神十分高涨，学生上课时的专心致志与partying or clubbing时的激情之间的戏剧性对比压倒了一切新托福句式的变换。

——Pat摄于Boston

TOEFL
iBT Writing Test

Day 7

What's Hot & What's Not
该出手时就出手：
考场里真正实用的写作句型

A fear of weapons is a sign of retarded sexual and emotional maturity.
——Sigmund Freud
founder of psychoanalysis

喜欢音乐的朋友们一定都听说过 the Woodstock Festival。其实 1969 年的第一场 Woodstock Festival 地点并非在 Wood-stock，而是在一个废弃的空军基地，and ironically（富有讽刺意味的是）：音乐会主题却是"Three Days of Peace and Music"。当时之所以被迫换地方也是典型美式理由：Woodstock 镇的居民一致反对在该镇举办音乐节。Even more ironically，音乐节火了之后，Woodstock 镇上的一切东西都立马儿开始跟这个不可错失的旅游业机会挂钩……

从中学时代就开始组乐队的 Pat 正失望地看到曾经那么帅的 rock 'n roll 反主流文化精神正在被吞噬一切的 American consumerism 无情地同化。

对于那些梦想着有一天自己也能写出一篇十分地道的英语文章的童鞋来说，精彩句型的积累应该是延续终生的任务。然而考试毕竟是很快就要去参加的，留美的计划也不能等下辈子再去实现。

本章中 Pat 推荐给大家的 172 个句子都是与新托福作文话题密切相关的加分武器，并且全部选自近一年内出版的最新英文原版文章或者书籍，仔细体会句型与例句必有所获。

A word of caution，though：正常人说话或者写文章的特点是多数内容一般般，只有少数内容才是亮点。新托福作文主要也是看是否流畅和自然，如果句句加分，那可就是句句恶心了，一篇 300 多字的作文里能用出来 4~5 句加分句型已经很好，否则肯定就不自然了。而且写句子本来就是一种综合实力——Day 4 的分类词汇以及总结出的动词、动词短语、名词和形容词表格都是大家盖房子用的砖，Day 5 的连词是帮您把砖绑合起来的钢筋，Day 6 的句式变换是赋予单调的砖墙以丰富色彩的颜料。而今天要学的句型则是 glass mosaic，是画龙点睛的手段，最重要的部分永远都还是前面的基础章节。

Truly hope that's not just wishful thinking.

北美写作 172 句型

※ 如果某些句型您觉得自己已经很熟悉，没关系，好好研究一下它们的例句，仍然会让你大有收获。Examining the illustrative samples will definitely add a new dimension to your sentence skills. ☺

前进类（论证 positive 方面常用）

❶ be supposed to 是在写作和口语考试中都可以用来替换 should 的美语极常用表达

例句：In fact，going on a diet is supposed to be more than just eating little. It should also be about eating healthily.

❷ hold fast to... 这里的 fast 不是"快速地"，而是"坚实地"。这个句型完整的意思是"牢牢地把握住……"

例句： In his biography, the message of perseverance and holding fast to one's dreams in the face of adversity is very strong. （本句的所有"生词"在 Day 4 的分类词汇中均已经出现过了）

近义： 其实在美语中，put a premium on / set considerable store （这里不是指商店） by / put a high value on / treasure（*vt.*）/ cherish（*vt.*）/ value（*vt.*）也都可以用来表达"珍视"的意思，没必要总是不停地用"put emphasis on"或者"attach great importance to"这些每个考生都在使用的表达了。

❸ bear in mind that... 牢记……

例句： ① Bear in mind that the next generation of cell phones is just around the corner（很快就要到来）.

② It's important to bear in mind that an assessment（评估）based on the data is only a prediction. The results are not carved in stone.

提示： ① be based on 也是新托福作文中很常见的句型，虽然是基础句型，但是出现频率很高。类似的还有 on the basis of... 基于……

② be not carved in stone 这个短语也很常见："某事不是一成不变的"

❹ There's no better way to... than to... ……是去做某事的最好方式

例句： There's no better way to connect with and truly understand the diverse experiences and talents of students and their families than to be a visible member of their community.

❺ go a long way 非常有效

例句： Sincere praise, encouragement and appreciation go a long way — even just saying "thank you" leaves a lasting impression.

比较： come a long way

例句： In 1858, the selling of human beings was legal in America. In January 2009, an African American officially became President of the United States. The country had come a long way.

❻ It's worthwhile to... 大家可能更熟悉 be worth doing sth. 这样的句型，但作文里也经常会用到 worthwhile 这个词

例句： Before you vote for a certain candidate in an election, it's worthwhile to find his/her true worth.

❼ give sb. the credit for... 把……归功于某人，相应的美语里还有 take the credit for...

164

例句：It's generally recognized that Edward Jenner should be given the credit for defeating the disease of smallpox.

⑧ enable sb. to do sth. / equip sb. with the ability to do sth. 让某人可以去做……

例句：Technically, the new bill enables the president to shut down the Internet when major threats to cybersecurity are identified.

⑨ draw on 借鉴（经验等）

例句：As a friend and mentor, she drew on humor, a beautiful spirit and her faith in the Aboriginal culture to accomplish her work.

⑩ boost efficiency / productivity 提高效率/生产率

例句：Automation（自动化）substantially（显著地）boosts productivity even though it may make jobs even more stressful.

⑪ give sb. a competitive edge 给某人竞争优势

例句：Foreign language skills give people a competitive edge in this age of globalization.

⑫ ... is a gateway to... ……是通向某一目标的途径（还有一个类似的句型叫 is a passport to... 这里 passport 就不是指护照了）

例句：Students' performance on standardized tests has become a gateway to the opportunities that lie before a student when they complete their studies.

⑬ enlarge one's outlook 开阔某人的眼界（那个 broaden one's horizons 明显已经被北京孩子使用得过多了）

例句：Encouraging students to study a foreign language is a way to enlarge their outlook and raise their cultural awareness.

⑭ is a good vehicle for... 这里的 vehicle 并不是交通工具，而是承载信息的手段

例句：Humor is generally considered a good vehicle for cross-cultural communication.

⑮ generate... (employment) opportunities 创造（就业）机会

例句：International trade can generate more employment opportunities for the domestic（国内的）job market.

⑯ dedicate A to B 把 A（金钱、时间、精力等）用到 B 这个目的上，写作里经常可以用来代替 spend A on B

例句：Multibillionaires like Bill Gates and Richard Branson have dedicated colossal（巨

大的）amounts of money to humanitarian initiatives（人道主义事业）.

类似句型： Our high school is committed to recognizing and responding to the needs of the local community.

⑰ assume / shoulder the responsibility for... 承担起……的责任，注意这里的 shoulder 是动词

例句： Educators should assume the responsibility for ensuring that cultural, language and learning differences are addressed in teaching.

⑱ be mindful of 基本就等于"关注……"，写作里用来代替 pay close attention to 挺不错

例句： The big companies should be more mindful of and sensitive to the environmental needs of the local communities.

⑲ a wealth of... 在地道英文里这个词组并不是指财富，而是指"大量（有益的东西）"，特别是当它后面跟一些抽象名词的时候

例句： The library brightened up the kids' drab lives, offering them a wealth of educational entertainment and an atmosphere in which they can enjoy it.

⑳ ... is a lifelong process 是持续一生的过程（比如积累好的英文句子就是！）

例句： Learning has become a lifelong process, not just because of the individual needs, but also because of the ever-increasing pressure.

㉑ put... into practice 把……投入实践

例句： Putting new ideas into practice is far more difficult than having them.

㉒ fulfill one's potential 发挥某人的潜力

例句： His management style derives from（某种抽象事物来自于……）the belief that working under pressure helps employees fulfill their potential.

近义： stretch sb. / make sb. stretch

例句： ① There is no shame in not meeting all of our goals, as long as our goals make us stretch. For example, if we want to run a marathon in under three hours, we'll train differently than if we want to run it in four hours.
② My present job doesn't stretch me, so I'm looking for something more demanding.

㉓ from within... 您可能觉得很奇怪：怎么 within 这个介词前面还能再加个 from？看似简单，其实这是个十分高端的惯用习语："来自内心深处"

例句： When you feel uncomfortable with your circumstances, listen to yourself, your own experiences, your own thoughts and your gifts from within, which are real and true.

㉔ remove the barrier for 为（发展、交流等）消除障碍

例句： Machine translation was intended to help remove the barrier for communication between people who do not speak the same language. （在美语中 help 的后面可以直接跟其他动词，而且 help sb. 也不加 to do sth.，而是加 do sth.）

㉕ be in tune with... 与……一致，与……和谐

例句： Some American scholars argue that John Dewey's thought is thoroughly in tune with the Asian philosophies.

㉖ keep pace with... 与……同步发展

例句： For the first time in five years, senior executives' salaries didn't keep pace with inflation（通货膨胀）.

㉗ promote the development of... 促进……的发展

例句： The extensive（广泛的）use of English as a global language has helped promote the development of a host of（大量的）international organizations.

㉘ raise people's awareness of... 提高人们的某种意识

例句： The electronic media, therefore, have the obligation to help raise the public awareness of the crisis.

㉙ ... has found one's niche 这是一个特美式的表达——找到了属于自己的一片天地，比如适合自己的工作或者事业等，或者公司找到了适合自己的定位

例句： Chris has found his niche as a high-school baseball coach.

㉚ be the cornerstone of... 是……的基石

例句： The strong belief in individualism has been the cornerstone of America throughout its history.

比较： be the bedrock of...：

例句： Marriage and children are the bedrock of family life.

㉛ be an essential ingredient of... 是……的必备条件

例句： The development of new products is an essential ingredient of corporate（公司的）success.

近义： ① play a pivotal/crucial role in 在……中起关键作用

例句： Architects（建筑师）play a pivotal role in the improvement of the modern cityscape（城市景观）.

近义： ② A is an essential/integral/ indispensable part of B. A 是 B 不可缺少的一部分

例句： Over the past decades, digital technology has emerged as an essential part of our everyday life at work and at home.
Parents are an indispensable part of preschool education.

近义： ③ is part and parcel of... 是……最核心的部分

例句： This program was part and parcel of his election campaign.

㉜ sharpen one's intellect 提高某人用知识去分析问题的能力

例句： Our friends are not all the same: One friend brings out our athletic side — we run or go to the gym together. Another sharpens our intellect with debate and discussion. Yet another is our favorite companion for going to the movies or out to dinner.

㉝ achieve and maintain sth. 实现并且保持某种状态

例句： One of the keys to achieving and maintaining a healthy weight is portion control.（注意这里的 to 为介词）

㉞ be a positive alternative... 某事是有益的替代方式

例句： Clearly, this is a positive alternative for motivated parents and their children.

对比： the mainstream of... 主流

例句： Due to the ever-increasing concern over climate change, environmental ideas have been absorbed（吸收）into the mainstream of American politics. But what truly matters is action, not talk, as President Obama aptly remarked about the Copenhagen Accord.

㉟ participate in 参与

例句： Encouraging kids to participate in an organized sport like soccer, gymnastics, ice hockey, or figure skating, is another great way to get them involved in physical activity.

近义： take part in

㊱ afford people the sense of belonging / the sense of fulfillment / the sense of achievement 给人们归属感/成就感，注意在写作里 afford 经常是"提供"的意思

例句： The sense of belonging to a team or a working community also contributes to job satisfaction as colleagues help each other enjoy their working lives.

㊲ ... is a main driving force behind... 是……的主要推动力

例句： Competition has been a main driving force behind productivity throughout the history of the market-oriented economy.

㊳ reverse the damage to... 挽回对……的破坏

例句： They're constructing facilities to reverse the flood damage to the town.

㊴ is a perfect complement to... 是对……的极好补充（注意 complement 的拼写要和 "compliment 夸奖"区分开）

例句： This system has the potential to develop into a perfect complement to antivirus software and firewalls.

比较： 形容词 complementary

㊵ be in accordance with 与……一致，符合。类似的表达还有 be in line with 和 be in keeping with

例句： The authorities must ensure that things proceed in accordance with the law.

反义： be incompatible with / be at odds with / clash with

㊶ catch a glimpse of... 很快地了解一下某种事物，像中文的"走马观花"

例句： Visitors to the gallery caught a glimpse of the painters' observations and fantasies.

㊷ integrate / incorporate... into... 将……结合进……

例句： This project brought together a group of teachers who created multimedia learning objects that incorporate innovative uses of technology into the curriculum to enhance students' learning and illustrate new ways of thinking.（如果 Day 4 里的教育类词汇您已经很熟悉，这句话不会有任何一个单词是生词）

近义成语： get the best of both worlds 很常用的美式表达，酷似中文里的"两全其美"

㊸ give priority to sth. 把……放在优先位置

例句： The finite（≈ limited）budget requires the government to give priority to the optimization（优化）of its financial resources.

⑭ inject... into... 把……注入，赋予……

例句： Even though the word fairness is somewhat elusive（飘忽不定的）, Americans have managed to inject many meanings into it.

⑮ explore every avenue toward... 去探索完成……的各种途径

例句： The American government will explore every avenue toward peace in this region.

⑯ awaken the conscience of society 唤起社会的良知或者责任感（这个句型看起来很大，但也是很地道而且常用的表达）

例句： They worked in Women's Shelter to protect the battered and abused women, to awaken the conscience of society and to arouse compassion（Day 4 里学过的单词：同情心）for the weak（Day 6 学过 the +形容词的用法）.

⑰ unravel the mystery / the detail of... 解释清楚本来很难理解的情况

例句： Life science has not completely unraveled the mystery of genes yet.

⑱ Far from being... 完全不是……，新托福作文中多用于正面论证，但偶尔也可用于负面意思

例句： ① Far from being amateurs（业余爱好者）, these kids know the game rules inside out.

know... inside out: 美语，对……了如指掌

② The space trash problem is far from being solved. In fact, all efforts to bring down space trash have failed glaringly and, ironically, have led to even more trash in the outer space.

fail glaringly: 惨重的失败

..., ironically, ... 有讽刺意味的是……

⑲ satisfy / accommodate the needs of... 大家都知道 accommodation 是住宿，但是您是否知道它的动词形式还经常用来表达"满足……的需求"的意思呢？

例句： We should make sure that the needs of individual students' are accommodated and the assessment practices are aligned to the learning process.（be aligned to: 与……一致）

⑳ are obligated to... 有义务去做某事

例句： In some American universities, graduate students are not obligated to have their advisor as their supervisor for their thesis.

㊿ make it a point to... 这句可能看起来很简单，但确实是地道的美语，而且如果能准确用出来肯定加分：确保去做某事（=make sure / ensure that）

例句：Journalists make it a point to know very little about an extremely wide variety of topics. This is how we stay objective.

㊾ ... is a milestone/milepost in... 在……的过程中是一个标志性（或者更严肃地说"是里程碑似的"）事件，但请注意这个句型并不只限于在新托福作文里举历史性例子才能使用，对生活影响较大的事情也同样可以用这个句型。milestone 英美通用，但 milepost 只有美语才用

例句：① Moving out of his parents' home was a milestone in the entrepreneur's life.

② The bill is an important milestone in preserving American natural resources.

㊽ ... is the cradle of... 是……的发源地

例句：Boston, or more specifically, Faneuil Hall, is sometimes referred to as the Cradle of Liberty. （or more specifically: 或者更具体地说，"句中做手脚"）

㊼ ... take sanctuary in... 在……中找到避风港

例句：If I want some peace and quiet, I take sanctuary in my study. （注意 quiet 其实也经常可以作名词使用）

比较：Home is my sanctuary, the place where I can escape the world. But it's also a convenient, comfortable place to introduce activity into my lifestyle.

㊻ gain / gather / lose momentum 这个 momentum 很像中文里的"势"，相应的这三个表达就是：某件事情的势头更强劲或者势头减弱了

例句：A switch to renewable energy resources has been gaining momentum in many portions of the Western U. S. in response to the environmentalists' concerns.

㊺ rise to the occasion 这个表达在写作里酷似中文的"迎难而上"

例句：Being prepared gives one enough confidence to rise to the occasion and deliver what he/she knows best.

㊹ exude confidence / sympathy / an air of wealth and power （某人)浑身散发着某种品质

例句：FDR was approachable（好接近的）and exuded optimism and vision.

㊸ a labor of love 是指那种发自内心心甘情愿地去做的努力

例句：He did all this as a labor of love. He didn't need any recognition for it.

(59) get into the swing of things 去努力熟悉、适应身边的事物

例句： Don't be too hard on yourself. Moving to a new country can be really stressful and it'll take a while for you to get into the swing of things.

倒退类（论证 negative 方面常用）

❶ be at risk 处在风险中

例句： If a company cannot keep profits well above the break-even point, its future is at risk.

近义： ① run the risk of... 冒……的风险

② be in peril 意思接近，但是语气更强，一般是很大的危险

③ be at stake，例如：Thousands of lives will be at stake if emergency aid（紧急援助）doesn't arrive in the city soon.

④ put... to the test 让……经受考验

❷ ... few of us have ever stopped to think about... 很少有人去考虑……

例句： Probably few of us have ever stopped to think about how our present-day concept of time and ways of measuring it came about（Day 4 学过的动词短语：逐渐成形）.

❸ be concerned about... 对……很关注，担忧

例句： Canada is deeply concerned about losing its professionals to the United States. Taxes are a big factor in this "brain drain". But the average families living in the United States are not necessarily better off in terms of disposable income（可支配收入）, than their Canadian counterparts.

❹ have a hard time doing sth. 很难实现或者完成某事，美语中极为常用的表达，而且不仅可以用于口语，新托福写作中也很常用

例句： You'll have a hard time falling asleep or wake up earlier than desired if you continue to think and worry.

❺ be at odds with sth. 与……不符，与……冲突

例句： Their findings were at odds with the previous research results, which suggested that there might be some problems with the methods used in the previous experiments.

近义： 动词短语 clash with sth. / be incompatible with

❻ be threatened with... 受到……的威胁

例句： Large numbers of animals and plants are being threatened with extinction, mainly as a consequence of human activities.

比较： 主动形式 pose a threat to... 对……构成威胁

❼ abide by / comply with / conform to 遵守（法律、规定等）

例句： We swear that we will take part in these Olympic Games in the true spirit of sportsmanship and that we will respect and abide by the rules which govern them, for the glory of sport and the honor of our country.

❽ ... very little, if any, ... 只有很少，如果有的话

例句： Some scientists believe that human activity has very little, if any, impact on the recent warming trend on Earth.

❾ be overly dependent/reliant on... 对某事过度依赖的

例句： Technology, originally intended to liberate we humans, has successfully made us overly dependent on it. （be intended to do sth.：被用来实现……的目的）

❿ be hard-pressed to... = find it difficult to...

例句： During the Christmas season, people are hard-pressed to find a nice restaurant with empty seats.

⓫ be in short supply 供应短缺

例句： In some developing countries, school classes are very large, ranging from 50 to 100 students and classroom resources are in short supply.

表示短缺的名词： lack / shortage / scarcity / dearth

⓬ widen the gap between... and... 加大两者之间的差距

例句： At present, the technology available to individuals is actually widening the gap between the rich and the poor rather than narrowing （narrow 在这里作动词） it.

反义： narrow the gap between / bridge the gap between / close the gap between

⓭ in part because... / partly because... 部分因为……

例句： In America, those who often move long distances are generally the kind of people who play the major role in holding the community together, in part / partly because they are more confident and have better career opportunities.

⑭ frown on... 对……皱眉头，反对（当你已经对 oppose, object to 这样的阶级斗争大词感到十分疲惫，frown on 就会显得平淡是真了）

例句：Many American citizens frowned on the astronomical budget deficit（天文数字的财政赤字）of their government.

⑮ If..., ... will ensue 如果……，某种结果将跟随而来

例句：Disasters will ensue if they remain unready like this.

⑯ ... hover at high levels ……居高不下

例句：The unemployment rate has been hovering at historically high levels this year.

⑰ be inundated with sth. / be saturated with sth. 充斥着……（一般跟负面的东东）

例句：The upcoming video game will be saturated with blood and nudity（裸露镜头）.

⑱ be subject to... 这里的 subject 是形容词，不是学科，而是 "经受、遭受……"

例句：Homeschooled children are less subject to the stress and pressure experienced by conventional students who spend six, seven, or eight hours a day with their peers.

⑲ A can be attributed/ascribed to B A 可以归因于 B，偶尔也用于正面含义，但多数时候都用于负面情况。

例句：Many cases of eating disorders can be attributed to anxiety or a sense of guilt.

近义：① A is attributable to B. A 的根源是 B。

近义：② B is the root cause of A. A 的根源是 B。

例句：The population explosion has been the root cause of the persistent water scarcity（长期存在的水短缺）.

近义：③ A stems from B. A 的根源是 B。

例句：Their disagreement mainly stemmed from misunderstanding.

⑳ be susceptible to 容易受到来自……的负面影响

例句：Children tend to be more susceptible to advertising, especially when they view the advertising alone.

㉑ distract sb. from... 分散某人的注意力

例句：There are educational video games that, instead of distracting students from their classes, actually make students more academically-motivated.

㉒ at the expense of... 以……为代价

例句： The economy should not be developed at the expense of reckless depletion（不顾后果的开采）of natural resources and degradation of the environment（环境的恶化）.

近义： at the cost of...

比较： be sth. down the drain 是白白扔掉的

例句： You've already spent a lot of money fixing your car. Spending even more will just be **money** down the drain.

㉓ run contrary to 与……背道而驰

例句： Their arguments run contrary to the overwhelming evidence that technology enhances efficiency in almost all fields.

㉔ erode the cultural identity / national pride 侵蚀文化特性/民族自豪感

例句： Extinction of native languages has been eroding the cultural identity of Native Americans.

㉕ It's wrong to equate... with... 把……等同于……是错误的

例句： It's wrong to equate **happiness** with a bigger house or a bigger bank account.

㉖ be confronted with sth. 面对挑战、危机、困难等，写作里经常可以用它来代替 face 这个大家最爱用的"面对"

例句： Today, the American parents who are confronted with a plethora of（过量的）violent and pornographic（色情的）TV shows are actually divided about this issue.

㉗ copy sth. mechanically 机械地抄袭

例句： Today, some public-school young teachers have no alternative（替代物）but to copy, very mechanically, the techniques used by their own teachers fifteen years ago.

㉘ ... is not a panacea for... 某种方案并不是解决某个问题的万能药

例句： Charter schools are not a panacea for the deficiencies（缺陷或不足）found in American public schools.

㉙ be addicted to sth. / be preoccupied with sth. 对负面事物上瘾，对应的还有 be absorbed in... / be engrossed in... 但这两个后面跟的不一定是坏事物

例句： Many American teens are so addicted to social networking websites like Facebook and Twitter they spend hours on them daily.

㉚ drive up the crime rate 导致犯罪率上升

例句： The unprecedentedly high unemployment rate is driving up the already alarming violent crime rate.

㉛ exert detrimental influence upon / have adverse effect on 对……有负面的影响

例句： Long-distance flights are a classic trade-off. On the one hand, they make things a lot easier for international travelers and multinational companies. On the other hand, a great deal of detrimental influence has been exerted upon the environment by the jumbo jets（巨型飞机）. trade-off 指为了获得好处而必须付出代价的处境，也可以用 "It cuts both ways." 等类似表达。北京孩子用得最多的则是 a double-edged sword

㉜ sth. is unwarranted / unjustifiable 某种做法很不合理

例句： Performance of experiments upon lab animals without effort to alleviate（减轻）their pain is unwarranted.

㉝ spin out of control 失去控制

例句： The demand for economic growth is helping make the American consumerism spin out of control.

比较： lose track of 失去对某事的管理

例句： It's easy for people to lose track of time when they use the Internet.

㉞ are not compatible with... / are incompatible with... 与……不一致或不协调

例句： We want to be safe, but we also want to be adventurous, even though the two don't seem compatible with each other.

㉟ be likely to fall prey to/ be vulnerable to 容易成为……的受害者（作文里经常当作比喻用法，比如暴力电子游戏或者环境污染）

例句： Some medical professionals assume（设想）that the elderly may be vulnerable to the side effects of H1N1 vaccination.

㊱ sth. should be condemned rather than condoned 某事应该被谴责而不是被宽恕

例句： The spokesman should be condemned rather than condoned for what were, essentially, racist remarks.

㊲ What's the good of...? 新托福高分范文中时常出现的反问句：……又有何好处呢？

例句： What's the good of having more advanced public transit if it's increasingly difficult to transport industrial and agricultural products?

㊳ live in poverty/ misery/ frustration/ anxiety 生活在贫穷/困苦/沮丧/焦虑中

例句： Living in misery, these people have no chance to receive education, which might be the only way that can lift them out of poverty.

㊴ diminish individuals' leisure time 减少人们的休闲时间

例句： The accelerating（加速的）pace of urban life seriously diminishes individuals' leisure time and causes psychological strain（持续的）心理压力.

㊵ stifle creativity 扼杀创造力

例句： In the same year, some scholars began to argue that copyright laws might stifle creativity.

㊶ be afflicted by 遭受……

例句： Interestingly, not just many women, but many men as well, are afflicted by compulsive shopping（不可控制的购物欲望，有这样倾向的人就叫 shopaholic。2009 年在美国还专门有部电影就叫 *Confessions of a Shopaholic*，情节老套但里面的名牌儿可真不少！）.

㊷ be oblivious to 对……完全无视

例句： Oblivious to our limits, we attempt things that we can't really handle.

㊸ cause grave concerns 引起严重关注

例句： The H1N1 epidemic has caused grave concerns and the elderly, pregnant women, children and health care workers have been encouraged to get vaccinated against the virus.

近义： Concerns have arisen about...

Legitimate concerns have been raised about...（legitimate：有根据的）

㊹ spell disaster / trouble for... 某事意味着灾难／麻烦

例句： The new policy could spell disaster for many businesses in this country.

㊺ deprive someone of sth. 剥夺某人的（自由、权利或者某种生活方式）

例句： As humans, we cannot function（*vi.*）properly when we are deprived of sleep.

㊻ take... for granted 这个大家应该很熟悉，而且它确实在美国相当常用

例句： Many young Americans take the comforts of living in America for granted. They would become more grateful for that if they saw more of the world.

㊼ poorly-informed, uninformed or misinformed about... 媒体类话题常用，（公众）关于某事了解很少，完全不了解或者错误了解

例句： Many Americans believe that they have been poorly-informed, uninformed or misinformed about the war in Iraq.

㊽ A has rendered B＋形容词或者名词作宾语补足语　A 让 B 变成某种状态

例句： New technology keeps rendering old computers obsolete（过时的，没人用了的）.

㊾ lower one's expectations 降低某人的期望值

例句： To keep from being disappointed, we sometimes lower our expectations or avoid taking challenges. There may be good reasons for this, but it can limit what we experience.

㊿ go from bad to worse 越来越糟

例句： Things went from bad to worse and in the end, Obama's Treasury Secretary nominee（财政部长提名候选人）apologized for tax mistakes.

(51) There's no guarantee that... 无法保证……

例句： There's no guarantee that the UN climate conference in Copenhagen can produce any concrete results.

最终达成的 the Copenhagen Accord 被很多环境科学家称为 "an abject failure"（惨败）

(52)（a certain problem）has reached such proportions that...　问题已经到了……的程度

例句： The H1N1 epidemic has reached such proportions that global control efforts must be made immediately. Otherwise, tourism, economy and public health may suffer irreparable harm（无法挽回的损失）.

中间类（论证不好不坏／可好可坏方面常用）

❶ on the basis of... 基于……

例句： The child laborers felt insulted when employers hired them solely on the basis of their size and appearance.

❷ are likely to…/ are unlikely to

例句： ① Men suffer from heart are more likely to disease, even though heart disease is still the number one killer of women in America.

② It's important to know events happening around the world, even though sometimes they are unlikely to affect your daily life.

名词形式： likelihood

例句： There is every likelihood that more jobs will be lost this year.

There is little likelihood now that interest rates will come down further.

❸ The +形容词比较级……，the +形容词比较级……　这个句型大家应该都很熟悉了吧：越……，就越……

例句： The greater the population there is in a locality, the greater the need there is for water, transportation, and disposal of refuse.

❹ old and young alike 年长的人和年轻的人都……，类似的在美语里还经常可以见到 friends and family alike，teachers and students alike 等写法

例句： The comic strip（报纸或者书里面那种一串小方块的连环画）is fun for old and young alike.（这里习惯上不在 old 前加 the）

❺ … is a fact of life. ……是必须面对的人生（事实）

例句： Outsourcing（外包）is a fact of life now in America and we can't escape it.

对比： … is a daily occurrence. 某事每天都在发生着。

例句： Even in a world where change is a daily occurrence, it's not easy to push forward reforms about healthcare and environmental policies.

❻ hinge on 取决于……

例句： Success of such efforts hinges on contribution from the authorities.

❼ It's little / no wonder that… 毫不奇怪，……

例句： ① It's little wonder that many female voters feel turned off by the male-dominated politics.

② It's no wonder that at class reunions, former classmates take it in turns to amuse one another with funny stories from bygone years.

❽ More than anything, … 最关键的是，……

例句： More than anything, the medical professionals debated the name of this health problem.

❾ This (trend) is not restricted to... 这个（趋势）不仅仅限于……

例句： This trend is not restricted to wealthy students who have the money to do this, but is also evident（明显的）among poorer students.

❿ It's rare for sb. / sth. to... 某人（事）很少会怎样

例句： It's rare for any type of market structure to run with absolute efficiency.

⓫ It's not uncommon for... to... 双重否定句型，就等于 "通常……"

例句： With the arrival of fall, it's not uncommon to see painters and photographers working on the sides of roads or shorelines capturing the scenery in New England.

⓬ ... may not... otherwise. 否则……就不会……

例句： Supporting children with mentors and after-school programs will give them opportunities and guidance that they might not receive otherwise.

⓭ make a difference 用于褒义比较常见：做贡献

例句： There are so many small things we can do to help preserve the earth, from turning the lights off when I leave a room to recycling cans and bottles to... These may seem insignificant, but if everyone acted in this way, it would make a big difference.

⓮ think in terms of... +名词或者名词短语　以某种方式思维

例句： Americans continue to think in terms of the "mainstream" and the "other". If we take a moment to think historically, we can see that our civilization is actually composed of many strands from diverse backgrounds.

⓯ be aimed at sth. 目标是……

例句： In the conventional classroom, most lessons are aimed at the middle level of ability. Thus, some students are dragged along much faster than is optimal（适宜的，最优化的）for them.

近义： target sth.

⓰ ... lie at the heart of... 处在核心地位

例句： Economic issues lied at the heart of the three Obama-McCain presidential debate.

倒装用法： At the heart of the function of these machines is motion（运动），which is the source of input to the machine.

⑰ the proliferation of... 名词短语：（污染、互联网等）的大量扩散

例句： The proliferation of fast-food restaurants in America has made it even harder for Americans to eat healthy lunches.

⑱ in all likelihood 很可能

例句： In all likelihood, these decisions would be made by government officials who don't necessarily understand the problems any better.

⑲ ..., by no means, ... ……绝不是

例句： Yet the U. S. is, by no means, the world's only economic dynamo（本意是发电机，这里指动力源）.

⑳ are not entirely unfounded 不是完全没有根据

例句： Persistent（长期存在的）American fears of being overshadowed（= seem less important because of sb. / sth. else）economically by China are not entirely unfounded.

㉑ put sth. in perspective 客观地看待……

例句： This important medical report has helped people put the medicine in perspective.

㉒ be interrelated and interdependent 相互联系，互相依赖的

例句： ① Everything in this world is interrelated and interdependent. Science suggests that something as trivial as the beating of a butterfly's wings in the Amazon can influence the formation of a tornado in Texas. Even our smallest acts can have major effects.

② Nations are increasingly interrelated and interdependent in this age of economic and cultural globalization, which means no matter how far away it may be geographically, no country is really isolated（孤立的）.

㉓ There's no substitute for... 某事物是无法替代的

例句： Vitamin pills are no substitute for a healthy diet.

㉔ cease to... 动词短语：不再……

例句： It should be noted that the Internet is in a constant state of change: While all the activities online have been based around websites with some stability, it's possible that some sites may cease to be accessible all of a sudden.

比较： has never ceased to... 从未停止过……

例句： Antonio Gaudi's poetic architecture has never ceased to amaze people.

㉕ can be traced back to... 可以追溯到……

例句： ① Comic books, graphic novels and the Sunday comics can all trace their heritage back to book illustrations, which have been around as long as the printed word.

② How did the English alphabet come about? It was based on Latin letters whose roots can be traced back to Greece and eastern Mediterranean.

㉖ It's no exaggeration to say that... 可以毫不夸张地说……（虽然这里是 say，但这个句型在书面文章里也经常会见到）

例句： It's no exaggeration to say that every human being is fooled by his/her own ideas once in a while.

比较： It's too simplistic to say that... 片面的（虽然 being simple 未必是缺点，但是 being simplistic 一般都是缺点）

例句： It's too simplistic to say that today's Republicans are yesterday's Hamiltonians and today's Democrats are descended from（是……的后代）Thomas Jefferson's party.

㉗ ... is an exception. 是一个例外

例句： ① Most people like to know they have a good sense of humor and pride themselves on making others laugh. Teachers are no exception.（不是例外）

② With the possible exception（可能出现的例外）of the Olympics, no other sports event in history has attracted as much interest from such a broad audience as the Super Bowl.

㉘ It's hard to overstate the significance of 怎样说……的重要性也不为过

例句： It's hard to overstate the significance of reading and writing skills in the twenty-first century.

㉙ a major shift in... 某方面的重要转变

例句： The last two decades have witnessed a major shift in the global distribution of economic power.（Kaplan）

㉚ sth. is consolidating its status as the... 某事物正在不断加固它作为……的地位

例句：English has been consolidating its status as the dominant（占统治地位的）language in the world.

㉛ require/necessitate/call for... 需要……（如果主语是人就只能用 need，但如果主语是事情，就可以用这三个词表示比较正式的 "need"）

例句：Reduction in government spending will necessitate further cuts in public services.

㉜ distinguish between A and B 区分 A 和 B

例句：The five-year-old's lack of capacity（能力）to distinguish between right and wrong should have been taken into consideration.

近义：differentiate between

例句：They don't differentiate between their workers on the basis of ethnic origin.

㉝ ... sound as if... 听起来似乎……（其实并不是那么回事儿）

例句：Days with no work to do sound as if they would be heavenly（天堂般的）. Usually, though, if we stay in bed or read a book for too long, our legs start twitching to get up and move about. And there's nothing good on television anymore.

㉞ is an important factor in determining... 是……的决定因素

例句：The scores that students receive on tests like the SAT or ACT are important factors in determining the college or university that a student attends in the United States.

近义：① is an important element of... 是……的重要因素

例句：Job satisfaction is an important element of individual wellbeing.

近义：② can make or break sth.

例句：Your decision can make or break this business.

近义：③ is a key determinant of sth.

例句：Nine years into the new millennium（千年）, we Americans are still divided over whether schooling can be a key determinant of individual success.

㉟ Quite the opposite, ... 正好相反，……

例句：Of course, equality in the classroom does not mean everyone receives the same amount of something or is treated exactly the same. Quite the opposite, to me, equality means students get what they need in order to create a learning experience that meets their individual needs.

㊱ is a hallmark of...　是……的显著特色

例句： Universal public education is a hallmark of American society. Across this country, a system of public schools ensures that all children have access to a primary or secondary education, regardless of their race, gender, intelligence, family income, social status or other personal characteristics.

㊲ be bent on / be bent upon...　全身心地投入去做某事（可好可坏），美式写作里极为常用的一个句型，但在国内却很少能看到有朋友用

例句： To develop the resources of a new country required energetic people, bent upon using their energies — not only for the rewards that would result to themselves, but even more importantly, to the community.

㊳ sth. is inherent in...　某种品质是……固有的

例句： No matter how efficient they are, how safe, or how inexpensive, trains simply cannot offer the thrill that is inherent in automobiles.

㊴ There's a definite link between A and B　在 A 和 B 之间有密切联系

例句： ① It has been scientifically proven that there is a link between the rise in global temperature and the increase of CO_2 emissions.

② In America, there's been mounting evidence of a link between obesity and some forms of cancer.

比较： link 也可以作动词：A diet that is rich in calcium has been linked to a markedly reduced risk of cancer.

㊵ sth. is sb. 's stock-in-trade　这个跟贸易没关系，而是指"某事是某人的拿手好戏"

例句： The journalist's work has been published far and wide（习惯用语：很多地方，到处）. Telling tales on the celebrities is his stock-in-trade.

㊶ A create（or bring about/ generate/ breed/ cause / engender/ spawn/ induce）B　A 产生 B

例句： Technological innovations（创新）have brought about profound changes to the political, economic and cultural arenas（领域）.

区分： create 后面可以跟的宾语比较广；bring about 通常是大范围内带来的结果；generate 后面一般跟 opportunities / tax revenue 这类词汇；breed, cause 和 engender 后面跟让人担心的事物多一些；spawn 跟新事物，比如 inventions；

induce 则跟抽象名词比较多，比如 induce drowsiness（困倦）。

近义： "领域" 除了 area 和 field，作文中还经常可以使用 sphere, domain, arena, realm 等近义词替换。

对比： is a contributing factor to sth. 是……的导致因素之一

例句： Any illness can be traced to one of three factors: genetic, environmental or poor nutritional habits. And of these, the food one eats or doesn't eat is the most important contributing factor to ill health.

⑫ someone would be well-advised to do sth. （＝sb. should）某人应该做某事

例句： People who have been infected with the H1N1 virus would be well-advised to stay home until the fever is gone.

⑬ resemble 动词：像……

例句： The city resembled a battle field after the devastating（破坏极大的）earthquake.

⑭ ... abound 动词：大量存在

例句： Old structures abound in many European cities.

比较： 它的形容词形式 abundant 也经常表示类似的意思

例句： Cheap consumer goods are abundant in this region.

⑮ reflect / represent / mirror / embody 动词：体现，反映

例句： The growth of sales of video games mirrored the rapid developments in computer technology that offers even the technophobes（恐惧科技的人们）entertaining introductions to the technological world.

⑯ sth. impels/ prompts sb. to do... 促使某人去……

例句： Peer pressure often impels youngsters to spend excessively（过度的）on fancy （新奇的）clothes and accessories（首饰）.

近义： spur（*vt.*）

例句： Spurred by her early success, Stephenie Meyer went on to write more novels, which were equally successful.

⑰ an indication of... 名词短语：显示出……，反映出……

例句： Success is normally an indication of human qualities such as intelligence, integrity, ambition and perseverance.

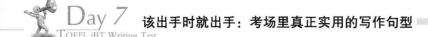

近义动词： reveal / represent / indicate / embody / mirror（这里是动词）

反义动词： conceal / mask（这里是 *vt.*）

例句： These statistics mask a troubling truth. For more than two decades, while household income and wealth may have been increasing, it was mostly the wealthiest Americans who benefited from the nation's economic gains.

㊽ be inseparable from... 与……密不可分

例句： Budget planning is inseparable from the strategy for reducing the deficit.

㊾ ... is inextricably intertwined with... 与……密不可分，如果用更地道的中文说法就是"与……有着千丝万缕的联系"

例句： All individuals are inextricably intertwined with their communities, regardless of their own competence.

㊿ eclipse sth. 动词：使……相形见绌

例句： ① The economy has eclipsed all the other issues during this election campaign.
② Twitter is sometimes described as the "SMS of the Internet" since the use of its application programming interface for sending and receiving short text messages by other applications often eclipses the direct use of Twitter.（这是书面语，在口语里用手机给人发短信一般就说"I'll text you."而不要过于实诚地说"I'll send you a short message."）

(51) be mutually helpful / beneficial / exclusive/dependent 互助的 / 互利的 / 相互排斥的/相互依存的

例句： Some Americans scientists have been trying to prove that science and religion are not mutually exclusive.

(52) is the exact antithesis of... 与……截然相反

例句： Jessica is so pretentious（Day 4 里学过的形容词：喜欢虚荣的）. She's the exact antithesis of what I would find attractive in ladies.

近义： represent the opposite end of the spectrum

例句： The two opinions represent the opposite ends of the spectrum.

(53) lean on... 本意是靠在某人身上，作文里经常作比喻用法，指依靠某种方式或者手段，有时候可以代替 depend on / rely on

例句： Obama's campaign leaned heavily on twenty-first century technology and techniques（Day 4 我们已经讲过这两个词的区别）, from sending Election Day voting reminders to cell phones to using websites to raise money and organize grassroots efforts（草根的、平民的努力）.

⑤④ beyond our wildest expectations 超出了我们一切的预期

例句：The pace of change has increased beyond our wildest expectations, which has been largely driven by technological breakthroughs occurring on an almost daily basis（=almost every day）.

⑤⑤ take steps / take measures to do sth. 采取措施去做某事

例句：Preventing a health problem is always better than treating it and there are some steps you can take to protect yourself from the potential damage.

⑤⑥ convert... into... 把……转变成……

例句："Let me assert my firm belief that the only thing we have to fear is fear itself — nameless, unreasoning, unjustified terror that paralyzes needed effort（导致必要的努力，陷入瘫痪）to convert retreat into advance. " — FDR

⑤⑦ be accountable to sb. / be accountable for sth. 向某人/某事负责。这个句型的意思很接近于 be responsible to sb. / to responsible for sth. ，只是语气更正式一些，而且主语也更多的是 the manager, the president, the administrators, the government, the organization, the hospital 等比较正式的职务或者机构

例句：The tax reform will make the government accountable for its spending.

⑤⑧ a variety of / a wide range of / a wide array of 各种各样的

例句：There're many things to like about fall — the huge variety of colors, the cool crisp air in the morning and of course the kids heading back to schools.

⑤⑨ the whole spectrum of... 其实就是 the whole range of... 的升级版

例句：① A wide spectrum of opinions was heard at the conference.

② The bill drew support from across the whole political spectrum.

⑥⓪ The bottom line is... 根本考虑因素是……

例句：The bottom line is that all students should be respected and be encouraged to learn how to apply the principles of equality so that each one of them can feel included.

⑥① Looking back, ... / In retrospect, ... 回过头来看，……

例句：In retrospect, my university years seem more enjoyable than they really were.

对比：With the wisdom of hindsight, I should have ... 其实早该……

例句： With the wisdom of hindsight, I should have taken the job.

⑫ be a watershed　说某事是 "重大转折"，各位都爱用 turning point，其实在美语里有个单词叫 watershed，在政治、经济和生活中都极为常见

例句： That year was a watershed in her life — she changed her career and changed her partner.

6 个俗不可耐却依然没被美国人淘汰的句型

❶ (develop / advance) by leaps and bounds　突飞猛进，这个短语已经俗到一定境界了，但在美国确实还挺常用的，语气更强的还有一个叫 a quantum leap forward

例句： The IT industry had grown by leaps and bounds in Silicon Valley until the dot-com crash.

❷ The advent of...　……的来临（引发了）……，同上面那句一样，这句也十分 corny（老掉牙的），但在美国还是被每天重复地写着

例句： The advent of automobiles greatly increased the demand for petroleum.

类似： the dawn of the new century

❸ embark on.../embark upon　进入（某个阶段）

例句： They have encouraged thousands of young Americans to embark on their own personal voyage of discovery.

❹ ..., and there seems to be plenty of research findings to confirm this.　看起来有足够的研究证明这个观点。其实是很空洞的话，除非后面确实能跟一堆研究成果

例句： Teaching students in groups helps them grow into social, responsible individuals, and there seems to be plenty of research findings to confirm this.

❺ is a blessing in disguise　表面上看是坏事其实却是好事，有一点像中文的 "因祸得福"。这个表达是俗，但是俗得很纯粹

例句： When we got there, that Greek restaurant was packed with people. But it was just a blessing in disguise: We found a better one.

❻ the social fabric / the fabric of society　这个句型国内的朋友们用得不多，但在美国已经被用烂了。fabric 本来指服装的面料或者纺织品，在这个句型里基本就是 "社会的凝聚力"

例句： Drug abuse poses a major threat to the fabric of our society.

课后练习

Take-Home Quiz

句子释义

请结合您在本章学习到的内容解释下面的句子:

We don't need special knowledge of the topics to answer the questions correctly. Rather, we should answer each question on the basis of what is stated or implied.

The current recession is putting even more pressure on the recent graduates who're already hard-pressed to find a decent job.

In fact, the quality of life we all enjoy today as Americans can, in many instances, be traced to the significant contributions made by Americans of different backgrounds throughout our history.

Bear in mind that some places are without public transit and/or only have very limited access to it.

Those who have spent some time traveling to other places have a broader view of life and better personal resources to draw on.

Advertising was spurred by the development of national media, such as radio and popular magazines, which made it possible to reach audiences from coast to coast.

The UN finally started to take action to curb（遏制）the proliferation of nuclear weapons: The Security Council unanimously backed a Resolution presented by the U. S. that ultimately involved laying the foundation for（为……铺平道路）a world free of the devastating（破坏力极大的）weapons.

Windows 7 is intended to be a more focused upgrade to the Windows line, with the objective of being fully compatible with applications with which Windows Vista is already compatible.

There's no guarantee that through space exploration, new food resources will be discovered and that habitable planets will be found.

Graduation and marriage are important milestones in people's lives.

The tragedy and the comedy of human existence are inseparable concepts.

The child ran into the road to get the ball, oblivious to the danger.

Young children are vulnerable to complications（并发症）from the flu, including pneumonia（肺炎）.

Unhappiness has been woven into the natural fabric of our lives.

A language is primarily a vehicle for thought.

It's not uncommon for people to choose the wrong communication channels simply because there're too many to choose from these days.

We need to be mindful of what we say — and what we fail to say.

Dogs are bred and trained to serve human needs in a variety of roles. For example, sled dogs are used in certain areas for hauling goods over snow. Herding dogs protect livestock. And there're also seeing-eye dogs that assist blind people by acting as their eyes to help them avoid dangers.

Teaching students in groups has the inherent advantage of helping schools use their equipment and facilities more efficiently.

Parents who choose homeschooling for their children may be attacked by others — for thinking that their children are better than anyone else's, for refusing to participate in an important social institution, or even for trying to destroy the public schools.

We make friends casually, but once they're part of our lives, we should be careful not to take them for granted.

Politicians should be held accountable to the public who elected them.

冬季的校园，貌似和49位诺贝尔奖获得者（最近的一位 laureate 就是那个拿了 2009 年 the Nobel Peace Prize 的哥们儿）、8位美国总统、辉煌、"炫"……完全不沾边儿. 可它偏偏就是那个以 "Let Plato be your friend, and Aristotle, but more let your friend be truth." 为 motto 的地方。　　　　——Pat摄

Day 8

Under the Microscope: The Introduction, Main Body and Conclusion
显微镜下的开头、主体与结尾

It's not true that nice guys always finish last. Nice guys are winners even before the game starts.

——Addison Mort Walker
American Performer

熟悉美国历史的朋友们都会深感，美国之所以在短短两百多年之内实现"飞跃"，与一系列的"幸运"密不可分：异常丰富的自然资源、几乎占到国土面积100%的可耕地（arable land），同时两次世界大战中受到的破坏相对较少，反倒是战时需求促进了经济和科技的发展，而且多次领土扩张都捡到了性价比极高的"便宜货"……更重要的是，在建国初期，美国有幸拥有了一大批 great minds and dedicated hearts，这些人为美国后来的持续发展建立了制度保障——从善于用人的 George Washington，到深思熟虑的 John Adams，从"自由战士"Thomas Jefferson 到"理财专家"Alexander Hamilton，从"宪法之父"James Madison 到最高法院院长 John Marshall……那真是一个英雄辈出的年代。一个好的开始，真的很重要。

Though no one can go back and make a brand new start, anyone can start from now and make a brand new ending. ——*Carl Bard*

TOEFL iBT
Writing Test

（上）万事开头未必难

Quit Waiting. Start Working.

大 家都知道英文里有句老谚语：A good beginning is half the battle. 这句话虽然已经过了鼎盛时期，但是依然生命力旺盛，经常被美国各路作家挪用到不同场合，改成 XX is half the battle. 用来吸引广大读者的眼球。

开个好头确实至关重要，新托福作文也是如此。考官毕竟也是人，也有人之常情，虽然一个好的开头未必真能像某些人描述的那样"决定全文的成败"，但至少会让考官愿意花更多的心思来阅读你的下文。

什么是开头段？

Pat 知道这个问题问得很弱智，但其实我想问的是："新托福作文开头段的实质是什么？"（同样弱智，sigh…）

考虑到考场里全篇文章只有 30 分钟去完成，也为了避免给主体部分造成过大的压力，新托福高分作文的开头段一般不宜过长，4~5 句话已经是很长的开头段了。而且高分作文的开头段实质上永远只会为下面 4 个目的中的某一个或者某几个服务：

（a）介绍社会、自然（比如环境类话题）或者生活背景，这个目的必要时可以忽略；

（b）介绍文中要讨论的话题，这个目的永远责无旁贷；

（c）转述原题中给出的关于这个话题的观点，这部分也经常可以省略，而且也有很多题本来就没给出观点；

（d）概括自己对讨论话题的态度。这部分在新托福作文的开头段一般都会直接或者间接地给出。

Pat's Tips

关于上面的（d），在 Day 1 中我们就已经明确指出：由于美国人与生俱来的直率性格，同时也由于新托福写作考试的生活化定位，多数高分作文都会在开头段就直接或间接表达出作者关于讨论话题的倾向性。

然而多数同学没有注意到的一个细节是：新托福作文中并不是只有使用 As far as I'm concerned/ In my opinion/ In my view/ To my mind 这些词组或者 I think / I believe/ I'm convinced that 这些句式才能引出作者自己的观点。有些高分开头其实是用比较不露声色的形式去表明态度的，反倒给考官更深刻的印象。这其实是一种新托福作文高分选手和考官间长期以来一直在进行的"第三类接触"。

Pat 建议大家逐字逐句地分析本节中的范例，思考它们到底精彩在何处。提高新托福写作能力应该是一个很具体的过程，而不应是空对空，否则永远只能是一个说客（a big mouth）或者一只"菜鸟"（a rookie）。写作是绝不能光说不练的，只有脚踏实地、多研究高分作品，并且勇于、勤于练笔，才会终有所成。对于已经铁了心要在作文里套模板的同学，也完全可以通过好好体会本节中的大量实例，从中选出两三种让你"有感觉"的开头，仿写出自己的开头段（但如果连这个工作都不愿意做，那就只能直接看 Day 9 最后的大表格了）。

美式议论文写 Introduction 的十四种方案

※下面高分实例中的大多数"生词"我们都已经在 Day 4 中学过了，牢牢把握核心词汇仍然是 the top priority。

※请大家在分析实例时特别注意开头段的那 4 个目的分别是如何被实现的，或者有哪一个/哪几个目的被自然地省略了。

※ 最好把十四种方法都泛读一下，对英文议论文开头有个宏观的把握，但对考试来说只需要精准地掌握其中的 2~3 种就够了。而且最好在进考场前就仿写出属于自己的这 2~3 种逻辑框架，为考场实战给出方向性指导。

1 赤裸裸型

这就是传统意义上的"开门见山"了。需要注意的是用这种方法的人必须胆儿大，因为直接亮明观点的开头段很可能比别人的开头段短，如果万一主体段的论证不够深入就有underlength 的可能。所以 Pat 觉得只有叫"赤裸裸型"，才能充分体现这种写法无怨无悔的流氓无产者形象。

比如 Michigan Guide 中的这个开头就十分赤裸：

There is a principal reason for agreeing with the statement that parents make the best teachers and it is the fact that children are closer to parents than to any other people.

（principal：primary／chief／main）

牛吧？整个开头段就这么短！虽然并没有用 From my point of view 这类其实是废话的提示词，但"牛眼看世界"的决心仍然明显。

下面这个 Media 类的开头段已经裸到了浑身只剩一根儿松紧带儿的程度：

The best way to know what's going on in a society is to study its popular media because social trends, people's fears and aspirations, the status of various groups and the power of the ruling elites can all be seen in the popular media of this society.

虽然看不到 To my way of thinking，也没见到 As I see it，但作者的倾向性依然不容置疑。

Though no one can go back and make a brand new start, anyone can start from
now and make a brand new ending.　　　　*——Carl Bard*

TOEFL iBT
Writing Test

（声明：Pat 并不是认为那些表示"在我看来"的词组不好，但如果每个考生的应试作文都是一堆"As far as I'm concerned"，"From my point of view"，"To my mind"……考官看着实在容易犯困不是么？）

下面这个关于"是否应该做自己不喜欢但必须做的工作"的开头段，明明已经脱至全裸还在继续挑战极限：

In reality, from time to time we all have to do things that we don't enjoy. And contrary to what many people believe, the fulfillment of obligation is actually more important to achieving job satisfaction than enjoyment at work.

赤裸裸型虽然相对来说篇幅较短，但比较适合美国人喜欢直接的性格，所以如果能够确保后面的主体段字数写够，也不失为一种好的开头形式，而且由于立场鲜明，尤其适合用来作"一边倒"文章的开头段（"一边倒"和"折中式"的区别我们将在 Day 9 深入讲解）。

2　缠绵型

与赤裸裸型针锋相对，缠绵型则显得十分小资。这种开头特别适合那些喜欢上"豆瓣儿网"的文艺青年，而且必须还得是自己有感而发原创出来的。如果一个本来就是鲁智深性格的人就绝对不能准备缠绵型开头。也正因为这种特点，缠绵型也可以叫做"Blues（蓝调）"型。

跟刚才的"赤裸裸"型的例子同样是写"家长是否是孩子最好的老师"的话题，下面这段萨克斯就把蓝调曲风发挥到了极致：

When we think about the relationship between parents and their children, we can say parents are the first teachers of their children, hence the idea of parents being the best teachers. There are several reasons for that, such as parents being the first people who their children met, children having spent most of their time with their parents and children having grown up with their parents' care as well.

（hence = therefore，但有时候 hence 后面也可以不跟句子或者从句，而仅跟名词，比如：His mother was Italian, hence his name — Luca. ）

下面这个 Media 类开头也是把一两句话可以说清楚的意思很曲折地表达了出来，最难得的是还不让人讨厌，已经完全是 *Killing Me Softly* 的风格：

In our media-intensive culture, it is not difficult to find differing opinions. Thousands of newspapers and magazines and dozens of radio and television talk shows all resound with differing points of view. So for the audience, now the difficulty lies in deciding which opinion to agree with and which "experts" seem the most credible. The more inundated we become with differing opinions and claims, the more essential it is to hone（磨练某方面的技能）critical reading and thinking skills for us to evaluate these ideas.

缠绵型既可以用于一边倒，也可以用于折中式，前提就是作者必须天生属于"慢性子"

（slowpoke）。

3 假惺惺型

与上一种方法的区别是：虽然都很假，但缠绵型是发自内心的，而假惺惺型则是一种斗争策略。这种开头的特点是在一开始就先把自己要驳斥的意见亮出来，甚至还"欲擒故纵"地说一两句可能用来支持它的理由。但之后就马上撕下伪装，开始用三个主体段铺天盖地地陈述反对的理由。

比如这个开头：

Some people claim that universities should allocate as much money to sports facilities as to the libraries because sports can help students keep fit and cope with heavy workload. But in fact, as academic institutions, universities do have the obligation to give higher priority to the funding of libraries than to that of athletic facilities.

下文就正式开始炮轰 some people 的观点了。

再比如这个开头段：

"Experience is the best teacher." is an old cliché. But it's nonetheless possibly true because the most important, and sometimes the hardest lessons we learn tend to come from our participation in situations.

真的够虚伪！英汉词典里把 cliché 这个词翻译成"陈词滥调"，其实这个词的地道英文意思只属于中性略偏贬义，就是不需要动脑子就能说出来的"套话"。作者先说这句老话压根儿就是一句套话，但紧接着又说其实这话还是挺有道理的，开始当仁不让地假惺惺了。

下面这个开头用的手法与刚才的那个就是 twins 或者 duo，只不过态度正相反：

There's an adage（老话，箴言）that says, "Knowledge is power," the implication（暗含的意思）being that knowledge breeds success. This adage is wrong. It's not knowledge that's power；it's the application of knowledge that provides the power which contributes to success. We all have encountered knowledgeable people are not nearly as successful as they should be.

而下面的开头则是先说二者之间密不可分，但紧接着就开始区别对待，也属假中高手：

Being a member of a group and being the leader of a group can both be desirable. Actually, I think these two roles are interrelated. However, it's very likely that being the leader can bring an individual more satisfaction and delight.

下面这个开头段更是直接让我联想到 Molière 的名作 *Tartuffe*（伪君子）：

Some people think that television has destroyed the communication among friends and family. It may be true that on average, most modern people spend a couple of hours in front of a TV set every night. But I believe it's an exaggeration（夸张）to say television has caused "communication breakdown" among friends and family members. Or even if it does, that only happens to those most passive, unthinking TV viewers who are not good at communicating with others anyway.

假惺惺型开头特别适合于驳论型的议论文，但不能用于完全赞成的文章。

4 忆苦思甜型

从标题就可以看出，这类开头的特点就是先感叹过去不堪回首，再对比今天"贫嘴张大民的幸福生活"，而作者的倾向性已经暗含其中。

比如下面这个讨论"是否应该经常搬家"考题的开头段：

For centuries, people have been moving from one part of the world to another. In the past, people moved mainly as a result of natural disasters or due to political upheavals（政治动荡）or wars. Today, though, we move to seek a fortune or better careers prospects, or just to see the world.

虽然作者并没有使用 I believe 这样的韩剧开头，但其对"生活真美好"的信念依然表达得十分鲜明，而且关键是很清爽，没有陈词滥调。

请大家再看下面关于"家长和教师是否有权决定孩子的未来"的例子：

During the Industrial Revolution, in many European countries children worked up to 19 hours a day in dingy（阴暗的）factories at a very early age and the factory owners could beat those who fell asleep at work or didn't work fast enough. But now even parents or teachers are not completely free to do things as they please to the kids because they're entitled to（有权享有……）protection and far more rights.

忆苦思甜是一种比较有"磁性"的开头，可以展现出作者的知识面比较广（其实也不用太专业，就写常识就很好了，但要用自己的话去写）。

这个方法比较常用的标志性词汇还包括：（指过去）Historically, / Traditionally, / used to… / It was not uncommon for… to…;（指现在）At present, / Currently, / In this day and age（固定短语）/ In present-day society, / These days / In today's society, / In the present age，以及各位已经耳熟能详的 In contemporary society 和 nowadays（请注意它的形容词是 present 或 current，而不是 nowaday，这个单词在英文里并不存在！）以上这些词组点到为止，不宜使用过于频繁。

忆苦思甜型开头特别适合用来讨论现在比过去有明显进步的现象，比如 Technology 类话题。

5 忆甜思苦型

这种手法在高分作文中远比"忆苦思甜型"更为常用，说白了就是忆往昔＋批判现实。

比如下面的这个 Media 类开头：

In a simpler time, advertising only called attention to the products. But now it manufactures a new product of its own: the consumers. That's because today advertising not just emphasizes the advantages of products, but also promotes ways of life.

虽然并没有用"In my view, ..."这样的大字报写法，但作者对于当代广告的批判态度依然很鲜明。

下面这篇 ETS 官方高分 Friends 类范文的开头段也是再典型不过的忆甜思苦型，上来就提出传统的美德——诚实，今天正在遭到越来越多的质疑：

The traditional virtue of telling the truth in all situations is increasingly doubted by many in today's world. Many believe that telling the truth is not always the best policy when dealing with people...

但后面接下来的主体段态度则是认为"还是诚实点好"（Honesty is still the best policy.），这就已经是"此地无银三百两"的高端忆甜思苦了。

再比如下面这个关于"writing skills 是否在今天比在过去更重要"的开头：

When we apply to a university, we are asked to present information that reflects our capabilities and talents. Not long ago, a transcript of test scores and letters of recommendation were all that were required to accompany an application. But now many universities have specific writing portfolio requirements that applicants must meet, which clearly indicates the increasing importance of writing skills.

"..., which clearly indicates..."这个句型虽然没有"My position is that..."那么强势，但是以理服人的意味反而愈加强烈。完全是在不经意间流露性感，已属闷骚主义者中的极品。

下面的这个 Princeton Review 中的关于 Adventure 的开头段也进行了集体忆甜思苦活动：

All of us crave adventure, at least at some time in our lives. Yet even though our ancestors had plenty of adventure, we can only find it on TV or the Internet today. Senior executives tucked away in offices, professors stranded in ivy-covered buildings and doctors overworked in emergency rooms all dream of mountain-climbing or deep-see diving or traveling through Amazon jungles.

通过对企业高管、教授和医生这些高收入人群的列举，唤起普通人对现代生活缺乏 adventure 的强烈共鸣。

忆甜思苦型开头特别适合用来讨论交通类、环境类、动物类或者涉及价值观（values）的改变等比较让人担忧的话题。

6　苦大仇深型

这种写法经常跟在忆甜思苦型的后面，进一步向考官灌输"人活着就是受苦"的佛家思想。

比如刚才大家见到的 ETS Friends 类满分范文开头忆甜思苦部分的后面就跟了一句苦大仇深的句子：

（接上文）Moreover, the line of a "truth" is becoming more and more vague（模糊的）……

下面这个 Education 类的开头则是整段使用苦大仇深的控诉方法，不过显得有点偏激。所以除非确信自己能在主体段展现出同等强烈的怨妇情结，否则将会人为增大主体段论证的难度：

I don't want to sound like a pretentious or rebellious teenager. But sometimes, schools do teach the wrong lessons, which range from teachers not knowing why they're teaching things that are too tough for their students, to having points taken off students' grades for being just one second late for class.

再看看这个"明星是否应该获得高收入"的开头，更是异常悲苦：

Without the sweat, blood and hard work of artisans, laborers, farmers, builders, technicians, domestic workers and all others who work with their hands, our country would come to a standstill. It's time for us to reexamine the gap between their meager（少得可怜的）wages and the astronomical（天文数字的）incomes of superstars.

有些苦大仇深的开头只写陈述句还嫌不过瘾，还要在开头段的结尾用反问句来提出质问：

Today, when celebrities like movie stars, famous athletes or rock singers say something, the whole world listens attentively. But when average people like you and me say something, only our loved ones genuinely care what we say. Is this how different opinions should be treated?

要注意苦大仇深型只能用于你确实感受比较强烈的话题，而不要让人感觉是在无病呻吟。

7　如数家珍型

这种开头写法的特点是把后面 body 各段的分论点在开头段就"陈列"出来。这样写的好处是显得特实诚，有一说一。但缺点则是开头和主体每段的第一句会略显重复，而且请注意这种写法仅限于"一边倒"的文章使用，但不宜用于"折中式"作文。

Barron's 中这类开头特别多，比如下面这个高分开头段：

Governments should definitely spend more money on improving all forms of public transit. The widespread use of private cars has contributed to some serious problems in society, including depletion（Day 4 学过的词：消耗）of natural resources, increased pollution and the loss of a sense of community. By encouraging the use of public transportation, governments can do a lot to counteract these problems. (*Barron's*)

（counteract：近义词 solve / combat / address / resolve）

接下来就在主体的三段分头开讲。

下面这个高分开头段也布局得像 art show 上的 showcase 似的，主体要讲的分论点在开头就已经一目了然：

People often behave differently, depending on what they wear. The reason is not that they have changed, but that people's reactions to them have changed. Strangers react to your appearance because it is all they know about you. A friend may be influenced by your dress also, if it is appropriate for a situation. In addition, appearance is almost always important at work. (*Barron's*)

又比如这个关于大学生是否应该 take part-time jobs 的话题，也同样是在开头就列举出了主体各段的分论点：

Some students who live at home with their family get part-time jobs during the school year to gain work experience. Other students save for things they want, like a car, or a holiday, or money to go to graduate schools. Still other youth（note: *pl.*）in school work just to earn some spending money. Many students even take jobs for a combination of all these reasons. Working part-time after school or on the weekends really make good sense.

有趣的是：有时候也可以用形容词或者副词排比来列举出主体段的几个分论点，比如下面这个关于"朋友和亲人谁对小孩的性格影响更大"的开头段：

Although friends definitely play a significant role in shaping teenagers' personality, it is the parents and siblings that have a far greater impact on the development of their personality traits. There're intellectual, emotional and financial reasons for my view. （你是否注意到了本段中的强调句？对特殊句式的敏感度一定要尽快练出来！）

8 顶牛型

与上一种开头只能用于"一边倒"截然相反，这类开头只能用于"折中式"作文，特点是在开头段就针锋相对地列出主体段双方各自的观点。**而且请注意**："顶牛型"是独立作文中少数的不一定非要在开头段表明自己态度，而是也可以选择等主体段对双方都进行过论证之后，最后在结尾段再给出自己倾向性的写法之一。

比如这个讨论美国文化多元化利弊的开头就挺"牛"的：

Many Americans feel that the Multiculturalism policy is essential to America because it has recognized different cultures, giving them equal importance and social representation.

In contrast, some other Americans have pointed out that the official Multiculturalism has reduced the essence of culture to outward, superficial symbols such as music, dance and food, instead of providing equal opportunity, status and power to the diverse groups. The American society is thus divided into the "mainstream", which has power, and the "multicultural minorities", which have no power.

再比如这个关于 History 话题的开头段也是这种顶牛型:

Some people think that the history of a country is only shaped by battles and political victories because they determine the course of history. Many others, however, think that a nation's history is also shaped by the underlying structures of culture, language and religion as they often reveal the key characteristics of the land that has molded a nation's past and present.

继续顶:

Many American companies have decided to outsource (外包) jobs performed by Americans to workers in other countries. This issue has fast become controversial, as some advocates of outsourcing see it as the only way to keep their companies competitive. Opponents, though, view it as the number-one reason for unemployment in the United States. Who's right? (*Kaplan*)

9 套磁型

正忙于 personal statement DIY 的同学们肯定对这种写法体会极深: 就是一上来就用自己的亲身经历现身说法, 凭真诚取胜, 比如下面这个 *Barron's* 的高分开头段:

The motto (座右铭) "if at first you don't succeed, try, try again" is a saying that I agree with. One example that comes to mind is a long-term struggle to maintain a healthy weight. Even as a child, I preferred sedentary activities to sports. Honestly, I would still rather have ice cream than an apple now. Nevertheless, I have launched several campaigns to lose weight. (*Barron's*)

还有下面这个著名的高分范文开头段也是典型的 P. S. 开头:

To answer the question of "What does the music of your country reveal about the culture of your country?", I would like to introduce myself. I am from Spain. I was born in a region called Catalonia, in a town near Barcelona.

下面这个讨论 "教育对 success 重要性" 的开头更是哭死招生委员会没商量的那种:

The grandson of impoverished peasants, the son of blue-collar parents who had to sacrifice their education to provide for their family, I trudged through school — like so many millions of others — with low aspirations and expectations, and, not surprisingly, with little achievement. Today, I'm pleased to say that eventually I came to realize the importance of schooling.

下面这个开头段则十分适合在 Thanksgiving 跟火鸡与 pumpkin pie 一起分享：

I'm blessed with great parents. They are understanding, intelligent and not overprotective. Throughout my life, they've been supportive of my endeavors and give me sound advice when I need it from them. I can say with conviction（信念）that parents make the best teachers for their children.

"套磁型" 比较适合用作 Success 话题、Work 话题、Money 话题或者 Family 话题的开头。

10 求知型

这种开头的标志就是问号，而且有时还是一串儿，目的就是呼唤考官的关注。需要注意的是：用这种方法在开头段提出的问题最好跟原考题的文字有一定区别，不要直接照搬原题或者仅仅是把原题的陈述句改为疑问句。

先看只提出一个问题的 Education 类开头段：

What should be the role of education in preparing young people to cope with the fast-changing new century? I believe tomorrow's society will be much more learning-oriented and education will increasingly be regarded as a lifelong process of adjustment, self-understanding and growth.

下面的 Environment 类话题开头段则是连续发问：

Can the planet's natural resources be allocated to meet the growing needs of our population while still being conserved in amounts enough for the unborn generations? Or are we exploiting them so quickly and wastefully that the decades ahead will find humankind impoverished?

如果您已经熟悉了 Day 4 的词汇，那么阅读上面这个开头一定是比较刺激的——好多词自己已经全都认识了。连续提出的两个问题，让我们立刻感受到了实现可持续发展的紧迫性。

下面这个 Media 类开头，虽然并没有提出问题，但仍然是充满探索意识的求知型：

The contemporary use of the word media still carries a trace of its original Latin meaning of "medium", which suggests a link between places or things. However, today the media no longer act simply as objective or neutral carriers of ideas, but are the manufacturers of ideas and meanings. Essentially, they have become central sources of power.

求知型开头可以用于各种作文话题，但需要提出的问题确实要有点儿意义，不要是太空洞的 small talk。

11 玩深沉型

这类开头的特点是听起来挺有哲理，其实仔细看看也就那样，并不是很深刻。比如下面这个关于 "technology 是否让生活更复杂" 的开头段：

People have often looked back longingly (*adv.* 渴望地) to an imagined Golden Age, especially in times when the idea of progress lacked proof. Today, with the limitations of technology becoming increasingly clear, many are yearning for (*v.* 渴望) a simpler life.

再比如这个 ETS 的满分开头段也是相当彻底地玩深沉：

There are certain considerations or factors that everyone takes into account in a relationship. People may look for honesty, altruism, understanding, loyalty, being thoughtful, etc. Everyone would more or less wish that the person he/she is dealing with has some of these virtues above. Putting them in an order according to their importance, however, can be very subjective and relative.

本来挺平常的一事儿，让他/她这么一说真变成了一失足成千古恨的大是大非问题。

下面更是一个彻头彻尾的 "大尾巴狼" 开头：

"Traveling around sure gets me down and lonely. Nothing else to do but close my mind. I sure hope the road don't come to own me…" These lines from Carole King have struck a chord (触动……的心弦) with millions of people. The frequent moving of modern people has resulted in the intermingling (融合) of races and culture around the globe. As philosopher Roland Barthes remarked, "Today We are all made up of tissues of quotations from the centers of many cultures."

"玩深沉" 比较适合那些影响全社会的话题，比如 Success, Technology 和 Money 类等考题。

12 显摆型（只限大牛）

这类开头在 GRE 阅读的段子以及少数新托福阅读段子中能见到，其特点是开头段就出现密集的例子，而且往往穿越时空，从 the Panama Canal 到 Nepal 再到 Florence，或者从 Thales 到 Charlemagne 再到 Medici Bank，让考官深感来者不善，从而为冲击 28 分以上的高分铺平道路。请看这个 Environment 类实例：

Not only is man the only creature capable of significantly improving the physical environment, he is also unique in his capacity to destroy it. As a litterbug he throws beer cans into the Grand Canyon while his kids decorate Highway 91 with discarded candy wrappers. His factories discharge a never-ending stream of industrial waste into the Ohio and Mississippi and have created patches of "dead water" in Lake Erie. Automobiles are the chief culprits (罪魁祸首) in producing smog in Los Angeles while offshore oil drilling have been guilty of polluting shorelines in the Gulf of Mexico and Nova Scotia.

下面这个 Education 类开头已经是毫无掩饰的显摆了：

I firmly believe children should be encouraged to read literature. Through literary works, children can travel around the world, visiting China in *First Apple*, India in *Binya's Blue Umbrella*, or Japan in *Great-Grandfather's House*. Also, folktale books introduce children to various cultures, from Native American legends to "pourquois" tales from Africa. Literature can even take children on adventures like the ones depicted in *The Bookstore Mouse* by Peggy Christian.

13　韦氏型

这种开头先对题目中的关键词下定义，然后再在此定义的基础上进行论证。给出的定义最好多少有一点新颖性，如果只是很泛泛地说一下对单词的大众理解，那就主动放弃了这种开头的得分点。比如这个关于 Work 的开头段就比较有意思，应该能让考官多看两眼：

All humans need incentives to keep working hard. That's my understanding of the word "promotion". Thus, it seems to me companies which implement merit-based promotions will have a competitive edge in attracting talent.

再比如这个关于"人类是否应该把动物当作食物来源"的开头：

Animals include wild creatures, pets and livestock kept on a farm. Even though humans raise pigs and sheep solely for meat, I don't think the same thing should be done to wild or domestic animals.

14　史诗型（正常人只可远观）

此种开头段气势宏大，上来就是电影 *Troy* 那种 blockbuster 的感觉。建议一般人不要去不自量力地模仿这种只有伟人才敢用的开头。比如下面这个关于 space research 的 opening paragraph：

Astronaut Armstrong and Aldrin set foot on the moon only two thirds of a century after the Wright brothers' first twelve-second flight at Kitty Hawk. Yet the exploration of space is more than simply an extension of air flight: It represents a new dimension in man's control of his environment.

下面这个关于"sense of humor 是否重要"的开头段，生生地把 sense of humor 和对人类的终极关怀给挂上钩了：

Can you imagine a more **dreary**（≈boring）world than one devoid of（≈lacking）**fun**? Can you imagine a human history without any **amusing episodes**（≈ events）? Luckily, our world is imbued with（≈ filled with）**humor** and it seems a sense of humor is an inborn human capacity, just like the ability to walk and to talk. In my experience, even people who **boldly claim to have developed a good sense of humor were actually born with this endowment**（≈ a natural ability）. Humor can bond people; indeed, nothing can glue people together better than shared moments of fun.

☆　　☆　　☆

虽然开头段足足有 14 种方式可供选择，而且在新托福作文中经常还可以穿插使用，排列组合之后可能性就更多。但是从实战角度来看，并没有必要把 14 种方式全都投入相同的精力去研究，除非你真的有志献身新托福写作培训。否则只要从中选择出 2~3 种比较适合自己平时的写作习惯和英语水平的，对这 2~3 种开头深入揣摩它们的逻辑关系，并坚持结合附录 C 和附录 E 的考题练笔，就完全可以做到进考场时心中有数了。对于基础过于薄弱或者备考时间超紧的同学们，也可以适当参考本书 Day 9 结束处提供的句型。

课后练习
Take-Home Quiz

判断练习

请快速判断下面的这个开头段使用了哪一种/哪几种类型的开头方式：

① In my country, people traditionally get married and have children in their twenties. There's no doubt that 25-year-old parents have more energy than those who are 45. However, energy doesn't necessarily mean better parenting skills. In my view, parents should have children when they're mature and can afford to raise them without poverty.（Eli Hinkel）

② Life has been filled with challenges and we always need to prepare ourselves on various fronts. Even though delightful activities are highly desirable, I believe sometimes we all need to commit ourselves to things that we don't enjoy.

参考答案

1　相当典型的假惺惺型开头

2　先玩深沉再假惺惺

Freshers' Week／Frosh就是北美大
学生活的"开头段"
——Pat摄

在美国经常会见到 NAACP 这个缩写，全称是 the National Association for the Advancement of Colored People。虽然看名字是为所有有色人种争取权利的，但这个组织主要还是为黑人（African Americans）争取平等。有历史学家很尖锐地指出：如果林肯总统没有被暗杀，那么在南北战争北方胜利后，他会如何对待被解放的黑人奴隶呢？林肯曾经很诚实地在一次演讲时说，"There is an unwillingness on the part of our people, harsh as it may be, for you free colored people to remain with us."（你看，毕竟是伟人，永远不会忘记用加分倒装句）。美国的肤色之争已经远远超越了一个 50% 非洲裔的总统所能带来的象征意义。Body 的颜色，难道真的这么重要么？

（中） Body 的诱惑

有句话说得好："身体是革命的本钱。"其实它还是新托福作文拿分的本钱——因为 body 最集中地体现出考生对于考题的理解和考生是否有深入论证话题的能力。

如果说文章的开头出于吸引考官注意力的目的，形式上允许用一些比较自由的话，那么主体最重要的要求则是逻辑合理（当然形式上也不一定非要很呆板，但每个论证环节是否符合逻辑一定是主体段压倒一切的首要要求）。

在本章里，我们就把英语议论文主体段的所有常见逻辑论证方式通过大量近期考题例文为大家做一个盘点。需要注意的是：本章中的绝大多数"生词"仍未超出本书前面核心词汇表中的范围。

Body Paragraphs 的展开路径详图

主体段展开方式	是否常用于"一边倒"文章的主体段	是否常用于"折中式"文章的主体段
段内顺延	√	√
段内并列	较少	√
段内递进	较少	√
段内因果	√	√
段内举例	√	√
段内类比	√	√
段内对比	√	√
段内转折	√	让步段中有时用到
段内让步	√	√
段内假设	√	√
段内下定义	√	√
段内耍赖	√	√

A person will sometimes devote all his life to the development of one part of his body — the mouth.

OEFL iBT
Writing Test

1　主体段内顺延（Extension）

这种论证形式的特点是：不使用明显的连词或者连词很少，句子之间仅仅凭语意自然地过渡，或者后面的句子 paraphrase 前面的句子。

比如，请仔细体会下面的 Education 类主体段：

I believe that parents' involvement in most American public schools has been declining. Today, parents are puzzled by all the new teaching methods and the new terminology（术语）used to introduce them. They can't find out what their kids are supposed to be learning, let alone whether or not they are being properly educated. The shortage of textbooks, the flexibility of standards, the lack of work coming home, the computerized report cards — all help to keep parents away from schooling. And well-intentioned teachers have been effectively discouraging parents from helping their kids at home on the grounds that the students may be confused by the different approaches. The result? Even more distance.

（let alone：更不用说，多用于否定句。比如：I wouldn't even date Katrina, let alone marry her.）

虽然全段并没有直接使用 linkers，但仍然层层推进，靠每句话的语意自然衔接。这种"踏雪无痕"的逻辑展开方式是一种比较高端的手法：它要求考生对自己在该段内想要表达的意思有深刻的领会，并且在开始打字前就对段落的内部结构做到心中有数，所以比较适合大牛使用。

不过对于水平一般的考生来说，段内顺延的缺点也是明显的，那就是模仿起来需要多花些功夫，只有把其中的妙处仔细揣摩透了才行。

请大家再认真研究下面的 Animals 类段内顺延实例：

Pets can substitute for the absence of other family members. Sometimes a couple who is unable to have children will adopt pets and treat them like babies. They shower on their pets the love that they might have provided a child and receive affection and companionship in return. Many people who live alone enjoy the companionship of a pet instead of loved ones who are at a distance or have passed away. The pet becomes a family member for these people and deserve the same kind of treatment that a family member would receive. (*Barron's*)

再请研读下面这个 Education 类很明显的段内顺延：

Other challenges that students face are the constant temptations that surround them every day. Cell phones, music players and even video games are all being carried into classrooms. With the general noise and confusion in today's classroom, it's easy to hide and even use them during class, which prevents the user and often people around them from getting the most out of the curriculum. (*Kaplan*)

值得大家欣慰的是：这种段内语句不用连词、自然衔接的本事即使在 native speaker 中也不是每个人都能掌握的。更多的美国人写 essay 时仍然会选择通过 linkers 来把主体段的逻辑串起来。下面的 11 种主体段展开方法在新托福作文里明显更为常见。

2 主体段内并列 Parallel Points/Listing

段内并列的特点是主体段内的几个分论点属于同级并列关系，这种逻辑写起来比较"顺手"，所以也被考生们用得最多。它的标志词就是大家耳熟能详的 First，（注意在美国仍用 Firstly 比较少）/ First of all，/ In the first place，/ To start with，/ To begin with，/ Second，/ Also，… / … as well. / …，too / Another reason is… / For one thing，… For another，… / Third，/ Lastly，/ Finally… 以及朋友们很偏爱的 Last but not least 那些，最后这个词组虽然在北美写文章时有时也会用到，但在 party 上介绍最后一位客人时用得更多。

段内并列的标志词最大的特色其实就是没特色。不过段内并列本来就是比较直白的一种逻辑，所以如果打算用就不必太介意标志词没个性，只要能把问题说清楚，而且深入论证时适当加些好句型和好词汇调节一下就可以了。

下面这个 Friends 类主体段就是明显的并列式：

Close friendships have numerous benefits. For one thing, loyal friends are always there to support each other, no matter what happens. Some friendships last many years, becoming deeper and more meaningful with time. Also, people can be themselves with friends. No one has to worry about not being perfect when he/she is among friends. Finally, nothing can be more satisfying than the intimate conversations that true friends can have. They can confide in and trust each other. (*Kaplan*)

Kaplan 中的这个主体段很明显地展示了段内并列的逻辑结构。请大家特别注意的是：在本段的分论点 1、2、3 之后各有一句支持句，用来支持这三个分论点。这也是美式议论文的基本要求：永远不要在写议论文时只写分论点却不写它的支持句，否则文章将会变成堆砌分论点的流水账，缺乏深入的论证过程。不过新托福作文的支持句也不需要太深刻，只要符合常识就好了。比如 *Kaplan* 的这段话里三个分论点后面的支持句就是没有什么深度的常识。

我们再看一个讨论 E-mail 弊端的段内并列实例：

Even though E-mail has the advantages of being convenient, speedy and economical, I believe E-mail has its downside, too. For example, there's no guarantee of（没有保证）privacy. If you use E-mail at work, the computer is your employer's property so he/she has the right to monitor it. Also, there may be misunderstandings because people often dash off quick E-mails to others. Since the recipient can't see or hear the sender, he/she may mistake the sender's tone for something that has not been intended. So E-mail is not really appropriate for formal business correspondence. Rather, it's only good for quick and informal messages.

还是非常明显：本段的两个分论点后各跟了 1 ~3 句支持句。并且请大家牢记：新托福写作主体段分论点后的支持句是全文中使用 linkers、加分句型和变换句式最为频繁的地方。

再比如这个 Technology 类主体段，还是段内并列，请重点体会分论点后的支持句是如何使用 linkers 的：

I believe technology can positively contribute to humans' keeping alive of traditional skills and ways of life. For example, the populations of some Pacific islands are too small to have regular schools. Their educational authorities have been able to use the Internet to deliver schooling online to the local kids rather than sending them to the mainland. Also, the modern refrigeration technology has been used to keep alive the traditional ways of producing salmon. As a result, they can now be ordered from and delivered to anywhere in the world.

段内并列的优点是在实战中操作方便，不容易出现失误。但缺陷是使用的考生较多，特色不够明显，而且比较适合用来写"折中式"作文的主体段，而不太适合写"一边倒"作文的主体段（"折中式"和"一边倒"的区别我们会在 Day 9 彻底搞定）。如果打算使用这种段内结构，那么分论点后面的支持句应该尽量多用些 linkers 或者好句型，以此来打破段内顺延比较呆板的先天不足。

3　主体段内递进（Sequential Arguments）

这种写法和段内并列有时候并没有本质区别，只是分论点间的层次感更加清晰。段内递进的标志词有 The primary（首要的）reason is... /... is primarily...（请注意 primarily 这个词一般是用在句中，极少用在句首）/ The principal（最主要的）factor is... / The main concern is... / The chief consideration is... / Moreover, ... / Furthermore, ... / Further, ...（用 Further 的考生明显要比用 Furthermore 的少，其实这个词在美国大学写作中也相当常见）/ Apart from..., ... / Aside from..., ... / Besides, ... /Besides..., ... / What's more, ... / Plus, ... / In addition, .../ Additionally, ...。

还有下面一些递进方式在新托福作文中也是可行的：

Worse yet, / ..., or worse yet, ...（更糟的是，）

Better yet, / ..., or better yet, ...（更棒的是，）

More exactly,（更准确地说）

More precisely,（更精确地说）

Specifically,（具体来说）

More importantly, ...（更重要的是）

The most significant reason why... is...（某方面最重要的原因是）

用段内递进的方法时，有时候第一个分论点前的标志词也可以自然省略，比如请大家仔细体会 Barron's 中的实例：

Many people enjoy participating in sports for recreation because it offers an opportunity to be part of a group. As a participant, you can join a team and enjoy all the benefits of membership, from shared experiences to a sense of belonging. Moreover, in training for a sport, an exercise routine contributes to your health.

Probably even more important than group identity and good health are the life lessons that participation in a sport provides. Setting a goal and working toward it, collaborating with others and putting a plan into action are all good lessons that can be learned on the playing field. (Barron's)

明显是省略了第一点之前的标志词。

下面这个关于 Transportation 的主体段也是再明显不过的段内递进：

I don't think biking is a safe means of transportation in America — for three reasons. To begin with, in my experience, many different pieces of bicycle equipment can be unreliable and may cause bike accidents. For instance, if a bike does not have good brakes, it cannot be stopped effectively. Similarly, a weak light will make it difficult for a biker to see at night. Aside from defective equipment, a biker may have difficulty controlling his/her bike when it's windy or rainy, which is common in many American cities. Under such conditions, water may obstruct the biker's view. And I believe most bike accidents are actually caused by bikers who do not stop at a stop sign or by bikers whose pants' legs get caught in the bike chain.

下面这个关于 Healthcare 的主体段仍是段内递进的典范，而且大量使用了我们在 Day 5 学习过的 linkers。请大家认真体会段内递进的结构，同时也注意各分论点后面的支持句是如何使用连词与句式变换的：

Socialized health care systems generally don't make sense. First, socialized medicine is extremely expensive — no matter how it is paid for. For example, in Sweden and Saudi Arabia, two medically socialized countries（句中插入短语）, the costs have increased to approximately（使用副词）40 percent of the budget of each country each year. Specifically（具体来说）, in Sweden, this money comes from high taxes while（对比）in Saudi Arabia, it comes from petrodollars. More than that, the socialized system is rarely efficient. Often（状语前置）, it's hard to find an appropriate doctor. Worse yet（更糟糕的是）, it's even harder to get examined by a doctor. According to one recent case in Algeria, a woman had to wait eight months just to have her tooth pulled out. That's because in countries with socialized medicine, everyone wants to go to the doctor or dentist, no matter how small the problem might be（让步）.

段内递进一般也多用于折中式作文，但较少用于"一边倒"文章的主体段。

4 主体段内因果（Cause and Effect）

因果关系是人类逻辑中最基础的关系之一，所以，在新托福作文主体段中也一再高调亮相（常用标志词请参考 Day 5 的因果关系部分）。我们多看几个实例。

Media 类段内因果实例：

I think serious TV shows can be used as supplementary（这个词的意思是"用来作补充的"）teaching tools. For many American students, once they get back home, the first thing that they do is to turn on the television. Therefore, recommending to their students serious TV shows that contain reflections on history, economy, science or social justice can really help teachers extend teaching into their students' leisure time.

与段内并列和段内推进不同，这段话只有一个论点（也就是全段的第一句），后面的句子都是它的支持句。这种写法是典型的"一边倒"作文的主体段写法。一边倒与折中式的区别我们会在 Day 9 彻底弄清。

再请看这个关于 Technology 的主体段是如何利用段内因果去论证的：

The benefits of computer skills for young children should not be denied. Their future adult world will be changing even faster than ours in terms of technology and lifestyle. Thus, it's essential that today, young children can learn at an early age to use the equipment for the storage（储存）and transmission（传输）of information.

下面这个主体段仍然是紧密依靠因果论证而出色地完成了任务：

Many immigrant parents think that their children should become Americans as quickly as possible and don't teach their children their native language or culture. I think this is a serious mistake. Immigrants are minorities in the U. S. , so keeping in touch with their own culture and ancestors is essential for keeping their sense of pride and security. Someday in the future the second-generation immigrant children will ask their parents where they came from and they will have a need to know their own culture. To understand that culture, they must learn their native tongue because the language is the most important element that forms the spiritual value and racial consciousness（意识）. Therefore, I believe while assimilation of the new language and culture should be encouraged, keeping the old one is just as important.

再看一个 Technology 话题主体段：

Technology makes it too difficult to censor（审查）material on the Internet. Every day, new computer programs are developed that make other programs obsolete. As soon as someone figures out（动词短语：理解，明白）how to censor material on the Internet, someone else can figure out how to break the code. As a result, a tremendous amount of money would have to be spent on developing new technology, and this expense would not be worth it.

再来一个：

One reason I believe it's a teacher's responsibility to help students learn is that many students are of a young age. A first — or second-grade teacher works with children who are only six or seven years old. At this age, a student is too young to recognize the value of education. Therefore, it should be the teacher's job to make sure the children can learn.

5　主体段内举例 Exemplification

举例的标志词和用法我们会在附录 A "妙手举例子" 中进行了详细介绍，请大家及时复习。

6　主体段内类比和对比 （Comparison & Contrast）

经过 Day 5 的集训，相信大家对这两种段内论证手段已经熟悉到了快要审美疲劳的程度，不过它们毕竟也是人类辩论了几千年后的辉煌成果，同志们（北京话说快了就叫 "徒儿们"）不可喜新厌旧：

（a） Education 类：

Taking a wide range of courses offers students more options for their leisure time. Past generations worked longer hours and their relatively short life expectancy（预期寿命） did not afford（提供） as many people the possibility of a long retirement. In contrast, today a large number of college graduates can expect to enjoy several decades of recreational（休闲的，这些可真都是咱们在 Day 4 讲过的词啊） activities after they stop working. The interests that they develop through exploring various academic fields can be very helpful in making their retirement more enjoyable. （Barron's）

（b） Leisure 类：

It's very interesting to discover the different personality of the Spanish regions by just listening to what their music sounds like. For example, in southern Spain, people are known for being very funny and for their good sense of humor. In this part of Spain you can find mainly two kinds of music: the Flamenco and the Sevillanas. Sevillanas has completly the personality of the Andalusian people as it is very cheerful. By contrast（这是个西班牙考生的作文，所以用了 By contrast 这样的欧式写法，在美国通常写 In contrast）, Flamenco sounds sad and deep. The reason is that although Andalusian people also have a good mood, they live in one of the poorest parts of Spain, and they express their pain through the Flamenco music.

（c） Success vs. Failure 话题：

All of us have had — and will continue to have — difficult experiences and failures. It's up to us（由我们来决定） to learn from them. One person who loses a job may become depressed, then withdraw, and finally start to blame others for his/her problems. In sharp contrast, another person who does not make excuses for failures may try to identify his/her own weaknesses, choose to go back to school or go to a refresher course, switch to another career path that is better suited to his/her potential, or relocate to a more prosperous area. Even though（让步）these two people have had the same failure, they will end up getting vastly different results.

7 主体段内转折 Dismissal

转折还是比较容易理解的，核心特征就是段中某个位置出现了 However, ... / But... / Yet... 这类词汇。但需要提醒大家注意的是：段内转折和段内对比间存在细微不同。

让俺用下面的表格来给您说明吧：

段内包含成分	段内转折	段内对比
A（位置在前）与 B（位置在后）	用 B 去证明 A 没有说服力	要证明 A 与 B 都是事实，但它们之间有差异，因此构成了对比

如果居然还觉得迷糊，那咱们就再用下面的 Government 类主体段说明吧：

Some（议论文里就是 Some people 的意思）argue that socialized medical care gives all the people a chance for health care rather than just the rich. This might be true.（此部分是 A）But we might ask, "What quality of health care does it give a chance for?" According to the American Medical Association, doctors in medically — socialized countries such as Canada possess（拥有）much less skill than doctors in countries with privately-financed health care. That sounds reasonable actually: If（假设）a doctor has a guaranteed supply of patients, what, other than self-satisfaction, does the doctor have to improve his/her skills?（此部分是 B。很明显：B 证明了 A 是不具有说服力的，因此属于典型的段内转折）

请您再研读下面的 Media 类段内转折：

Many people argue that educational media programs are too commercialized today. It's true the media have noticed the demand for adult education as a leisure-time pursuit and often speak in the language of education even while promoting their routine fare（常规的收费）. However, I believe that educational programming in its best sense does exist. For example, a large number of excellent nature documentaries now sit comfortably in the prime-time（黄金时段）schedules of broadcasters. Sizeable（可观的）quantities of serious literature have found their niche（还记得 172 中的这个句型么：找到合适的定位）in publishing companies' lists with increasing book sales. And on the Internet, surfers can visit thousands of specialized websites featuring visual arts, poetry and classical music. All these alternative sources of art would have been very difficult to locate for all but the experts just ten years ago.

请再体会一个关于 Taking risks 的主体段：

Yes, most wealthy people tell us stories of the giant risk they took on the way to extraordinary success. But don't jump to the conclusion that the willingness to take risks is a key to success. It's deceptive（有欺骗性的）because we only hear about the people who successfully take risks but we don't get to hear about the thousands who take similar risks and lose. We know about the $50 million lottery winner but we don't know about the far more than 10 million people who took the uninformed risk of 5 dollars trying to win.

还有下面的关于"Moving to a new country"的主体段内转折实例：

We will meet many new people. At the beginning, we probably will feel a bit disoriented and won't be able to remember everyone's name, their roles and how they might affect us. But later on, our classmates or co-workers are going to ask us about ourselves. After all, people are always curious about someone new. So we'll get a lot of opportunities to socialize with them, which will really help us get used to the unfamiliar things in a new country.

"有幽默感的教师教学是否更有效" 这个难题的一个高分主体段：

In a sense, educators are also performers who are on display all day long. They need to engage their students, motivate, inspire and support them. Sometimes they think that humor is the way to go and enjoy seeing the magic that shared laughter can create. However, reactions to humor are highly individual indeed. What one student finds funny, another may think of as being stupid or even offensive. Humor and jokes are the hardest concepts to translate and the most difficult to understand in a language that is not one's own. Also, they're always rooted in age, sex, culture, language and religion. Therefore, American teachers who often teach ethnically diverse classes often find themselves inadvertently（不经意地）wading into dangerous waters（复数指"水域"，这里是比喻用法）when they attempt to use humor in their classroom.

8　主体段内让步 Concession

让步逻辑我们也已经在 Day 5 深入接触过了，现在放到主体段逻辑的角度来分析。

标志词（除 Day 5 已经给出的让步关系 linkers 之外）：

Granted, ...（诚然……）

Admittedly, ...（我承认……）

I tend to agree that...

It's true that...

To be sure, ...

Surely, ...

Few can deny that...

需要提醒各位的是：新托福作文中主体段内一般都是通过这些词制造出虚假妥协气氛，之后通常都还要用下列词汇转折：

However, ...

Yet...（注意 Yet 后面不要加逗号）

Nevertheless, ...

Nonetheless, ...

Even so, ...

Still, ...（这里不是"仍然"而是"尽管如此"的意思）

Despite that, ... 等

比如，请您认真体会这个关于 Transportation 的主体段：

I don't think cars are necessarily "greener" than airplanes. Granted, one flight consumes more fuel and causes more pollution than a single car journey. However, air trips carry far more passengers than car rides. Therefore, given the amount of pollution produced per passenger per kilometer travelled, a car journey is no more fuel-efficient or environmentally-friendly than a flight.

又比如，下面这个关于 Taking risks 话题的主体段同样是"以退为进"：

No matter how much afraid we are of taking risks, we'll have to take them from time to time. I admit this is a cliché（套话），but it's nevertheless true. Risk-taking is not necessarily the same as rash（匆忙的）and reckless（不考虑后果的）gambles that never pay off. It's just an inescapable（无法逃避的）fact of life. Even to possess the most treasured things in our lives at the same time means that we have to risk their loss. If we constantly assume that we can't accomplish anything, we almost certainly won't. But if we believe that we can, at least we'll make the effort. Those who we think of as being lucky are simply those who have been willing to take calculated risks（这里并不是"经过计算的风险"，而是"经过慎重权衡的风

险"）and to put themselves on the line（put... on the line 是美语：用⋯⋯去冒险）.

下面这个高分主体段仍是在让步的同时话锋一转：

In my opinion, music tells us a lot about a culture. For example, one can learn a lot from the Spanish culture by just listening to Spanish music in his/her room. Even so, it is not easy to collect a representative sample of the Spanish music because of its enormous variety: every region of Spain has its own music that sounds completely different from the rest. And in some regions, there are even more than one type of typical music. This variety is very important because it shows that Spain is a country of various cultures, each one with a particular personality.

9　主体段内假设（反证）Supposition

对于新托福作文来说，主体段内的假设除了可能用到 Day 5 讲过的假设关系连词外，还有一大特色就是经常用到虚拟语气：

（a）*Barron's* 的高分范例

Taking a variety of subjects provides a common core of knowledge for all educated people. If students limited their courses to their major fields of study, they would not have a broad view of the world. Their vision would be very narrow and they would not be able to exchange views with others whose education had been limited to the study of a different field. (*Barron's*)

（b）再比如下面这个 Education 类主体段也是相当典型的段内假设（反证）：

The reason I prefer that teachers encourage their students to be skeptical about what they're taught is that in education and science, many things we think that are true are really not. An example — for many years it was thought that the earth was flat. But it turned out that the earth was round. If education had never encouraged students to question what they were taught, this discovery might not have been made. (*Princeton Review*)

另外，对于艺高人胆大的高分考生来说，段内反证还有一种极有魄力的形式——使用反问句。不过需要注意，即使打算用也不要全段都只用反问句，否则会显得对你的阅卷人挑衅性过强，甚至形成一种视觉调戏。一般如果打算用段内反问，也都是在一些陈述句后面再适当使用 1~3 句反问句。

（c）比如 *Kaplan* 的这个关于"个人是否对解决环境问题有责任"的段落：

We've all heard countless advertising campaigns warning us not to litter. Yet some people still think nothing of throwing a soda can out of their car window onto the highway or dropping a candy wrapper on the sidewalk. In fact, most of us realize that we are upsetting a delicate ecological balance when we don't dispose of our trash properly. Why do people continue to litter? (*Kaplan*)

（d）再比如下面这个关于 Friends 的 ETS 官方高分作文主体段：

In any relationship of mine, I would wish that first of all, the person I'm dealing with is honest. Even if he/she thinks that he/she did something wrong that I wouldn't like, Later on if I find out about a lie or hear the truth from someone else, that'd be much more unpleasant. In that case, how can I ever believe or trust that person again? How can I ever believe that this person has enough confidence in me to forgive him/her and carry on with the relationship from there?

请注意上面的段落其实是很典型的高分写法：不仅使用了反问，而且虚拟、让步等手法也交叉使用。任何一篇高分范文都是多种手法的综合体，这也就要求我们对前面的核心词汇、linkers、句式变换等章节的内容都要尽可能熟练。

（e）继续发问：

We all understand that the truth often may not be a very nice thing to either hear or say. Lies or white lies often have their advantages. The manipulation of white lies is the most obvious in the business world. How many times have we heard that a certain product is "the finest" or "the cheapest"? How many times have we heard that products have such and such "magical functions"? Advertising is about persuasion, and many would agree that if a company is to tell the absolute truth about its products, no one would be interested in even having a look at the products.

10 主体段内下定义 Definition

在 Day 5 讲 linkers 的时候我们也讲过了：下定义是一种体现考生对话题的理解比较深入的抢高分方法。我们看一下这种手法在建构主体段逻辑时的应用：

（a）

Successes in our lives are hugely influenced by the quality of our thinking, which means how we view the world, how we interact with the world and what we think of our own actions and thoughts. Without proper thinking, people who are financially rich may find themselves having a poor quality of life.

（b）

In addition, social skills are very important to achieving success because people enjoy being around socially-skilled people. Social skills are, essentially, the abilities to manage relationships and the emotions of others. Every time we interact, we have the potential to make others feel better — or worse — than they did before, depending on what we do and how we do it. Socially-skilled people know emotions can be contagious（本来是指有传染性的，这里指有感染力的）and always try to make others feel good. Who doesn't want to be in the presence of those who make them feel good? Who hasn't had the experience of witnessing how a spark of laughter lightened the mood of a whole room?

（C）

I believe vacations are essential to modern life. When work is too hard or so easy that it becomes repetitive, we feel we must escape. We have become so fascinated with the "time out" that we yearn for（渴望）them all year long and would be outraged（愤怒的）if anyone tried to take them away from us. To many of us, vacations are the time when we're "forced" to take it easy, to spend the money we have devoted most of our lives to earning, and to feel that we are truly alive — as compared with the rest of our existence, and by far a greater part of it, that we spend at work.

11　主体段内耍赖 Playing Dumb

在讲 linkers 那章的时候我们已经提到过，高分范文里经常有一种不是关系的关系：似乎一直在振振有词地论证，可仔细一看，其实只不过一直在 paraphrase 转述。对于新托福 essays 这样比较生活化的作文来说，"耍赖"其实不失为在实在想不出支持句时还能让主体段（显得）很充实的一招妙棋。

标志词：

In other words, ／ — that is, ／ — that is to say, ／ — i. e. , ／ By that I mean, ／ What is meant by that is... 等。

下面这个主体段就是异常明显的耍赖式论证：

Another reason I'm against students being in control is that it means students won't study as much. By that I mean if students get to pick the program, they'll only pick the areas they like. Maybe one student will only study history, another chemistry. This can be good, but a student should study all subjects. Teachers can make sure the students study everything and get a better education. (*Princeton Review*)

乍一看蛮有理，可仔细一分析，竟然每句话都是不折不扣的反复论证。事实上，我们不应该小看"不是关系的关系"，它存在于大量高分范文中。"说废话"的本事，其实是搞定新托福写作这种语言水平测试而非思维水平测试必备的一种技能（当然也不能 300 多字全是废话，否则考官可不跟你废话，直接低分了）。

☆   ☆   ☆

新托福写作的主体段论证手法并不是一成不变的，实战中经常是一段话里兼有 N 种论证方法的"大杂烩"型（Fusion-Style）。在今天给大家布置的课后练习题和明天我们要学习的内容中，您将更深刻地体会到多种论证手段在考场实战中的综合运用。

课后练习

Take-Home Quiz

判断练习

请快速判断下面的主体段综合使用了哪几种论证方法：

① North Americans work extremely hard. We work for long hours and with remarkably short holidays. If we compare our employment patterns with the workday of a hunter-gatherer in the Peruvian forests (three to four hours), the average work week in pre-revolutionary France (four days), or the annual number of work-free days in fourth-century Rome (a hundred and seventy-five), we seem a very hard-driven lot.

② Most immigrants in America, regardless of their social or economic status, are torn between cultures — what they feel they have left behind in their country of origin and what they have adopted in their new homeland. The nostalgia, love and pain of missing home, friends and even family are often a very strong emotion for newcomers. The lifestyle, the streets and cafés, the weather and climate, the dress and the customs, the seasons, the sweet smells of food, fruit and flowers all trigger feelings of remembrance. On the other hand, when the immigrants return to their native land, they find that everything has been changed. The total sense of belonging is missing. Friends and family have moved on, streets and cities look unfamiliar and the culture they missed so much when they were in America have been Americanized too.

③ Culture is never static（静止不动的）. It's always changing, evolving and growing, just like us. More importantly, individuals don't only have one identity, but multiple identities. Therefore, immigrants who are adaptable enough can still maintain a sense of cultural identity wherever they live. Why should immigrants in America define themselves as being "Canadian", "Portuguese" or "Indian", when they actually are all influenced by several cultures and each of them have a different story?

参考答案

① 顺延，假设，对比

② 下定义，顺延，对比

③ 顺延，递进，因果，反问

后现代主义的woodpecker，好在新托福的所有满分范文都是遵循常规逻辑论证方式，绝没有哪一篇使用了"意识流"。

——Pat摄

国 内的朋友很多对 Native Americans 的话题感兴趣。在美国虽然这已经不能再算是严格意义上的 touchy issue（敏感话题），但 Native American kids 的教育问题以及由此导致的 truancy（逃学）、年轻人就业问题甚至 drug abuse 的问题在美国还是会时常引起关注。

其实 Native American 文化曾为美语输送过大量词汇，比如 turkey, tobacco, chocolate 甚至 potatoes 和 tomatoes 这些常用词。但它的影响力随着印第安人口降至美国总人口的 1% 以下已经越来越少地被展现了。我想这并不是对 Native American 曾经受到不公正待遇的一个合理的 conclusion 吧。

（下）蛇尾还是豹尾

A Hit or a Flop?

新 托福作文结尾段的意义绝不仅限于对上文的总结。它同时也是你利用考场上仅存的几分钟再去多抢点分儿的最后机会。永远不要让你的结尾段成为开头和主体段句子的机械重复，那样的结尾放在阅卷人嘴里实在味如嚼蜡，甚至有可能破坏你的文章本来已经在他/她的心目中建立起的健康形象。

我们现在就来把貌似千变万化的新托福高分作文结尾看个明明白白，真真切切。想总结属于自己的结尾段框架的同学，可以从下列大量范例中挑出一两个比较适合自己水平的来仿写，并仔细体会每个高分范例中的彩色字部分。

结束全文的五种方式

A 领导式　Bossy Style

领导就是领导，一拿起话筒就特有"范儿"。新托福作文的领导式结尾一般都是回顾主体段的观点，偶尔高兴了还会再小展望一下未来。

比如 Kaplan 中这个关于"班级规模到底应该多大合适"的结尾段就是纯粹的领导式（但是请注意它没有照搬上文的词句，而是 paraphrase 和 summary，这一点请要当"领导"的朋友们切记）：

Reducing class size is not just a matter of relieving（减轻）pressure. It will enhance what a student learns and even the person they learn it from can learn from this process.（The End）

很大牌吧？两句话就结束全文，根本不给你反驳的机会。

再看这个处级干部：

In conclusion, university education should not be made free. I believe in that because the colleges need the money to make them better. If the universities are free, taxes will be raised and people will have to pay for things they might not use.

（群众掌声……）

此外，领导式结尾中还有一种极度嚣张的形式，已经接近给读者最后通牒，所以这样的结尾也可以称为"大爷式"。

比如 *Princeton Review* 中的这个结尾段，就是典型的 mogul style：

In conclusion, I have shown that it's better for teachers to encourage their students to question things. Without curiosity there can be no education.

领导式结尾非常适合作 "一边倒" 作文的结尾段，不过要注意这种写法除了转述上文外，最好能再深入写一点相关的引申，这样显得结尾更充实。

B 家长式 Tender-Loving-Care Style

家长式结尾也同样带有较强的概括性，但语气比领导式温馨很多，有坚实的群众基础，让考官接受起来不会有屈辱感。

比如下面这个 Education 类结尾：

For those reasons, we can safely conclude that classmates are too important a factor to ignore and they have more important influence than teachers on students' success at school.

是不是？完全以理服人。

再请看同样是 Education 类的另一个结尾：

There's nothing wrong with studying on your own. For the best possible learning, though, a teacher is the biggest help you can have. (*Barron's*)

这个家长在提出自己的建议前还要先强调一下对方其实也没错，实在是 "循循善诱"。

又比如这个 Family 类的结束语：

Therefore, even though many jobs come together to make a house a house, a house becomes a home only when people who live in it try to make it a place where they truly belong.

虽然也是摆条件，但并没有像领导式那样强加于人，而是通过描绘出美好前景来引诱读者，这跟家长们从口袋里掏出的 candy bar 实在没什么区别。

还有这个 Friends 话题高分结尾段：

So we should really allow ourselves to make new friends. New schools, new workplaces and even new countries are all going to create opportunities for us to expand our pool of companions. Don't just socialize with old chums? — it's good to branch out（进入某个新领域）and have friends who are separate from your core social circle.

句句都是暖人心的话。由于家长式结尾特有的温情一面，它既适合一边倒的结束语，也适合作折中式的结尾。不过需要注意：家长也毕竟还是有决策权的，不能完全让孩子（你的读者）去自己选择，所以家长式结尾还是要有明显倾向性的，只不过是用比较容易接受的方式说出来而已了。

C　愤青式　the Beat Generation Style

看名字就很好理解：对话题冷眼看待，有一种自命清高的书生气。但如果确实语言功底不错，而且确信能把自己不同流合污的价值取向表达清晰，用这种结尾倒真是相当不俗的。多给大家看几个例子：

愤青甲：

Needless to say, both sources are important to us. But in my opinion, knowledge from experience is even more important because without experience, it's almost impossible to understand knowledge from books or to understand how to apply this knowledge in real life.

这种结尾通常是先用 Apparently, … / Clearly, …/Needless to say, …/ It goes without saying that… 等表达在结尾段首对辩论话题表示不屑，然后再用 However, … / But… / Yet… / Nevertheless, … / Still, … 这类词汇引出一两句表明自己态度的结束语。

愤青乙：

At one time, people said that computers could not have emotions. But now it seems that scientists are trying to develop computers that have emotions and are smart enough to have the potential to be humans' friends. Still, what are the benefits of having a friend that's essentially a machine? I truly wonder what the rationale (*n.* 合理因素) is behind this development.

下面的年轻人也很 cynical（愤世嫉俗的）：

The elderly are a valuable part of society and deserve to be treated as such, not to be put in a home somewhere forgotten about because people think they are a burden. The elderly should be able to live comfortable and productive lives, surrounded by their loved ones for whom they once cared. (*Kaplan*)

接下来的愤青式结尾更带有鲜明的批判现实主义色彩：

I don't think we should categorize people before we listen to their views. NFL superstars are not necessarily more capable than average people in terms of judging the value of a water treatment plant. When celebrities advocate a cause, their opinions should be only one of the many factors that we consider in evaluating that cause.

下面的"大愤"相当精彩地陈述了自己对"科学家是否应该对自己的研究带来的后果负责"这道考题的见解：

Hence, even though science creates a power through its knowledge — i. e. , we're able to do things after we know something scientifically, science does not carry instructions about whether we should do good or do evil with it. Therefore, contrary to what many people believe, I would argue that the moral choice about the application of science is independent of scientists' work，which means scientists shouldn't be held accountable for their own discoveries or inventions.

与家长式的"可正可反"不同，愤青式特别适合一边倒的高分作文结尾段。但注意写好它的关键并不是激动地发泄对社会的不满，而是有论证依据的、建立在充分说理基础上的表达改变现状的合理愿望。

D 小秘式　Gold-Digger Style

这种结尾的特色就是"顺着说"，比较适合已经放弃了努力去改变社会的幻想、等着社会来改变自己的考生。

比如下面这个高分范文结尾段：

I would like to say that I personally agree with the statement that music tells us something about a culture，and with my example I wanted to illustrate how much of the culture of a country it is possible to learn about just listening to its music.

再比如这个关于"教育重要还是让小朋友多玩儿重要"的结尾：

I agree that formal education at an early age offers children benefits at all levels and therefore is more important than letting them play. After all，kids can always play after school but learning at school stimulates（激发）their brain growth and puts them in competitive social settings，which is indeed irreplaceable experience for such a critical stage of life.

（irreplaceable 这个词用得很妙——不可替代的，嘴这么甜的小秘一定人见人爱吧?）

Pat's Tips

上面讲的四类结尾是新托福作文考试中最常用的四种结尾手法。但请注意：如果你的作文主体用的是"折中式"写法，那么在结尾通常还是要重点倾向于其中的某一方，而不是双方各同意50%，否则你的结尾将转化成下面这种类型：

E "和稀泥"型　Goodie-Goodie Style

这种文章在结尾还是不表明任何一种态度倾向，完全是"大团圆"。请看下面关于"远程教育好还是到教室上课好"的结尾段实例：

Given all the advantages of both types of courses，I think that students would be wise to register for distance-learning courses and traditional classroom courses as well during their college experiences. By participating in distance-learning courses，they can work independently in classes that may be more difficult for them，repeating the lectures on computers at convenient times. By attending traditional classes，they can get to know the teachers personally and will have good references when they need them. They will also make friends in the class. Also, by sharing information with other students, they can organize their schedules for the following semester, choosing the best classes, including both distance-learning and traditional courses.

客观地说，这个"稀泥"和得不错，主要因为对两方都表示接受后还分别点出了接受的理由，所以仍然算是以理服人，而不是无原则的两面派。如果打算一起和的朋友们请牢记这个特点。

下面 ETS O. G. 中的满分范文结尾段更是"和"中高手：

The time to live independently depends on the person himself. He must decide whether they're ready to leave their parents to have an independent life or not. The decision will vary from one person to another. A person should judge that he's capable of fulfilling his needs without being dependent on his parents; this indicates that he's ready for his independent life. Otherwise he might need to stay longer with his parents.

先用 3 句绕口令似的句子，最后提出到底应该何时开始独立取决于孩子自身的判断能力。depends on 往往是"和稀泥"式的标志词。

F 开放式 Open-ended Approach

且慢！刚才说好了只学五种结尾，怎么又偷偷加重学习负担？

呵呵，主要是因为这种结尾虽然确实在美式议论文里存在，但 Pat 并不是很推荐大家在实战中使用。了解一下还成，但如果在考场那么紧张的状态下采用这种开放式写法，有可能会陷入"虚无主义"。

请看下例：

The controversy over whether or not TV programming should be censored（审查）and be made more "wholesome"（Day 4 学过的词，你是否还记得是什么意思？）will likely continue. At the heart of the debate lies the question of what impact TV shows have on young viewers' values and behavioral tendencies.

先是声明讨论话题仍会继续引起争议，这会让期待作者态度的读者产生挫败感。不过好在接下来还是很实诚地提出了解决问题的关键到底在哪里，比较成功地扭转了败局。

又比如这个结尾：

Arguments on this issue still continue today and I do believe that there's an ongoing need for dialogue（对话）between those who produce our food and those who protect our health.

开放之后又提出双方需要更多的对话，最终积极的人生观还是战胜了"Let it be."的列侬曲风。

还可以更多：

Therefore，**happiness** is a concept that can be interpreted in myriad（美语写作词汇常用：大量的）ways. Actually，it has been the **incredible diversity of individuals' understandings of this concept** that（典型的强调句）has led to the amazing variety of human pursuits，which are，after all，exactly what have made life rewarding（有回报的）and worthwhile.

把开放式结尾和多样性扯到一起，让读者相信"开放"才是新世纪人类生活的 central theme。

Pat's Tips

"一边倒"作文不要用 open-ended 结尾，否则会让考官感觉包容力过强的结尾段和旗帜鲜明的主体段严重冲突。

☆　　☆　　☆

从（上）到（下），我们分别分析了开头、主体和结尾段各自的常用写作手法。在下一章里，我们将统揽全局，从文章的角度彻底看清新托福作文的整体结构。

学有余力

lrs. ed. uiuc. edu/students/fwalters/toeflwrite. html

互联网上有很多关于合理英文段落安排的好资料。比如这个网站下方的 Lesson 1-4，对于形成属于自己的个性化（personalized）写作框架就很有好处。Pat 坚信：有特色的逻辑框架对于新托福这样的生活化作文来说，远比 200 字的模板更靠谱。

课后练习

Take-Home Quiz

判断练习

请快速说出下面的结尾段属于何种结尾：

The pace of life is increasingly fast，but we still have good food. So I think overall，the food-preparation technology is desirable，even though we should also try to make sure that we have a healthy diet and better nutrition.

参考答案

如果只看前两句感觉像是"领导"来了，但是看到 even though 后面的内容可以断定原来是"和稀泥"型。

这年头儿开Oldsmobile的估计是老"愤青"了吧!
　　　　　　　　　　——Pat摄

Day 9

Getting the Big Picture
独立作文的结构与解构

Nothing is static. Even Mona Lisa is falling apart.

——Chuck Palahniuk
American Journalist

很多新托福考生也需要参加 SAT 考试。Pat 经常听到北京的孩子们把这个词连读为 sat，第一次听的时候真是愣了一下，因为在美国这个考试永远都被拆开读做 S-EI-T。☺

到底是拆开好还是合并好呢？在本章里，咱们两件事情都要做。

上一章为大家展示了新托福作文开头段、主体段和结尾段的全部写作手法。在本章中，我们将从总体的角度去把握新托福独立作文。

在正式开始学习之前，请大家先熟悉下面的 4 个事实：

A Nice Warm-up ⇩

◆ 官方高分范文最常见的段数是 4 段或者 5 段，6 段比较少，而 3 段更少。其他段数几乎百年不遇；

◆ 虽然确实有少数官方高分范文采用了把开头和主体融合在一起，或者是把主体和结尾融合在一起的写法，但绝大多数范文均有明确的开头、主体和结尾；

◆ 官方范文中"一边倒"的写法明显多于"折中式"的写法；

◆ 即使采用"折中式"写法的新托福范文，除极少数特例（比如 *Kaplan* 中的少数范文），一般也都会明显偏重论述其中一方，而对另一方的论证篇幅则较短。

新托福独立作文结构详表

	一边倒	折中式
开头段结构（参考 Day 8 上）	社会或生活背景（可省略）+ 引出要讨论的话题（必写）+ 一方的观点（可省略）+ 自己的态度（一般不省略）	社会或生活背景（可省略）+ 引出要讨论的话题（必写）+ 双方各自的观点（可省略）+ 自己的态度（一般不省略）
开头段不宜使用的形式	顶牛式	如数家珍式
主体段个数	3 ~ 4	2 ~ 3
主体段态度	各主体段的态度一致，即"都支持"或"都反对"；	各主体段的态度不一致，可以选择：(a) 倾向的一方写一段，写得长一些，不倾向的一方也写一段（即"让步段"），但写得短一些；(b) 倾向的一方写两段，让步段写一段

（续表）

	一边倒	折中式	
主体段结构（参考 Day 8 中）	主体段1： 理由句 +2 ~4 个展开支持句 主体段2： 理由句 +2 ~4 个支持句 主体段3： 理由句 +2 ~4 个支持句 ※ 不管打算采用何种形式，每一个理由句后面的支持句永远是全文中最应该多用 linkers 和加分句式的地方	写法（a）主体段1：段首表明倾向一方的观点，段内写2 ~3 个理由句，每个理由句后面各跟 2 ~3 句支持句；让步段：段首表明不倾向一方的观点，段内写1 ~2 个理由句，每个理由后跟 1 ~2 句支持句	写法（b）主体段1：段首表明倾向一方的观点，段内写第一个理由句，后面跟 2 ~3 句支持句；主体段2：段首写倾向一方的第二个理由句，后面跟 2 ~3 句支持句；让步段：段首写不倾向一方的观点，段内写一个理由句，后面跟 1 ~2 句支持句
遇到难题时主体段理由思考方法	裸奔法，分类法	裸奔法，替代法	
结尾段结构（参考 Day 8 下）	改写或概括全文观点，并适当延伸	改写或概括倾向一方的观点，并适当延伸	
结尾段较少使用的形式	和稀泥式	领导式	

* 但请不要相信"美国人都是直线思维，所以必须把让步段放在后面写"的忽悠。真相其实是：在美国大学里，无论把让步段放在前面还是放在后面的写法都允许，纯属个人偏好，跟文化完全没关系。只要主体段的连接词能够确保段落间逻辑衔接顺利就行。

* 基础较好的考生在写让步段的时候还可以选择先论证几句让步的观点，但接着再指出这种观点存在的缺陷。具体实例请看本章后面的折中式范文（一）。

最简单也最困难的"一边倒"

在台湾，有段时间大大小小的商店里都能听到一句歌词："嘿！蛋炒饭，最简单也最困难……"

"一边倒"——或者说得更精确点就是：完全支持或者完全反对某种观点，而对其他的视角全都不予考虑。这么听起来，"一边倒"其实挺可怕的，因为世界上很少有绝对正或者绝对负的东西。可这恰恰就是 TOEFL iBT Writing 和 GRE Issue 的区别：成功的 GRE Issue essays 一定要给阅卷人一种"get involved"的感觉，换句话说就是必须要看起来很客观（尽管不可能绝对客观），而且对各方的理由都不要完全排斥。而新托福独立写作作为主要目的是语言能力测试的考试，则明显更"自我"，只要确实体现出了用 American English 去"自圆其说"的能力，就是一篇好文章。

☆　　☆　　☆

新托福高分范文中常见的"一边倒"是写 3 个主体段（如果确实写 high 了也可以写出 4 个主体段，但两个主体段的一边倒高分范文则很少）。

之所以说一边倒的写法简单，是因为它从头到尾态度都很一致，"一根筋"，只要认准倾向之后执着地把文章写出来就好了。

说它困难，则是从文章的字数来考虑的。这明摆着：全世界任何一个命题，正反两方都讨论肯定比只讨论其中一方能写出的字数要多。但好在字数并不是新托福作文的主要矛盾，只要大家把之前学过的主体段内逻辑关系真正掌握熟练，能确保每一步的逻辑清晰，写到 320 字左右或者再多一点 350 字左右就已经不算短了，并不需要追求一些人梦想中的 400 字长篇大论。真正了解美国社会的人都能感觉到：它对"废话"（就是谁都知道的 common sense）还比较容忍，如果你能说得非常漂亮甚至还可能得到掌声，前提是你说话的目的必须是明确的。而美国社会对"空话"（就是什么目的都没有，或者跟目的完全不沾边儿的 baloney）却是 zero tolerance——零容忍度。

"一边倒"范文分析

下面我们一起来看一下高分范文的结构版和解构版，请大家阅读时重点体会：

❶ 一边倒的整体布局；

❷ 以前学过的词汇、句式和句型的熟练运用；

❸ 自圆其说的能力，把其实没什么道理的观点却证明得有理、有力、有节。

⦿ Money 类考题：

Do you agree or disagree with the following statement:

It's unfair that successful sports professionals earn huge amounts of money today.

题目分析：

这其实是近年来在美国一直存在广泛争议的话题。职业体育明星的收入确实挺让人"眼红"的，更不要说他们/她们除了 base salary 外，还有那么多的 endorsements（代言）和 winnings（获奖收入）。在美国连 Muhammad Ali 这种出了名儿的巨有个性的运动员，退休后都靠把自己的名字让厂商使用每年净赚 0.55 亿 USD。但在本文中，作者却 go against the grain（美语：不盲从大众），有力地论证了相反的见解，素材则是使用"裸奔法"中的 Skill、Tenacity 和 Enjoyment 3 条理由在 1 分钟内搞定的。不吹了，还是看文儿吧：

开头段

It's not uncommon today that elite sporting stars earn top salaries while professionals in many other important fields such as medical care and laboratory research make much less. Clearly, these distinguished athletes and first-rate players are not overpaid.

主体段 1

Even though it's likely the world population will top seven billion in two years, those who are truly athletically talented will remain very rare. Preeminent sportspeople such as LeBron James and Scott Gomez are so uniquely gifted that we ordinary individuals can never be trained to reach comparable levels. Thus, they are supposed to be highly paid due to the rarity of their talent.

主体段 2

Aside from genetics, it takes extremely hard work for sportspeople to make it to the top of their professions, regardless of their age or gender. To improve performance, dedicated athletes have been in constant training, mostly from their childhood onward, and can only enjoy a minimal amount of leisure time. Besides, they frequently have to put their bodies at risk and, even more frequently, cope with recurring psychological strain as a consequence of unusually stiff competition. Still, these incredible people simply don't waver from their goals. In short, I would argue all their commitments and sacrifices deserve abundant rewards, of which substantial sums of money may be just a token.

主体段 3

Most importantly, sports celebrities' salaries are set by the market. Sports have always been one of America's favorite pastimes and we have to face the fact that now professional sports are a major source of entertainment and inspiration for Americans. Big names like Peyton Manning make fortunes by getting their fair share of the profits that come from ticket money, merchandise sales and endorsements. I really don't see anything wrong with the top sports performers getting recognized and paid dearly as top entertainers and, often, very effective motivational speakers.

结尾段

Therefore, the unique talent, extraordinary willpower and immense marketing appeal that sports stars exhibit are all compelling justifications for the size of financial compensation they receive. (326 words)

如果您还没看清楚门道，请再来看下面的"解构版"，几乎全是我们学过的东西：

It's not uncommon today that（双重否定即肯定）elite sporting stars（Day 4 已经学过 elite：精英）earn top salaries while professionals in many other important fields such as medical care and laboratory research make much less.（背景与讨论话题合并成一句了）Clearly, these distinguished athletes and first-rate players are not overpaid. （明确表明倾向性，Distinguished 在 Day 4 已经学过："卓越……" 可不是广告~）

Even though it's likely（172 句中的）the world population will top seven billion in two years, those who are truly athletically talented will remain very rare（理由 1：体育明星拥有稀缺才能）. Preeminent sportspeople such as LeBron James and Scott Gomez（真的不想再举 Kobe Bryant 或者 Tiger Woods 那些俗例了，而且这两位在美国也是鼎鼎大名的）are so uniquely gifted that we ordinary individuals can never be trained to reach comparable levels（so… that… 讲过的因果关系标志词，同时这句也用了段内举例）. Thus, they are supposed to be（172 句里的）highly paid due to（因为）the rarity of their talent（rarity 也在 Day 4 学过了：稀缺性）.

Aside from genetics, it takes extremely hard work for sportspeople to make it to the top of their professions, regardless of their age or gender（理由 2：除基因外，个人努力也是体育明星成功的关键。regardless of 也是学过的，加分 linker: 不管……）. To improve performance（这是 "状语前置"）, dedicated athletes have been in constant training, mostly from their childhood onward（这是 "句中做手脚"）, and can only enjoy a minimal amount of leisure time. Besides（典型的段内推进结构）, they frequently have to put their bodies at risk（172 句里的：冒风险）and, even more frequently（又是一只 "句中的手"）, cope with recurring psychological strain as a consequence of unusually stiff competition（as a consequence of 学过的表示因果关系的标志词，标注的单词都已经学过）. Still, these incredible people simply don't waver from their goals（incredible 在美语中经常用作 "好得超出想象的" 的意思，waver from 则是 "动摇"）. In short（又是状语前置，注意 in short 这个词组不一定只能用于结尾，主体段结束处同样也能用）, I believe all their commitments and sacrifices deserve abundant rewards, of which substantial sums of money may be just a token.（用了 which 引

导的定语从句，token 是一种象征性的奖励，在北美坐地铁时买的小圆片也是 token）

Most importantly, sports celebrities' salaries are set by the market（一边倒的第三个理由，义无反顾：市场这只"无形的手"才决定是否公平）. Sports have always been one of America's favorite pastimes（Day 4 讲过的词：业余消遣）and we have to face the fact that now professional sports are a major source of entertainment and inspiration for Americans. Big names like Peyton Manning（在美国的电视广告上总能看见此人，是橄榄球明星，顺手拉过来做例子）make fortunes by getting their fair share of the profits that come from ticket money, merchandise sales and endorsements（门票钱、体育商品销售和代言收入，这句用了 that 引导的定语从句）. I really don't see anything wrong with the top sports performers getting recognized and paid dearly as top entertainers and, often, very effective motivational speakers（注意 pay sb. dearly 的意思并不是很亲密地付钱，而是付重金。motivational speakers 就是北京的新华书店里不停播放的讲成功哲学的演讲者了）.

Therefore, the unique talent, extraordinary willpower and immense marketing appeal（巨大的市场吸引力）that sports stars exhibit（在这里是动词：展现出）are all compelling justifications（强有力的支持证据）for the size of financial compensation they receive.（纯领导式结尾，舍我其谁，再也不给读者留下任何质疑的余地）

真的要是写 High 了怎么办？（仅适合考前 Dove 摄入过多的童鞋们）

前面谈到过要是在考场里确实写"高"了收不住笔了，那么一边倒也可以写出 4 个主体段，每段各论述 1 个支持（或者反对）的理由，那就形成加开头、结尾一共 6 段的结构。

比如上面这篇范文，如果写兴奋了也可以再加一段谈关于 patriotism（体育明星的爱国主义）的主体段。请看：

主体段 4

And let's not forget the contribution that international-event medalists like Roger Federer and Kerri Walsh make to their home countries. The honor they bring is invaluable. In terms of the national pride that their triumphs can generate, these national icons compete for their people. Through sports games, they enhance the image and the status of their countries in the international community, which, in most cases, brings an increased sense of unity to their fellow countrymen and countrywomen alike.

也来看个解构版吧，给个理由先：

And let's not forget the contribution that international event medalists like Roger Federer and Kerri Walsh make to their home countries. （理由 4：体育明星也为国争光了，举了实例。

Roger Federer 是瑞士人，但因为世界排名极靠前，所以在美国的知名度相当高，考官只要看过 ESPN 或者 *Sports Illustrated* 肯定了解此人）. The honor they bring is invaluable （长短句结合的原则——这儿来句超短的）. In terms of the national pride that their triumphs can generate, these national icons （Day 4 媒体类中学过这个词：国家、社会或者文化的象征者） compete for their people （In terms of 是学过的 linker："从……的意义上来讲"。虽然美国的职业运动已经彻底商业化了，但即使对职业运动员来说，能够为国争光毕竟也是让人高兴的事儿）. Through sports games （状语前置），they enhance （增进）the image and the status （地位）of their countries in the international community，which，in most cases，（又是"句中的手"）brings an increased sense of national unity to their fellow countrymen and countrywomen alike （172 句中的）.

※ 再次强调：与偏重学术风格的 GRE 和 IELTS 写作考试相比，新托福写作的特色是"接受废话，但不接受空话"：某些句子意思相近甚至 paraphrase 是完全允许的（在过去的"段内耍赖式"中我们已经见过了）。特别是对于一边倒的文章来说，毕竟在 30 分钟里写 300 多字而且还不停地说新东西也很难，只要多用些 linkers，让考官觉得逻辑关系是通顺的，而且废话别太多就好了。但是另一方面，新托福考官不喜欢没有任何意义的"万金油式"空话，所以建议大家即使打算用模板，也绝不要像老太太的裹脚布那样又 X 又 X。

中立但不中庸的"折中式"写法

"折中式"——如果说得更准确一点就是：不是双方各占 50%，而是倾向于其中的一方，但对另一方也适当加以论证，而最终落脚点则仍然是你倾向的那一方的写法。

"折中式"范文分析

（一）四段折中式范文

刚刚谈到了：折中式文章写成四段和五段都可以。先请大家看一篇 Pat 在北京时帮一个大学生修改的四段折中式作文：

◎ Environment 类考题：

Do you agree or disagree with the following statement:

Environmental problems should be solved with international effort.

题目分析:

当时这位同学的习作问题是:字数较少,只有 270 多个字。而且对 linkers 掌握不熟练,简单句太多。更关键的是,文章句式基本全都是单调的主谓宾加句号,缺乏句式变化,十分枯燥。另外,这个大姐虽然当时也举了一个例子,可惜还是国内同学们人见人爱的环保类例子 the Kyoto Protocol 京都协定。既然在北京人见人爱,那考官肯定晕菜,所以替换掉了,文章的结尾也帮她扩展成了传说中的愤青式。

请大家仔细体会修改后文章中的四段折中式布局:

A variety of environmental challenges, from the smog (烟雾) clouds to toxic groundwater to the Antarctic ozone hole, have been presented to the world. I believe many of these challenges should be met with collaboration across national boundaries (界限).

开头段介绍了背景,并把要讨论的话题和作者的态度融合成了一句话。

Environmental issues should be addressed through joint efforts from countries for two main reasons. First, now the impact of problems like oil spills and dust storms is so widespread that it can hardly be confined (限制) to one single country or region. Thus, it's crucial that these problems be solved with international efforts. What's meant by this is that each country and person should be made aware of their unique roles in environmental protection. Second, given that each country has its own weaknesses in environmental protection, cooperation between countries normally leads to more effective measures in confronting (面对) global environmental issues. For instance, even though the industrialized countries possess advanced technology and more financial resources for environmental preservation, many of them are big contributors to environmental problems such as emission-induced (尾气所导致的) climate changes and the depletion of fossil fuel reserves as well. Reducing those problems may slow down their industrial production and lessen their people's comfort and convenience so the lack of motivation to change may be their weakness. In light of this deficiency (n. 不足), other nations and international organizations have their roles to play in ensuring that these countries fulfill their environmental obligations (责任).

第一个主体段先提出了作者更倾向的观点,然后先后给出了两个理由,而且每个理由之后分别都跟了支持句,支持句里密集使用了我们过去学过的 linkers 并举了例子。

I admit there may be practical problems related to international cooperation in improving the environment. For example, countries may have different views on environmental issues; therefore, to achieve consensus (意见一致) on the steps that they should take definitely will take time. Even so, the willingness to join hands at least will put them on the right track in seeking solutions.

这是让步段，先提出了作者并不是很赞同的观点，并且论证了一句它的合理性，但接下来在 Even so 后面又适当地指出了这种观点的不足之处。

In conclusion, I would argue that more concerted（协调一致的）efforts should be made by the international community before the deterioration of the ecosystem becomes irreversible. (307 words)

结尾段总结了自己的看法，但并不是简单照搬前面的措辞，而是进行了改写和引申，并在文章最后用"在生态系统恶化变得无法挽回之前"表达了适度的愤青理想。

注：上文主体中的让步段如果不采用这种对让步观点先支持再反驳的写法，而是在让步段先后写对让步观点的两个支持理由，但同时确保第一个主体段比第二个主体段的论证明显更有力也更充分，那就也是可行的写法。另外上文中标出颜色的部分大家也可以用本章最后"致反动派的公开信"里的词句去替换，只要逻辑是正确的就可以理直气壮。

（二）五段折中式范文

○ Media 类考题：

Do you agree or disagree with the following statement:

Advertising makes people buy things that they don't need.

题目分析：

广告可以促销肯定没争议。但广告是否可以让消费者去买自己不想买的东西，这很有争议。这道题容易被写成"广告只是参考，真正掏钱的人才是爷"。但 Pat 认为：成功广告的厉害之处，就在于它可以在不知不觉中让消费者调整自己的期望，明明是买了和自己开始的预想不同的东西，还乐呵呵地以为自己占了便宜……

先看结构版：

Advertisements have been breaking old norms and generating new trends in North America. Now it seems the consumption of goods and services is spurred more by advertising power than by the real consumer needs.

Few would deny that advertising heavily influences consumers' decision-making process as it puts people in touch with the latest products and technology available. With the help of advertising, there are more chances for cutting-edge products like Blu-ray discs and Windows 7 Home Premium to be understood by the target customers. In this sense, advertising creates consumer needs.

Further, advertising contributes to the growth of popularity and trustworthiness of brands.

Take TV advertising for example. The more commercials on air, the better consumers get to know the brands featured in these commercials. Gradually, consumers build up their trust in these brands and will, consequently, purchase more of the products. More importantly, people tend to adjust their demand after viewing advertisements, which is precisely why some ads highlight inferior aspects of the target consumers. An example that aptly illustrates this point would be the marketing strategy of Vichy, which exposes some of women's skin flaws in its advertising, followed by solutions that Vichy offers to remedy the imperfections.

Meanwhile, people are truly able to discover their own needs and to satisfy themselves even without being informed by advertisements. Humans are born with the natural desire to lead a better life. Apart from the basic necessities, we tend to search for what our peers own and try to possess those things if we have the purchasing power. Also, customers' social status matters when they make purchase decisions. People prefer to own things matching their status. For instance, in the U. S. , the wealthy are more likely to buy luxury cars such as Jaguars, Mercedes or Porsches as their private vehicles, even if they are not exposed to any related advertising.

Overall, I believe advertising plays a critical role in creating profitability for companies, which has been empirically proven by the ever-increasing marketing and sales budgets in most industries. Although some people do recognize their needs, this recognition may be modified or reversed by effective advertising, and thus is not the main driving force behind the high sales of consumer goods. (365 words)

再来看它的"解构版":

Advertisements have been breaking old norms (normal 的名词形式, the norm 在美式英语里极为常用) and generating new trends in North America. Now it seems the consumption of goods and services is more spurred (*vt.* 激励) by advertising power than by the real consumer needs.

开头段先介绍了背景, 然后把要讨论的话题和自己的观点合并到了一句话里。

Few would deny that advertising heavily influences the consumers' decision-making process as (学过的 linker: 因为) it puts people in touch with the latest products and technology available. With the help of advertising, there are more chances for cutting-edge products like Blu-ray discs and Windows 7 Home Premium to be understood by the target customers (目标客户群). In this sense, advertising creates consumer needs.

第一个主体段提出广告让消费者了解最新的产品与服务, 因此在一定意义上创造了本来并不存在的用户需求。举了 Blu-ray 和 Windows 7 的例子。

Further, advertising contributes to the growth of popularity and trustworthiness of brands. Take **TV advertising** for example. The more commercials **on air**, the better（两个比较级连用的句式） consumers get to know the brands featured in these commercials. Gradually（状语前置）, consumers build up their trust in these brands and will, consequently, purchase more of the products. Even more importantly, people tend to adjust their demand after viewing advertisements, which is precisely why some ads highlight inferior（不如别人或别的事物好的） aspects of the target consumers. An example that aptly illustrates this point would be **the marketing strategy of Vichy, which exposes（暴露） some of women's skin flaws in its advertising, followed by solutions that Vichy offers to remedy the imperfections（不完美）.**

主体第二段提出广告提升产品的可信度，而且还让一些消费者认为自身存在缺陷。这些始终都是紧紧围绕"广告促使消费者购买自己并不需要的产品"来展开的，而且两个理由后面都跟了支持句。举了化妆品的例子。

Meanwhile, people are truly able to discover their own needs and to satisfy themselves even without being informed by advertisements. Humans are born with the natural desire to lead a better life（长短句结合，这里用个短的）. Apart from the basic necessities（状语前置）, we tend to search for what our peers（Day 4 也讲过的词：同龄人，同辈） own and try to possess those things if we have the purchasing power（购买力）. Also, customers' social status（学过：社会地位） matters（≈counts） when they make purchase decisions（又是一个短句，这个 purchase 作名词）. People prefer to own things matching their status（连续第二个短句，好文章真的不需要每句话都是长句，虚虚实实才够内行）. For instance, in the U. S. , the wealthy（the + 形容词，指一类人） are more likely to buy luxury cars such as Jaguars, Mercedes or Porsches as their private vehicles, even if they are not exposed to any related advertising.

本段是让步段，承认消费者有一定的选择能力，举了些好车的例子。虽然让步段写了两个理由，但总体上看，全文对第一、第二个主体段的论证还是明显比让步段中的论证更强势。

Overall（总体上来看，折中式结尾常见的副词）, I believe advertising plays a critical role in creating profitability for companies, which has been empirically proven（已经生活实践证明了） by the ever-increasing marketing and sales budgets（预算） in most industries. Although some people do recognize their needs, this recognition may be modified or reversed（Day 4 讲过：逆转） by effective advertising, and thus is not the main driving force（172 句里的） behind the high sales of consumer goods.

这里用了以理服人、比较温和的家长式结尾，提出消费者的需求确实会受到广告宣传的调整甚至转变，倾向前两个主体段观点的态度依然非常明确。

致"反动派"们的一封信

（适合基础薄弱或者备考时间极短的"小白"们）

虽然 Pat 已经一再大声疾呼："与 GRE Issue 或者 IELTS Writing 这些偏重学术风格的作文考试不同，新托福写作这类生活化风格的作文考试真的不需要用模板，踏踏实实地提高自己遣词造句的能力并真正理解托福作文的逻辑结构才是唯一万能的备考方法。"但彻底改变顽固分子的想法应该也不是那么容易的，否则世界上就不会有"反动派"（reactionaries）这个词了。

Fair enough.

如果您铁了心要用模板，那么至少请确保下面三点：

（1）模板里一定不要充满惊天地泣鬼神的大词或者让考官读到三分之二就已经窒息身亡的长难句，模板难度必须是和你自己的用词造句水平接近的。模板（Templates）只能当小菜儿，但不能当主食。你想想：如果两口子吃的小菜儿都是法式焗蜗牛，主食吃的却是烙饼卷大葱，吃不到一半俩人就得离吧？考官看作文也是一样：只有你的模板和你填的内容能衔接起来，才能不被发现；

（2）不要用超长无敌模板。最"万能"的模板也一定是最容易跑题的模板，因为它排除了一切其他的可能性。应该把模板看成一种逻辑结构而不是凑字工具，这样才能在遇到不同题型时适当作出调整，去适应具体题目的要求；

（3）力争确保模板里的英文没错误。基础薄弱的同学考前至少应该把自己的模板给英语功底好的朋友或者老师看看，改一改语法和词句。

下面 Pat 给那部分不用模板怎么也写不出作文的朋友们设计了一些句子，供你在修改自己模板的时候参考。唯一目的是帮大家更深入地体会作文的逻辑结构。

新托福作文模板工具箱

◎ 一边倒和折中式作文的开头段都适用的句型

（a）Describing the General Background 开头段介绍背景

It's widely / commonly / extensively / generally accepted that... (accepted: believed / recognized / acknowledged)

It's generally arguable that... (请特别注意这句话的意思很容易被误解，它并不是"引起争论的"，而是"It's probably true that..."的意思)

e. g. It is arguable that the organization has failed in this regard.

We are all agreed that... (固定用法：If two or more people are agreed, they have the same opinion.)

It's a well-known fact that...

It's popular/common belief that...

另外，如果要在背景中表示"在当代"：

At present，/ Currently，/ In this day and age (固定习语) / In present-day society，/ These days，/ In today's society，/ In the present age，以及各位早就耳熟能详的 In contemporary society 和 nowadays (后两个已被国内考生严重透支，不推荐在应试时使用)

(b) Expressing Optimism / Approval 开头段表达乐观或认可

... has revolutionized / transformed / fundamentally changed our lives.

... is advancing / progressing by leaps and bounds. (这里 progress 作 *vi.*)

... plays an increasingly important / significant role in...

... continues to advance at a staggering / an astonishing rate.

The progress / The progression in... has enabled us to...

... has assumed /played an increasingly essential role in...

With the immense world shrinking (收缩) into a tiny village, ...

Today the... (communication / exchange) has been intensified.

The impact of... on... has been massive indeed.

Gone are the days when... 意思是：……的日子已经一去不复返了。

(c) Expressing Concern 开头段表达担忧

The issue of... is increasingly disturbing / worrying / worrisome / severe.

... has been deteriorating at an alarming rate.

One of the most pressing issue of our time is...

The issue of... has drawn widespread attention.

... are increasingly prevalent / ... are increasingly pervasive. (有时也可以用于积极方面)

... is having profound impact / repercussions / implications on... (有时也可以用于积极方面)

With..., the problem of... has been thrown into sharp relief. (这里的 relief 指 "突出的位置")

The swift changes in... have brought the issue of... into sharp focus.

Today, there are a multitude of competing claims on the limited resources of...

With the incidence (发生率) of... hovering at high levels, many people have become alarmed (警觉的).

The incidence of... has been on the rise.

... is, doubtless, the predominant... in today's world and its ascendancy has sparked off much discussion and debate.

As an inevitable consequence of... (作为……的不可避免的结果), ……

The proliferation (扩散) of... has rendered many citizens apprehensive (担惊受怕的) / fearful.

People tend to... when asked about...

(d) Introducing the Topic 开头段用来引出讨论的话题

The debate over whether... has been raging for some time.

People remain divided over whether...

people are divided over whether...

There is no consensus on whether... yet.

Whether... is an issue open to debate.

Whether... is a boon or bane is still open to debate. (a boon or bane: bane 前一般不再加 a, 美国习惯用语 "是好事还是坏事", 类似 a blessing or a curse, 但注意 curse 前的 a 则一般不能省略)

The issue of whether... has triggered intense debate.

The issue of whether... has caused quite a stir.

Whether... has been a highly debatable issue.

Whether... has aroused heated debate.

These days, public debate has been going on over whether...

One of the most bitterly-contested disputes has been about whether...

When it comes to…, people tend to hold different views.

One of the lasting public controversies in my country is the one concerning whether…

One of the most enduring public controversies in my country is the one regarding whether…

There has been much discussion revolving around the issue of whether…

Today, an issue that has given rise to much debate is whether…

People tend to have mixed opinions on…

There have been mixed reactions to…

There has been mixed response to… (注意这里的 response 一般不加复数)

◎ 仅限一边倒文章使用的开头段句型

（a）Expressing Agreement　表达同意

I tend to agree with…

I think that's a valid point.

I entirely agree with…

I'm in favor of…

I tend to agree with… and I would go further and say…

Personally, I think their view has considerable merit.

think / believe /say /argue / maintain/contend/ assert/ insist/ aver (语气很强) / claim…

（b）Expressing Disagreement　表达不同意

I'm afraid I can't agree with…

I don't share their point of view.

I can't go along with…

I don't think that ideas will work.

It seems to me that there may be other possibilities.

I'm afraid I had different experiences.

I would say the exact opposite.

◎ 多用于折中式作文的开头段词句

（a）Expressing Choice　在开头段表达自己在两方中倾向哪一方

be in favor (*n.*) of / favor (*vt.*) / side (*vi.*) with / incline toward / tend to support 这些词组都是"倾向于……"的意思。

the former view 前者的观点/ the latter view 后者的观点

(b) Only Expressing Partial Agreement　表达部分同意

Theoretically, that may be true. But in reality, …

That may be true to a certain extent, but we also have to consider…

That might have been the case once (曾经), but now…

As I see it, there is more to it than that.

They may have a point there, but…

I admit there's an element of truth in… (an argument).

Personally, I agree with their view, but I would qualify it to some extent. (Here qualify means

limit the strength or meaning of a statement.)

Speaking for myself, I agree with their proposition, with certain qualifications.

I can agree with their view, but with reservations.

(c) Casting doubt　(表示主要反对)

What if…?

I would say this does not sound very convincing because…

Nevertheless, one apparent problem with this view is that…

Personally, I would say that actually depends on…

Even so, it can be argued that…

People don't necessarily…

It shouldn't be overlooked, though, …

However, I have to emphasize the fact that…

That isn't strictly true.

That's not always the case.

That's highly debatable.

That's highly unlikely.

I think their view is only partly/partially true.

Personally, I find this view ill-founded.

I think this view is specious at best.

I think this view overlooks some important factors of this issue.

I think their view is overly simplistic.

I think their view is overgeneralized.

I find their view unconvincing (or unpersuasive/problematic/somewhat) untenable.

I think their view amounts to an oversimplification.

○ 一边倒和折中式作文的主体段都适用的句型和路标词：

（a）First, … / First of all, / To begin with, … / To start with, … / To start off with, … / In the first place, …

（b）Second, … / Also, (这个最简单，但也最特别，因为别的考生们已经都去追求"最长"的词了☺) / In the second place, … / … as well. / …, too. / Further, … (如果只为了考试实战，那么在 Further 和 Furthermore 之间宁可选择 Further，因为可以少打四个字母，还可以减少跟别人重复) / Furthermore, … / Moreover, … / Aside from… / Apart from… / In addition to…/ Besides… （除……之外）

注意：Besides 也可以不跟宾语而直接加逗号。上面的表达大家最多用熟其中的两三个就足够了。

（c）下面的副词或者词组也都可以在一边倒或者折中式作文中引出主体段。它们的优点是都具体摆明了该段会从哪一个视角来论证问题：

Intellectually（从头脑与知识的角度来看），… **请比较**：Psychologically（从心理的角度来看），Academically， = From an academic viewpoint（从学术或者学习的角度来看），

反义：On a more day-to-day level,（从更日常的角度来看）……

Socially（从社会角度来看），… = From a social perspective（从社会的角度来看），……

Economically（从经济的角度来看），…≈Financially（从金融或者资金的角度来看），……

Professionally（从职业的角度来看）， = From a professional standpoint, …

Personally（就个人生活而言） = From a personal angle, … / Our own experience has revealed that…

（d）下面的句型或者副词也可以用来引出主体段，特点是比较强势，相应的紧接着的主体段的理由句和支持句也应该力争写出说服力，支持句多用些 linkers

It's clear that... = Clearly, ...

It's obvious that... = Obviously, ...

It's apparent that... = Apparently, ...

It's evident that... = Evidently, ...

It's manifest that...（用得比较少）

It's self-evident that...（用得更少）

Convincing /Compelling（有说服力的）arguments can be made that...

○ 仅适合"一边倒"主体段开头使用的词汇或者词组

Third，/ Finally，/ Lastly，...

Above all，/ Most importantly，这两个可以放在第三个主体段的开头，表示这一段要论证最重要的一个理由。

Additionally，/ In addition... 如果第三个主体段只是补充说明，就可以用它们来开头。

下面的几个句子也可以用来引出"一边倒"文章的主体段，它们的优点主要是可以在三个主体段间形成一种鲜明的秩序感：

① The chief / principal /primary / first and foremost / main reason for... is ...

② A second / Another factor that should be taken into account is... 也比较具体（这里一般还不用 The second...）或者 Another point that we should not overlook is... / An even more important aspect of the issue is... / Another argument in support of my view is...

③ A third / Yet another thing we should consider is...（这里的 Yet 不是转折，而是递进）或者 A third argument that we should not neglect is... / The most significant aspect of this issue is...

○ 多用于折中式让步段的词汇或句型

（a）Expressing Concession 表达让步

Admittedly，/ Granted，/ To be sure，/ Undeniably，/ Indisputably，/ Of course，/ Certainly... 后面几个听起来貌似挺强硬的，其实在新托福议论文中还是用来放在让步段开头引出让步段。

I concede（承认）that...

I recognize that...

It may be tempting to argue that...

It may be true that...

This is reasonable to the extent that...

This is valid insofar as...

This argument has considerable merit in that...

　（b）Expressing Rebuttal　用来引出让步段内后部的反驳让步段观点的部分

Nevertheless, ...

Nonetheless, ...

However, ...

Yet / But... （一般直接跟后面的句子，不加逗号）

Still, ...

Despite that, ...

But closer examination would reveal that...

But further analysis would make it clear that...

Having said this, however, ...

◎ 一边倒和折中式作文的结尾段开始处都可以使用的词汇与句型

In conclusion, / In summary/ To sum up/ In sum/ In the final analysis/ Based on the arguments offered above/ On the basis of the above discussion/ Accordingly, / Hence, / Thus, / Therefore,

　※ 不鼓励国内同学再使用 In a nutshell，本来它是一个挺轻松的偏口语化表达，但被太多人用过之后却显得异常沉重。至于 All in all，更是早在通货膨胀之后就严重贬值了。

◎ 通常只用于一边倒作文结尾段的开头

For these reasons, ... / Based on all these arguments, ...

◎ 通常只用于折中式结尾段开头的词句

On balance / Overall / Having considered all the arguments above, ...

今天的最后还是要跟大家再次强调：模板只是一个逻辑框架，可以用来控制考场中行文的大方向，但如果把它作为凑字数甚至把考官"拿下"的手段，那只能是自我欺骗。只要基础不是太"潮"，备考时间也还够，那么仔细研究新托福作文的核心词汇、linkers 的逻辑关系、172 个加分句型、开头、主体、结尾的结构安排、附录 B 的素材段落等，并积极实践、多练多改，才是对付 TOEFL iBT essays 的"万能模板"。

学有余力

more. headroyce. org/research/writing/argumentation/argmainpage. html

在美国国内，对新托福写作这个层次的 essays 教学研究非常深入，相应的网络资源很多。比如上面这个小网站，虽然并不是针对考试，但对于帮助大家把握美式议论文的结构还是挺有用的。类似的资源在 Internet 上可以用"海量"来形容，大家也可以发挥能动性多找一找，不必追求"高大全"，适合自己的就是最好的。另一方面，美国国内对于 GRE 和 GMAT 等级的议论文研究得则要少得多，而且去读 graduate school 对极度务实的普通美国人来说，跟国内的"考研"完全就是不同性质的两件事。就像本书 Day 1 所说的："新托福作文的关键在语言能力和真情实感，GRE 作文的关键在思维能力和以理服人。"这就是为什么 Pat 建议大家不要在新托福独立写作考试中过度依赖"模板式作文"的道理。

课后练习

Assignment

请大家认真阅读下面的文章，并仔细体会每一段的结构、论证方法和连词。（倒立文字部分为参考答案）

We Americans（Abbreviated version）

G. D. Couts

We Americans are a blend of people from many countries. We have a very short history that can properly be called "American"; therefore, it is hard to find characteristics that apply to all Americans. Nevertheless, we can make some generalizations concerning our main characteristics, including individuality, a combination of idealism and practicality, materialism and a lack of parental influence, all of which permeate our lives.

（permeate：渗透到……的各个角落）

参考答案

。承开庭主"经套族代"，十"武前的转"的题话陪普本

We Americans value individuality. Our country was founded by strong individuals and we do not like to be forced into conformity; thus, we insist on having a great deal of freedom. Interestingly, as a consequence, most Americans use this freedom to behave very much like most other Americans. For instance, early hippies were individualists, but most Americans did not like them. By the same token, we consider ourselves very faithful to the laws of our country but there are few among us who would not break one if it was felt that no harm would be done by doing so, such as by exceeding the speed limit or failing to report informally-received cash on tax forms.

参考答案

。容内不余

正面句的对转长存中，系关充补示表和给上承示表，"子例的" 举、面下了用使

Second, we Americans are both practical and idealistic. We place great value on doing things for ourselves, for this is what our pioneer ancestors were forced to do. As a result, many foreign visitors are so surprised to find that many couples of comfortable means do their own yardwork, their own housework and their own repairs. On the other hand, we are very idealistic: We think we have the best political, social and economic system and we expect everything to go smoothly. Due to our idealism, we are easily disappointed, which is why so many marriages end in divorce — young couples' expectations from marriage are often unrealistically high. Similarly, it helps to explain the dissatisfactions of many young people, and even elderly people, who enjoy one of the highest standards of living in the world.

参考答案

。系关等靠递充补示表和对、比对、折转了用使

A third characteristic of us Americans is that money is more important than fame to us. People work extremely hard but so many, unfortunately, either have little leisure time or do not know how to enjoy it. Why do we have to work so hard then? It is not because we want to achieve greater status or prestige, but simply to have more of the material objects and comfort that money can buy.

参考答案

。系关对的了用使

Finally, our parents have less influence on us than parents do in other countries. Many children are left in day-care centers by their working mothers or with babysitters when their parents go out at night. Further, peer pressure is great because children's feelings and desires are taken very seriously and they are given a lot of freedom to form strong personalities. Then, we leave home at a relatively early age, usually after high school, to take jobs and have our own apartments or to go to college where we are allowed a great deal of freedom. After that, we choose our own spouses, even if our parents object. And, later in life, when our parents are old and helpless, we tend to live far away from them: Many prefer to put them in nursing homes rather than to have the responsibility of caring for them daily.

参考答案

经由连接词的回收使用了 "排例子" 和因果论述。

Foreigners may find this practice of treating parents heartless, and I suppose it is, but like many other qualities we Americans share, it is subject to change over time.

参考答案

"综合式"并融合 "加强论述",结尾 it is subject to 的句型自己经在 Day 7 对大家进行了详述。

超级大木桩上趴着一只后现代主义的wood-pecker。好在新托福的高分作文从来都是用经典逻辑结构就行，官方满分范文没有任何一篇使用了"意识流"的…… ——Pat摄

A Thorough Checklist for the Independent Writing Task

下面的 10 个问题是帮助你检查自己的独立作文是否能达到高分作文要求的 checklist。大家可以在考前每次练习完一篇作文之后都拿它对照一下（当然最好还能找有经验的写作老师帮你修改）。这样在进考场的时候，这些要求你应该都十分熟悉而且可以应用到实战中了。

从本书 Day 1 中你被问到的 10 个问题，到 Day 10 后面的这 10 个核对问题。We've come a long way...

□ Your answer focuses on the topic question.

□ Your main arguments can be easily found.

□ Your introduction is not unbearably long.

□ Your paragraphing is logical.

□ Your linking of ideas is easy to follow.

□ Your range of vocabulary is not too limited. (You don't have to be a walking dictionary, either.)

□ Your use of sentence structures is varied.

□ Your examples can ALWAYS support your ideas.

□ Your errors in grammar are NOT frequent.

□ Your essay is NOT underlength.

Day 10

You Are the Template for My Integrated Writing

那些年，我们一起追的综合写作模板

We had a group called The Citations, but after a while we all had to get jobs, so we couldn't really pursue it.

——Joe Griffo
New York State Senator

平心而论，美国确实是一个充满机遇的地方，即使这两年财力确实不如以前了。R&D 的经费也还是给得很足。Obama 的那句话还是比较符合事实的，"If there's anyone out there who still doubts that America is a place where all things are possible... tonight is your answer." 但同时，美国文化里有很多东西也真是挺表面化的。例如，Frank Gehry 的设计在美国已经火得不行，但他的作品在欧洲却经常被人指责为"外表与功能严重脱节"（incongruity between the exterior and the function）。

Frank Gehry 设计的 MIT Strata Center，Pat 摄

听 起来很像一个 paradox（悖论）：既然是综合的，怎么又会是单一的呢？但这就是新托福的综合写作（Integrated Writing）。

之所以叫综合写作，是因为在形式上看，它采用下面的形式：

The Reading Passage

第一步，考生会被要求先用 3 分钟阅读一篇学术文章（里面肯定有生词，不要奢望每个词都能看懂哈～）。全文都需要泛读，而且重点看开头、主体段每段的第一句，以及主体段内出现的 linkers（联系词）后面紧跟的句子。如果还有结尾段就再扫一眼，但也有一些文章没给结尾段。阅读文章时允许在 scratch paper 上记录关键词或词组（记录时最节省时间而且能减少混乱的方式，就是阅读文章的时候把文章中的 3 个分论点写在 scratch paper 的左侧，而听录音段子的时候把对应的 3 点记在右侧）。

在第一步你的核心任务是：找出这段话中的讨论话题（用 1～2 句话概括），文章的总论点（也用 1～2 句话概括）和 3 个分论点（即用来支持总论点的 3 个理由，肯定是 3 个，真题里从来没有出现过 4 个）。

The Lecture

综合写作考试的第二步中，你会听到一段关于同一话题的大约 2 分钟长的 lecture。说话者会提出对你刚阅读的学术文章里 3 个分论点的态度（而且绝大多数都是对那 3 点的反驳。如果是提出对那 3 点的附和，那么你就可以去买体彩了，甚至可以考虑买福彩……）在这一步，同样允许在 scratch paper 上记录关键词或词组。而且很棒的是：说话人讲的 3 个分论点和相关支持与阅读段落中提出的 3 个分论点在顺序上是一一对应的，从来没有出现过把反驳第一个分论点的理由放到后面或者把反驳后面分论点的理由提到前面来的"杯具"。

Writing the Essay

正式开始写作（打字），这一步要求你用 20 分钟在电脑上完成一篇短文（官方建议的长度是 150～225 字，少了不好，多了时间未必够），介绍刚才讲话的人用哪 3 个理由分别驳斥（或者极少出现的支持）了阅读段落中的 3 个分论点。让人欣慰的是，这时阅读文章仍然在你的屏幕左侧，可以随时参考，但是最好不要参考次数过多，否则速度就慢了。

所以从形式上来看，Integrated Writing Task 确实很综合。特别是听录音的时候，需要大家调动自己通过准备新托福听力而得到提高的听力理解能力和快速记录关键词的能力。

在听录音时可能用到的速记符号	
缩写	**含义**
+	and
/	or
−	except / except for
:)	agree, approve（of）
: (	disagree, be against, disapprove（of）
w/	with
w/o	without
w. m.	which means
∧	表否定、转折或让步这类接近的含义 = no, not, doesn't, isn't, however, but, yet, nevertheless, even so
N/A	本来指 not applicable，但综合写作中可以用来指 nothing
abt	about
cuz	because
n/t	next
=	is, are, means, refers to
≠	is different from（其实在美国更多的时候说 be different than）
→	leads to, causes, results in, shows, represents
←	comes from, is a result of, is a consequence of
#	number
@	at
e. g. （如果时间太紧张连这两个点也可以去掉，一切为实战服务）	for example
btw	between / by the way

☆　　☆　　☆

　　而说综合写作是单一的原因也很简单：与独立写作的"自圆其说"主观性写作相反，综合写作则是纯客观性写作，不要用 I 或者 me（是的，坚决不要用！*The Official Guide* 在介绍综合写作时明确指出：*Remember that you are NOT being asked for your opinions.* 而至于 *we*，虽然严格来说不能算错，但如果能避免最好还是避免，除非你非要强烈暗示考官"偶是菜鸟"）。

过去的老托福是没有综合写作部分的。非常明显，ETS 之所以要添加综合写作，目的就是针对很多美国大学对老托福提出的"高分低能"现象做出纠正，让 TOEFL iBT Writing Test 能更好地反映考生在进入美国大学之后的实际语言应用能力会怎样，所以综合写作的全过程其实酷似上课的过程：好孩子在课前一般都先要读一下课本或者资料的相关章节"预习"一下，然后去教室听老师讲课，最后把自己所学到的知识，通过写作业或者是写论文应用出来，这个学习过程跟综合写作的三步是完全吻合的。

但国内考生往往不理解的是：Integrated Writing 最核心的目的还不是这些，而是要考查：

两种"特美国"的能力

（1）summarization skills（概括能力）。凡在美国读过书的人，特别是上过 graduate school 的人都会深有体会：快速把握核心信息的能力在美国实在是学术生存的关键。不论是恐怖的 reading list，还是课前发的充斥着 awe-inspiring words 的 handouts，再或者 seminars 前的准备工作……一切都在逼着人去 summarize everything。在美国 "Get down to the nitty-gritty." 完全是想顺利毕业而不被中途累死必备的大学求生法则，这与你是否刻苦无关；

（2）Citation Skills（引证能力）。这种技能有一点接近 paraphrase，但不同之处在于：citation 是有着强烈目的性的 paraphrase，是为了让文章更充实、更连贯而做出的有严密选择的改写。

写论文的时候，不管你的教授是指定 APA，MLA 还是其他的 format（格式），除了 bibliography/references（参考文献）在文章后面或者书后必须出现之外，文章中的 citation&quo-tation（间接转述和直接引用）也是 crediting resources 的重要形式。新托福考生需要特别注意的是：虽然这两种引用形式在美国大学中都极度常见，但在综合写作考试中却只允许 citation，而不允许 quotation。如果照抄阅读原文中的 6 个或者更多连续单词，一般来说就算是违反考试要求的 quotation（原文直接引用）了。但如果是通过明显地改变原句表达方式或者浓缩、提炼核心意思去改写原文，那么就还算是遵纪守法的 citation。还有，如果仅使用阅读文章里的 1~5 个连续非关键单词一般也还是可以算 citation 的。特别是对于比较生僻的专业术语来说，少量的直接引用更是合理合法的（对听力段子里的直接引用倒不是大问题，而且即使真想大段照搬听到的内容也很难实现，除非我们的大脑拥有复读机功能）。

正是由于综合写作的本质就是对上述两种学术技能的测试，考生在 20 分钟里只能选择就事论事，进行"忘我地"客观概述与引证，才决定了最优秀的 Integrated Writing 反而是"单向"的写作。

☆　　　☆　　　☆

写好新托福综合作文的核心是要注意：一种文，两类人，三重门。

◆　**一种文**　　内行其实一眼就可以看出来：新托福综合写作，在一定意义上就是 GRE Argument 的初级版！只不过 Argument 作文是要作者自己去发现错误，并且自己进行论证，思维难度要大得多。而新托福作文主要是语言能力测试，所以是由听力段子告诉考生错误在哪里，让考生转述出来。因此，对于想冲击新托福综合写作高分的筒子们来说，其实 GRE 的 200 多道"阿狗"题是非常难得地训练自己给人挑逻辑毛病能力的好素材。

◆　**两类人**　　想写好综合作文，还必须看清两类人：写阅读文章的人和讲听力段子的人。考前就必须要非常熟练地掌握他们/她们各自的英语称呼，否则到考场里很容易写混。

(a) 对阅读文章（或者写阅读文章的人）的称呼：the reading passage / the reading / the brief reading passage 都可以。或者指人也可以，那就叫 the author of the reading passage 了。但请注意：严格来讲，阅读段子不能只简称为 the passage，因为听力段子其实也可以叫做 the listening passage；

(b) 称呼听力段子或者讲话人的方式也很多，比如指讲话者：the professor, the instructor, the speaker, the lecturer, the presenter。事实上 instructor 和 lecturer 都是美国大学里的两种初级职称，但在 Integrated Writing 里都可以用来指讲话的那个人。指听力段子：the lecture, the speech, the professor's talk（注意 talk 未必一定是 conversation，在美语里很多时候 talk 就是 speech 的意思），the presentation（北美大学里也常常把类似的学术报告称为 presentation）。

◆　**三重门**　　是指各位同学们要写好综合作文必须跨过的三个"坎儿"：

(a) 一定一定一定要看清阅读文章里讨论的总体话题到底是关于什么的。阅读文章里的 overall topic 跟听力段子里的 overall topic 是一致的，所以在听录音的时候还可以再确认一次，当然也可以在 scratch paper 上作简要记录；

(b) 特别注意 reading passage 和 lecture 中的逻辑关系词，因为它们前后的信息往往是你的加分武器（高分考生还可以参考今天最后的大表格）；

(c) 写综合作文的时候一定别忘了语法问题。Pat 在北京的时候见过很多孩子准备的"综合写作秘制模板"，甚至还亲眼见过一个同学从书包里把他的模板和一卷卫生纸一起掏了出来，可见模板在大家的心目中有多重要。可惜仔细一看，模板里的英文多数都有明显的语法错误或者用词错误。高深的错误不谈，但至少请大家一定要确保写的是成分完整的句子，绝不能只是把一个词组或者几个单词就当成一句话。本书前面独立写作部分讲过的大量 linkers，照样可以在综合写作里用来拿分。

另外还要提示大家两个拿高分的秘诀：一是综合写作是客观性学术写作，文风和独立写作是明显不同的，一定要避免缩写：高分的综合作文一般都不用缩写，因为这是美国大学中学术写作的基本要求。比如 don't 就必须拆开写成 do not；二是综合写作中不要出现 I，me，you，we 和 us 这类主观词。其实在北美近几年来的趋势是大学论文里也开始逐渐能见到 I 这类词了，但新托福综合写作中我们还是最好避免。

Integrated Writing 的结构与怎样编写个性化模板

由于和独立写作性质不同，综合写作的结构相对比较单调（但换句话说也就是更严谨）：一般都是开头交待 overall topic/subject（总的话题）和 central argument/thesis（总论点）。而主体最清晰的写法是写 3 段，分别用 professor 的三个分论点及其支持句去批驳阅读文章里的三个分论点。结尾段按照官方范文的标准是允许省略的，如果打算写的话，也就是再重申一下 professor 的话确实有道理。

相应地，由于新托福综合写作的逻辑结构比较固定，所以建议大家最好不要在考场里"突发奇想"。Integrated Writing 考试的重点本来就不是考查学生的思维独特性，而是重点考查 citation 和 summarization 的学术能力。也正是由于它的逻辑结构相对固定，所以与独立写作正相反，Pat 非常建议大家考前认真准备一个综合写作结构模板，为考场里集中精力看文章、听录音和准确建立反驳关系留出宝贵的时间。不过当然，理解了文章逻辑结构之后自己编写出来的个性化模板才是最好的模板。

大体来说，好的综合写作模板有三个原则：

（a）逻辑必须严密，这是最首要的要求。好的模板应该每句话之间有合理的承接顺序和紧密的衔接关系，并且能帮助考生把阅读和听力段子里自己能大致理解的部分充分展示给考官；

（b）但同时，模板逻辑也不要太"绕"，否则在考场里有忙中出错的可能。填写综合写作模板需要一遍成功，如果中途发现逻辑填乱了再去改，将会对考生的心理甚至生理造成巨大压力；

（c）字数不宜过多，否则肯定有废话；当然字数也不宜太少，否则……那就不叫模板了。

下面的综合写作模板逻辑很严密，而且内容也比较好填，还提供了大量同义词替换，供同学们在准备自己的个性化模板时参考：

第❶段 The reading passage explores the issue of... The professor's lecture deals with the same issue. However, he/she thinks that..., which contradicts what the reading states. And in the lecture, he/she uses three specific points to support his/her idea.

第❷段 First, even though the reading passage suggests that..., the professor argues in the lecture that... This is because..., which means... Obviously, the professor's argument disproves its counterpart in the reading.

第❸段 Moreover, despite the statement in the reading that..., the professor contends that... Then he/she supports this point with the fact that... In other words, ...

第❹段 Finally, the professor asserts that... whereas the author of the reading claims that... The professor proves that this claim is indefensible by pointing out that — i. e. , ...

第❺段 In conclusion, the professor clearly identifies the weaknesses in the reading passage and convincingly shows that the central argument in the reading, — that is, ... is incorrect.

综合写作模板之解构版

开头段

The reading passage explores the issue of（of 后面转述总的讨论话题，语法上需要填名词、名词短语或者 how / what / whether / why 引导的从句）. The professor's lecture deals with the same issue. However, he/she（请注意你只能根据说话人的声音在这两个性别间选一个）thinks that（这里填入"叫兽"关于讨论话题的总论点）, which contradicts what the reading states. And in the lecture, he/she（这里当然也只能选择一个代词）uses three specific points to support his/her（仍然只能选一个）idea.

主体段 1

First, even though the reading passage suggests that（此处转述阅读段落中的第一个分论点，后面如果还跟有支持的句子也不妨从阅读段落里再转述一两句支持句过来，拿分啊）, the professor argues in the lecture that（"叫兽"的第一个反驳分论点）. This is because（转述 professor 第一个分论点后面的支持句）, which means（最好能再深入写半句 professor 对其第一个分论点的支持句，但如果实在写不出了，就把前半句再转述一下）. Obviously, the professor's argument disproves（v. 证明……不正确，学术写作中的常见词，不过生活里不太常用）its counterpart（对应物，这里就是指 reading 中的第一个分论点）in the reading.

主体段 2

Moreover, contrary to the statement in the reading that（转述阅读段子里的第二个分论点，如果后面还能从段子里转述过来一两句引申最好）, the professor contends that（转述"叫兽"的第二个反驳分论点）Then he/she supports this point with the fact that（professor 对其第二个分论点的支持句）In other words,（继续转述）

主体段 3

Finally, the professor asserts that（转述第三个反驳分论点）whereas the author of the reading claims that（转述阅读文章作者的第三个分论点）. The professor proves that this claim is indefensible by pointing out that（"叫兽"第三个分论点的支持句）— i. e.,（如果这里能再引申 1~2 句就非常棒了，但实在填不出那就结束，应该字数也够了）

结尾段（这段也可以选择不写）

In conclusion, the professor clearly identifies（*v.* 确定）the weaknesses（*n.* 弱点）in the reading passage and convincingly shows that the central argument in the reading，— that is,（转述阅读文章对讨论话题的总论点）is incorrect.

综合写作模板同义词替换全集

大家还可以用下面的同义词去替换自己模板里的表达，以形成专属于你自己的个性化模板。如果能在理解了综合作文逻辑结构的基础上参考下面的加分词，"磨"出一个最适合你自己的版本，那就真万无一失了。

---

explores:

analyzes, examines, deals with, is concerned with, is about, focuses on, concentrates on, investigates（这个词在学术写作中往往不是"调查"，而是"深入研究"）

issue:

subject, topic

professor:

lecturer, speaker, instructor, the presenter

lecture:

speech, talk, the listening passage, the presentation

deals with:

analyzes, examines, explores, is concerned with, is about, focuses on, concentrates on, investigates

However:

But / Yet / Even so, / Despite that,

---

thinks:

believes, argues, asserts, claims, contends, maintains（这个词比较大，但在写 citation 或者 quotation 时常能见到）, insists, states, indicates，另外还有两个意思类似的词 note 和 remark，不过它们虽然在新闻报道引用中很常用，但在学术论文中引用时并不太常见

contradicts:

challenges, directly contradicts, clashes with, conflicts with（在这里是 vi.）, denies, opposes, is opposed to, runs counter to, is exactly the opposite of, is precisely the opposite of, makes… seem weak, makes… seem incorrect, makes… seem inaccurate, makes… seem wrong, proves that… is specious, makes… seem dubious, makes… seem doubtful, raises doubts about, puts… in doubt, throws… into doubt

states:

见前面 thinks 的替换选择

use three specific points:

makes three specific points, uses ample evidence, offers plenty of evidence, presents sufficient evidence, provides some compelling arguments, shows enough evidence / reveals three pieces of evidence

support

confirm / back（在这里是 vt.） / back up / buttress / strengthen / bolster / advocate

idea:

view, opinion, viewpoint, point of view, understanding, perspective, conception, notion, belief, position

First:

可以用独立写作讲过的那一堆"首先"的同义词去替换

even though:

although, while, whereas（虽然后面两个词是对比关系，但填入这句话中也完全符合逻辑）

because:

due to（但注意如果改成这个，那后面就只能直接跟名词而不能直接跟从句了，具体语法请看 Day 5，还有很多表示"因为"的 linkers，但注意语法首先必须正确才行，否则宁可不换）

… which means…:

… which suggests that… / and this means that… / — that is to say, … / — i. e., / In other words, / Specifically,（但如果用这后两个替换就要断句，前面改为句号）

Obviously:

Apparently, Evidently, Clearly, (更多替换形式还可以参考 Day 9 结尾处)

disprove:

见上文 contradict 的替换词

Moreover:

替换方式见独立写作部分（Day 8 和 Day 9）

contrary to:

in opposition to, in sharp contrast to, in stark contrast to, in marked contrast to, in noticeable contrast to, despite, in spite of

contends:

见上文 thinks 的替换

Finally,:

替换方式请看独立写作部分（Day 8 和 Day 9）

asserts:

替换方式请看上文 thinks 替代

whereas:

while / In contrast, (但如果这么换这里就必须改用句号形成断句) / even though / although

proves:

shows, confirm, verifies

indefensible:

very weak, specious, spurious

In conclusion,:

这个大家太熟悉了，替换方式请看独立写作的 Day 9 结尾部分

clearly:

请注意这个 clearly 的意思并不是 "显然地"，而是 "清晰地"，所以同义词不要再用上面的 obviously 那些替换了，而要用 precisely, exactly, correctly 等替换

identifies:

finds, determines, pinpoints, ascertains, discovers, discerns weaknesses:

flaws, weak links, 另外当然 problems 在这里也可以用来指阅读段子里的论证失误

convincingly:

compellingly, forcefully, successfully, impressively

show:

prove, reveal

central argument:

fundamental argument, main idea, main argument, main point

incorrect:

inaccurate, wrong, indefensible, inadequate, specious at best（这里的 at best 很像中文的 "充其量也就是……"）, unconvincing

注:

(a) 如果指听力段子时主语不打算用 The professor's lecture，而改为用人称作主语，比如 The professor/ The lecturer 等，那么后面也可以用 … talks about / … delivers a lecture about… 等的表示说话人的动作的句型来引出讨论话题。切记：一个好的模板中前后逻辑和语意的一致是编写个性化模板时的首要任务。

(b) 另外，像下面这些句型在综合作文里也都十分常见，希望大家多注意积累。而且这些句式大家来北美读书的时候都还是经常会用到的，掌握它们不会是浪费时间。

… offers the ideas that…

According to the professor, …

… brings up the issue of …

… raise the issue of…

It is said in the lecture that…

Based on these reasons, …

… differ with sb. / … differ on sth. …

… disagree with sb.

… argues against sb.

The lecturer does not subscribe to the idea of … （注意这里的 subscribe to 并不是订阅杂志，而是正式写作中的 "赞成某种观点"，而加上 does not 就是不赞成了）

… have differing views on sth. …

… have divergent views on…

… have conflicting views on…

… have contrasting views on…

… don't match.

… is at odds with…（略显不正式）

The professor's counterargument to/ rebuttal to / objection to…（对……的反驳）

The presenter expands on / elaborates on this point（对某一点进行详述）by saying that…

The speaker stresses / emphasizes / high-lights（强调）the fact that…

（c）过去极少数综合写作考题的 lecture 中曾出现听力段子对阅读原文的少量内容持部分支持态度的情况。如果真的出现了这种"整体反对，但局部承认"的极端特例，那么除了承认自己 RP 还不够需要继续积累之外，还可以在结尾段中的"In conclusion,"之后加入这样一句话：Even though the professor admits in his/her（选一个）speech that the ideas in the reading passage have some positive attributes, such as … and …, overall, … 后面仍然接我们的模板中结尾段后面的内容就好了。

The Devil Is in the Details（高分内容）

这个标题是美语里很有名的一句 proverb。这句话其实对于在综合写作中夺取高分还挺关键的：好的模板确实可以保证综合作文的逻辑通顺，字数也会够。但是如果真想拿到 top-tier 的分数，那么对 lecture 和 reading passage 里面论证细节的把握，包括对两方，特别是对听力段子里分论点后面的支持理由的进一步深入和具体化、数据、例子的大致描述（不用太精确），以及积极调动在独立写作部分学过的 linkers，将明确地告诉考官你对听力和阅读信息的理解高于普通考生，并充分展现出你写学术复杂句的能力（当然也不用全文转述，只是适当深入一些细节就好了）。

下面这个表格里的单词和词组前后很可能会出现细节或者其他关键信息：

提示逻辑顺序的路标词	
First of all, …	First, …
Second, …	Also, …
Besides, …	Furthermore, …
Moreover, …	Another（reason 等）…
In addition to…	Finally, …
… and by the way, …	
提示存在因果关系	
…, because…	Since…, …
… so…	Consequently, …
… and, ultimately, …	… so that…
… so… that…	

后面肯定跟某个人的理论	
According to…,	In…'s theory,
In…'s view, …	

后面肯定是超级细节	
（极度精密的细节虽然并不是考生必须复述的，但是如果能准确地写出来一般都是加分点，比如78%，3-5 years，1939等）	
… which we call… 后跟专业名词（如果不会拼写一般都可以在阅读段子中找到）	… that… / … where… / … who… 定语从句，后面跟的肯定也是细节
The fact that… is further evidence of…	We may find that…
This suggests that…	…, which means…
And that means that…	…, … in which…
（听力段子中）I mean… 后跟细节	（听力段子中）…, I mean… 之前是细节
And what about…? 问题后面会是细节	Why do…? 问题后面也会是细节
Can you guess…? 问题后面也会是细节	When we…, …
New…	Old…
… in the past…	Now…
The best…	The worst…
形容词比较级比如 greater / more quickly / less stress 等	advantages…
disadvantages…	Sometimes…
… is more likely to… 更有可能去……	… not only…, but also…
… not merely… / but… as well.	In effect, … 实质上……
… essentially… 本质上……	… will no doubt…
virtually / almost	every / each / all

后面跟的肯定是例子	
In the case of…	For example, …
, … including…	（lecture中的）Let's say… （后跟假设性例子）

后面肯定跟的是对比或者转折

... whereas...	... while...
However, ...	But...
On the other hand, ...	

后面肯定跟让步

Although..., ...	Still, ...
Even though..., ...	Even if..., ...
In any case, ... / At any rate, ...（在任何情况下）	

后面跟的肯定是替代

Instead, ...	Rather than..., ...
... instead of... / Instead of..., ...	In other words, ... 后面跟转述
In a sense, ... 后面跟更具体一点的转述	... namely,（也就是）...
By that I mean...	

后面跟的肯定是某种结果或者原因

... lead to...	... cause...
... give rise to...	... create...
... generate...	... result in...
... arise from... / ... result from...	

学有余力

mitworld. mit. edu/

　　Integrated Writing 的实质就是考查学生快速概括学术信息并且对其转述后再加以应用的能力的过程。所以，如果能通过经常到 MIT 去听课来准备新托福综合写作应该是很不错的选择吧？当然，除非听到的 lecture 的内容正好和你的专业相关，否则你的目的应该仅仅是准备新托福，不要陷入专业知识的纠结当中去。练习的方法是：每听 2~3 分钟后就 pause 一下，然后在纸上自己写 summary（不必过多纠缠于专业生词），然后再听一遍 lecture，核对自己的正

确率。经常做这样的练习，不但会让你对新托福综合写作的准备相当充分，而且到北美之后的
第一堂课你也将能听得兴趣盎然。

已经记不清曾多少次从这里飞过，一个即使在盛
夏也是被冰川覆盖的地方。但每次飞越Alaska的
时候依然会感到震撼，而且确实能看出那些冰川
正在减少。中美间的无数航班每天都从这里跨越，
承载着一批又一批寻梦的人们。

——Pat，2011年1月12日

附 录

Appendix A-H

附录 A　美国考官喜欢看什么样的例子

附录 B　新托福写作中的偏题、难题原创素材库

附录 C　新老作文话题总 PK（上）

附录 D　新老作文话题总 PK（下）

附录 E　北美在行动

附录 F　新托福写作 211 同义词重点替换词全集

附录 G　名人眼中的新托福写作

附录 H　新托福写作常用备考网站

附录 A
美国考官喜欢看什么样的例子

州终于破产了！当年施瓦辛格以 GOP 党员身份，在曾经一直是 Democrats 天下的加州击败身为州财政厅长的对手，早已为后来的加州政治与经济问题埋下了无数隐患。虽然曾经赢得 body-building contest 的冠军称号，并被粉丝亲切地称为 "Arnold Strong"，这个顶级肌肉男也无法再挽回 California has gone broke. 的悲壮局面。

把这个例子用在去年底的新托福作文题： *Good clothing and appearance are more important to success than good ideas.* 中作为反驳的论据怎么样，够酷吧？

在这个附录中咱们就来看看到底怎样才能举出纯正"美国味儿"的例子。

妙手举例子

关于模板，有一句精辟到骨髓的话："其实世上本没有模板，用的人多了，也就成了模板。"

其实作文里举例子又何尝不是如此呢？

Galileo，Copernicus，James Watt，Thomas Edison，JFK，FDR，the Watergate scandal，the Chernobyl disaster，Mother Teresa，Nelson Mandela，Pavlov's research on the reflex system 以及 the Boston Tea Party 等等，本来都是伟大的作文例子。但是当 GT 前辈们群起而用之、这些伟大的例子一再地被当成大白菜甩向考官的时候，如果你再扔同类诱饵，考官们得到的将不再是惊喜，而是惊慌甚至惊恐。

举例子 ≥ For example

很多同学一想到举例就自然地把 For example 摆出来，当然这两个词没错，而且很常用，但举例的手段远远超出这个词组。

A 明例子

最常用的一种举例手段，如有需要就可以把 For example 自然摆出。当然，这两个词没错，甚至就是明确告诉考官："你准备好了，我可要举例了啊。"用来举明例子的标志词有八大金刚，其中前四位长相最普通的反倒是最常登场的。"外貌协会"的会员们不可歧视它们。

1 For example, …

例句： Since the U. S. market was a dominant（统治地位的）force in the world economy, when its financial institutions foundered, its credit markets dried up and its consumers spending shrank, other countries felt the pain, too. For example, in Iceland, the government had to nationalize the country's three biggest banks.

2 For instance, …

例句： Avoiding the virus is by far the best way to prevent the H1N1 flu, but this isn't always possible. Schoolchildren, for instance, can't always hide in a closet while school is in session.

3 like…（稍有点口语化，在学术论文中不要用来举例，但是在新托福写作中大家可以尽情使用，即使满分范文中也随处可见）

例句： Investing in education is a wise long-term investment for everyone. Students who are better educated will be better able to solve problems, like the decline of rainforests.（Kaplan）

4 such as…

例句： Success is normally an indication of human qualities such as intelligence, integrity, ambition and perseverance.

5 Take / Consider… for example. 注意省略号中填入名词或者名词短语

近义句型： To give a specific example, …

6 … is a case in point. 意思是：……是一个恰当的例子

7 This point is best illustrated with the example of… 意思是：这个观点可以用……的例子最有力地证明，注意后面跟名词或者名词短语

8 This point can be confirmed by the example of… 意思是：这个观点可以通过……的例子得到支持，后面也是跟名词或者名词短语

另外有时"明例子"也会有别的"变体"，比如：If JFK was a fresh face in the White House, his successor（继任者），Lyndon B. Johnson, was a classic example of the old school（很美国的一个概念：守旧派）of U. S. politics.

B 暗例子（高分内容）：

这种例子就没有那么直截了当，而是有计划有预谋地默默推出例子。客观来讲，这种举例方法在美式议论文里并不像明例子那么常见，但是一旦能够用好却更拿分。举暗例子常用的

"暗器" 有:

(a) 惯用句型引例子

This is proven by the fact that...

Nowhere is... more evident than in... (……在……中看得再明显不过了)

In some/most cases, ...

... tend to... (……多半会……)

The majority of... (多数……都)

For the most part, ... (ditto)

... largely... (……大部分)

In general, ... (通常来讲,)

Generally, ... (ditto)

请看下面的 "美句":

After the Civil War, most blacks and many whites couldn't afford to buy land of their own, so the new form of sharecropping became the basis of the Southern agricultural economy. But in most cases, the sharecropper had to borrow money to make ends meet (保持日常收支平衡) until the next crop was harvested.

Physical activity can help us get in shape. In general, when we climb a flight of stairs, walk to the store, or play in the courtyard, our health and fitness levels improve.

(b) 巧用 ":" 和 "—" 引例子

请看下例:

And what does writing mean to us today? We're surrounded by writing at every turn. We use it, often unconsciously, in daily activities — in the kitchen, at the job or on the road.

Technology is essential to modern life: Every morning, people wake up to the built-in alarm in their cell phone and then go to work on a bus, in a private car or ride the subway, complete tasks with PCs or laptops during the day and watch cable channels at night.

(c) 巧用动词 "带" 例子

❶ encompass (跨越, 覆盖)

例句: This study encompassed the social, political, economic and cultural aspects of the situation.

❷ involve (涉及)

例句: The new proposal not only involves students, but teachers, parents and school administrators as well.

❸ concern（这里指"关于"，也可以用形容词形式 be concerned with...）

例句： Her new book concerns distribution of welfare and social injustice.

❹ affect（影响）

例句： This plan, when carried out, will affect physicians, nurses and paramedics.

（d）活用介词"串"例子

❶（range）from... to:

接着捧起爆米花看"美句"吧：

例句： In the 19th century, the American ideas about what they should do with the "Indian problem" ranged from complete extermination to setting up reservations to forcing the white culture onto Native Americans.

Humor often stimulates laughter, which covers a wide range, from a belly laugh to a chuckle to a smile.

The development of easier connections, more user-friendly software and cheaper access has opened up the information highway to everyone, from children — both at home and at school — to homemakers to professionals in all fields.

❷ include / including（包括）...

例句： Some American presidents, including Theodore Roosevelt, JFK, Bill Clinton and Barack Obama, took the Oval Office in their forties.

可以看出，这里的 including 已经很接近 such as 的作用了。

例句： Causes of high blood pressure include genetics, eating too much salt, being overweight, drinking excessive amounts of alcohol and certain medications.

（e）不管不顾直接给例子

这种略显"粗暴"的举例手法在新托福高分作文中偶尔也能见到。比如请看下面这个"关于举例的举例"：

例句： In spite of the fact that humor depends on so many variables（age, era, culture, etc.）, many humorous works（作品）do survive the ages. We all know that Shakespeare's romantic comedies are still produced quite often, as are French playwright Moliere's short plays. And of course, our most revered author in America was essentially a humorist, Mark Twain.

下面则是一个"明、暗交织"的相当复杂的例子：

例句： A well-balanced meal will include one portion of protein like meat, fish or chicken, two portions of colored fruit and vegetables and one portion of starch such as bread, rice, pasta, corn or potatoes.

如何挑选新托福作文的例子？

引出例子的手段已经明确，就要提高对美式例子的欣赏水平了。

先请看 the Michigan Guide 给出的满分范文中的一个例子：

The most important languages in the world, and the ones that we should be focusing our attention on, are languages that are dying. For example, Navajo is a Native American language that is dying as Navajo children learn English in order to be successful in the larger U. S. economy and culture. As a result, many Navajo children lose their Navajo, which causes the language to slowly die. （这 4 个蓝色单词或词组都是 Day 5 中我们学过的 linkers）

为什么说这个例子对于新托福作文来说是很成功的呢？因为它有 3 个特点：

1）它是为美国大众所熟知的例子。Navajo 是美国最重要的印第安部落之一，普通的美国人一般都听说过一些关于它的情况，Pat 还认识一个在 ASU 读书的 Navajo 朋友。如果非要把这个例子改成一个很冷僻的南美印第安人部落的例子，虽然意思差不多，但是考官绝对得不到"于我心有戚戚焉"的感受；

2）但同时，它并不属于托福考生人所共知的"大白菜"（a-dime-a-dozen）例子。毕竟对于美国本土以外的考生来说，除了有些上过新托福阅读班可能接触过关于 Navajo 的知识外，一般考生应该是想不到去举这个例子的；

3）它并不只是简单的一笔带过，而是有适当的分析与讨论。很显然，这个例子虽然仅有两句话，却连用 4 个在 Day 5 讲过的 linkers。即使不深入看文字，仅仅从 linkers 的频率也能明显感到其逻辑论证有一定的复杂程度。

分析完了满分例子，我们来归纳一下好例子的可能性到底有哪些吧。

下面四种例子都是托福写作中的顶级例子：

（a）被美国公众所熟知的社会潮流

（trends）或者具体事件（a specific event）。这类例子并不一定要特别新，否则是不是已经构成了社会潮流就很难讲了，但是它必须要跟你的论证紧密相关。

举这类例子的好处是有强烈的"美国风情"，并且具有普遍性，而不是一两个人的特例。而且北美的例子让考官更容易产生认同感。事实上，普通美国人对全世界的兴趣远远少于美国政府对全世界的兴趣。

（b）自己生活中经历过的事情

这类例子的好处是有真情实感，容易写具体。但同时需要注意几点：

一是必须要扣题，如果感觉不是很 to-the-point 那么宁可不举。

二是在这类例子后面最好再写一些分析引申的句子，以防止你的作文成为琐事的堆砌。

三是要具体才会可信，比如写 one of my relatives 就不如写 my soon-to-be twelfth-grader cousin；写 go to a good university 就不如写 attend a prestigious medical school 或者干脆写出校名，甚至还可以再加个括号写出校名缩写来表示童叟无欺；写 failed an exam 就不如写 failed his midterm anatomy exam（the written part）等等。请注意这几个写法只是示范，不必挪用。

（c）不是例子的例子

用英文讲这叫 common denominator，说白了就是公众普遍都相信的东西。比如下面这个例子就属于这一类：

Doing things that we don't like builds character and helps us mature. For instance, when parents have their first baby, they are forced to give up their freedom in order to look after the child. There are times when parents hardly get enough sleep and still have to get up and go to work in the morning. But they nonetheless feel rewarded and handle pressure better in their later lives.

举这类例子的好处是可以比较放松，信手拈来。但需要注意的是也不能太空洞，而且数量应该适可而止。如果此类例子过多，那你的文章就变成了流水账（rambling pieces）。

（d）化腐朽为神奇的例子（高分内容）

这种方法很有特色，就是"把老例子举出时代感。"但这类例子对作者水平的要求最高，相应的如果举好了的话也就容易最出彩儿。

比如国内同学都爱举 Gettysburg Address 来说明林肯的伟大。但你是否知道，林肯在那次演讲之后对自己一再重复的一句话竟是，"I failed."因为那次演讲他准备的时间很短，而且只讲了 3 分钟，268 个词，而爱抢镜头的哈佛校长 Edward Everett 为那次精心准备的演讲长达 2 个多小时，1500⁺个词。这个视角新颖的例子如果用来论证 2009 年下半年的大陆考题：*It's better to achieve high efficiency with possibly more mistakes than to work with lower efficiency but possibly fewer mistakes.* 绝对能起到让考官眼前一亮的效果。

再比如同样是关于林肯的，还可以把他著名的幽默感跟战时南方联盟（the Confederate States of America）的"总统"Jefferson Davis 著名的 humorless 风格作比较，来论证"humor 对成功的重要性"这个本来很有难度的新托福作文话题。

再比如，各位提到富兰克林·罗斯福（FDR），一般都是跟 New Deal 相关。其实为什么不换一换视角呢？比如不妨举一下战时 The American media avoided taking pictures showing that he walked with crutches（拐杖）这个事实来说明 media 对公众意见的巨大影响力；或者也可以举 FDR 的夫人 Eleanor Roosevelt 的例子。她在抚养了六个孩子，丈夫出现多次外遇（affairs，对于 FDR 的这一"成就"历史学家们已经有定论）之后，却并没有轻言放弃，继续协助丈夫在战时的伟大事业，最终成了美国历史上最受公众尊重的 first ladies 之一。甚至还可以引用 FDR 在 1940 年的演讲词（Pearl Harbor 事件发生在 1941 年圣诞节前夕），"While I'm talking to you, mothers and fathers, I give you one more assurance. I have said this before, but I shall say it again and again and again: Your boys are NOT going to be sent into any foreign wars." 这么强有力的"保证"和后来美国积极参战的鲜明对比，充分证明了 FDR 这样的伟人为了国家利益也曾经 told some white lies（Barack Obama 也讲过无数的"white lies"，请看 barackswhite-lies. blogspot. com）。

而下面这些名人的例子也同样可以帮我们在写 Success 话题的时候把旧题写出新意：

1. Einstein was four years old before he could speak and seven before he could read.

2. Isaac Newton did poorly in grade school（elementary school）.

3. When Thomas Edison was a boy, his teachers told him he was too stupid to learn anything.

4. A newspaper editor fired Walt Disney because he had "No good ideas".

5. Bill Gates dropped out of Harvard.

6. Steve Jobs dropped out of Reed.

7. Michael Dell dropped out of University of Texas at Austin.

8. Larry Ellison dropped out of University of Chicago and also University of Illinois.

另外 www. adhdrelief. com/famous 上还有对很多其他名人成功前的"惨状"描述。

在北京的时候，曾听说过有的考生因为托福没考好就悲观地觉得靠自己的努力出国已经无望，甚至产生了"轻身"（倒不是"轻生"）的念头。可跟上面那些天才们遭受的来自小混混的侮辱比起来，一次考试成绩算得了什么？更不要说 Larry Ellison（Oracle 甲骨文公司的 CEO）还是双料冠军！

反面教材

除上面四类很赞的例子外，Pat 发现巨多的国内考生喜欢在托福作文中把编写数据作为"杀手锏"（aces up their sleeves），而且乐此不疲。

坦白地说，这种编出来的"统计数据"是真是假 Pat 基本上一秒钟就能看出来，考官们这些阅托福作文无数的家伙更是心明眼亮。除非你真的是个中高手，否则你编的不是数字，是寂寞。

请看：下面的数字是真实的官方统计，所以勉强还能对付过去：

Countries like America and Canada have been built by immigrants from all races, creeds and cultures. Survey results from the U. S. Bureau of Labor Statistics have confirmed that by 2005, every group in the American workforce had become a minority. Still, Americans continue to think in terms of the "mainstream" and the "other". If we take a moment to think historically, we can see that our civilization is actually composed of many strands from diverse backgrounds.

而下面这个关于 happiness 的例子，虽然也是 100% 真实的调查结果，但是如果用在考试中就已经显得比较生硬了：

Today, British people don't feel as happy as those who lived in the 1950s, even though they have three times more wealth than people had at that time. According to a GfK NOP survey, 52% of the people in 1957 indicated that their lives were "very happy." while today only 36% of people have the same feeling. In America, similar research has revealed the same result.

下面这种编数字的方法好一点，因为它并不是编造统计数据，而是作为一种假设论证出现，还使用了虚拟语气，本质上已经不是典型的例证了：

In a 50 minute class with an average sized class of 30 students, if a teacher spent 20 minutes teaching a particular lesson, he/she would have just one minutes to spend per student.

自己写的时候不觉得，看别人写的就能看出编出来的数字是多么容易被看穿了。所以 Pat 真的并不推荐大家把编数字当成 "可爱" 的例证手段，因为它再可爱也只不过是装嫩。除非你实在想不出任何其他例子了，否则尽量不要依靠编造统计数据来凑字，更不要让它成为你作文中 "阿喀琉斯的脚跟" （Achilles' heel）。

☆　　☆　　☆

但如果您真地发现自己已经对编机构统计数据中毒太深，无药可救，不编不行，那么好吧，下面是与新托福作文话题最直接相关的一些美国联邦机构（机构名称前均需加上 the U. S. ）：

Census Bureau

Commission of Fine Arts

Department of Health and Human Services

National Aeronautics and Space Administration （它的缩写大家很都熟悉了）

Department of Education

National Center for Education Evaluation and Regional Assistance

National Center for Education Statistics

the American Association of University Professors（这个不是联邦机构，所以不需要加 the U. S.）

建立起属于自己的作文例子库

下面的两个大表格是 Pat 精选出的：

（1）美国人非常熟悉的一些社会现象或者运动；

（2）美国人同样非常熟悉的、在新托福作文里还没有上镜过多的名人。

由于出版社规定了本书的篇幅，Pat 无法把所有国内同学们还不熟悉的美国名人都收入本书，在这里只能是给大家示范一下如何积累例子。希望大家尽快建立名人档案。根本不必去考虑别人对这些人或事情的解释是怎样的，因为每个人的出发点也不同，解释就不会完全一样，能够自圆其说就好了。而且在建立名人档案库的时候最好多参考本书附录 C 和附录 E 的话题，这样你的资料库的建立过程也就同时成了你不断思考新托福作文话题的过程。您今后一定会相信 Pat 的话：这个不断思考的过程本身才是最大的收获。

Pat's Tips

Please feel free to use Wikipedia, Britannica, www. reference. com, www. encyclopedia. com, www. answers. com, www. infoplease. com（the MSN Encarta Encyclopedia was shut down at the end of 2009）or any other online reference sources to assist with the construction of your personalized pool of examples.

Table 1

事件/潮流	参考关键词	适用的新托福话题（仅为参考建议，大家完全可以自己去研发不同的用途）
Louisiana Purchase	Thomas Jefferson, unconstitutional, opposition, at a critical juncture	自己做决定的重要性
Alaska Purchase	"Seward's Folly", gold was discovered in Alaska in 1897, the deal paid off thousands of times over	take risks 的意义
the founding of the Library of Congress	no books or not even any building to put books in when the resolution was passed	果断行动的必要性

事件/潮流	参考关键词	适用的新托福话题（仅为参考建议，大家完全可以自己去研发不同的用途）
Mt. Rushmore National Memorial	*originally intended to be a tribute to figures from the Old West*, *ended up with George Washington, Abraham Lincoln, Thomas Jefferson and Theodore Roosevelt*	按计划工作还是有创意的工作
the Twenty-First Amendment	the repeal of Prohibition, drinking alcohol was legal again, poorly-planned, only 550 agents enforced the ban in the whole country	政府与个人 leisure 的关系／计划的重要性
Marbury vs. Madison	the basis of judicial review	个人经验 vs. 他人建议
the Underground Railroad	Black slaves, abolitionists, secret routes	过去和现在成功难易度比较
the Bay of Pigs（这个可跟猪流感没什么关系）	the entire world was on the brink of nuclear war, destruction of the sites might trigger World War III, doing nothing means exposing America to possible nuclear destruction	高效率不完美 vs. 低效率完美
Sputnik	Soviet satellite, shocked Americans, efforts to catch up with the Soviet Union in space	太空研究
Model T	assembly lines, mass production, effective advertising	广告和产品的相互依存关系
Monopoly	At first, the game was described as "too long, too dull and burdened with 52 fundamental play errors" by a game company.	没想到吧？连"大富翁"游戏的成功也充满了曲折
latchkey kids	lack of parental supervision	工作与家庭的关系
empty nest syndrome	the extended family is less common; loneliness	年轻人与老年人的关系
the Three-Mile Island accident	the safety of nuclear plants; relatively low levels of radiation; no new nuclear plants were built in America since the accident	科技对生活的改变是利还是弊
the Exxon Valdez Oil Spoil	the ship's captain, negligence	个人对于环境可能造成的影响

事件/潮流	参考关键词	适用的新托福话题（仅为参考建议，大家完全可以自己去研发不同的用途）
the impeachment of Bill Clinton	"I want you to listen to me. I'm going to say this again ... I never told anybody to lie a single time. These allegations（指控）are false and I need to go back to work for the American people. "	lies & truth
the digital divide	gap；access to more information	科技让生活更简单还是更复杂
Child pornography	proliferation	互联网的利弊
Obama Girl	an Internet celebrity, I got a crush on（暗恋）Obama	媒体的影响
the Challengerdisaster	broke apart, seven crew members	太空研究
the Mars Exploration Mission	the Spirit Rover & the Opportunity Rover	太空研究
the national debt topped $11.4 trillion	credit, emergency	plan & risk 话题
Bankruptcy of Lehman Brothers	"Your company is now bankrupt, our economy is in crisis, but you get to keep $480 million（£276 million）. I have a very basic question for you, is this fair?"	"有米"是否是成功的唯一标准
the subprime mortgage crisis	high-risk loans, uncalculated risk	risk 话题
Google Earth	convenience, great accessibility	科技是否让生活更复杂
An Inconvenient Truth / Our Choice	Al Gore	个人与环境的关系
American Idol	Simon Cowell	是否应该总讲真话/cooperation
Haiti earthquake	catastrophe humanitarian	是否应该关注与我们生活不直接相关的时事

名人	关键词	相关新托福话题
Andrew Carnegie	industrialist, philanthropist（我们在第4天学过 philanthropy，还记得么?）/ passion for reading / By 1897, he controlled almost the entire steel industry in the United States. philanthropist donations	读书的意义/儿童业余时间工作的利弊/过去成功容易还是现在成功容易（类似的个人几乎控制整个行业的例子当然还有 J. P. Morgan）
Alan Greenspan	Federal Reserve, excess liquidity（流动性过剩）	risk 话题
Andrew Jackson（他就是 20 块美金正面的那个"卷毛儿"）	rotation in office, the spoils system, ordered that all public land could be sold only for silver or gold, the bank panic, the Indian Removal Act, Trail of Tears	学习历史可以更好地解决当代问题
Andy Warhol	"In the future, everybody will be world-famous for 15 minutes." commercialization	媒体的影响力
Ben Bernanke	an expert on the economic and political causes of the Great Depression	了解历史是否帮助解决现在的问题
BlackBerry	smart phone	这个可是"一代名机"，用它来论述科技相关话题很棒
Bono	third-world debt relief / Africa	成功的标准
Bruce Barton	The Man Nobody Knows, sold 700,000 copies in two years, whether advertising was wasteful and dishonest	广告与产品的关系
Clara Barton	the "Angel" of mercy; at first, the Red Cross only assisted soldiers; the new clause in the Red Cross Constitution that provided for civilian relief	工作的意义应该只为了金钱么
Carly Fiorina	failure to communicate with her staff, departure from HP	与他人合作的能力是否越来越重要

名人	关键词	相关新托福话题
Charles Lindbergh	American aviator; the first solo nonstop flight across the Atlantic Ocean	冒险的意义
Donald Trump	real estate, The Apprentice, reality show, "You're fired."	电视节目对年轻人的影响
Edgar Allan Poe	tales of mystery, financial difficulty	是否只看写实的书/人该为了什么工作
Elizabeth Blackwell	was rejected by 17 medical schools before she got admitted to New York's Geneva Medical College and graduated at the head of her class and became the first woman to receive a medical degree in America	成功需要的因素
Evan Williams	Twitter, Blogger, "What we have to do is deliver to people the best and freshest most relevant information possible. We think of Twitter as it's not a social network, but it's an information network. It tells people what they care about as it is happening in the world."	科技让生活更复杂还是更简单
George Lucas	*Star Wars* / financial success / being imaginative / special effects	严肃电影 vs. 娱乐电影
Herbert Hoover	who was blamed (somewhat unfairly) for the Great Depression	了解历史才能更好地处理现在的问题
Harper Lee	*To Kill a Mockingbird*, Presidential Medal of Freedom	"I never expected any sort of success with *Mockingbird*. I was hoping for a quick and merciful death at the hands of the reviewers." Harper Lee 这样评价自己的作品。用途：不凸显个性是否更容易成功
Johnny Appleseed	a media-made legend	信息来源是否真实

（续表）

名人	关键词	相关新托福话题
Johnny Cash	"Man in Black"	着装对成功的影响
John Cheever	short stories, "the Chekhov of the Suburbs"	现在还是过去更容易成功
John Dewey	educator / progressivism	学生应该只学少数课程还是广泛学习
J. D. Salinger	*The Catcher in the Rye*, his struggle with unwanted public attention	对幸福的理解
Jesse Jackson	passed up a pro baseball contract, became a preacher instead, "the president of Black America"	决定对人生的影响
Jack Kerouac	*On the Road*, the false legend that the book was written in three weeks	信息来源的真实性
John McCain (当每个人都开始研究 *Barrack Obama* 的时候，你就该开始研究失败者和他的战友 *Sarah Palin* 了)	*a Naval veteran / one of the oldest candidates / prefer chatting with small groups to public speeches*	媒体的重要性
Jeannette Rankin	"*Few members of Congress have ever stood more alone while being true to a higher honor and loyalty.*" — JFK	听从他人建议还是坚持自己的判断
John Scopes	*the Scopes Monkey Trial, the teaching of the theory of evolution, the fight against fundamentalism*	教师是否应该把自己的政治或者社会观点带入课堂
Jack Welch	"Change before you have to." CEO of GE, winning	计划重要还是随机应变（be spontaneous）重要
Les Brown	motivational speaker	成功的因素包括哪些
Michael Dell	dispute with Apple, "un-innovative"	创意的重要性
Mark Twain	这位名人貌似已经被国内考生用得超多了，不过我们完全看看他说的这句话，"Lies, damn lies, and statistics."	信息来源太多，无法判断是否真实

287

名人	关键词	相关新托福话题
Muhammad Yunus	banker / microcredit / "create economic and social development from below"	坚持做好一件事 vs. 快速做好大量事情
Mark Zuckerberg	Facebook，born in 1984，passion for computerized networking since childhood，a program to help the workers in his father's office communicate	成功是过去容易还是现在容易
Neil Armstrong	first moon walk, Apollo 11, "That's one small step for a man, one giant leap for mankind."	政府是否应该投资太空研究
Oprah Winfrey	talk show, getting people to talk about their lives, the decision to end her show in 2011, a humble beginning, rags-to-riches story, extremely hard-working	媒体的影响/做决定应该听别人的意见还是自己做/成功的要素
Patrick Henry	"Is life so dear or peace so sweet as to be purchased at the price of chains and slavery?"	跟俺重名儿的名人哈~Patrick Henry 的这句名言可以在论证 take risks 的必要性时用。而紧跟这句话的下一句就是极有名的"Give me liberty, or give me death."了
Richard Branson	virgin，adventures	冒险的意义
Rachel Carson	*Silent Spring*, the ban on DDT	个人对于环境问题是否可以有贡献
Rudolf Diesel	a believer in social engineering，a machine that could be built by average engineers，to compete with big businesses	成功的标准只是金钱还是有别的衡量标准
Robert Lee	the Civil War / was asked by Lincoln to take over the Union / his loyalties were to the South	影视作品是否应该总是让好人上天堂、坏人下地狱

名人	关键词	相关新托福话题
Rupert Murdoch	"He who controls the media controls the mind."	媒体的影响
Rosa Parks	大家都喜欢举 Martin Luther King 的例子，难道这位 refused to betreated as a second-class human being and give her seat on a bus to a white man 最终导致了最高法院裁决公交上实行种族隔离违宪的黑人阿姨不值得我们尊敬么？	2005 年 Rosa Parks 以 92 岁高龄去世，Pat 在 Arizona 看电视上播放这个消息的时候心中一凛：不走寻常路，造就女英雄……
Randy Pausch	Carnegie Mellon professor, the last lecture, great sense of humor, an inspiration to millions	幽默的教师 vs. 严肃的教师
Ronald Reagan	"the most successful actor in the American history", served two terms as President of the U.S.	敢于挑战自己的重要性
Ralph Waldo Emerson	the leading voice in the American intellectual culture, dreamed about helping to free slaves, abolitionist	"To be great is to be misun-derstood." 个人开心是否比责任更重要
Samuel Adams	a total failure at business, helped organize the Sons of Liberty, the Boston Tea Part, the minuteman	成功需要的素质
Sergey Brin	"Knowledge is always good, and certainly always better than ignorance." / Google / access to information	科技是否减少创造力
Steve Jobs（可以不知道美国副总统是谁，但是绝不能不知道他是谁）	creativity, marketing prowess（造诣）	娱乐的重要性
Steven Spielberg	a science fiction fan when he was little	是否应该只读关于事实的书
Theodore Dreiser	An American Tragedy, based on a real-life criminal case	看关于事实的书还是虚构的书

名人	关键词	相关新托福话题
Thomas Jefferson	cut off all U. S. trade with foreign countries to stop the British and French raids on American ships / seriously damaged the American economy	历史的教训帮助解决今天的问题
Thomas Paine	"These are the times that try men's souls." / the American Revolutionary cause / Common Sense / signed over all the royalties（版税）to Congress	工作难道只为了金钱
Theodore Roosevelt (*Teddy*)	a "human dynamo" / progressivism/ America's youngest President at 42 (Barack Obama is the fifth-youngest President, at 47.) / the Panama Canal	old vs. young
William Faulkner	the deep South, Yoknapatawpha county, a fictional county	只看有事实的书么
Washington Irving	short stories and historical works, his stay in Europe inspired some of his greatest works	写实的书 vs. 虚构的书/出国旅行的好处

学有余力

（适合备考超过三个月的"闲人"）

经常登录下面这些网站并阅读相关文章也可以帮助你对西方社会，特别是对美国社会逐渐形成自己的深刻见解。

http∶//online. wsj. com/home-page

http∶//www. washingtonpost. com/

http∶//www. nytimes. com/

http∶//global. nytimes. com/? iht

http://www.latimes.com/

http://www.usnews.com/

http://www.reason.com/

http://www.economist.com/

www.americanthinker.com

课后练习

Take-Home Quiz

判断练习

请判断下面的主体段使用了何种举例手段（倒立部分为参考答案）：

(Hinkel, E.)

Raising a child can be really expensive. For example, in my country, most young parents cannot afford to buy a house or to send their children to private schools. In most cases, few people in their twenties have not made enough money for those things. As a consequence, in general couples who have children early cannot give them the best of what comfortable living has to offer.

（明例子与暗例子都用上了。）

分析练习

请指出下面的这个例子为什么是失败的：

One of the most interesting classes I have ever attended was one on computer science by a guest lecturer. The guest lecturer was a renowned professor. He started the lecture with some basics of computer science and then talked about the rapid developments in this field. I felt I learned so much from his presentation.

（明显属于自己亲身经历的实例，却又不够具体，导致了本来是"个人例子"但看起来缺乏 personal appeal）

你看你，就是不肯涂防晒霜（sunscreen），被UV晒黑了吧，下次写作文儿的时候就拿你当保护ozone layer重要性的反例。

——Pat摄

附录 B （高分内容，基础薄弱的同学挑选出好单词和句型用来攒 RP 就可以了）

新托福写作中的偏题、难题原创素材库

对 于新托福写作中的偏题、难题，很多同学都有这样的感觉：即使有了思路，但还是不知道该怎样用英文准确表达出来。可是一看高分范文，又发现其实高手用的多数单词和句子自己都认识，就是几个特别关键的"点睛"部分自己是无论如何也想不到的。

下面的这 66 个段落都是 Pat 自己针对新托福考试中比较难的考题为大家原创的高分段落（之所以是 66 个倒真不是为了凑一个 lucky number，而是写完之后一数不多不少正好是 66段）。需要提醒的是：下面的段落都比较"冻人"，只适合功底好的同学深入研究。对于英语基础还不太扎实的同学，Pat 的建议则是研究一下其中的关键词汇和表达以及整体思路就好了。当然最重要的还是实践：把好单词或者好句型积极运用到你自己的文章里去（直接照搬就免了吧，Day 1 里早就跟大家提过 E-rater 的事儿了）。

而且为了帮助大家开阔思路，多数话题 Pat 都同时写了正反两方面的观点及各自的支持理由。对于喜欢写一边倒的同学，也可以只阅读其中一方的论证。深入研究这些段落的英文表达和思路，对于作文目标在 26 分以上的考生会有重大意义，同时对大家今后到美国大学读书时从事一定深度的学术文章写作也将会产生深远影响。

新托福作文偏题、难题的 66 个高分段落

去影院看电影还是在家看

1

Few things can be more magical than enjoying a movie in a movie theater. Watching the characters on a giant screen helps us better appreciate the cinematography and makes us feel we're genuinely (≈ truly) part of the story. The booming surround sound* further enhances that effect, not to mention the soundtracks are always pleasantly clearer. Aside from those blessings, we share our viewing experience — the joy, sorrow, frustration, anger, excitement, or thrill and sensation, with a large audience. In that sense, movie theaters are nice gathering places for social events. And although movie theaters actually lure us with a combination of things, most importantly they are indeed places where we can escape from the daily grind of life and get transported into the past, the future or the present in a different setting.

＊ Technology that enriches sound quality with additional speakers, commonly used in movie theaters.

2

It's true that today people can see a movie on Blu-ray or HDTV while listening to a home theater system with multiple speakers and munching on homemade popcorn. But movie theaters are evolving, too. In fact, they've never failed to integrate and deliver innovative audio-visual technology. For example, in Disney's *A Christmas Carol*, the IMAX 3-D technology has made it seem as if Jim Carrey would fly right out of the screen, which has definitely made the animation even more entertaining. And comparison between viewing the immersive IMAX 3-D warfare in *Avatar* and watching the conventional 2-D version would reveal how fundamentally technology has revolutionized the cinematic experience. Incidentally, the snacks that concession stands in movie theaters offer are always more than just popcorn.

3

I prefer to enjoy flicks in a movie theater, simply because the psychological and physiological effects it can have on us remain superior to what we can get from watching DVDs at home, despite the fact that there's sometimes sticky chewing gum on the theater floor. ☺

大家是否都应该学历史

1

History is important as it shapes our nation today. It is a mirror reflecting us and thus is essential to our self-identity. After all, the best approach to knowing and judging ourselves is seeing ourselves in others. A. E. Stevenson was definitely right in stating, "We can chart our future wisely and clearly only when we know the path which has led to the present."

2

All students should be required to take history classes, regardless of their own academic interest. Like it or not, we're all travelers in time who constantly draw on our past individual experiences in judging the present; and if we haven't individually experienced anything similar to the present situation that we're in, we draw on our collective memory-the very thing that we call history. And since we view present occurrences from this time perspective, the past decisions and actions also set precedent for our future options and precautions. Why are we intensely concerned about the mass killings in Rwanda? That's because we know about the atrocities of Hitler and Mussolini. Why are there on-going, concerted efforts to curb the spread of AIDS across the world? That's due to the lessons we have learned about the ravages of the Black Death and TB*. And why do we believe lofty statesmen are just human? Partly thanks to our knowledge about Thomas Jefferson's love affair with Sally Hemmings and the impeachment of Bill Clinton. Hence, it seems the American philosopher George Santayana was right in saying, "Those who cannot remember the past are condemned to repeat it."

TB*: *Tuberculosis*

History is appealing. It's the story of a myriad of people, famous and infamous, intelligent and brainless, industrious and negligent. It's the story of what these people contemplated, did or attempted to do but failed. It's the story of what angered, saddened or pleased them. Granted, this story is not always entertaining or uplifting. Some parts of it can be even shady, miserable, heartrending or make us ashamed. But overall, I feel history is fun, not to mention the enlightening quotes and the mini-profiles of semi-obscure people.

"History will always tell lies", wrote George Bernard Shaw in his play "*The Devil's Disciple*". The so-called "historical facts" are essentially false assumptions people believe to be true; therefore on the whole, history is the subjective interpretation of historical events where bias keeps sneaking in. As a consequence, conflicting versions of the same historical event can often be found. For example, back in the 18th century, colonial conquests were a matter of pride and glory for the colonist countries. Yet if history can be rewritten from the viewpoint of those who were forcibly colonized, it would definitely reveal an entirely different story of invasion and brutality. In 1992, during the 500th celebration of Columbus' discovery of America, in stark contrast to the conventional approach, numerous scholars presented findings about the inhuman atrocities of the colonizers, which appalled many Americans. Such reexamination and reevaluation of history will shed new light on our past and our future.

History classes are not all they're cracked up to be. In reality, they're largely real academic punishments. Students are force-fed with a bewildering assortment of dates, movements and trends that are barely relatable or relevant to them and taking history exams basically means mere regurgitation of mindless text. The historical figures have had their personality drained away in the textbooks and come across either as being distant and aloof or just as bizarre characters from a costume party. In class, the well-intentioned teacher often has a hard time making history come alive, mainly because it's almost impossible to strike a sensible balance between imparting rigid facts and making history his-story (or hers) that can keep students attentive and motivated.

学生是否都应该学习基础科学

1

Teaching basic science in elementary and secondary schools is essential to fulfilling their purpose of preparing students to be scientifically literate citizens. In the U. S. , it was not until the former Soviet Union launched Sputnik into orbit that educators began to feel that Americans were slipping way behind in basic science education. In a science class, students not only can learn about physical principles, chemical reactions and biological experiments, but can grasp the process of analyzing hypothesis and demonstrating evidence as well, which is crucial to the fostering of a scientific worldview.

2

Another rationale for students taking basic science class is although it may sound drab and dreary to some students, science can actually stimulate their imagination because it not only explains and predicts, it can be completely unpredictable and pleasantly surprising sometimes. For example, these days some smart American chemistry teachers even use Harry Potter style magic in their class to show to their students how fascinating the chemical world can be.

3

Yet another reason why the basic science class should be taken by all students, regardless of their future career plans, is that it helps young people put science in perspective by making them aware that science cannot provide answers to all questions we humans face. For example, in the U. S. , students in science classes are taught there are generally-accepted moral rules regulating scientific research, including efforts to avoid the adverse effects of scientific inquiries and the ethical treatment of experimental subjects. Therefore, they will understand that even people as powerful as scientists don't have absolute freedom in pursuing their dreams.

教师是否应该把自己关于政治或社会的观点带入课堂

1

I don't see why teachers shouldn't give their own political or social opinions in class as long as they allow opposing voices to be heard. After all, the First Amendment ensures their freedom of speech. And keep in mind that the "Monkey Trial" defendant, John Scopes (Please refer to the list of examples in Chapter 6) was never really punished for teaching Darwinism in class. The court ruling against him was overturned afterwards.

2

Such subjectivity in teachers' lectures, even when it's flawed, can lend a human touch to their classes and help students better understand that teachers are not really supermen or superwomen, but some people they can relate to, which will surely make them teachers more approachable to students.

3

On the other hand, I would say if a teacher uses his/her class as a platform to promote his/her own political or even religious pursuits, to impose his/her own social belief on the students, or to make the class a process of ideological indoctrination instead of just sharing his/her interesting thoughts about current events with students, then the school administrators and parents should remind him/her immediately that he/she should stick to the curriculum and stop brainwashing the kids.

4

We all agree that teachers are just humans. Their own views on politics or social issues may be unconvincing or even biased. But simply because of their special status — the authority figures who give lectures to the kids rather than individuals who are on an equal footing with the kids, their opinions may carry more weight with young and impressionable students than they actually deserve. So I strongly believe teachers should stay out of political discussions in a classroom setting.

应该先掌握概念还是先掌握事实

1

Without the prior learning of concepts, the learning of facts would be reduced to mere rote memorization of rigid sets of data and would serve no useful ends other than honing students' memorization techniques. Concepts, either quantitative or qualitative, are like roadmaps. They provide students with a conceptual framework for them to better comprehend the facts they will deal with. Concepts present logical rules that underlie facts and summarize how facts have been sampled, measured or experimented with. Also, they facilitate students' understanding of facts by familiarizing them with the key terminology and fundamental guiding principles in the related fields.

2

The ultimate aim of concepts is to reduce complex realities to simple, easy-to-understand statements that specify relations between variables. Concepts tend to be more systematic than facts and therefore describe things in more organized ways. They are overarching rules guiding or explaining a variety of processes. They are also more reliable sources of knowledge than people's experiences, beliefs or traditions. Some concepts are abstract and provide general information on common subjects while others are highly specific and detailed and can be applied immediately to improve or justify a particular practice.

3

Knowledge about concrete facts can really turn theories into things that we can relate to. Without them, abstract concepts would become so drab or even soporific. I still remember how our math teacher taught us about vectors by first showing us a Kleenex box and analyzed its different dimensions. The fact that many things in this world had three dimensions made her subsequent explanations about the vectors so vivid and easy to absorb.

学生是否应该选择有挑战性的科目

1

Learning how to handle academic challenges and difficulties is like lifting weights: The more we do, the stronger and tougher we become. None of us ever wish for difficulties because of the hassle, disappointment and even grief they may bring but sometimes they do come along. Then we can take solace in knowing we have gained enough coping skills before they actually come that will help us overcome them.

2

Survey results have consistently shown that students who take advanced algebra, trigonometry or literature courses in high school are more likely to get excellent grades in college. This is because tough terms, complicated ideas or abstract concepts make students more intellectually involved in their studies and effectively motivate them to utilize as many resources as possible to meet these challenges. Also, the more knowledge students have acquired, the more likely they will be able to link the new information to the knowledge they have already accumulated, which will definitely make learning new things easier. Further, the experience of conquering a series of difficulties boosts their self-confidence and enhances their self-esteem. As a result, eventually taking demanding courses will pay off both intellectually and emotionally.

I admit that giving students high expectations is an important aspect of challenging them to perform to their full potential. Yet this alone may not be sufficient unless teachers can purposefully create and engineer opportunities that can extend students' levels of cognitive and intellectual development. The realities in American public schools simply don't make me think that's achievable. I'm not blaming the teachers, who are generally considerate and hard-working front-line workers. Nevertheless, they're just like pawns in a big chess game: The entire public education system is wrapped up in cult-like enthusiasm for "progressive" child-centered learning. In such a system, teachers, no matter how motivated they are, are programmed to respond passively to requests for information rather than to create needs for information actively. It's almost like a stage where students are the directors, the parents are the producers while teachers are the actors and actresses, the principals and the school board officials being the backstage crew. I would be hard-pressed to imagine that any major challenges can be realistically posed to the students on such a stage. And in many present-day American public schools, the child-centered report cards are just like press release that makes students' academic performance and prospects look much rosier than they really are.

小组成员是否应该获得相同的成绩

It's a highly egalitarian approach when all the group members get the same grade for their work. This practice strengthens their sense of "being in the same boat" and thus naturally cultivates trusting relationships. Only through assigning the same grades can teachers guarantee that the difficulties are shared equally among the members and the challenges are met with all students whole-heartedly pooling their intellectual resources. Otherwise, it would almost be inevitable that some group members would hide valuable discoveries as "secret weapons" just to get more favorable scores. Also, a sense of competition and rivalry would linger on if individual members were well aware that they would not be awarded the same scores for their group work, which would definitely cause clashes and hurt feelings.

2

Giving each member the same grade is unfair and defeats the purpose of collaboration. It is unlikely for all groups to be composed of students with exactly the same academic abilities or the same levels of engagement. As a consequence, they will surely make unequal contributions to completion of the assigned work. How ridiculous it would be if the slackers end up with the same scores as the truly hard-working members do? Even worse, chances are that those most intelligent and motivated ones will feel highly frustrated as a result of such unjustified egalitarianism and may even become freeloaders themselves in future group work.

学校教育的必要性

Today, truly well-rounded education holds the key to opportunities and to people's living out their dreams. All school-aged young individuals should set specific goals for their education, such as to excel in their academic studies, to learn about fresh and stimulating thoughts, to appreciate fine arts and performing arts more fully, to get involved in school life like extra-curricular activities, to get prepared for future professional careers or to identify things that they're genuinely passionate about rather than just dabble in a hodge-podge of things.

学习艺术的好处

1

Knowledge about arts and art history can effectively elevate students' cultural awareness, such as their understanding of the historical context of customs and rituals, their appreciation of ethnic handicrafts and their interest in trans-cultural and trans-generational communication. Also, learning about arts can promote personal development. For example, working on a design project in groups may make children more collaborative while reading novels, watching drama and memorizing poetry tend to make them more reflective. And auditioning for a school musical or singing in a school choir may well give young people fresh means of self-expression. In addition, art classes can improve the emotional well-being of students as they offer creative outlets for their energy, stress, tension or even aggressiveness.

2

Art classes can bring practical benefits as well, even though they are not directly related to numeracy, scientific know-how or even literacy which many parents believe are essential in preparation for employment. For example, playing musical instruments can train students' eye-hand coordination, which can be really useful for careers as medical professionals, engineers or technicians. Also, pottery or porcelain making can enhance the cooperation between the left brain and the right brain, thereby enabling students to come up with more creative solutions to problems. Moreover, art classes actually open up opportunities for certain internships, jobs or careers, like performing artists, graphic artists, composers and architects.

竞争的意义

1

We are living in an age when the "jungle law" and the "survival of the fittest" rule prevail. Now practically everything must be competed for before we get it. Kids compete for good grades, and then compete for awards and merit-based scholarships. In the workplace, adults compete for jobs, for promotion and for pay raises. In social life, men and women compete for attention, status and even love and romance.

2

To compete with others means to try to excel and achieve a sense of superiority. To dominate our rivals or opponents, we exert ourselves and can't afford to settle for mediocrity. The urge to win can compel us to become more original or at least more innovation.

3

Individuals, companies and nations all compete with each other. The burning desire for appreciation, recognition, rewards or supremacy may all be the driving forces behind competition. Personally, I believe that as long as the competition is fair and square, it is actually the only effective way to ensure fulfillment of potential and realization of dreams. What we should do is not to blame competition for all the rivalry or confrontation it may involve, but to guarantee that it is played out on a level playing field — i. e. , even though not every player has an equal chance to win, but at least we all abide by the same set of rules.

科技是否让生活变得更加复杂

1

Technology not only makes our options more diversified, but complicates our lives as well.

The other day, I saw an electric fireplace in Sears. Just like any regular fireplaces, it would give the users physical warmth during wintertime. But it had so many buttons, dials and meters on it that the contrivance really lacked the psychological warmth sitting around a fireplace with a cozy fire burning could give us. Also, think about the digital books that so many students rely on today. Yes, now we have more alternatives than just going to a bookstore or a library. But that often means we have to sacrifice the simple leisure of curling up with a good book. Instead, to stare at the computer screen and scroll the sidebar up and down daily, which simply hurts our eyes and makes our neck stiffen. Likewise, inventions like the electronic keyboard, PSP and Blackberry really make our lives unnecessarily complex and drag us away from the simple enjoyment of playing the piano, building sandcastles or writing letters to our loved ones.

On a more spiritual level, with the boom of technological innovations, the computer-enhanced productivity, the computer-boosted mechanical precision and the fascinating computer-generated advertising, people become increasingly preoccupied with material possessions. Technology has, in effect, caused us to be more competitive and aggressive. Today, insomnia is a chronic condition that plagues millions of people in the world, largely due to the insecurity brought about by the modern complexity that not only means more inventions and more choices, but also means more greed and more jealousy. Technology may bring us comforts, but the breakneck speed of the technology-centered, highly-charged modern life has taken away our peace of mind that has been necessary to enjoy these comforts.

Technology is further complicating the challenges confronting humans as new problems have been popping up due to technological advancement and many of them remain unresolved. For example, the waste gas and water discharged by modern factories have been linked to the extinction of many wild species and are threatening the human existence too. Even things as simple and basic as fresh air and clean water are hard to come by these days. Also, the urban expansion facilitated by the advances in construction technology is encroaching on the countryside and the rustic and peaceful lifestyle rural communities represent. It seems true that humans, through modern technology, are getting many complicated new comforts at the expense of the past simple comforts, which may even mean self-destruction in the long run.

Those who think technology is making our lives more complicated are reactionaries. Yes, technology has brought about dazzling arrays of choices to us. Yet it just serves to simplify things rather than renders our lives inconvenient or confusing. For example, people used to communicate with each other with "snail mail", which means they had to go to the post office, bought a stamp and an envelope, licked the stamp and stuck it onto the envelope before they finally could get their mail into the mail bag. Now telecommunications technology has streamlined the process to the extent that we're just a-click-of-a-button away from the intended recipients. Also, customized BlackBerry and iPhones enable us to remain on top of what really interest us besides helping us reach out to our loved ones on the go. Inventions like lawn mowers and leaf blowers make our yard maintenance easy and digital cameras have turned the daunting photography classes into enjoyable sessions when we can fulfill our photographic potential without having to struggle with the mechanical details of a camera. Medical innovations like laser surgery is helping doctors immensely simplify operations that used to involve complicated use of scalpels. In short, technology not only brings us more comfort and more leisure time, it makes our lives much simpler than before with enhanced productivity and better reliability.

科技是否减少学生的创造力

1

Three-dimensional computer-generated graphics offer vivid and precise images, which can be really helpful in illustrating abstract physical, chemical and biological concepts to the students. Plus, multi-media devices are mostly interactive, which can stimulate children's visual and spatial imagination more effectively. Also, search engines and Internet-based encyclopedias put more options at children's fingertips, thereby substantially enhancing their ability to come up with innovative approaches to problems-solving processes. Most importantly, modern technology allows school kids to memorize far less, thanks to the ready availability of the information stored in their PC or laptop. Thus, the kids can break away from the restrictions of rote learning and start to think independently.

2

The famous Austrian educator Rudolf Steiner once observed, "I've often heard that there must be an education which makes learning a game for children and schools must be all joy. This is the best educational principle to ensure that NOTHING at all can be learned." Today, high-tech devices in classrooms dull the students' minds with graphical teaching where quick answers replace true understanding. Students are not given time for reflection or critical thinking. And thinking, after all, involves originality and the courage to challenge conventions. In the end, students suffer from intellectual passivity — the lack of desire to explore serious subjects.

电影应该严肃还是应该搞笑

1

Reality is rough. To help us avoid facing reality, comedies sugarcoat the harsh facts for us. By contrast, serious movies tend to show us the reality or the dark side of society and prompt us to reflect on life. Ultimately, reality has a way of catching up with us; therefore, it would be a lot easier to face when we recognize it through serious movies. For example, Clint Eastwood's last movie, the award-winning *Gran Tarino*, realistically depicted the racial conflicts in America. But in essence, it encouraged Americans of different races to grow more open to one another in the new century. Also, some serious movies, such as many historical and autobiographic movies, teach moral lessons in thought-provoking ways. There is no doubt that movies like *A beautiful Mind* definitely showed us fresh ways to understand humanity and ourselves. In a sense, serious films afford us very healthy exercise of the mind and thus constitute a form of entertainment in their own right.

2

Comedies normally throw a whole bunch of mismatched things together, thereby producing an outlet for releasing our daily pressure. They are entertaining and offer us good and healthy ways to escape from reality for a couple of hours. Some amusing films teach moral lessons too. For instance, Jim Carrey's *Yes Man* vividly showed us the crucial importance of being true and honest to ourselves in a melodramatic manner. Amusement does not always have to be mindless anyway.

读写能力在今天是否比过去更加重要

1

Individuals today need reading and writing skills to participate in modern society, whether it is to understand a bus schedule or to enjoy a celebrity magazine, to operate a computer or to use a cell phone to text our colleagues, friends and family members. Being able to read and write is fundamental to our lives as students, employees, supervisors or citizens.

2

For individuals, zero or poor reading and writing skills may mean low incomes and chronic psychological strain due to the social exclusion that illiteracy can incur. For communities, residents' low reading and writing skills may mean poor school district performance and low property value. For societies and nations, citizens' low literacy skills may mean a serious lack of productive work force.

The worldwide proliferation of voice telecommunications and digital graphics makes textual communication seem largely irrelevant to many of us. For example, according to a survey conducted by the US Census Bureau in 1960, nearly 77% of American households back then preferred mail over other means of communication. In stark contrast to this allegiance to correspondence, it was reported by NBC in March 2009 that three out of every four Americans today identified cell phones as their primary communication tools.

年轻人当中流行的网站的利和弊

Video sharing websites like YouTube are Internet destinations where people can watch and share video clips on almost every topic imaginable, from Cartoons to sporting events, from music performances to horrific car crashes. They create a sense of community — i. e. , they allow us to upload our talents, interests and experiences and share them with other viewers from across the world.

2

Social networking websites like Facebook and Twitter actually bring trouble to our lives. For example, our personal information is often misused by companies for commercial purposes and as a matter of fact, these websites themselves are often used for excessive advertising, which makes me feel utterly annoyed. Also, as members of those websites are driven by the desire to become popular, we tend to find ourselves forced to interact with many people we don't really know well and that simply wastes our time and energy. And worse yet, those sites have the potential to turn our friends and partners into nosy parkers and let them get to know things we don't want to disclose to them, let alone the confusion or even animosity that identity theft may cause us.

参观博物馆的好处

1

Today, most museums have a central theme to them. Exploring those theme museums in a foreign country can be really informative and entertaining as well. It helps us grasp the culture of that country, from prehistoric times to the present day, from rites to rituals, from antiques to handicrafts, from food to clothing, from architecture to vehicles, from war to peace-making. By touring foreign museums we can see the origins of things, the historical debris and the facts and factoids about the current society there. They are like encyclopedias about a nation's glories, mysteries and sometimes failures.

2

The most essential difference between visiting local museums and reading history books about a foreign country is that museums are not just about the famous and infamous (meaning notorious). Many of them are actually about the obscure, average people — their customs, costumes, artifacts and preferences in everyday life. Besides, today many museums do not just recount things. They are more closely connected with the audience than before. For example, many of them are interactive, through which visitors can feel the local culture even more vividly. Also, many museums offer public presentations and lectures on a wide variety of subjects and that makes them great educational tools for parents. Further, the comparisons and contrasts that museum exhibits can present are far more visual and more memorable than the two-dimensional illustrations in any history books or TV shows.

3

When I attended the ASU (Arizona State University), my favorite place on campus was the Art Museum, which was named "the single most impressive venue for contemporary art in Arizona" by Art in America magazine. I still remember all the peace and quiet I enjoyed there, and the exquisite artworks showcased in that museum. And now I still often visit museums when I travel to other countries because they tend to slow me down and calm my racing mind. They enable my imagination to create its own virtual worlds instead of keeping it reliant on TV programs.

钱应该花在短期享受（比如 vacation）上还是花在可以长久保存的物品（比如 jewelry）上

1

I prefer things that last longer because in today's world of breakneck speed, when so many things are technological, disposable or even virtual, more durable things such as silver pendants, gemstones, souvenirs and antiques can slow me down and calm my anxious and wandering mind.

2

Initially durable items may cost even more than short-term pleasure such as a vacation. But in the end, they give us greater contentment. They show us that happiness does not have to be fleeting or circumstantial. The contentment they afford can last very long indeed, even a lifetime. Do we really need a gas-guzzler SUV? Do we really need a walk-in closet full of stylish clothes? And do we have to eat out in an upscale restaurant every weekend?

提高油价是否是解决环境问题的好方法

1

Raising the price of fuel will definitely drive up the price of many other things on the market, from vegetables to dairy products, from clothing to electronics, from imported beers to package tours, as their transportation costs will grow up accordingly. This will be a chain reaction that only exacerbates the already high rate of inflation.

2

Necessity has always been the mother of inventions. Maybe the demand for cheaper sources of energy will motivate scientists to come up with fresh solutions to the problem, such as the development of more efficient wind turbines or breakthroughs in producing more dependable hydrogen-driven cars.

3

Higher prices of fuel make drivers more aware of the environmental costs that driving incurs. There will be less market demand for gas guzzlers like SUVs and pickup trucks. Public transit and the notion of "going green" will be more popular among the middle-class adults and the kids, some of whom will hold the key to the future environmental problems.

人类今后是否不再需要印刷的书籍

1

Computers have much greater storage capacities, which means you'll have far better selections if you choose to read e-books instead of conventional books. And the Internet further expands your pool of information as search engines put tons of data, facts and theories at your fingertips. More importantly, you can download e-books and edit or even copy them very easily.

2

Think of all the trees chopped down for the making of paper (Yes. Today, a still very low proportion of books are printed on recycled paper). But the environment should not be something to be subjugated or exploited. Books are by no means eco-friendly when you take into account the colossal amount of paper they consume. Actually, whole areas of tropical rainforests are disappearing because of this each year. And as a matter of fact, information stored in books is not so durable because books can be easily torn, worn out or even burned. I believe books should only be part of our past and present, but surely not the future.

3

When you read a book, you never have to worry about the viruses, worms or hackers plaguing millions of computers in the world. And who wants to curl up with a PC screen and read a romantic love story on it? Realistically, no screens today are good enough to avoid glare or eyestrain for the users completely. Even if you can settle for all the insecurity and discomfort reading e-books may bring, it's very likely that you may find the e-books you've downloaded turn out to be incompatible with the software on your laptop. And don't forget that so far, all the devices for reading e-books use power, which means exclusively relying on them is an eco-unfriendly practice.

可再生能源的优势

1

Renewable resources have been the fastest-growing sources of energy in many industrial countries. Their primary advantage is obviously their sustainability. Scientists have been worried that the reserves of petroleum, natural gas and coal on Earth will be exhausted by the end of this century if the world population continues to grow at the current rate. Renewable sources of energy, such as solar energy and hydropower are desirable alternatives to these conventional resources as their supply is abundant and is theoretically inexhaustible

2

Further, these new sources of energy are largely clean, which gives us another compelling reason for phasing out the fossil fuels in the 21st century. For example, wind energy never pollutes the environment as it does not require any fuel like coal-burning power plants do. Nor does it produce toxic emissions that cause acid rain, which, consequently, reduces the health costs many societies have to bear as a result of air pollution.

乘客是否应该为公交付费

Free public transit will definitely encourage citizens to use it more. As we probably all know, one of the major threats to the environment today is global warming caused by heavy use of motor vehicles in cities. As a matter of fact, the soaring fuel price has been making drivers think twice about their loyalty to their private cars. If all modes of public transportation can be accessed free of charge, more car owners will be won over and go green and more fossil-fueled vehicles will be locked in garages, which will surely ease the flow of traffic as well.

Fully-subsidized public transit makes sense in that it is service aimed at the majority of the citizens who are taxpayers at the same time. Being available for free to all citizens instead of just to the elderly and the disabled, it will encourage equality in the sharing of municipal resources and promotes easy and laid-back communication between people.

The buses, subway trains and ferries are very expensive to purchase or to lease. If no users paid for their service, the government would have to rely on tax revenue to pay for it. And with the growth of cities, the transportation network needs to be upgraded and expanded too. Where will this follow-up investment come from? Obviously, all the citizens will have to face increased tax rates if some of us wish to enjoy free public transit. So my view is that only senior citizens and children should be entitled to lower fares, but not completely free either.

了解时事的重要性（即使它们并不直接影响我们的生活）

They are always good for a conversation over a cup of coffee. More importantly, discussing or even just chit-chatting about current events with your friends and family members will not only satisfy your curiosity about the world, it will make your mind more analytical and insightful as well. Also, you can better understand the community and city life around you through keeping track of current events happening in the world. After all, they're all stories of people — how people trust, cooperate or compete with, or confront one another. It's no exaggeration to say those who don't know about anything going on in the world may be entirely cut off from society.

Even seemingly unrelated things are actually interrelated in this age of sweeping globalization. For example, the US-led war on Iraq seemed to have no bearing whatsoever on the lives of the taxi drivers in Madrid. But the following wild fluctuations in the oil price have definitely made them feel the repercussions. And the Swine Flu once confined to Mexico eventually forced so many to be hospitalized or have to wear a mask on a subway train regardless of how stuffy it feels across the world. Being "blissfully ignorant" can be really risky in today's world.

对动物的研究是否可以帮助人类更多地了解自身

1

Animal research on primates and other mammals has substantially increased humans' understanding of our own behavioral tendencies and the basic principles that underlie our lives, such as the learning process and the sensory processes. For example, recent research of chimpanzees has highlighted the close link between anxiety and physical illnesses. Also, over the past decade, medical research on mice has been critical to pharmaceutical progress in the relief of mental disorders, cancer treatment and the alleviation of alcohol and drug addiction.

2

On the other hand, regulations about laboratory animal care should be issued and enforced to ensure the best conditions and the most humane research methods for the lab primates, rodents and birds, especially those regarding the levels of pain and other sufferings inflicted.

是否有必要经常和家人一起吃饭

1

As with many people who have left home, I sorely miss eating meals around a table with my parents and my siblings. Even though Chinese food is widely available in America, I still find myself constantly longing for the food my parents cooked and the experience of having breakfast and dinner with my family. That was when I didn't have to gulp down endless variations of burgers without even chewing them. During the meals, we caught up on the day, shared our joys and frustrations, talked about our achievements at school or at work, or even settled arguments we had before.

By eating meals together, we learned table manners such as always keeping our elbows off the table and never talking with our mouths full, and also skills like how to set the table with candles. And my parents always managed to surprise us with a variety of colors, forms and textures. We could really taste the flavor of love in the dishes we shared as a family. I feel lucky not having been raised on frozen meals in front of the television although honestly, now I have to wolf down sandwiches while talking on the cell phone over lunch regularly. I firmly believe families that do not eat together tend to fall apart gradually.

食品生产方式的变化

Now crops can be selected to make sure that they are best suited to certain climatic and soil conditions. Then they can be distributed easily thanks to the advancements in transportation. The refrigeration technology has made possible long-distance shipment of perishable food. Pasteurization helps us keep milk and other diary products fresh for a long time. New meatpacking methods have transformed home-based industries into mass production in factories, which not only exponentially increases the productivity, but makes the processing of meat more hygienic.

自己在家做饭的好处

1

Cooking can actually be therapeutic. After a hectic day in the workplace, what a relief it can be to be your own boss and "call the shots" in the kitchen! You can do whatever you want to and don't have to ask for anybody's permission. And you just don't have to be concerned about the food hygiene as many customers do in restaurants because everything is taken care of by yourself.

2

Cooking for your loved ones can really strengthen the ties between you and them. People naturally feel delighted and gratified when they have someone they care about cook for them. That's probably how we got the well-known saying, "The best way to a man's heart is through his stomach."

3

Cooking can tell a lot about one's personality. For example, those who stick to vegetarian recipes are very likely to be animal-adorers and environmentally-conscious. For real cooking-lovers, we're not just what we eat, we're what we cook as well.

Bonus Samples

是否应该养宠物

1

Those who detest pet-free lives tend to stress (=emphasize) the emotional needs pets can satisfy. They would argue that we humans are social creatures and naturally crave companionship. Then when human company is impossible, regardless of the causes, pets can drive off our loneliness, make us feel wanted and comfort us at times of sorrow.

2

The opponents have some legitimate concerns. There're always stray pets roaming the streets. Take cats for instance, when some irresponsible people find out that these little creatures have such an amazing speed of reproduction and it becomes hard to keep them anymore, the next step may be tossing the kittens onto the street rather than finding adoption for them or sending them to a pet shelter, which not only betrays the affection and companionship that pet raising is all about in the first place, but poses very real health risks to the city residents as well. Even if pets stay with their masters, they misbehave at times, which may disturb neighbors, make a mess of the sidewalks or even cause accidents. In extreme cases, pet attacks can actually kill as deadly germs may be spread from pets to humans who are not necessarily immune to these germs.

3

It all comes down to how pet owners understand their responsibilities. Pets are, by definition, animals that afford humans pleasure but at the same time rely on their masters for food and shelter. So raising a pet is, after all, a luxury. Not just because in most modern cities pet owners have to buy a license for their pets, but because of the love, attention and devotion pet keeping calls for. Keeping pets on a leash when they are outdoors can effectively prevent them from attacking people or wandering off. Also, picking up pets waste dutifully can help clean up the city. And if all pet owners can get their pets the mandatory (=required by the law or the rules) shots (It means vaccines here.) and take them to the vet (=pet doctors) regularly, viruses in pets would be put under control immediately.

是否应该把动物关在动物园里

1

In most cases, it's better for wild animals to live in a natural environment with access to appropriate food and shelter. For example, living in the wild enables social animals such as lions and dolphins to play appropriate roles within groups, while keeping them in the zoo may eventually cause the disappearance of many traits that are helpful for their survival.

2

However, today the natural environment is increasingly threatened by pollution, deforestation and global warming. In fact, most animals live longer in captivity today because normally keepers are available to take care of their health and diet. And if animals are sick, there are veterinarians in zoos to help them, which can substantially extend the lifespan of these animals.

3

Establishing and maintaining zoos are a way for us humans to atone for the destruction of the land, the forest, the river and the sea. There have been joint programs among zoos to increase our knowledge about animals that used to live in the wild, such as how to preserve, breed, and care for them. And nowadays, some rare species only exist in zoos, which also makes zoos an essential part of wildlife preservation.

Reason to switch #9:
Advice that makes sense for me.

Switch your chequing account and get up to $250. Ask us how.
Visit www.tdcanadatrust.com/reasons or call 1-800-268-6611 today.

北美的生活中随处可见本书给大家讲过
的词汇与短语……

——Pat摄

313

新老作文话题总 PK（上）

2006 ~ 2011 年大陆机考话题全集

　　机经一直是朋友们比较关心的问题，下面的题库覆盖了从 2006 年下半年直到 2011 年初的国内独立写作全部话题。为了表示对 ETS 知识产权的尊重，本题库使用中文对话题进行简要描述。并且 Pat 还按照 15 类常见话题对题目方向进行了分类，供大家参考。重复出现的题目均只列出一次。

　　另外，大家还可以在本书的附录 B 中看到大量机考"难题"的原创高分段落。

序号	话题
2006 年	
2006 年（1）	新闻与信息过量是否会导致人们无法判断这些信息的可信度。（Media）
2006 年（2）	最重要的教育是否发生在教室。（Education）
2006 年（3）	20 年后人们将会减少汽车使用，同意吗？（Transportation）
2006 年（4）	学习到的知识比创造力更有助于个人成功。（Success）
2006 年（5）	一生只为一个老板工作是不现实的。（Work）
2006 年（6）	可再生资源将会迅速取代非可再生资源。（Environment）
2006 年（7）	小组成员应得到相同的分数。（Education）
2006 年（8）	工作中获得幸福感比银子重要。（Work）
2006 年（9）	选自己感兴趣的学科比选有前途的学科更重要。（Education）
2006 年（10）	分数可以鼓励学生去努力学习。（Education）
2006 年（11）	给人类用地比为动物保留栖息地重要。（Environment）
2006 年（12）	有智慧的朋友比幽默的朋友更好。（Friends）
2007 年	
2007 年（1）	司机在繁忙时段出行应交纳一定费用。（Traffic）

（续表）

序号	话题
2007 年	
2007 年（2）	多数人会让别人帮自己做决定，同意吗？（Friends）
2007 年（3）	口头表达重要还是写作技能重要？（Success）
2007 年（4）	看电视比读书学的多？（Media）
2007 年（5）	咱们的生活比祖父母年轻时要好。（Old vs. Young）
2007 年（6）	现在与别人合作的能力比过去更重要了。（Success）
2007 年（7）	老师帮学生提升自信比讲知识更重要。（Education）
2007 年（8）	严肃电影比娱乐电影好。（Media）
2007 年（9）	影视是否对年轻人的负面作用多于正面作用？（Media）
2007 年（10）	每天发生很多事，咱们无需都知道。（Media）
2007 年（11）	老师应该挣和医生、律师、企业高层一样多的钱吗？（Work）
2007 年（12）	20 年后人们将有更多休闲时光。（Leisure）
2007 年（13）	过多的影视节目使家长觉得很难掌控孩子。（Media）
2007 年（14）	做完一件事再去做另一件好还是两件一起做好？（Work）
2007 年（15）	允许朋友犯错比终止友谊好。（Friends）
2007 年（16）	非理科专业的大学生也应该上基础科学课。（Education）
2007 年（17）	报纸可以帮助人们真实地获取新闻。（Media）
2007 年（18）	在今日社会，年轻人应有计划和组织能力。（Success）
2007 年（19）	大学生必修历史课。（Education）
2007 年（20）	再过 20 年学生不会用纸质书了。（Education）
2007 年（21）	最有效节能的方法是提高油、电价。（Environment）
2007 年（22）	年长朋友的建议更有价值。（Friends）
2007 年（23）	学校不应太关注常规科目而应帮助学生就业。（Education）
2007 年（24）	老师有与学生沟通的能力远比教授知识重要。（Education）
2007 年（25）	和别人一起工作比单干好。（Work）
2007 年（26）	家庭观念没以前那么重要了。（Family）
2007 年（27）	休息的时候有些人喜欢独处好不好？（Leisure）

315

序号	话题
2007 年	
2007 年（28）	大学生应上有关外国文化的课程。（Education）
2007 年（29）	有钱花在旅游度假上比存银行好。（Leisure）
2007 年（30）	教师应按其学生的成绩发工资。（Education）
2007 年（31）	因为有钱而不工作的人很少会快乐。（Work）
2007 年（32）	广告使产品看起来比它们本身要好。（Media）
2007 年（33）	20 年后人们会用更少的时间准备食物。（Food）
2007 年（34）	应不应付公交费。（Transportation）
2007 年（35）	广告没意义因为顾客已经知道自己想要什么。（Media）
2007 年（36）	学生理解思路和想法比知道事实更重要。（Education）
2008 年	
2008 年（1）	即使得不了高分，大学生也应选难度大的课程。（Education）
2008 年（2）	高分促进学习。（Education）
2008 年（3）	最好的旅游方式是有导游的团队游。（Travel）
2008 年（4）	人们花太多时间享乐而不是在应做的事情上。（Leisure）
2008 年（5）	老师有必要每天给学生留作业吗？（Education）
2008 年（6）	科技使小孩没以前有创造力了，对吗？（Technology）
2008 年（7）	政府应支持艺术发展还是体育场馆建设？（Government）
2008 年（8）	通过自己的经验解决问题比听取他人意见好。（Friends）
2008 年（9）	小孩是否应打电游。（Media）
2008 年（10）	政府改进医疗需要做的最重要的事是改善环境。（Government）
2008 年（11）	大学教育是成功的关键因素。（Success）
2008 年（12）	20 年以后人们会有更多的休闲时间。（Leisure）
2008 年（13）	严肃的老师比幽默的老师教学效果好。（Education）
2008 年（14）	有人认为孩子应该学和玩，有人认为孩子应做家务。（Education）
2008 年（15）	不突显个性更易成功。（Success）

序号	话题
	2008 年
2008 年（16）	人们在自己的国家旅游比在国外旅游收获大。（Leisure）
2008 年（17）	高中毕业生上大学前应有一年去工作或旅游。（Education）
2008 年（18）	科学家该为其发明所带来的负面影响负责。（Technology）
2008 年（19）	小孩子运动是为兴趣还是为了进比赛？（Leisure）
2008 年（20）	老师比朋友对学生的影响更大。（Education）
2008 年（21）	把钱花在有价值的物品上还是在花在短时间的享受上。（Money）
2008 年（22）	有不同兴趣的人不能做朋友。（Friends）
2008 年（23）	针对幼儿的电视广告应被允许。（Media）
	2009 年
2009 年（1）	一家人经常一起吃饭很重要。（Family）
2009 年（2）	应通过不同媒介得到更全面的信息。（Media）
2009 年（3）	电视的目的应是教育而非娱乐。（Media）
2009 年（4）	政府应更注重环保而不是经济发展。（Government）
2009 年（5）	老师应把自己的社会或政治观点告诉学生吗？（Education）
2009 年（6）	科技使人们的生活变得更复杂。（Technology）
2009 年（7）	职业上的成功更多取决于与别人交往而不是在校刻苦学习。（Success）
2009 年（8）	相比认真计划，创造性思维更能使人们找到解决方案。（Success）
2009 年（9）	人在何时更有满足感：完成挑战性的任务还是解决了简单的问题？（Work）
2009 年（10）	有可能犯错误但效率高比正确率高但效率低更重要。（Work）
2009 年（11）	以前人们更友善。（Old vs. Young）
2009 年（12）	现在人们比过去更容易成功。（Old vs. Young）
2009 年（13）	在家或电影院，哪个看电影更好？（Leisure）
2009 年（14）	参观博物馆是了解一个国家的最好方式。（Leisure）
2009 年（15）	好的外表与着装比好想法对成功更重要。（Success）
2009 年（16）	家长该鼓励孩子打工。（Education）

序号	话题
2009 年	
2009 年（17）	搬到新地方会失去老友。（Friends）
2009 年（18）	今天的父母相对于 50 年前的父母与孩子更少相互了解。（Family）
2009 年（19）	现代生活越来越复杂，年轻人更需要计划与组织能力。（Success）
2009 年（20）	读写能力比过去更重要。（Young & Old）
2009 年（21）	对人们在学习或者工作时的着装进行规定十分重要，是否同意？（Education & Work）
2010 年	
2010 年（1）	孩子是否应该选择从事和父母的工作相近的工作。（Education & Work，这是今年全年的第一道考题，难度偏低）
2010 年（2）	集中完成一项任务是否比同时做多件事情好（Work，没有任何悬念了：第二道题是考过无数次的老题，清晰地预示着 2010 年的 killer 考题并不会太多。James Cameron 十年时间才拍出一部 Avatar 就完全可以作为这道题的最新例子）
2010 年（3）	环境问题越来越复杂，凭个人能力无法解决。（Environment，果然，今年的第三道考题也是祖爷爷级旧题）
2010 年（4）	为了成功必须与他人相似，而不是特立独行。（Success）
2010 年（5）	儿童应该为了娱乐而不是为了比赛而参加运动。（Leisure）
2010 年（6）	了解过去是否能帮助我们解决当代与未来的问题？（Success）
2010 年（7）	最好的培养儿童责任感的方式就是让他们养宠物。（Animals）
2010 年（8）	多数商人均是被金钱所驱使（Warren Buffett 最近连续说美国经济存在二次探底（double-dip recession）的风险，新托福写作就跟着考 Money ☺）。
2010 年（9）	职业运动员是否应该获得高薪？（Day 9 范文里的原题）（Work）
2010 年（10）	保持自己的房间干净整洁的孩子是否会更加成功（一屋既扫，可否扫天下）？（Success & Family）
2010 年（11）	电视对人类生活的影响比电话更大么？（Media）
2010 年（12）	成功的领导会让团队的其他成员感觉自己也能够参与决策。（Success）
2010 年（13）	看电影或读书比体育锻炼更让人放松么？（Leisure）

序号	话题
2010 年（14）	让你的经理或主管了解你的长项和成就是否会助你成功。（Work & Success）
2010 年（15）	为提升教学质量，大学应该加大对于教授们工资的投入么？（Education & Work）
2010 年（16）	每周工作三天、但每天都长时间工作是否比每周工作五天、但每天只工作较短时间更舒服？（Work & Leisure）
2011 年	
2011 年（1）	过去人们吃的食品是否比现在的食品更健康？（Food）
2011 年（2）	对于像毕业和生日之类的庆祝聚会，多邀请一些人比仅仅邀请家人和朋友更好。（Family & Friends）
2011 年（3）	世界的变化日新月异，人们不再像以前一样快乐了。（Old vs. New）
2011 年（4）	在这个拥挤繁闹的社会里，我们不应该期望人们对他人都保持礼貌。（Old vs. New）
2011 年（5）	如今在人们作出的可以改变世界未来的重要决定中，年轻人的意见没有任何影响力。（Young vs. Old）
2011 年（6）	即便国外的产品价格会更便宜，人们也仍应该购买本国产品。（Money）
2011 年（7）	人们如果没有任何财产，会活得更快乐一些。（Money）
2011 年（8）	年轻人应该在决定从事哪个行业之前多试试各行各业的工作。（Work）
2011 年（9）	政府应该花更多资金来兴建博物馆和画廊而不是游乐设施。（Government）
2011 年（10）	和现如今相比，过去人们更容易断定哪种工作是成功稳定的。（Work）
2011 年（11）	一个人的衣着能反映出他/她的性格特点。（Clothing）
2011 年（12）	所有学校都应该把经济学定为基础课。（Education）

更多的 2011 年真题您还可以在 Pat 博客上找到 blog. sina. com. cn/toeflwizard。

新老作文话题总 PK（下）

老托福的 185 话题

在本书第一天中，我们已经向大家介绍过：精确统计后可以发现，老托福 185 题在机考中完全重复出现的概率低于 2%。但把这些老话题用来作为思维训练的素材还是不错的。为了表达对 ETS 的尊重，这里也采取对 185 话题进行中文提示的形式。如果大家还想看原题请登录 ETS 官方网址 www.ets.org/Media/Tests/TOEFL/pdf/989563wt.pdf。

1.	上大学到底为什么？
2.	父母是不是孩子最好的老师？
3.	快餐是否改善了我们的生活？
4.	学习是该读万卷书还是该行万里路？
5.	你是否愿意有工厂建在你家附近？
6.	你最愿意帮家乡改变的事情是什么？
7.	电影电视对人们生活的影响有多大？
8.	电视是否雪藏了亲友关系？
9.	繁华大都市 vs. 小城故事多，更喜欢哪个？
10.	成功是否真与运气无关？
11.	对待体育活动和图书馆建设，大学是否应在资金投入上一视同仁？
12.	为什么有人旅游时喜欢参观博物馆？
13.	喜欢在家吃还是下馆子？
14.	大学生是否应有权选择课程？
15.	远亲不如近邻？怎样才是一个好邻居？
16.	你是否愿意在你家附近新建一家餐馆？
17.	求师不如求己，你是否同意？
18.	什么样的老板才是好老板？
19.	政府为了改善交通是应该修路还是建公交？
20.	小孩在农村会比在城市成长得更好吗？

21.	为什么现在人们越来越长寿了？
22.	你最喜欢哪种性格的同事？
23.	十几岁的孩子是否应该边上学边上班？
24.	你的一位朋友要搬到你的城市里来，你觉得他（她）会喜欢这座城市的哪一点、会不喜欢哪一点？
25.	你是否会对在你家附近新建购物中心感到高兴？
26.	你是否会对在你家附近新建电影院感到高兴？
27.	人们应该有时强迫自己做自己不喜欢做的事情吗？
28.	媒体对名人私生活过于八卦了吗？
29.	人类到底是在改善地球还是在毁灭地球？
30.	你是否会对在你家附近新建一所高中而感到高兴？
31.	你愿意定居一处还是云游四方？
32.	是做月光族还是为今后存钱？
33.	珠宝和音乐会之间你更喜欢哪个做礼物？
34.	谈谈你对"铁饭碗"的看法。
35.	观看现场表演比看转播享受得多吗？
36.	谈谈这种交通工具对人们生活的影响（可选：汽车、自行车、飞机）。
37.	进步是否永远是件好事？
38.	以史为鉴，价值几何？
39.	随着科技的发展，当今学生能够更有效地学习吗？
40.	你是否认同应该"永不放弃"？
41.	有人认为人类用地比挽救动物栖息地更重要，是这样吗？
42.	哪种技能将会是在当今社会的成功之匙？
43.	为什么会有人从事各种危险的运动或冒险？
44.	你更喜欢群体出游还是独自旅行？
45.	你喜欢早起还是当夜猫子？
46.	什么是做一个好儿女的标准？这些标准在你的文化中有没有逐渐改变？
47.	你更愿意在大公司还是小公司工作？
48.	除了挣钱，人们工作究竟还为了什么？
49.	面对面的交流才是最有效的交流？
50.	向未知领域冒险还是只做自己拿手的？

51.	成功究竟是来自于创新冒险还是细心计划？
52.	什么样的变化能使你的故乡更为年轻人所爱？
53.	挣多少银子是一份工作好与不好的最重要标准？
54.	人真的不可貌相吗？
55.	人不应该独自做出重大的决定吗？
56.	支持艺术与保护环境，你觉得哪个更需要社会支持？
57.	电影引发的思考与带来的娱乐，你更倾向于哪一种？
58.	利润应该是生意场上的唯一动力吗？
59.	你更喜欢快节奏的生活吗？
60.	成人也需要玩游戏吗？
61.	家长、亲戚应该替 15~18 岁的孩子做关于他们的决定吗？
62.	智慧的朋友，幽默的朋友，可信赖的朋友，你最想要哪一个？
63.	吃一堑，长一智吗？
64.	打工还是自己干，金融危机下的烦恼。
65.	一个城市是否该保留其中的古老建筑？
66.	在校园生活中，好同学胜过好家长吗？
67.	作为老板，你更愿雇个低薪菜鸟还是高薪能手？
68.	每天的家庭作业对孩子是否真的必要？
69.	如果你可以选一个永远没有机会学习的科目来学习，你选哪个？
70.	汽车的发展是否带来很严重的后果？
71.	选工作时，有钱没闲 PK 有闲没钱？
72.	分数是学生学习的第一动力吗？
73.	电脑使生活更简单还是更复杂了？
74.	有导游的组团旅行是最好的旅游方式吗？
75.	大学应该让学生学广还是学精？
76.	小孩应该一入学就开始学习外语吗？
77.	男生女生是否应该分校学习？
78.	团队工作能力和独立工作能力哪个更重要？
79.	你愿为哪位本国英雄立纪念碑？
80.	描述一种你愿意为外国人所接受的本国习俗。

81.	科技使世界更美好吗?
82.	想了解一个国家，看她的广告吧。
83.	现代科技造成了世界文化大同吗?
84.	因特网所带来的信息爆炸的利与弊。
85.	帮一个外国朋友策划一个你的家乡一日游。
86.	如果你可以选择回到某一时间某一地点，你想回到哪里?
87.	在过去的 100 年里，哪种发明最造福人类?
88.	电邮和电话是否反将人们的距离拉远了?
89.	如果你能穿越历史见一位古人，你愿意见谁?
90.	你愿意与哪位文体明星见面?
91.	你可以问一位名人一个问题，你会问哪一个?
92.	相比气候稳定的和气候多变的环境，你更喜欢哪一种?
93.	什么样的室友是个理想室友?
94.	舞蹈是否是一种文化的重要组成部分?
95.	政府应该大力投资外太空探索还是更多投资基本民生?
96.	告诉我们你的减压秘诀吧。
97.	学生应该按学会多少知识来付给老师工资吗?
98.	选一种可以代表你的国家参加国际展览的事物。
99.	关于室友，你愿意自由选择还是学校包办?
100.	国家应该更重视电脑科技还是基本民生?
101.	你更喜欢手工工作还是用机器工作?
102.	学校应该让学生给他们的老师"打分"吗?
103.	哪种品格是成功的最重要条件?
104.	艺术家和科学家，谁对社会的贡献更大?
105.	住寝室还是租公寓?
106.	你会选择哪种交通工具去一个离家 40 英里的地方?
107.	高等教育应该是大众教育还是精英教育?
108.	生活的知识是来自于别人的教导还是自己的经验?
109.	到国外是否应该入乡随俗?
110.	你喜欢独处还是和朋友在一起?

111.	你更喜欢和三两知己在一起还是宾朋满座的感觉？
112.	幼儿时期应该用来系统学习还是玩耍？
113.	你对于在你家附近新建大学的看法是什么？
114.	家庭与朋友，谁对年轻人的影响更大？
115.	你会为自己的假期活动做计划还是随性而行？
116.	你认为知识应该来自于实践、书本，还是别人的经验呢？
117.	你更倾向于与你相似的朋友还是与你不同的朋友交往？
118.	你喜欢生活充满变数还是一成不变？
119.	你是否认同人们"穿什么衣服做什么事"？
120.	你是否认同人们快速作出决定时总是错误的？
121.	你认为以第一印象评价他人是否准确？
122.	人永远不安于现状吗？
123.	是否应该只读真人真事的书？
124.	文科的学习比理科更重要吗？
125.	所有学生在中学时都必须学习美术与音乐吗？
126.	年长人从年轻人身上学不到东西吗？
127.	读小说比看电影更享受吗？
128.	体育课是否应成为必修课？
129.	商业研究中心或农业研究中心，你更希望国家建立哪个？
130.	小孩花长时间进行体育运动的利与弊是什么？
131	金钱是评判成败的唯一标准吗？
132.	你最想发明什么东东？
133.	1～12岁是人一生中最重要的时间吗？
134.	小孩应该在力所能及的情况下尽量完成家务吗？
135.	学校要求穿校服是否必要？
136.	只有赢，游戏才有意思吗？
137.	高中是否应让学生选择自己喜欢的科目来学习？
138.	做个组员比做领导要好吗？
139.	你觉得哪间房间在一个家里最重要？
140.	你更喜欢手工制作的东西还是机器制作的？

141.	如果你可以给母校做一项改变，那么会是什么呢？
142.	一件好礼物会帮助小孩子更好地成长，你会选择呢？
143.	你认为学生应该每年有一次长假还是几次短假？
144.	传统小屋与摩登公寓，哪个是你的最爱？
145.	广告是否鼓励我们购买不需要的东西，或告知新产品信息？
146.	你在空闲时间是喜欢在外面还是当宅男（女）？
147.	你的学校收到了一笔赠款，你觉得学校应该怎么花？
148.	游戏如人生，它教给了我们很多道理吗？
149.	如果你是一个大地主，你愿意如何利用手里的地？
150.	电视对儿童是否起坏作用？
151.	在你的国家里，哪种动物最重要？
152.	谈一种在你国家里正在迅速流失的资源。
153.	动物园没有用处吗？
154.	吸烟是否应在大多数公共场合被禁止？
155.	你认为哪种植物对你和你的国家最重要？
156.	假如给你两周时间出国旅游，你选择哪里？
157.	将来远程教学是否能胜过传统教学方式？
158.	是否应听信文艺名人的意见？
159.	你认为哪种改变最能代表20世纪中的变化？
160.	如果需要投诉，你更喜欢写投诉信还是以面对面的方式解决？
161.	为什么人们收到别出心裁的礼物后会一直铭记于心？
162.	你觉得文体明星的高收入是否合适？
163.	读写能力是否在当今变得更加重要了？
164.	你保持健康的秘诀是什么？
165.	你要怎样做能让你的社区变得越来越好？
166.	男孩要走多少路才能成为男人？
167.	你认为学校应该先投资电脑还是图书？
168.	为什么学生要去国外留学？
169.	为什么音乐对人如此重要？
170.	为什么身处小组或团体对人们如此重要？

171.	如果你要离家旅行一年，除了必需品你还想带哪一件？
172.	学校该如何帮助外来学生的"水土不服"？
173.	君子之交不借钱？
174.	你和你家长一代有多大的代沟？
175.	相比讲师一人授课与互动型的课堂，你倾向于哪一种？
176.	如果可以创建一个新节日，你希望它的意义何在，人们怎样来庆祝它？
177.	你会建议你的朋友花钱度假还是买车？
178.	你觉得21世纪的到来会带来什么变化？
179.	作一个好家长的特质是什么？
180.	解释电影风靡全球的原因？
181.	土地是否应保持自然状态或为人所用？
182.	人是否应视宠物为亲友？
183.	从看一个国家的电影中可以学到关于这个国家的什么？
184.	你更喜欢独自学习还是小组学习？
185.	如果你有足够资金，你愿意用它来买房还是创业？

北美在行动

  去年的部分大陆作文题与去年和前年的一些北美题出现了重合的情况。其实不仅是去年，这个规律一直都存在：大陆的"新题"经常是 10~18 个月前北美新题的再现。甚至也有过像 2009 年情人节那天中国和北美同考一道题的超级 coincidence。我们应该研究北美考题，但也不要把全部希望"寄托"在考题重现上。即使你真的知道考题是什么，如果没有基本功那还是写不出精彩的托福作文。

  下面的 2008~2011 北美题库也采用中文对话题进行了提示，但前两个附录里已经出现的考题就不再收入。Pat 也按照 15 类话题对考题方向进行了归类。

序号	话题
2008 年	
2008 年（1）	有挑战性的工作更让人快乐吗？（Work）
2008 年（2）	成功需要敢于冒险？（Success）
2008 年（3）	家人应该经常一起进餐？（Family）
2008 年（4）	有创意的方案比有计划的方案更容易解决问题？（Work）
2008 年（5）	针对儿童的广告应被禁止？（Media）
2008 年（6）	科技让生活更复杂？（Technology）
2008 年（7）	解决现在的问题需要了解过去？（Old vs. Young）
2008 年（8）	人们普遍认为开心比责任更重要？（Work）
2008 年（9）	个人无法解决环境问题？（Environment）
2008 年（10）	学校有权规定着装？（Education）
2008 年（11）	解决环境问题是政府改善公众健康的最好方法？（Government）
2008 年（12）	科技减少学生创造力？（Technology）
2008 年（13）	政府应该发展交通而不是互联网？（Government）
2008 年（14）	现在的家长没有过去的家长了解孩子？（Old vs. Young）
2008 年（15）	电话比电视对生活影响更大？（Media）

序号	话题
2008 年	
2008 年（16）	过去比现在更容易成功？（Old vs. Young）
2008 年（17）	书比电视对社会影响大？（Media）
2008 年（18）	小孩运动应该为了玩还是为了竞争？（Leisure）
2008 年（19）	人们应该总在一地生活而不是搬家？（Family）
2008 年（20）	老师对学生的影响大于朋友？（Education）
2008 年（21）	体育教给我们人生道理？（Leisure）
2008 年（22）	锻炼对老人比对年轻人更重要？（Old vs. Young）
2008 年（23）	公交上该不该打手机？（Transportation）
2008 年（24）	在本国旅游比去国外旅游给人的收获更大？（Leisure）
2008 年（25）	保持房间整洁的学生更容易成功？（Education）
2008 年（26）	看电影在家好还是在电影院好？（Media）
2008 年（27）	科学家应该对成果带来的负面影响负责？（Technology）
2008 年（28）	个性不同也能做朋友？（Friends）
2009 年	
2009 年（1）	国家成功关键在教育？（Education）
2009 年（2）	广告是不健康饮食习惯的根源？（Media）
2009 年（3）	人们应该从不同媒体获取新闻？（Media）
2009 年（4）	读报纸杂志是了解外国的最好方式？（Media）
2009 年（5）	假期多的工作即使工资不高也更值得干？（Work）
2009 年（6）	失败时乐观比成功更重要？（Success）
2009 年（7）	教师上课是否应该公开政治观点？（Education）
2009 年（8）	人们应该从小理财才会有财务上的责任感？（Money）
2009 年（9）	职业运动员应该拿高薪？（Work）
2009 年（10）	小孩应该学艺术和音乐？（Education）
2009 年（11）	大学生应该兼职？（Education）
2009 年（12）	家长应该让孩子自己决定未来？（Family）

序号	话题
	2009 年
2009 年（13）	政府应该更多投资在艺术场所上而不是运动设施上？（Government）
2009 年（14）	低工资但稳定的工作更好？（Work）
2009 年（15）	家长应该鼓励孩子兼职？（Family）
2009 年（16）	政府应该更多投资于美术馆和音乐厅而不是游泳池或者活动场？（Government）
2009 年（17）	搬到新的国家或地区将会失去老友？（Friends）
2009 年（18）	政府该更关注儿童教育而非大学教育？（Government）
2009 年（19）	影视作品总是让好人上天堂、坏人下地狱？（Media）
2009 年（20）	拥有财产（possessions）越多的人幸福就会越少？（Money）
2009 年（21）	在本国旅行比出国旅行收获更大？（Leisure）
2009 年（22）	人们都该买本国货，即使别国的产品更便宜。（Money）
	2010 年
2010 年（1）	为了培养财务上有责任感的成年人，是否应该从小就让儿童管理自己的财务？（Money）
2010 年（2）	离开村庄（village）的人是否比一直生活在村儿里的人更加成功？（Success）
2010 年（3）	政府是否应该资助没有实用性的科学研究？（Government）
2010 年（4）	一群持有不同意见的人无法作为团队而成功。（Success）
2010 年（5）	是否所有高中生都该学习经济学课程？（Education）
2010 年（6）	关于未来，是有挑战性的计划好还是现实的计划好？（Success）
2010 年（7）	如果家长希望让孩子成绩好就该减少他们/她们看电视的时间么？（Education）
2010 年（8）	人们可以自己或者通过家人的帮助解决问题，因此无需政府帮助。（Government）
2010 年（9）	为了让自己快乐，应该首先学会让别人快乐。（Leisure）
2010 年（10）	人们的爱好应该与他们/她们的工作内容不同。（Leisure）
2010 年（11）	人们的衣着能够很好地体现他们/她们的性格。（Leisure）
2010 年（12）	家长培养孩子责任感的最好方式是让他们/她们爱护动物。（Animals）
2010 年（13）	在家里通过电脑或电话上班比在办公室上班好吗？（Work & Technology）

序号	话题
2010 年（14）	你在和他人讨论有争议的问题时，会使用电子邮件或者手机短信还是会使用电话或者语音信箱？(Media)
2010 年（15）	越来越多的人把钱花在养宠物上面，尽管还有更好的花钱方式。(Animals)
2010 年（16）	人们对于公众认可度比对赚钱更加在乎。即使无法盈利，能够获得公众认可也会让人们更勤奋地工作。(Work)
2010 年（17）	与生活在城市的人们比起来，生活在乡村的人们可以更好地照顾家庭。(Family)
2010 年（18）	祖父母们提出的建议没有价值，因为世界在过去的 50 年中已经发生了重大变化。(Old vs. Young)
2010 年（19）	为了提高教学质量，大学应该花更多的钱在提高教授的工资上面。(Education)
2010 年（20）	两人即使贫富不均仍可成为朋友。(Friends)
2011 年	
2011 年（1）	大学教授应该把更多的时间花在研究上还是花在教育学生上？(Education)
2011 年（2）	如今社会的飞速发展是一种积极的趋势。(Old vs. New)
2011 年（3）	世界的变化日新月异，人们不再像以前一样快乐了。(Old vs. New)
2011 年（4）	成功领袖的一个显著性格特征就是能对自己的错误负责任。(Success)
2011 年（5）	家长应该允许孩子犯错误，并让他们从错误中吸取教训。(Family)
2011 年（6）	当今世界最重要的一个课题就是解决我们的寿命问题。(Present vs. Future)
2011 年（7）	在可以保证毕业生找到好工作的大学和拥有诸多著名教授的大学之间，你更倾向于哪一种？(Education)
2011 年（8）	我们可以从一个人交什么样的朋友来了解这个人。(Friends)

附录 F（适合骨灰级玩家）
新托福写作 211 同义词重点替换词全集

美 语里有句很俗的话，"Variety is the spice of life." 也有句很不俗的话， "The less routine, the more life." 但说来说去都是同一个意思：多样性很重要。写作中除了词汇的数量和准确度，还有一个更高的境界：用词的新颖程度。下面表格的左侧单词都是新托福考生在作文中最容易用词出现"撞车"的单词。其实很坦诚地说：一个单词容易出现"撞车"，也恰恰说明了这个单词是常用词，之所以要去替换这词，仅仅是为了避免用词跟其他考生的用词过于重复而已。

211 同义词工程学习说明

❶ 由于新托福作文的风格是比较生活化的，因此换词并不需要过于频繁。比如 about，大家在托福作文中第一次用就并不一定非要替换成 regarding/ concerning。但如果你的文章里已经连续用了 3、4 个 about，那么就真该考虑是不是该换换写法了。学习本附录里的这个表格既可以从头到尾，也可以只挑出你一直使用并已经厌烦的词汇，看看该如何替换。

❷ 本附录选词的原则是：（a）首先必须是地道的英文。编写这个表格的目的，绝不是鼓励大家片面追求"大词"，而是鼓励大家增加用词的多样性；（b）所选词在意义上尽可能接近被替换的词汇。很多网络同义词汇存在的共同问题是：貌似"同义词"给了一大堆，深入分析却有很多词在地道的英文里根本不是同一个意思甚至完全不沾边儿。在下面的这个表格中，有些 items 也没有强求完全同义，倒不是因为找不到同义词，而主要还是考虑单词的得分效果；（c）必须是容易使用正确的词汇——是的，单词无论多酷，如果非常 tricky 导致你的用法是错的，结果也只能是扣分而非拿分。

❸ 高分考生仅了解单词的中文意思仍然是不够的，至少还应该知道词性，最好还能够再深入了解同义词（或近义词）的用法（或语义）的区别。下面这个表格在篇幅允许的情况下已经尽可能详尽地给出了用法区分。另外大家还可以登录 www. ldoceonline. com（注意第一个 dot 后是字母 l），超级好用的朗文词典官方网站，结合例句进一步学习词汇的用法。

❹ 下面这个表格是专门针对新托福写作的要求整理的，有些词汇在口试中不宜使用。

❺ 这个词汇表最开始的时候是包括 211 个写作重要同义替换词，现在经过"扩招"，又增加了 171 个词。但为了向过去的工作致敬，还是叫它"211 重点替换工程"吧。

❻ 这个表格无论从单词的覆盖量还是内容的实用性来讲，相信在中国英语教学界都是属于开创性的。Pat 会不断努力，让这个表格越来越全面。大家在写作实践中如果遇到自己希望替换的表达，可以发邮件至 toeflessays@ sina. com，如有时间定当回复。

331

写作 211 同义词重点替换词全集

Synonyms That Can Spice up Your Writing

	国内考生常用的表达	更得分的表述方式
		名词
1.	things that one tries hard to do	one's undertakings / one's commitments
2.	The fact is that…	The reality is that…
3.	joy	happiness / delight / enjoyment
4.	sadness	sorrow / grief
5.	danger	hazard / peril（后面这个词语气很强，危险程度非同一般）［派生］dangerous: hazardous
6.	education	≈ schooling（指学校教育，家庭教育则用 upbringing / parenting）［区分］家庭教育的两个词 upbringing 和 parenting 的区别在于：upbringing 是从孩子的角度说的，比如 children's upbringing；而 parenting 是从家长的角度来说，比如 sensible parenting.
7.	advertisement/ advertising	如果你写过关于广告的题目，就一定体会过不停轮换使用 advertisement/ advertising 有多郁闷。其实主体段论证中完全可以把广告种类细化，比如 commercials（电视或者互联网上的广告），flyers（传单广告，北京最常见的形式就是"136＊＊＊＊，办证儿"），billboards（巨幅的广告牌）或者 non-profit advertisements ＝ public-interest advertisements（公益广告）
8.	car	automobile
9.	economic crisis	economic meltdown（很接近）/ recession（这个一般仅仅还是衰退）/ the Great Depression（这个则是特指 1929 年开始的那次了）
10.	famous people	celebrities（单数为 celebrity）

332

	国内考生常用的表达	更得分的表述方式
		名词
11.	human beings（被考生使用过多）	humanity（注意这个词的单数指人类，复数指人文学科）/ the human race
12.	wealth	fortune(s)（fortune 作财富的意思时可以加复数）
13.	［相关］rich	wealthy / affluent（*adj.*）
14.	skill	≈ technique（注意这个词的正确解释是技能或者方法，而不是 technology 科技）
15.	［派生］skilled	adept / adroit（*adj.*）
16.	method	methodology（美国大学里超级常用的词，其实严格来说应该是一套方法的体系，但在实际应用中已基本沦为了 method 的"耍酷"版）
17.	field	sphere / domain / arena
18.	understanding of	≈ grasp of / command of
19.	choice	option
20.	cooperation	≈ collaboration
21.	basic structure in a city or a country	infrastructure
22.	tiredness for a long time	fatigue
23.	is a must for	is a prerequisite for（是……的必备先决条件）
24.	the Internet	≈the information highway（一篇考生作文里 Internet 被使用十几次是常事儿）
25.	honesty	≈ integrity
26.	strong belief	faith（in）
27.	aim	intention
28.	worries	anxieties（是的，这两个词的确都可以加复数）
29.	influence	impact / repercussion / implication
30.	influence on each other	mutual influence（类似的表达还有 mutual respect, mutual trust 和 mutual understanding / interaction between A and B / interplay between A and B

	国内考生常用的表达	更得分的表述方式
		名词
31.	many different kinds of…	a variety of… / a wide array of… / a wide range of…
32.	wrong ideas held by many people	misconceptions
33.	fame	prestige / sterling reputation
34.	range	≈ spectrum
35.	sense	≈ recognition
36.	part	component（这个词不仅指零件，在学术写作中也经常指"部分"）
37.	wise	［相关］sensible（*adj.*）
38.	gap	disparity
39.	a system for a particular purpose	≈ a mechanism for…
40.	a solution to sth.	a remedy for sth.（生活中经常指一种病的治疗方法，但学术写作中经常用来指某种问题的解决办法，注意搭配的介词不同）
41.	bad students	≈ unruly students / disruptive students
42.	bad behavior	unethical behavior / immoral behavior
43.	organizations that help poor people	charities / charitable organizations
44.	difference	distinction
45.	［派生］be different from	be distinct from（*adj.*）
46.	person	individual
47.	personality	≈ disposition
48.	businesses	enterprises（这里指企业）
49.	prices that are too high	exorbitant prices
50.	the rate of…	the incidence of…（后面一般跟坏事儿，比如 unemployment / crime / a disease）
51.	intense enthusiasm	zeal / passion

	国内考生常用的表达	更得分的表述方式
名词		
52.	cultural globalization（有过多人使用这个词）	global cultural homogenization
53.	a thing that is necessary	a necessity
54.	a thing that is new and interesting	a novelty
55.	a thing that is rare	a rarity
56.	things that people are not sure about	uncertainties
57.	a world language	a universal language
58.	friends	companions
59.	relaxation	≈ recreation
60.	self-respect	≈ self-esteem and dignity
61.	respect sb. / sth.	hold sb. /sth. in high regard
62.	[反义] look down on…	treat… with contempt = despise（v.）
63.	self-control	self-discipline
64.	criminal	convict
65.	prisoner	inmate
66.	drinks	≈ alcoholic beverages
67.	people who walk on the street	pedestrians
68.	old generations in history	ancestors
69.	a person who benefits from sth.	a beneficiary of sth.
70.	a disease that spreads quickly	an epidemic（注意这个词虽然是-ic 结尾，却不是形容词）
71.	a very unpleasant way of life	misery

	国内考生常用的表达	更得分的表述方式
	名词	
72.	a task that requires lots of effort	an arduous task
73.	emotion	≈ sentiment
74.	enemy	≈ opponent / foe
75.	narrow minds	insular minds（狭隘的头脑或者观念）
76.	a way to do sth.	a approach to doing sth. / an avenue towards sth.
77.	hobby	≈ pastime / diversion
78.	progress	progression（经常指抽象的进步，比如写关于 society/ career/technology 的话题）
79.	failure	setback（注意作名词的时候中间不要加空格）
80.	importance	significance（当你用了一次 importance 之后，第二次不妨用这个）
81.	duty	obligation（用于比较重要的责任）
82.	difficulty	hindrance / impediment / hurdles
83.	pressure from your class-mates	peer pressure
84.	citizens who can work	labor force / workforce（都是总体概念，而且注意后面这个词的标准写法中间没有空格）
85.	problems or diseases that exist for a long time	persistent problems / chronic diseases
86.	a life without regular exercise	a sedentary lifestyle
87.	result	consequence（表示消极的结果更多一些）
88.	thoughts	≈ considerations
89.	the lack of knowledge	ignorance（注意在地道英文里，这个词经常并不表示"忽视"，而是表示"无知"）

	国内考生常用的表达	更得分的表述方式
		名词
90.	harm（ *n.* ）	adverse effect
91.	harm（ *vt.* ）	damage destroy／ruin（这两个词比 damage 程度更重）spoil（后面跟 the cityscape／scenery／environment）undermine（后面跟抽象概念，比如 stability／social order／harmony）jeopardize（后面跟抽象概念，比如 one's future／one's career）tarnish（后面跟 one's reputation／image）sap／dampen（后面跟 one's enthusiasm／interest／confidence）
92.	［派生］harmful	detrimental（ *adj.* ）
93.	［派生］be harmful to	≈ pose a threat to
94.	bad luck	misfortune
95.	trouble	adversity／dilemma／predicament／hardship
96.	crime	offense／criminal act
97.	youth crime	≈ juvenile delinquency
98.	criminal	offender／≈ culprit／≈ perpetrator
99.	serious crime	heinous crime／felony
100.	a minor crime	a misdemeanor
101.	shortage（of）	scarcity（of）／dearth（of）
102.	the only one	an exception
103.	places where animals live	habitat
		形容词
104.	worrying	≈ disturbing
105.	very popular	prevalent／ubiquitous
106.	true	genuine（truly／genuinely）
107.	deep	profound（深刻的，后面经常跟 wisdom／truths／understanding／impact／thoughts）

	国内考生常用的表达	更得分的表述方式
		形容词
108.	strong	powerful / mighty
109.	weak	≈vulnerable
110.	hard-working	industrious（注意不是 industrial，而 diligent 那个词在美语中是个挺大的词）
111.	very disappointing	lamentable / pathetic
112.	be good（for）	be beneficial（to） = be in the best interests（of）
113.	be not as good as	be inferior to
114.	be better than	be superior to
115.	uninteresting	mundane（注意这个词其实在美国很多时候并不是"世俗的"意思）/ humdrum
116.	many	numerous（注意要跟可数名词）
117.	complicated	intricate
118.	strange	odd / bizarre / eccentric（单 weird 有点过于口语化了）
119.	cannot be turned back	be irreversible
120.	produce useful results	productive
121.	practical	≈realistic
122.	mature	sophisticated（这个词指人的时候意思是思维成熟老练的）
123.	selfish	self-centered/ materialistic
124.	proud（贬义）	conceited
125.	suitable	fitting
126.	most suitable	optimal
127.	lonely	≈ isolated / alienated
128.	alone	solitary
129.	be easily influenced by sth.	be susceptible to sth.（一般是坏事情，比如 a disease / attacks）
130.	is better than	is superior to

	国内考生常用的表达	更得分的表述方式
形容词		
131.	not as good as…	is inferior to
132.	be the same	be identical / be homogenous / be uniform（后面两个词比较正式，一般是说 cultural globalization 的时候常用，现在理解为什么校服的名词叫 school uniforms 了吧，就是让大家都看起来一样的衣服 ☺）
133.	interesting	≈ stimulating
134.	boring	≈ monotonous / repetitive
135.	useless	redundant
136.	smart	intelligent
137.	famous	renowned
138.	positive	≈ desirable / encouraging
139.	happy	delighted
140.	enjoyable	delightful
141.	can be used	be available
142.	hard to understand	bewildering / baffling / confusing
143.	(laws / rules / people) not strict	lenient
144.	healthy	wholesome（注意说人的健康还是要用 healthy，但是如果说事物有益健康，就可以用 wholesome）
145.	good for the environment	eco-friendly（比如 Biking is far more eco-friendly than driving their SUVs.）
146.	nervous / anxious	≈ apprehensive
147.	doubt sth.	be skeptical about sth.
148.	fair	≈ justified
149.	unfair	≈ unwarranted / unjustifiable
150.	huge	enormous / massive / vast/ colossal

	国内考生常用的表达	更得分的表述方式
	形容词	
151.	small	tiny / miniscule（后面一般跟抽象名词）
152.	have many different abilities	be versatile / be well-rounded
153.	be familiar with	be well-acquainted with
154.	very successful / admirable	distinguished
155.	proper	appropriate
156.	typical	quintessential（这个语气非常强）
157.	exact	precise / ≈accurate
158.	ugly	unsightly
159.	poor-quality	substandard（housing / accommodation / work / goods / machines）
160.	the present...	the current... / the existing...（比如 the current financial crisis / the existing environmental problems）
161.	outdated	antiquated / obsolete
162.	highly-respected	esteemed
163.	complete (*adj.*) / whole	entire
164.	spend a lot of money	lead an extravagant /a lavish life
165.	open	enlightened / progressive（开明的，进步的，经常用来形容 government 或者 society）
166.	sth. must be carried out	sth. is compulsory / sth. is mandatory
167.	with long history	time-honored（后面经常跟抽象名词，比如 tradition / practice / methods / heritage）
168.	continuing forever	perpetual
169.	important	significant / essential / vital（这三个词的重要性依次递增）
170.	very attractive	very appealing / fascinating / captivating
171.	very careful	cautious

	国内考生常用的表达	更得分的表述方式
		形容词
172.	be very interested in	be absorbed in / be engrossed in
173.	be qualified for	be eligible for
174.	disappointing	frustrating
175.	wrong	erroneous
176.	long and a bit annoying	lengthy
177.	very difficult	daunting / formidable
178.	being spread in an un-controlled way	rampant（后面经常跟负面现象，比如 crime, pollution 或者 discrimination）
179.	cruel	≈ inhumane / merciless
180.	fat	overweight / obese（后面这个已经胖出病了）
181.	having wrong opinions	skewed / biased（这两个词一般在媒体类话题使用，表示"有偏见的"）
182.	including many things	comprehensive（综合的，全面的）
183.	enough	adequate / sufficient / ample / abundant（注意这四个词的语气是逐渐递增的）
184.	too much	excessive
185.	very little	minimal（注意不是 minimum）
186.	cause bad effects	counterproductive（其实地道英文写作里这个词不见得和生产有关，只要阻止人们达到目的，都可以写它 counterpro-ductive）
187.	strict	stringent（后面一般跟 laws, measures 或者 rules）
188.	urgent	pressing（problems）
189.	quiet	tranquil and serene（美语中这两个词经常可以连在一起用）
		动词
190.	make sth. strong	strengthen / reinforce sth.
191.	make sth. weak	weaken / erode（侵蚀）

	国内考生常用的表达	更得分的表述方式
动词		
192.	make sth. better	enhance / better（很少看到国内考生用 better 当动词，其实在学术写作中 better sth. 是挺常见的表达）
193.	make sth. worse	aggravate / exacerbate sth.
194.	control ...（a negative trend）	curb...（crime / pollution / economic recessions）
195.	stop	cease
196.	manage sth.	≈ regulate sth. / oversee sth.
197.	appear	emerge / arise（后者的主语一般是抽象概念，比如 debate）
198.	die out	go extinct
199.	fail to see	neglect / overlook
200.	set... free	release（prisoners / stress）
201.	begin	commence / initiate（后者跟抽象概念更多，比如 initiate conflict）
202.	narrow / bridge the gap between A and B（注意这里 bridge 作动词）	[反义] widen the gap between A and B
203.	be forced to to sth.	be compelled to do sth.
204.	keep complaining about sth.	grumble about sth.
205.	try hard to do sth.	≈ pursue sth.（one's goal / one's career / business interests / maximum profit / hegemony）
206.	do sth.	≈perform / conduct（注意这里的 perform 不是"表演"而是"从事"）
207.	do not do sth.	refrain from doing sth.
208.	carry out	implement
209.	turn... into...	convert... to / into...

	国内考生常用的表达	更得分的表述方式
		动词
210.	decrease	decline / dwindle（特指逐渐缓慢的减少）/ dip /slip（后两个词用来指短促的下降）
211.	make a crime	commit a crime（注意作文中不要用 make a crime 这样不地道的英文）
212.	commit a crime again	revert to crime（这里的 crime 作不可数名词）
213.	punish	penalize
214.	［派生］punishment	penalty
215.	spread	propagate / disseminate（这两个词后面经常跟 information / ideas / belief 这类名词）
216.	develop fast	flourish / thrive
217.	develop（这里作"培养"的意思）	cultivate / foster / nurture（这三个词后面经常跟和教育有关的名词，比如 an interest in social issues）
218.	［相关］fast-developing	burgeoning
219.	accept	adopt（注意这个词不是 adapt 适应，而是接纳，采纳的意思）
220.	build	construct
221.	gather	garner，但这个词只能用在很正式的意思，而且略有贬义，比如 garner funding, garner support during the UN climate conference at Copenhagen
222.	measure	gauge，比 measure 稍正式一点
223.	teach sth.	≈ impart sth. / inculcate sth.（注意如果 teach 后面是人则不要替换）
224.	start	initiate（*formal*）多用于政府类话题
225.	support	espouse，后面跟某种重要的事业，类似的还有动词 champion（作动词不是冠军的意思了）和动词 sanction（它作名词则变成了"制裁"）
226.	praise	≈compliment / extol（后面这个语气很强）
227.	support	≈buttress / bolster
228.	prove / confirm	verify

	国内考生常用的表达	更得分的表述方式
		动词
229.	create	generate（一般是大规模的产生，比如 generate employment opportunities / generate tax revenue / electricity）breed（经常是产生消极的东西，比如 conflict / crime / resentment）spawn（一般是产生新事物，比如 spawn inventions/innovations）
230.	use	≈utilize / exploit
231.	use… again	recycle
232.	work hard	work assiduously
233.	get	≈acquire（注意 acquire / gain knowledge 比 learn knowledge 在地道英文中更加常见）
234.	consider	contemplate / reflect on /ponder
235.	meet	encounter，多用于政府，文化或者 success 这样偏大一些的话题
236.	provide sth.	afford sth.（在正式的英文写作中，afford 经常可以表示"提供"
237.	need	require（注意主语如果是人称则一般还需要使用 need，但如果主语是事物，则可以改用 require）
238.	like sth. very much	≈ have an affinity for sth. / have a strong attachment to sth.
239.	be unhappy about	complain about (*v.*) / be discontented with (*adj.*)
240.	ask for	request
241.	raise	elevate，就是正式版的 raise，但只是"提高"而不能表示抚养小孩的意思
242.	look like sth.	resemble sth.
243.	treat… poorly	mistreat… / abuse…
244.	consider sth. valuable	value sth. / treasure sth. / cherish sth.
245.	keep	≈maintain / preserve（这个词后面经常跟 traditions / cultural heritage / wild animals/ natural resources 等）

	国内考生常用的表达	更得分的表述方式
		动词
246.	mix... together	blend / combine / synthesize
247.	solve	tackle / combat / address
248.	notice	discern
249.	understand... to mean... / to be...	interpret... as... （很多时候这个词并不是口译，而是把……理解为……）
250.	choose sth. / choose to do sth.	opt for sth. / opt to do sth.
251.	achieve	fulfill（one's dream / one's goal / one's potential / one's obligation / one's promise / one's task）
252.	appear in large numbers	sprout up / mushroom
253.	make... less serious	relieve / ease / alleviate（作文中经常用到的搭配有 relieve stress / alleviate poverty / ease the traffic congestion 等）
254.	pay... for（one's loss）	compensate... for...
255.	pay... for（one's effort）	reward... for...
256.	make sth. faster	accelerate sth. / speed up sth.
257.	join	participate in
258.	outweigh	exceed（大家应该已经注意到了，新托福议论文的题目中经常出现 outweigh 这个词用来比较事物的重要性或者利弊，在作文中最好不要重复考题中出现过的特征词汇）
259.	contribute to	promote / facilitate（注意这两个词都是及物动词，所以不需要跟 to）
260.	prevent the development of...	hinder / impede / inhibit / obstruct...
261.	find out	≈ identify
262.	encourage sb. to...	≈ motivate sb. to...
263.	like sth. very much	adore sth.
264.	dislike sth. very much	abhor / detest / loathe

	国内考生常用的表达	更得分的表述方式
		动词
265.	hate	resent / hold a grudge against
266.	limit	restrict / constrain
267.	avoid	≈ bypass / eschew / shun
268.	is not limited to…	is not restricted to… / is not confined to…（经常用来描述一个 trend 不仅限于某个范围）
269.	be so surprised	be astonished / be astounded / be startled
270.	decide	determine
271.	move to…	relocate to… / have been relocated to…
272.	come from…	originate from / in…
273.	improve	boost / enhance（比如 boost solidarity 增进团结/ enhance productivity 提高生产率）
274.	waste	use… lavishly
275.	attack	assail（语气更强烈）
276.	reduce	curtail（多用于政府投资类话题）/ diminish（多用于文化类或者发展类中的抽象话题）
277.	increase	augment（多用于政府投资类话题）
278.	help	assist
279.	help（n.）	assistance
280.	set up	establish
281.	try to do sth.	attempt to do sth.
282.	try hard to do sth.	make a strenuous / an arduous / a painstaking effort to do sth.
283.	change	alter
284.	change… a lot	fundamentally change… / radically change… / transform…
285.	solve	address / combat
286.	correct（vt.）	rectify（a mistake）
287.	take down	demolish / raze（谈到拆老建筑的时候常用）

	国内考生常用的表达	更得分的表述方式
		动词
288.	obey	abide by / comply with / conform to（后面跟 the law / rules / regulations 等）
289.	ban	ban… altogether / strictly prohibit…
290.	criticize	condemn / denounce（这两个词一般用于政府类话题，但不要用在教育类）
291.	increase	show an upward trend / be on therise 反义：show a downward trend
292.	depend on	hinge on = be contingent on（意思是：取决于……）
293.	depend on	rely on（意思是：依靠……）
294.	deal with	cope with
295.	do one's best to do sth.	commit oneself to doing sth. / strive to do sth. / do one's utmost to do sth. / spare no effort to do sth.
296.	use up	exhaust（energy / resources）/ stretch（resources）to the limit
297.	report the details of sth.	report sth. in graphic detail
298.	prevent sb. from focusing on…	distract sb. from…
299.	spend A on B	≈ dedicate A to B
300.	use too much…	stretch… to the limit / put a strain on…
301.	pour	discharge（排放，环境类话题常用，比如 discharge chemical waste into rivers，streams and lakes）
302.	get used to	get accustomed to
303.	die out	go extinct
304.	continue to exist	persist
305.	come with…	be attended by / be accompanied by…
306.	broaden one's horizons	expand one's outlook / enlarge one's vision（broaden sb. 's horizons 这个本来真心不错的句型已经因为连续多年被考生过度使用而在作文考试里惨遭贬值了）

	国内考生常用的表达	更得分的表述方式
		动词
307.	break the law	violate the law
308.	put sb. in prison	incarcerate sb.
309.	make laws against...	legislate against...
310.	［相关］law	legislation（名词，注意 law 在特指具体的法律时可以用复数，但是 legislation 不能用复数）
311.	make sth. active	stimulate（后面经常跟 imagination / creativity / interest / economic growth 等词汇）
312.	make one's dream come true	fulfill one's potential / attain one's goal
313.	have the right to do sth.	be entitled to do sth.
314.	lead to change in	act as a catalyst for change in...
315.	stick to	adhere to / cling to（注意后面这个有时候略带贬义）
316.	deal with the need	meet the demand / satisfy the need
317.	take... away from sb.	deprive sb. of...（省略号中可以填入 freedom / leisure time / the right to 等值得拥有的内容）
318.	give sb. the ability to	enable sb. to
319.	get a clear idea of	get a clear perspective of
320.	be lost	go astray（作文中如果写青少年"误入歧途"，就不要再写 get lost 了）
321.	spend too much time on	be addicted to / be preoccupied with / be obsessed with（这三个词组的语气越来越强）
322.	prepare for...	pave the way for... / lay the groundwork for... / lay a solid foundation for...（为……打好基础）
323.	break the balance	upset the balance
324.	balance A and B	strike a balance between A and B（在 A 和 B 之间争取一种平衡）
325.	catch	capture

	国内考生常用的表达	更得分的表述方式
	动词	
326.	think of... as	regard... as / view... as / perceive... as
327.	get rid of	eliminate / remove
328.	get rid of	abolish（多用于政府类话题，废除）
329.	make... higher	drive up（后面经常跟 the crime rate / unemployment rate）
	副词	
330.	more and more + *adj.*	increasingly + *adj.* 但要注意如果后面不是 *adj.* 而是 noun，那么就可以用 an increasing number of（跟可数名词）/ an increasing amount of（跟不可数名词）来代替
331.	mainly	primarily / principally / chiefly
332.	In the old days, ...	Traditionally, ... / Historically, ...
333.	now	≈ currently
334.	Actually, ...	≈ Technically, ...（严格来说它的意思并不是"事实上"，但在学术写作中它是一个表示"精确地说"非常棒的词汇）
335.	very soon	immediately
336.	not often at all	rarely
337.	completely	entirely
338.	do sth. without careful thought	do sth. impulsively
339.	blindly	indiscriminately（不加选择的）/ mechanically（机械的）
340.	only	≈ merely（注意只有 only 作副词的时候才可以替换）
341.	a little / a bit	somewhat（注意只有 a little / a bit 后面跟形容词的时候才可以这样替换）
342.	mainly	primarily / principally / chiefly
	短语或句型	
343.	about	regarding / concerning / with respect to / with regard to
344.	before...	prior to...

	国内考生常用的表达	更得分的表述方式
		短语或句型
345.	a few	a handful of（请注意在仅指少数时，a couple of 容易被挑剔的考官判为过于口语化）
346.	Although ..., the real situation is...	Hypothetically, ... / Theoretically, ... / In theory / Ideally, ... → But in reality, ... / But in actuality, ... / But in practice, ...（Ideally 指 "理想化地说"）
347.	Most young people...	Young people tend to... = Young people typically...（tend to 和 typically 都是表示某一类人多半会怎样做的常用表达）
348.	needs to be changed	is crying out for reform（固定短语）
349.	be punished by the law	be brought to justice
350.	do sth. together	make a concerted effort to do sth.
351.	It is common for sb. to...	It is standard practice for sb. to...
352.	is based on...	is predicated on...（*formal*）
353.	have no choice but to...	have no option but to... / have no alternative but to...
354.	be worth the effort	be worthwhile
355.	and so on	etc.
356.	become more than	exceed / surpass
357.	grow fast	grow dramatically /soar / rocket
358.	fall fast	fall drastically / plunge / plummet
359.	much higher	considerably / substantially/ significantly higher
360.	a little higher	marginally higher / slightly higher / fractionally higher
361.	is closely connected with...	is intrinsically linked to...
362.	through	by way of（*formal*，介词短语）
363.	on the whole	overall

	国内考生常用的表达	更得分的表述方式
		短语或句型
364.	because of	due to / owing to（新托福作文中这两个词组后面经常是跟负面含义的名词）
365.	before（时间）	prior to
366.	in this aspect	in this regard/ in this respect（这里不是尊重的意思，而是指某方面）
367.	despite / in spite of	notwithstanding（请注意这三个词都是后面必须紧跟名词或者名词短语，而不可以直接跟从句）
368.	in fact	as a matter of fact ≈in essence / essentially（in essence / essentially 的意思是"本质上"）
369.	besides	apart from
370.	about / around	approximately
371.	It is obvious that…	It is evident that…
372.	sth. stops.	sth. comes to a standstill
373.	be similar to…	be akin to…（学术写作中相当常见的句型）
374.	A is as… as B	B is… A is equally…
375.	It is impossible that…	It is highly unlikely that…
376.	A has made B + *adj.* / *n.*	A has rendered B + *adj.* / *n.*（注意这里的宾语 B 后面只能是跟形容词或者名词，而且经常是负面含义）
377.	A has made B do sth.	A has prompted / impelled sb. to do sth.（注意这两个词后面的宾语之后不能省略 to）
378.	sth. does not always remain the same.	sth. is not carved in stone（某事物并非一成不变）
379.	A high percentage of…	The proportion of… is very high.（……的比例很高）
380.	The cause of… is…	can be attributed to / can be ascribed to…（可以归因于……）

	国内考生常用的表达	更得分的表述方式
	短语或句型	
381.	no matter	regardless of
382.	talking about… / speaking of	in terms of…（经常用来限制一个命题的适用范围，比如 In terms of culture, this city is fascinating. But the traffic in this city is a nightmare.）

这么可爱的RCMP Moose, 快买一个带回家玩儿吧！
——Pat摄

名人眼中的新托福写作

名人名言对写好新托福作文的重大意义是不言而喻的：往轻里说，展现了一个人的文化素养；往重里说，能折射出一个人的历史责任感和对人类命运的终极关怀。

很多寄托们依然痴迷于早已被用滥的 "Ask not what your country can do for you, but what you can do for your country." 和 "Government of the people, by the people and for the people shall not perish from the earth." 并坚信这些闪光句会给自己带来好运。

但你是否知道考场里坐你右侧的那个 RP 大爆发的 DX 早已经偷偷地把他的装备升级成了 MH-53？赶快 upgrade your arsenal 吧，趁着还不算太晚……

※ 本节收入了与作文话题密切相关的名言。而对于在作文中有兴趣使用 proverbs 或者 idioms 的同学，还可以看附录 H 中的网址（但注意不要用得过多，否则就显得 "痞" 了）。

Education

"A child miseducated is a child lost."

— John F. Kennedy

"Education is not the filling of a pail, but the lighting of a fire."

— W. B. Yeats

"Technology is just a tool. In terms of getting the kids working together and motivating them, the teacher is the most important."

— Bill Gates

"Educating the mind without educating the heart is no education at all."

— Aristotle

"The solution to adult problems tomorrow depends in large measure upon how our children grow up today."

— Margaret Mead

"Every child is an artist. The problem is how to remain an artist once he grows up."

— Pablo Picasso

"The important thing is not to stop questioning. Curiosity has its own reason for existing."

— Albert Einstein

"A child becomes an adult when he realizes that he has a right not only to be right but also to be wrong. "

— Thomas Szasz

Technology

"The greatest danger in modern technology is not that machines begin to think like people, but that people will begin to think like machines. "

— Albert Einstein

"As we go forward, I hope we're going to continue to use technology to make really big differences in how people live and work. "

— Sergey Brin

"Advances in computer technology and the Internet have changed the way America works, learns, and communicates. The Internet has become an integral part of America's economic, political, and social life. "

— Bill Clinton

"The world has changed far more in the past 100 years than in any other century in history. The reason is not political or economic but technological — technologies that flowed directly from advances in basic science. "

— Stephen Hawking

"If a man will begin with certainties, he shall end in doubts, but if he will be content to begin with doubts, he shall end in certainties. "

— Sir Francis Bacon

"Everything is being transformed under the magic influence of science and technology. And every day, if we want to live with open eyes, we have a problem to study, to resolve. "

— Pope Pius VI

"Whenever you take a step forward, you are bound to disturb something. "

— Indira Gandhi

"What is now proved was only was imagined. "

— William Blake

Media

"He who controls the media, controls the mind. "

— Rupert Murdock

"I do not read advertisements. I would spend all of my time wanting things.

— Franz Kafka

Success

"Start by doing what's necessary, then what's possible, and suddenly you are doing the impossible. "

— St. Francis of Assisi

"You can do anything in this world if you are prepared to take the consequences. "

— W. Somerset Maugham

"I have chosen this, that I might illustrate in my death the principles which I advocated through a long life: Equality of Man before his Creator. "

— Thaddeus Stevens

"Our life is frittered away by too many things simplify. "

— Henry D. Thoreau (the 16th American President)

"Success is the ability to go from one failure to another with no loss of enthusiasm. "

— Winston Churchill

"Achievement is the knowledge that you have studied and worked hard and done the best that is in you. Success is being praised by others. That is nice, but not as important or as satisfying. "

— Helen Hayes

"Big shots are just little shots who keep shooting. "

— Christopher Morley

"No great thing is created suddenly. "

— Epictetus

"The unfortunate thing about this world is that the good habits are much easier to give up than the bad ones. "

— W. Somerset Maugham

"What after all has maintained the human race on this old globe, despite all the calamities of nature and all the tragic failures of mankind, if not the faith in new possibilities and the courage to explore them. "

— Jane Addams

"Nothing can stop the man with the right mental attitude from achieving his goal; nothing on earth can help the man with the wrong mental attitude. "

— Thomas Jefferson

"The problems of the world cannot possibly be solved by skeptics or cynics whose horizons are limited by the obvious realities. We need men who can dream of things that never were. "

— John F. Kennedy

"Faced with crisis, the man of character falls back on himself. He imposes his own stamp of action, takes responsibility for it, makes it his own."

— Charles De Gaulle

"The way a team plays as a whole determines its success. You may have the greatest bunch of individual stars in the world, but if they don't play together, the club won't be worth a dime."

— Babe Ruth

"It is our attitude at the beginning of a difficult task which, more than anything else, will affect its successful outcome."

— William James

"Life is like an onion; you peel it off one layer at a time and sometimes you weep."

— Carl Sandburg

"I figured that if I said it enough, I would convince the world that I really was the greatest."

— Muhammad Ali

"We must have strong minds, ready to accept facts as they are.

— Harry S. Truman

"A great many people think they are thinking when they are merely rearranging their prejudices.

— Edward R. Murrow

"It is not the strongest of the species that survive, nor the most intelligent, but the one most responsive to change."

— Charles Darwin

"It doesn't matter how many say it cannot or how many people have tried it before; it's important to realize that whatever you're doing, it's your first attempt at it."

— Walley Amos

"The 'how' thinker gets problems solved effectively because he wastes no time with futile 'ifs.'"

— Norman Vincent Peale

"Has fortune dealt you some bad cards? Then let wisdom make you a good gamester."

— Francis Quarles

"If I had my life to live again, I'd make the same mistakes, only sooner."

— Tallulah Bankhead

"One reason why birds and horse are not unhappy is because they are not trying to impress other birds and horses. "

— Dale Carnegie

"Regardless of how you feel inside, always try to look like a winner. Even if you are behind, a sustained look of control and confidence can give you a mental edge that results in victory. "

— Arthur Ashe

"You got to be careful if you don't know where you're going, because you might not get there. "

— Yogi Berra

"A goal without a plan is just a wish. "

— Saint Exupery

"If a man does not know what port he is steering for, no wind is favorable to him. "

— Seneca

"Yesterday is ashes, tomorrow wood. Only today does the fire burn brightly. "

— Eskimo proverb

"It's not whether you get knocked down, it's whether you get back up. "

— Anonymous

We can't get into top-tier or find a high-paid job if we don't try. Those that we think of as being lucky are often simply those who have been willing to take a chance, to put themselves on the line.

— Anonymous

Work

"Nothing is particularly hard if you divide it into small jobs.

— Henry Ford

"When I hear somebody sign that life is hard, I am always tempted to ask, Compared to what?"

— Sydney J. Harris

"The best way to have a good idea is to have lots of ideas. "

— Linus Pauling

"Look at a day when you are supremely satisfied at the end. It's not a day when you lounge around doing nothing; it's when you had everything to do and you've done it. "

— Margaret Thatcher

"Both tears and sweat are salty, but they render a different result. Tears will get you sympathy; sweat will get you change."

— Jesse Jackson

"Where I was born and where and how I have lived is unimportant. It is what I have done with where I have been that should be of interest."

— Georgia O'Keefe

"In the field of observation, chance favors only the prepared mind."

— Louis Pasteur

"Work banishes those three great evils: boredom, vice and poverty."

— Voltaire

"What we obtain too easily, we esteem too lightly."

— Thomas Paine

"If men could regard the events of their own lives with more open minds, they would frequently discover that they did not really desire the things they failed to obtain."

— Andre Maurois

"Change before you have to."

— Jack Welch

"Love and work are the cornerstones of our humanness."

— Sigmund Freud

"When you're following your energy and doing what you want all the time, the distinction between work and play dissolves."

— Shakti Gawain

"The really idle man gets nowhere. The perpetually busy man does not get much further."

— Sir Heneage Ogilivie

"Never fail to know that if you are doing all the talking, you are boring somebody."

— Helen Gurley Brown

I can think about money as something that helps me do good things for myself and others, not as a goal in itself.

— Anonymous

Government

"Millions of individuals making their own decisions in the marketplace will always allocate resources better than any centralized government."

— Ronald Reagan

"The problem is not that people are taxed too little, but that the government spends too much."

— Ronald Reagan

"The will of the people is the only legitimate foundation of any government."

— Thomas Jefferson

"Globalization is not something we can hold off or turn off. It is the economic equivalent of a force of nature — like wind or water."

— Bill Clinton

"Arguing against globalization is like arguing against the laws of gravity."

— Kofi Annan

Friends

"We make friends casually, but once they're part of our lives, we should be careful not to take them for granted."

— Ralph Waldo Emerson

"Sometimes your joy is the source of your smile, but sometimes your smile can be the source of your joy."

— Thich Nhat Hanh

"People, even more than things, have to be restored, renewed, revived, reclaimed, and redeemed; never throw out anyone."

— Audrey Hepburn

"The best way to cheer yourself up is to try to cheer somebody else up."

— Mark Twain

"Friendship makes prosperity more shining and lessens adversity by dividing and sharing it."

— Circero

"People offer to share their experiences with us, and this can be helpful. But sometimes other people's experiences can hold us back from trying things that we might otherwise succeed at."

— Anonymous

"Life is an adventure in forgiveness."

— Norman Cousins

"Sharing food with another human being is an intimate act that should not be indulged in lightly."

— M. F. K. Fisher

"We are all something, but none of us are everything."

— Blaise Pascal

"If a man does not make new acquaintances as he advances through life, he will soon find himself left alone. At the same time, a man should keep his friendships in constant repair."

— Samuel Johnson

"Every man takes the limits of his own field of vision for the limits of the world."

— Arthur Schopenhauer

"That is the best — to laugh with someone because you think the same things are funny."

— Gloria Vanderbilt

"When a friends is in trouble, don't annoy him by asking if there is anything you can do. Think up something appropriate and do it."

— E. W. Howe

"Courage is what it takes to stand up and speak; courage is also what it takes to sit down and listen."

— Anonymous

"The more faithfully you listen to the voices within you, the better you will hear what is sounding outside."

— Dag Hammarskjold

"We are all full of weakness and errors; let us mutually pardon each other our follies; it is the first law of nature."

— Voltaire

"I'm treating you as a friend, asking you to share my present minuses in the hope that I can ask you to share my future pluses."

— Katherine Mansfield

"A true friend is the greatest of all blessings, and that which we take the least care to acquire."

— Francois De La Rochefoucauld

"Listening, not imitation, may be the sincerest form of flattery."

— Dr. Joyce Brothers

"The easiest kind of relationship is with ten thousand people, the hardest is with one."

— Joan Baez

"Our friends are both like us and not like us, and it is the ways they are not like us that stimulates and awakens new possibilities in ourselves."

— Anonymous

"Friends of varied backgrounds and experiences make us more aware of how limited our viewpoint is. "

— Anonymous

Old vs. Young

"Friends are an aid to the young, to guard them from error; to the elderly, to attend to their wants and to supplement their failing power of action; to those in the prime of life, to assist them to noble deeds. "

— Aristotle

"I know elderly people who have so lived in their long lives. Today, they find great pleasure in each and every day. "

— Loretta Young

"It is difficult to live in the present, ridiculous to live in the future, and impossible to live in the past. Nothing is as far away as one minute ago. "

— Jim Bishop

"The Past: Our cradle, not our prison; there is danger as well as appeal in its glamour. The past is for inspiration, not imitation, for continuation, not repetition. "

— Anonymous

Transportation

"We willingly pay 30,000—40,000 fatalities per year for the advantages of individual transportation by automobile. "

— John von Neumann

Environment

"Many anthropogenic activities foul the air, contaminate the water and devastate the forests. "

— Newsweek

"Don't blow it — good planets are hard to find. "

— Time

"We do not inherit the earth from our ancestors. We borrow it from our children. "

— Native American Proverb

"How many times have we walked past a piece of litter on the ground, cursing whoever was so thoughtless as to drop it and wondering when someone would come by to clean it up? It wouldn't be hard for us to bend over and pick up the litter, then drop it in the nearest waste bin, after all. "

— Anonymous

Money

"There was a time when a fool and his money were soon parted, but now it happens to everybody."

— Adlai E. Stevenson

"Often people attempt to live their lives backwards; they try to have more things, or more money, in order to do more of what they want, so they will be happier."

— Anonymous

"The real measure of your wealth is how much you'd be worth if you lost all your money."

— Anonymous

"Money and success don't change people; they merely amplify what is already there."

— Will Smith

"Only after the last tree has been cut down, only after the last river has been poisoned, only after the last fish has been caught, only then will you find that money cannot be eaten."

— Anonymous

"When I get a little money I buy books; and if any is left I buy food and clothes."

— Desiderius Erasmus

"It is more rewarding to watch money change the world than watch it accumulate."

— Gloria Steinem

"A wise man should have money in his head, but not in his heart."

— Jonathan Swift

Leisure

"Arts bring you hope when you feel hopeless, give you comfort when you're anxious and support you when you're defeated."

— Rodin

"The world is a book, and those who do not travel read only a page."

— Saint Augustine

"As the traveler who has once been from home is wiser than he who has never left his own doorstep, so a knowledge of one other culture should sharpen our ability to scrutinize more steadily, to appreciate more lovingly, our own."

— Margaret Mead

"Culture means the widening of the mind and of the spirit."

— Ruth Benedict

"The solution to adult problems tomorrow depends on large measure upon how our children grow up today."

— Margaret Mead

"Happiness is a perfume you cannot pour on others without getting a few drops on yourself."

— Ralph Waldo Emerson

"Early to bed and early to rise, makes a man healthy, wealthy, and wise."

— Benjamin Franklin

"Nature uses human imagination to lift her work of creation to even higher levels."

— Luigi Pirandello

I always try more often to reach for a book instead of the television remote control.

— Anonymous

Family

"The bond that links your true family is not one of blood, but of respect and joy in each other's life."

— Richard Bach

"To put the world in order, we must first put the nation in order; to put the nation in order, we must put the family in order; to put the family in order, we must cultivate our personal life; and to cultivate our personal life, we must first set our hearts right."

— Confucius

"The soul is healed by being with children.

— Fyodor Dostoyevski

Animals

"The greatness of a nation and its moral progress can be judged by the way its animals are treated."

— Gandhi

"The most important thing is to preserve the world we live in. Unless people understand and learn about our world, habitats, and animals, they won't understand that if we don't protect those habitats, we'll eventually destroy ourselves."

— Jack Hanna

Food

"What garlic is to food, insanity is to art."

— Augustus Saint-Gaudens

"His house was perfect, whether you liked food, or sleep, or work, or story-telling, or singing, or just sitting and thinking, best, or a pleasant mixture of them all."

— J. R. R. Tolkien

"Learning acquired in youth arrests the evil of old age; and if you understand that old age has wisdom for its food, you will so conduct yourself in youth that your old age will not lack for nourishment."

— Leonardo Da Vinci

"Food is an important part of a balanced diet."

— Fran Lebowitz

History

"The past is never simply the past. It always has something to say to us; it tells us the paths to take and the paths not to take."

— Pope Benedict

"History has been written by rulers and soldiers rather than average citizens and it is, for the most part, about follies, crimes and bloodshed. It mainly shows us how self-absorbed humans have been."

— Thomas Macaulay

"Every history should be written in a wisdom which divined the range of our affinities and looked at facts as symbols. I am ashamed to see what a shallow village tale our so-called history is."

— Ralph Waldo Emerson

Challenge

"I ask not for a lighter burden but for broader shoulders."

— Jewish proverb

"Character cannot be developed in ease and quiet. Only through experience of setbacks and suffering can the soul be strengthened, ambition inspired, and success achieved."

— Helen Keller

"If you would hit the mark, you must aim a little above it."

— Henry Longfellow

"Don't bother just to be better than your contemporaries or predecessors. Try to be better than yourself."

— William Faulkner

Seeking challenge is a way of focusing thought and motivation.

— Anonymous

附录 H
新托福写作常用备考网站

① www.ldoceonline.com

一直很奇怪，这么好的网络资源为什么很少有人去用？这是朗文词典的官方网站，最棒的是每个词都给出了对应例句，这对提高写作用词的准确度至关重要。

② www.m-w.com

美国最权威的韦氏大词典的官方网站，一大特色是提供真人发音的红色按钮，带你朗读每个单词学习地道发音。

③ www.wordreference.com

最好的英语学习交流网站之一，遗憾的是，到目前为止还很少有大陆的同学使用它。有很多 well-educated native speakers 回答你提出的问题，而且完全免费。

④ www.usingenglish.com

类似的好网站，也是让 native speakers 帮你解除英语学习中困惑的好选择，而且跟上一个网站可以配合使用，两个都贴上你的问题，说什么也会有热心人帮你回答了。

⑤ www.gettoefl.com/twe/essay.htm

很多朋友希望在考前就能模拟机考写作的实战感觉，其实这类软件挺多的。除了官方资源之外，很多网站也提供类似的设置，而且利用 Google 也不难找。比如上面这个页面看着还比较舒服。如果想写别的题目，只要把方框里的题目改成你自己要练的题就好了，计时也可以选择用自己的时钟或者手机。当然，大家还可以去寻找更适合你自己的界面。这类网页在视觉上都和大家在考试中看到的界面有些区别，不过从练习机考打文章的感觉上来说已经接近了。十分渴望体验真实考试感受的童鞋们还是依靠 ETS 吧。

⑥ www.livejournal.com

这里的 journal 并不是指杂志，而是日记。这是美国人用得最多的写日记网站，很多感悟都可以用到新托福写作里当素材的，而且其实你自己也不妨从此养成用英文记日记的习惯，这对英语水平的提高将是最持久的。

⑦ http://www.vocaboly.com/vocabulary-test/

非常实用的 vocabulary 自测网站，不仅准备托福可以用，准备其他的北美留学考试也都可以用，而且还有 quick，medium 和 thorough 三种类型供你选择。不过需要注意的是，它不仅是针对写作的，所以有些词汇写作不一定有用，但是对阅读考试却很有帮助。

⑧ http://thinkexist. com/topics/

准备名人名言最有用的网站，覆盖了与新托福写作所有常见话题相关的名言。

⑨ http://www. learnenglishfeelgood. com/americanidioms/

从 A 到 Z 开头的大量美国常用成语包括在这个网站里。Pat 仔细看了这个网站上的全部 idioms，确实都是美国人和加拿大人常用的。虽然你也可以找到 armed to the teeth 这样的说法，但仍然是因为它是地道的美式英语，而不是因为它是"武装到牙齿"的机械翻译。背谚语必须坚决反对背过于初级的，比如"There's a will，there's a way."这种虽然不会扣分但肯定也不拿分的东东，就完全是浪费宝贵的备考时间，更少的工作量还不如背一个更精辟的 You reap what you sow。我们永远应该把有限的精力花在性价比最高的资源上，比如讨论学生是否应该选择更 challenging 的课程，用这个 proverb 就不错：Ask not for a lighter burden，but for broader shoulders。

⑩ http://homepage. smc. edu/reading_lab/american_english_proverbs. htm

收集了 101 个美国 proverbs 谚语，可以让你最快地了解最常用的美国谚语。如果你竟然还嫌 101 个太少，就看 http://www. goenglish. com/Index. asp 吧，proverbs 和 idioms 大全，足够你背上几个月了。

⑪ http://leo. stcloudstate. edu/style/transitioncues. html#forward

专门用来学习 linkers 的网站，帮你把英文写作连接词一网打尽。

⑫ www. newsinsider. org

提供大量美国新闻的深度报导，很多都可以用作新托福写作的例子。还有这个网站也类似 globalvoicesonline. org。虽然它们的更新不算太及时，但是毕竟新托福作文也不要求你时刻盯着 CNN，www. foxnews. com 或者 www. theonion. com 吧？

⑬ www. popsci. com

介绍很多最新的科技发展，而且是用外行人能看懂的语言，对于长期提高自身的科学素养也是很不错的选择。另外，经济学家杂志的科技版也提供对最新科技的跟踪与分析 www. economist. com/sciencetechnology/，还有科学美国人的官方网站也不错 www. scientificamerican. com。

⑭ www. topics-mag. com

一份网络的免费英文杂志，超级多的内容都可以在新托福写作里借鉴。

⑮ http://owl. english. purdue. edu/owl/

比较适合高端选手，页面右侧的导航会带你到不同的写作领域深入探索。

⑯ www. accd. edu/SAC/english/mgarcia/writfils/

希望深入学习英语写作的高端考生，不妨把这个网站的每个主题都浏览一遍，英语写作所有的要素都包含在里面了。更棒的是这个网站是专门针对 academic writing，百分百符合新托福考试的要求，对你今后到大学里写 paper 也有很大益处。

⑰ http://www.infoplease.com/

这个网站的信息比较杂，但是只要你愿意多花点时间研究它的 links，就会发现真的特酷。

⑱ www.videojug.com/webvideo/how-to-write-a-toefl-essay

这个关于托福写作的 video clip 虽然表述得很浅显，但传达的信息是正确的，那就是对于高分作文：Details Reeeeeeally Count！

⑲ www.yelp.com/locations? return_url =％2Fhome

美国年轻人很喜欢上的一个点评网站，很有点像国内的"大众点评网"。注意上面那些帖子的英语风格就不要在备考写作时模仿了，但这些讨论可以让你极其深入地了解美国年轻人中的流行与时尚。而且更棒的是到了美国之后还可以接着用，甚至用得更频繁，比如www.yelp.com/topic/chicago-americas-favorite-cities 这一页就可以当成在美国各城市旅行的指南用了。

⑳ 最后一个，但并不是最次要的一个：encarta.msn.com/thesaurus_/thesaurus.html

MSN 的同义词词典，可以让你很快地替换那些你觉得已经烦了的写作词汇。不过它的小缺点是少数同义词意义和用法上还不够"同义"。对于新托福作文同义词为说，意义准确并且掌握用法的细微差异才是最重要的，关键还是要注意平时阅读时的积累，并且学好本书中的附录 F。

☆　　☆　　☆

本节的最后，还是要向大家真诚推荐 Pat 的新托福写作博客：

blog.sina.com.cn/toeflwizard

结 束 语——To the next step.

一直以来，国内的同学们学英语存在的一个严重问题，就是把英式、美式、中式和应试英语全都混在一起学，最后导致失去方向甚至信心崩溃。Pat 真心希望本书能够成为大家学习美式＋短期应试英语的实用指南。

10 年前，Mary Schmich 在 *Chicago Tribune* 上发表的 *Everybody's Free to Wear Sunscreen* 被 Baz Luhrmann 唱得火遍全美大学校园，势头比当时国内流行的"同桌的你"有过之而无不及。那时的我缺乏人生阅历，不是很能理解歌词中的深刻含义。现在回头来看，句句都是过来人的真实体验。我决定把它放在本书最后，送给各位来美学子（正文中蓝色的单词都是我们在本书里学过的词汇、句型和变换句式等手法，现在您终于应该相信：本书里教的内容都是真正实用的美语了……）。

Everybody's Free to Wear Sunscreen

(*Abbreviated Version*)

If I could offer you only one tip for the future, sunscreen would be it. The long term benefits of sunscreen have been proved by scientists whereas the rest of my advice has no basis more reliable than my own experience

Enjoy the power and beauty of your youth; you will not understand the power and beauty of your youth until they have faded. Trust me, in 20 years you'll look back at photos of yourself and recall how much possibility lay before you and how fabulous you really looked: You're not as fat as you imagine.

Do one thing everyday that scares you. Don't be reckless with other people's hearts and don't put up with (=tolerate) people who are reckless with yours, either.

Don't waste your time on jealousy; sometimes you're ahead, sometimes you're behind... The race is long, but in the end, it's only with yourself.

Remember the compliments you receive. Forget the insults. Keep your old love letters. Throw away your old bank statements. Don't feel guilty if you don't know what you want to do with your life The most interesting people I know didn't know at 22 what they wanted to do with their lives. Some of the most interesting 40-year-olds still don't.

Enjoy your body. Don't be afraid of what other people think of it. It's the greatest instrument you'll ever own. Dance, even if you have nowhere to do it but in your own living room.

Don't read beauty magazines. They'll only make you feel ugly.

Be nice to your siblings; they are the best link to your past and the people most likely to stick with you in the future.

Work hard to bridge the gaps in geography and lifestyle because the older you get, the more you need the people you knew when you were young.

Live in New York City once, but leave before it makes you hard; live in Northern California once, but leave before it makes you soft.

Respect your elders. Don't expect anyone else to support you. Maybe you have a trust fund. Maybe you have a wealthy spouse; but you never know when either one might run out.

Advice is a form of nostalgia, a way of painting over the ugly parts and recycling it for more than it's worth. But trust me on the sunscreen...

参考文献

Bibliography

[1] Behrens L, Rosen L J. *Writing and reading across the curriculum* [M]. New York, NY: Pearson, 2008.

[2] Educational Testing Service. *The official guide to the TOEFL iBT* [M]. Princeton, NJ: McGraw-Hill, 2009.

[3] Farthing J, Lobato T, Ostrow C. (Eds.) *TOEFL iBT* [M]. New York, NY: Kaplan Publishing, 2006.

[4] Gear J. *Cambridge preparation for the TOEFL Test* [M]. Cambridge, UK: Cambridge University Press, 2006.

[5] Kaplan. *TOEFL iBT* [M]. New York, NY: Kaplan Publishing, 2009.

[6] Loughheed, L. *Barron's writing for the TOEFL iBT* [M]. New York, NY: *Barron's* Educational Series Inc. , 2008.

[7] Mazak C, Zwier L J, Stafford-Yilmaz L M. *The Michigan guide to English for academic success and better TOEFL test scores* [M]. Ann Arbor, MI: University of Michigan Press, 2004.

[8] Princeton Review. *Cracking the GRE* [M]. New York, NY: Princeton Review Inc, 2010.

[9] Princeton Review. *Cracking the TOEFL iBT* [M]. New York, NY: Princeton Review Inc, 2010.

[10] Sharpe P J. *Barron's TOEFL iBT Internet-Based Test* [M]. New York, NY: *Barron's* Educational Series Inc. , 2006.